REVISED AND U...

JOSE

RETURN OF THE KING

HARRY HARRIS

JOHN BLAKE

Published by John Blake Publishing Ltd,
3 Bramber Court, 2 Bramber Road,
London W14 9PB, England

www.johnblakepublishing.co.uk

www.facebook.com/johnblakebooks 𝐟
twitter.com/jblakebooks 𝐭

First published in hardback, as *Jose Mourinho: Simply the Best*, in 2007
This revised, expanded and updated paperback edition published in 2014

ISBN: 978-1-78418-000-3

British Library Cataloguing-in-Publication Data:

A catalogue record for this book is available from the British Library.

Design by www.envydesign.co.uk

Printed in Great Britain by CPI Group (UK) Ltd

1 3 5 7 9 10 8 6 4 2

Papers used by John Blake Publishing are natural, recyclable products made from wood
grown in sustainable forests. The manufacturing processes conform to the
environmental regulations of the country of origin.

Every attempt has been made to contact the relevant copyright-holders, but some were
unobtainable. We would be grateful if the appropriate people could contact us.

Dedication
To the Blues in my family (Linda, Ken, Jean, Uncle John) who love
Jose Mourinho's winning ways.

Acknowledgements

To my publisher, John Blake, whose son, Adam, is such
a big Chelsea fan – no wonder he keeps commissioning me
for books on Chelsea!
To my editor at John Blake Publishing, Steve Burdett, and
Michelle Signore for putting the book together.
Special thanks to FA Cup sponsors E.ON and their PR Tim Collins
for the invite to the FA Cup Final at the new Wembley to record Jose
Mourinho winning his full house of domestic prizes.
And a wonderful thank you to Mark Mitchinson of Chelsea
sponsors Samsung and his lovely wife Lynn.
Plus another special mention for Andy Sutherden and Steve
Bradley at Hill & Knowlton for their help on the Carling Cup.
However this book wouldn't be worthwhile without the
charismatic Jose Mourinho and his wonderful way with words.
This book is a tribute to the Special One.

Contents

PART THREE: RETURN OF THE KING

Introduction

For most managers, it would have been the perfect moment. Jose Mourinho and his players had just walked up the 107 steps of the new Wembley Stadium to collect their winner's medals and the FA Cup from Prince William.

Turning to the crowd, Mourinho held up six fingers to signal his achievements – he has now landed a clean sweep of all English football's domestic prizes, but there is no doubt his future at Chelsea still hinges on landing the Champions League. Mourinho has yet to mastermind the sort of dominance in Europe which Chelsea's owner Roman Abramovich both craves and demands.

Reflecting on the fall-out from his most frenzied season yet at Chelsea, Mourinho's enthusiasm in planning Chelsea's next title tilt was more than matched by satisfaction at their last. 'I used to say that in football the worst thing is when you lose and realise you could do more. Now I don't have that feeling. We did everything we could. A bad feeling was that I lost because I didn't do my best, because I didn't have enough motivation, because I slept in the shade of my success. We tried everything. I'm happy that we're not happy as it means we want more. But the FA Cup, in a historic moment, was a good reward for the club and ended a period of three years where we won everything in England.

'Winning is a habit, winning is culture, winning has a lot of mental preparation and I am very happy with it here. I just feel the last step is to take this feeling, or this little bit of luck, into European competition. Chelsea played three Champions League semi-finals in the last four years, which is fantastic, but couldn't play one single final. This club wants more and we want more. I won it before, but past is past. I want to do it with Chelsea. The players, they want to do it, but we have to do it without being obsessed because being obsessed doesn't help.'

After a rocky period, a truce has now been brokered between Mourinho and Abramovich. Season 2006–07 was a rollercoaster ride of emotions, controversy, rows, accusations and disciplinary hearings as each of Mourinho's seasons with the Blues has grown more controversial than the last. The highly charged Mourinho, often likened to the late Brian Clough, has never wandered far from the back-page headlines.

He admitted that there has been a change in spending policy at Chelsea, but denied, contrary to reports, that this had anything to do with Roman Abramovich tightening his purse strings. 'Roman is the boss, that doesn't change. He's the owner and the top man in the club. The change in philosophy is not because Mr Abramovich turned off the tap. The philosophy is we spent money before, built the squad for a long time and don't need to make big investments season after season. We will basically have the same squad, which is young and can be together for a few more years, so we don't have big needs. If you don't have big needs, why spend big money?'

Mourinho is already planning ahead to win future trophies by bringing in youngsters such as 16-year-olds Danny Philliskirk from Oldham and Jacob Mellis from Sheffield United. 'If we can do it in a good way – calm, not noisy, not expensive, keeping a good balance in the team – then we don't need big transfers.'

The most expensive product of the owner's previous approach, Andriy Shevchenko, who cost over £30m from Milan, contributed just four league goals. Mourinho was not prepared to spare the Ukrainian's blushes. 'Shevchenko did not have a good season. When we signed him we were searching for a top striker. The club decided to invest that money on a big player, and we did not get a big Shevchenko. It's very important that Sheva is not happy and wants to fight, to recover the prestige he had. Next season we hope it's better.'

At the beginning of the season, the self-proclaimed 'Special One' considered he had spent money wisely on a squad capable of winning all four major trophies – not just the Premiership crown – for a third successive year. But robbed of the services of several of his main assets – John Terry, Petr Cech and the flying Dutch winger Arjen Robben – the Quadruple was first to disappear from sight, followed quickly by the Treble, leaving Chelsea with 'only' the Double after wins in the Carling and FA Cups.

Rendered mortal by his failure to win his fifth league title in a row, Mourinho has started toning down the comments which once made him seem too brash. 'I don't think I am the greatest coach of this generation. But I belong to an elite group of young coaches who have chalked up important successes and made a huge impact. The elite group are Rafa Benitez, Frank Rijkaard and Carlo Ancelotti and we are sharing the best trophies in Europe among us. There are others I would not like to mention and I don't think I am the best. But I want to stay in the group. I want to stay among the top.'

Over the course of three seasons, many of Mourinho's methods have leaked out. One of these is the fact that he writes a report for owner Abramovich each week outlining the reasons behind his team selection, tactics and substitutions. 'He wanted the best for the club,' Mourinho said about the Russian billionaire. 'So did I. He wanted to know the club life. From that point I told him he will know why every decision was made. Why do you want Paulo to be your right-back? Why do you want Ricardo Carvalho to be your central defender? I have to explain – more than explain – I have to give a written report where they can understand and I can commit myself with that responsibility.'

In the early stages of his Bridge career, Mourinho observed, 'If I am in Chelsea for 10 years like Arsène Wenger with Arsenal, in my 10th year I won't have to spend so much money, because by then we will have built an academy and a scouting network. It's not fair when people speak about Chelsea's amount of money, but I cannot be a hypocrite because it is easier to work with a person of his economic power where you can say, "I'd love to have this player."

'I put myself [in the firing line] straight away by saying things that some people understand and some don't. I might have put myself in the spotlight but, at the same time, I woke up my people. And I put them also under a little bit of pressure. I said, "All of you are top players, but nobody won a Premiership or a Champions League, and you are not successful players until you win." So I made them think. I hurt them a bit, but I created a big ambition in the team. It was risky, but it worked.

'The first step is to make the big guys understand and accept and be on my side. Once they accept this rule, it's easy to manage the group. I couldn't be luckier than when I got Terry and Lampard and, immediately behind them, Makelele. They are the perfect example of big players with a notion of the needs of the club.

'The Italian League is the tactical league. The Spanish League is the technical league. The English League is about passion. When I thought I could have success here, it is because I thought I could mix that English passion with tactical organisation, and so our team became tactical. Boring for some – I don't know why – but tactical. To be fair, I think we are the best team in history, because we beat the record.'

After adjustments for games played and changes in points awarded for wins, in 2004–05 Chelsea achieved the best top-flight record in England since 1888–89 – with 95 points and only 15 goals conceded – but their pursuit of the European Cup has come grinding to a halt three times in the semi-finals, which means the pressure is really on for season 2007–08. Still, things have worked out better for

Mourinho than they might have done. At Christmas 2006, the critics all thought Jose would be collecting his designer coat, hailing a taxi and heading out through the exit door. Not so.

But is this going to be Jose's final season? If so, it promises to be just as high profile and controversial as the last three – perhaps even more so if his past record is anything to go by.

Introduction to the updated edition

Jose: Return of the King recalls in graphic detail Mourinho's first period at the Bridge, but updates all the dramatic details of his trials and tribulations, trophies and controversies in Italy and especially in Spain, and how he came much closer than anyone expected to becoming England manager – talked out of it only at the last minute by his wife.

Now he is back. Peter Osgood used to be the King of Stamford Bridge in the era of Charlie Cooke and the Swinging 60s. Then it was Franco Zola, then Didier Drogba, perhaps even lovely Frank Lampard, but in terms of management there has been – and once again is – only one King, Jose Mourinho. There has been a procession of A-listers in the hot seat, but no one compares to Mourinho.

Mourinho might have fancied managing Manchester United, but the Chosen One there turned out to be David Moyes, the choice of Jose's pal Sir Alex, although that didn't last long. Now Mourinho has taken up the reins again at Chelsea he will be locking horns with one man whose CV he envies, Louis van Gaal, Moyes' replacement at United.

Mourinho tried to reinvent himself in his first season back at his 'home' in west London as 'the Happy One'. That season disintegrated into its usual round of squabbles and strife, perhaps nowhere near some of his more embarrassing escapades, but on the field, he took the team much further than could have been anticipated given the limitations of the squad he inherited. He and Chelsea had their moments, ripping apart the eventual champions Manchester City at the Etihad and destroying Liverpool's title aspirations, beating the top teams at will, but just falling short of a title haul, yet still progressing in the Champions League.

Most un-Mourinho like, though, was his openly savaging his lack of genuine goalscorers, and writing the word 'Balls' on a scrap of paper when asked to assess his side's deficiencies after losing to Palace. Some of his fencing with journalists was classic Mourinho, and my thanks go to the likes of the *Daily Telegraph*, *Guardian*, *Daily Mail*, *Independent* and numerous online sources for so often reporting in full some of those exchanges.

Close, but not good enough, left Mourinho trophyless and determined to recruit the high-end individuals with whom he could forge a new Chelsea team in his own image.

After cheekily dismissing his squad as 'little horses' against some big-spending thoroughbreds, Mourinho was out to deliver the club's first Premier League crown since 2010, and he set about the task with his astute, and early, player purchases and pre-season planning.

Mourinho is pinning a great deal on Diego Costa, an expensive purchase from Atlético Madrid, to resolve Chelsea's biggest problem in putting away the moderate Premier League teams which was their failing the previous season, while the surprise but popular return of Drogba was needed as back-up with Samuel Eto'o departing along with Ashley Cole, Lampard, and Romelu Lukaku. The arrival of Cesc Fagregas more than softened the blow for the loyal fans who would have wanted Lampard to stay. Arsène Wenger passed up the opportunity to re-sign his former captain but Mourinho didn't hesitate to invest £27m, nor did he disguise the importance of recruiting such a dynamic midfield player. Mourinho observed, 'He is the missing piece of our engine. I see him everywhere because he can play everywhere. His best quality is the speed at which he analyses the game and executes. He rarely loses the ball or makes the wrong decision. He can accelerate the intensity of the game or he can reduce it. He's very intelligent and he has goals, and the players have a fantastic feeling around him as they really feel that he sees football too fast.'

The previous season was the first since 2002–3 that he did not score at least 10 league goals. While Terry signed a new one-year deal, Lampard and Cole could have stayed too. Mourinho revealed, 'They were [offered new deals]. We were in this process until the end, but you arrive into a moment [where you ask] what's the best for the team? What's the best for the other players? What's the best for them? And it depends also on their mentality. Lampard and Ashley, they will be until the last day players to compete, to play every game, to be involved. I think they are happier – in spite of their love for Chelsea – in this new situation for them. The best way for competitive people like them to be happy, to enjoy the last part of their career, is to go and play. I think Frank knows clearly he can come back to Chelsea. We are clear about that in the club. Mr Abramovich has it clear: "Be back when you want, be back where you want. And decide in which area you want to develop yourself after being in New York as a player." With Frank going to play there is about an adventure, an experience. In this moment he wants to play football for two or three more years.'

As for the 33-year-old Terry, the manager said: 'John last year had the sort of season where I can't remember him having had a better one. That's the point. Last season he played basically every match at a very high level, so when you have a player able to perform during the whole season, it's because you believe the next season he can do the same. That's the contract he got: one based only on performance, not based on status or captaincy or anything like that. I think he knows me. He knows the club. He just has to be worried about performing. We think these one-year contracts are a very good way to deal with these players.'

While there was reason to rejoice in recruiting Fabregas, it wasn't so fab for the fans to see Lampard leave at the end of his contract, when he signed for Major League Soccer side New York City, a new franchise albeit with the same owners as Manchester City. Much harder to stomach was that City then signed Lampard on loan for the first half of the season until the MSL season kicks off in March 2015. Pat Nevin said: 'It won't damage the way Chelsea fans feel about him long term.' Chelsea fans' groups gave the move a mixed reception. David Johnstone, spokesperson for 'cfcuk' fanzine, pointed out that Lampard made it clear that he would not play for any Premier League side other than Chelsea. 'He told me in the first week in July that he would not go to any other Premier League club and that he had season tickets for this year at Stamford Bridge and would come down,' he said. 'But he is an absolute professional and if New York City want to loan him out he will do as he is told. He is the greatest player of my generation – a credit to Chelsea and England, and for English football as a whole.' Chelsea Supporters' Group chair Trizia Fiorellino said, 'You always get one or two idiots but the majority of fans will not go against him. It will be strange to see him in a Manchester City shirt but I could not begrudge him.' Lampard scored 211 goals in 649 matches over 13 years, to become the club's record scorer. Since making his international debut in 1999, Lampard won 106 England caps, nine short of David Beckham's outfield record.

Real Madrid boss Carlo Ancelotti, who worked with Lampard while in charge of Chelsea between 2009-11, was surprised, 'I'm really surprised because I thought he was coming to the USA to play. But he's a good signing for Manchester City.' City were sanctioned by UEFA for breaching financial fair play (FFP) rules, with a £49m restriction on their net spending during the summer transfer window, and have named a reduced 21-man Champions League squad, to include five home-grown players. City own New York City in the States, Melbourne City in Australia, a minority share of Yokohama F Marinos in Japan. Arsène Wenger could resist getting involved as he said: 'It is a surprise after the statements we heard. It looks like all these City clubs will feed the main club. They bought the New York franchise for $100 million in the States to play next season and, at the moment, the players they sign cannot play until next year. I heard they want to buy five clubs all around the world. The players will register in the clubs where they will put them and they can get out on loan. Is it a way to get around the fair play? I don't know.'

The hugely popular David Luiz was sold off to Paris Saint-Germain in a remarkable £50m pre-World Cup sale, but if any Blues fans questioned Mourinho's sanity in dispensing with such a highly gifted individual his defending for Brazil in the World Cup illustrated the manager's wisdom. Luiz helped Chelsea win the Champions League in 2012, but when Mourinho returned he had his suspicions about the Brazilian's defensive qualities, trying him in the holding role, but again was concerned about his discipline in that position. Mourinho trusts veteran John Terry and Gary Cahill far more in the heart of his defence. PSG's world record for a defender came with interest from Bayern and Barca, yet Mourinho trusted his judgement, which was vindicated in Brazil's 7–1 defeat to Germany in the semi-finals. Mourinho revealed, 'Last season he was not regular first-choice for us. David did important things here, was always a good professional and we will miss him as a good guy when he was with us. But from a football point of view we believe our squad is stronger this season than it was. As a central defender he was not at all [first-choice], it was John and Cahill during the whole season. In midfield he was a physical guy and gave us some important things, especially when we played in the Champions League when Nemanja Matic couldn't play. But this season Matic can play in the Champions League so we don't lose that physicality. The fact we also have Cesc Fabregas moves us in a different direction and we want to move in a different direction. It's something that our football needs and we want to go in that direction.'

The third significant signing was Filipe Luis, a Brazilian full back who can defend, and who therefore might have been a better option for Big Phil Scolari, Brazil's manager and short-lived former Chelsea boss, to have had in the ill-fated tournament.

The tough call for Mourinho was that Petr Cech confronted real competition from Thibaut Courtois. Mourinho recalled the Belgium international, after three successful seasons with Atlético Madrid. For 10 years Cech has been undisputed No 1 and is not prepared to accept being relegated to the bench. With clubs allowed only 17 foreign players aged over 21, Mourinho might have shifted Torres if the price was right, but instead, had a tricky call to make about his goalkeepers. Mourinho said: 'I have to do what I think is the best and the fact we have two fantastic goalkeepers is not a problem for me. I was never afraid to make decisions and in the end it will be my decision and not that of anybody else. They have to work and work hard and wait for my decision, then fight against my decision if it is against one of them. The only way to fight is to work. It was logical that Courtois had to be back. It would make no sense to have such a fantastic young goalkeeper and not have him back so that decision was an easy one to make. If I have to make the decision of Petr on the bench, it's not a problem for me. Everybody says the same [about not wanting to be on the bench]. If somebody says I'm happy to be on the bench what are you doing here? Petr says the obvious, Courtois says the same. Mark Schwarzer is 42 and he will say he's not happy being the third choice and will fight hard to try and be No. 2 again.'

Fernando Torres endured a confidence-shattering spell but Mourinho said: 'Nando is a good player. Maybe the self-esteem in terms of a goalscorer is not at the top. All eyes are on him and when he misses a goal, everybody remembers. But his work for the team is fantastic and because of that we can play with two of them at the same time, that is no problem. Nando will always be a choice and a very useful player for us. When you look at your three strikers on paper, it's a hell of a strike force. They have different qualities which is very important.'

Mourinho was bullish about his prospects for the new season, 'We are strong. I don't want to speak about the others because obviously the others are strong too. But we are going to be stronger. We needed to transform our squad a bit and especially the striker and midfielder positions. We identified clearly the profile of the players we needed. With Diego Costa, we always had the feeling from six or seven months ago that we could possibly get him. And we thought that it would be good for us not to buy a striker in January because we knew we could get the striker in June. Cesc Fabregas was just a consequence of what was going on. The profile was clearly identified but I always thought Cesc would be a Barcelona player because he is so good and being a Catalan and with the end of Xavi's career coming, I thought that Fab would stay, but it was about him being so strong about this position and coming back to English football, a bit like me. I was in a big club and he wanted to be back. He was at a big club and wanted to be back. So when he heard that information he'd decided to come back to London, we knew he was there and he was the one we wanted.'

Mourinho once described his earlier Chelsea as 'untouchables', and he is once again feeling the winning potential, the vibes are good. He said: 'Our squad has been built in a way that we are strong now but yes, we are also strong in the future. The point is that I'm in a club I want to be. If you gave me every club in the world to choose from I'd choose Chelsea and the Premier League. I'm so happy to be in England and Chelsea and while he [owner Roman Abramovich] is happy to have me as coach I will stay. I don't have other targets or a next move. I'll stay as long as he wants me.'

'For myself, for myself,' is how he described the need for another trophy. He doesn't like the term 'trophyless'.

HARRY HARRIS, August 2014

Jose Mourinho

*'THERE'S A BIT OF THE YOUNG CLOUGH ABOUT HIM. FOR A START, HE'S
GOOD LOOKING AND, LIKE ME, HE DOESN'T BELIEVE IN THE STAR SYSTEM.'*

Brian Clough on Jose Mourinho.

Designer stubble, expensive grey overcoat and scarf, brooding, explosive, animated, flashy, arrogant, young and glamorous. But Jose Mourinho has proved to be more substance than style.

Mourinho was voted the best club coach in the world in 2004 by the International Football Federation of History and Statistics, finishing well ahead of Arséne Wenger and Didier Deschamps of Monaco, and the nomination came just as he was on the verge of engineering a shift in power within English football away from Highbury and Old Trafford.

It's incredible to realise that Mourinho has performed a meteoric rise – six years ago he was a glorified interpreter at Sporting Lisbon, Porto and Barcelona.

Some say Mourinho's defining moment was when his Porto team won the Portuguese League Cup for the second year running, and then overwhelmed Monaco for the European Champions title last May. Perhaps, though, his seminal moment had come in Lisbon four years earlier when, after just nine matches, he walked out on the famous Benfica club. 'It wasn't right,' says Mourinho. 'I could have stayed around, but I knew my work could not prosper there. My ideas could not develop.'

When Roman Abramovich interviewed Mourinho on his yacht moored in Monte Carlo, the Chelsea owner had had 24 hours to read a document sent to him by his prospective coach. It was a stunning appraisal of the situation of the club that had become the richest in the game.

English football writers put to Mourinho some theories about the course of English football, which has been so dominated by Chelsea. They spoke of a renaissance at Arsenal and a rally by Manchester United. Mourinho frowned. 'Do not tell me about your movie. I am in a movie of my own.'

The choice of metaphor is not accidental. Mourinho loves films. On away trips he carries his Sony Vaio laptop with him – the night before Porto's 2004 Champions League final he planned to watch a DVD of *The Punisher,* starring John Travolta – and when he describes meeting Abramovich it's like a scene from a James Bond flick: the French Riviera, the speedboat, the monumental yacht. And the pressure Mourinho is under? That brings another screen reference. 'Worthy of Don Corleone,' he says.

Mourinho is star-struck. 'I don't have many invitations to social events in London,' says the workaholic, not previously known for his liking for parties. When he arrived in June he moved into a flat in Eaton Square, Belgravia. In Eaton Square, with its Doric columns across terraced facades, his neighbours include Abramovich and the former 007, Roger Moore. 'English actors know me,' he says proudly. 'But the Americans don't. We can meet on the street, because we all live near. It is usual to be walking down the street and cross paths with Sean Connery. One of my deputies, Brito, lives in the same building as Monica Bellucci. Jeremy Irons lives near me also.'

If Mourinho's life is a movie, then its pre-production has been extensive. 'He's an overnight sensation who is twenty years in the making,' says Andy Roxburgh, UEFA's technical director. Roxburgh has been acquainted with Mourinho all that time. It was through Roxburgh that Mourinho acquired his first coaching badge, when he attended a Scottish Football Association course in Largs, Ayrshire. 'We used small-sided games on that course and it had a profound effect upon him. I know that players appreciate his training methods and attention to detail. He is also very personable and has good communication skills.'

For Roxburgh, Mourinho was a willing, enthusiastic and, above all, interested student. His public image – ice-cool, dispassionate, detached – is misleading, though even his wife, Tami, has said she had to learn to 'decodify him'.

Roxburgh says that far from the public perception, Mourinho does not 'need the limelight'. 'With big-name players you sometimes see that they do,' Roxburgh adds, 'but because of his background that's not the case.'

Mourinho enjoys the good life, but sees it as merely a reflection of success. 'I have a good car, but only one at a time. I like good holidays with my family, I like us to live in a nice place [Eaton Square], but as a football man the most important thing is to be working with the right people and with the right approach to things,' he says.

There is a little secret to his success. He calls it his 'methodology.' Mourinho calls it his ability to 'smell' what to do. 'There is an impression that he is a purely analytical robot,' Roxburgh says. 'The enigma is that he is all that but is also very passionate and emotional.' Mourinho himself appears to concur, 'I have a new way of thinking the game, the players and the practice,' he says. 'I defend the globalisation of the work, the non-separation of the physical, technical, tactical and psychological. The psychological is fundamental.'

Mourinho's ideas are stored on his laptop. He used the machine to make his famous 'Power point' presentation to Abramovich in which he analysed Chelsea's strengths and weaknesses with forensic detail. Also, on the computer is Mourinho's 'bible': an extraordinary document that contains his theories about teamwork (its first line is 'The team is more important than the player'), his philosophies, beliefs and even his definition of what the role of club chairman should be. He never shows it to anyone. It's his secret – as are the notebooks he keeps hidden in his coat and his private diary.

There is a locked cupboard at Chelsea's training ground full of dossiers and DVDs, many of them compiled by Andre Villas, a reformed addict of the Championship Manager computer game, who heads what Mourinho calls his 'Opponent Observation Department.' Villas takes four days at a time to compile detailed reports on forthcoming opponents. Mourinho used to do the same for his father. Sometimes each player receives a document running to ten pages, sometimes it is simply a DVD showing which way a player turns or shoots. Villas is just twenty-eight and is known as 'Mini Mourinho', and, like all of Mourinho's staff has known his boss for several years. 'With my staff things are clear in one respect – they grew up with me,' says Mourinho.

It is the same with some of the players. He signed four from his homeland in his first season, but resisted the urge to acquire more. 'The core had to be English. I wanted to show my players that I could build a team without the need to bring in all my "children".'

What strikes all who encounter him is his remarkable belief in himself – a belief that allows him, unusually among managers, to sleep easily. 'I think it's normal that a coach – the night before a match – doesn't sleep well,' he says. 'Some sleep badly because they are afraid but, since I do not sleep badly, I don't consider it to be normal.'

But his wife Tami is really in charge. When she ran out of cigarettes, there was no argument over who nipped out to their local in Belgravia in the cold and wet, still wearing his slippers. Mourinho says, 'It's a fantastic life in England but it's difficult. I have been to a pub only once, the one near where I live. My wife sent me out to buy a packet of cigarettes. I didn't have a drink. I just used my coins to buy cigarettes from the machine.

'I am enjoying life in England but it has been difficult to distinguish the main differences between English life and Portuguese life because I do not have much contact with the reality of the daily thing as work and family take up almost the entire time I have. In Portugal, I am what is known as the three F's. Fatima – Portugal's best known shrine – Family and Football. First and foremost, I'm a family man, but I am religious and Catholic and I'm from football, no doubts about that. I can be a good Catholic but I have not been to Fatima for six months.

'I'm not stuck to the symbolic thing. There are times I go to church and others not so much. At Porto I was going to Fatima once a month; at Leiria, my previous club, every week. I have full days. I wake at 7.15am and I leave home not long after that. I usually arrive at Chelsea training ground around 8.30am and have breakfast with the players and my assistants. I meet my assistants after that to organise work and then I meet the medical staff. Around 12.15pm, I end the training session and, if I don't have to go to a Press conference, I have lunch. If I don't have an afternoon session I leave at about 5pm to be with my wife and kids. Sometimes we go out together or we stay at home. Other times I just go out with my wife, to the movies or for dinner. I never go to bed until around midnight.

'It will be very difficult to go back to Portugal. Yesterday I was in my house looking at a Portuguese Cup quarter-final. In the Benfica stadium, which holds 87,000, there was just 12,000. I prefer it here, with the enthusiasm, the atmosphere. Every stadium is full; every team can fight for a result. Every country is different and the professionals have to adapt to the country, not the other way around. I have to respect what is important for the people who rule football here. In the future, I know if I do things on the touch line I will be punished. So I will not do them again.'

Mourinho's favourite hobby is quad-biking, and he enjoys skiing and snowboarding. He admits, 'I love quad-bikes but the guys from the insurance company which covers Chelsea told me "no way", otherwise I would be breaking the contract. I have a lot of hobbies but I don't have the time to practise them. I love snow, but I only had the chance to do snow sports when I left Benfica. I also love the summer and everything related to water, like swimming, but there is never any time for me to enjoy these things. Any spare time left over from my professional life is spent with my wife and kids.'

Mourinho also indulges in more genteel pastimes such as reading and going to the theatre. 'I like to go out for dinner, to go to a show or read a book. My wife suggests books for me to read because she is an insatiable reader. My latest is the autobiography of Colombian Nobel Prize winner Gabriel Garcia Marques. Reading allows me to distract my mind from the rest of my worries.'

In an interview with UEFA's technical director, Andy Roxburgh, the former Scotland manager, the Chelsea coach reveals his international ambitions and also laughs off suggestions that he is arrogant. Mourinho points to the way he was encouraged to develop when assistant manager at Barcelona, first to Bobby Robson and then Louis van Gaal as a key period in his career.

'Louis gave me the responsibility of taking the team in some friendlies or cup games and he monitored the way I handled things,' he says. 'I was prepared to take charge of a team; I had developed my know-how and confidence. Confident? Yes. Arrogant? No. My friends laugh when they read articles which label me as arrogant – they know it is not true. When I say I think we will win, I am only saying what most coaches think before a match.'

After his time at Barcelona, Mourinho returned to Portugal, ready to become a coach in his own right, and he admits it was not all plain sailing at Porto, with whom he would go on to win the UEFA Cup and Champions League. 'The first six months were difficult because the club and the team were in a very bad situation. I changed players and reorganised the team – it was a crucial period of rebuilding. The next season was fantastic because we won the UEFA Cup and the treble in Portugal. It was a great process, but it did not happen by chance. I have been influenced by some people, although I have never been the type to just accept the truth of others.'

Mourinho is an assiduous note-taker, but only during the first half of games. 'During the half-time team talk I try to control my emotions and be what the team needs me to be – this means I can be cool or I can be emotional because the team needs a certain response. There is always something to tell them at half-time, but after the match not one word, because the players are not ready to be analytical at that moment.' Instead, he analyses the second half at home.

'I am very demanding during training. We go for quality and high intensity during short periods. Players want to work, as long as the training is well organised and serious, and they know the purpose of the exercise.'

Mourinho took a gamble by recruiting Didier Drogba for £24m, but believed he had similar attributes to Thierry Henry – power and speed. Drogba reveals that Mourinho banned running during training, unless the players have a ball at their feet. 'I haven't jogged a single step since I got here,' says Drogba. 'We never run, except with the ball.' Talking about his first day of preseason training, he adds, 'I turned up with jogging trainers on. Mourinho looked at me with surprise and said, "You can put them back at the bottom of your bag. With me you'll never be needing them."'

Mourinho took more pleasure from winning the UEFA Cup – when Porto beat Celtic – than he did from the club's triumph in the Champions League. 'The emotion was much greater when winning the UEFA Cup than beating Monaco in the Champions League final because of the game of football. The match against Celtic was dramatic until the last moment. But after the dust has settled, the Champions League title is the greatest prize. The night we won it was difficult because I was full of conflicting emotions, knowing that I would be leaving the team.'

He possesses a meticulous attention to detail when discussing what he looks for in a player. 'I have produced profiles for each position in terms of personality, athletic qualities, technical skills, etc. If a player lacks speed he has no chance at the top level.' Mourinho gets frustrated by some aspects of the English game. In particular, he believes it is unfair that Chelsea counter-attacks are often stopped by 'technical fouls', with most referees failing to issue yellow cards, and he joins the chorus of managers demanding that action be taken on the offside rule. 'The interpretation of the offside law is very confusing and it must be very difficult for officials to make decisions.'

His new-found fame has come at a price, but he has few complaints. 'My life has changed. It is part of the job to deal with the demands. However, a principle for me is that I never miss a training session due to other claims on my time. Professional duties always come before external business requests. Football is my job but also my passion.' He is ambitious and desperately wants to repeat the success he achieved at Porto with Chelsea. And then? 'One day I would like to be the head coach of Portugal, but not now. I would not like to retire without having been the Portuguese manager.'

Spirit, motivation, togetherness. It used to be the prerogative of 'The Invincibles,' as Arséne Wenger's players indulged in on-the-pitch pre-kick off huddles. For Jose Mourinho the bonding takes places in the privacy and sanctuary of the dressing room. Just before the players go out, they take it in turns to deliver a brief motivational speech.

Frank Lampard explains, 'It's about bonding and it's a way of bringing out people's character. We stand in the dressing room, put our arms around each other and one of us says a few words and finishes by asking, 'Who are we?' Everyone shouts, 'We are Chelsea.' There are a few lads who are a bit quiet, and it's a way of bringing them out of themselves as well as getting everyone motivated.

'John Terry swears an awful lot when he does it. There was a pre-season game against Celtic and he was effing and blinding and I was thinking, "Hang on, John, it's only a run-out!" Scott Parker did the best one at Newcastle in the Carling Cup. It was the most aggressive speech I've ever heard, about being ready for battle. We already had a good spirit but the manager has taken it a step further.'

In his pre-Premiership existence he was 'sent off' and subsequently suspended for preventing an opposition player (Lazio's Lucas Castroman) taking a throw-in at a crucial moment during a UEFA Cup semi-final game. He explains, 'I did it by instinct. It wasn't that I was waiting for a chance to interfere with the game and stop the opponents' throw-in.'

That suspension meant that Mourinho was not allowed to communicate with his players after arriving at Lazio's stadium in Rome for the second leg of that tie. For the coach it was more than an inconvenience. 'What it came down to was that I wasn't going "into battle" with them,' he recalls in a book, written with a Portuguese journalist friend, Luis Lourenco. 'I cried because I couldn't be in the war with my men.' To overcome such an adversity, he watched the game from the stands, aided by a 'small, sophisticated communications device' to enable him to keep in touch with his coaching staff.

There is no room for jokes, raised voice or any other gimmick in Mourinho's team talks. 'He is simply meticulous,' says Lampard. 'Everything is explained in such detail that the minute he does make a change, we can adjust. We're able to do it because he leaves absolutely nothing to chance; he even tells us how to play if we go a goal up or down. He knows every opponent inside out. Even their subs. He talks to us as a team but also individually. No player likes to be blanked by the manager because even if you're playing well, you still wonder what he's thinking.'

Dressing room fun and games sum up the camaraderie in Mourinho's squad. Terry says, 'The team spirit we have here is great. There are PlayStation competitions, we go go-karting and paintballing together. Going into the games we all want to fight and die for each other. We also have the pre-match talks now, when everyone has their turn to say something. I had to do it in the first game under Jose, against Celtic. Mine was all effing and blinding but other lads will read out a quote. It always gets us pumped up. Jose's so thorough. He always wants to win. Even in training he doesn't like players conceding goals. We know what the opposition are about before we go into the game. And we always know what the boss wants you to do.'

Lampard expresses how much the atmosphere has changed due to Mourinho's regime, and how much Chelsea have raised their expectancy levels and status, 'Fans and other players are always asking the same thing: "What's it like at Chelsea? What is the manager like? What's Roman Abramovich like?" Even on England duty, people like David Beckham, Gary Neville, and Wayne Rooney all ask about it. It just shows the level that we have reached now at Chelsea, and it is terrific. There's an amazing buzz about the place. The buzz of a club that's going places, where something big is happening, and we have become such perfectionists about everything we don't feel it strange to look down and see Manchester United and Arsenal below us. Right now I think Chelsea is the most exciting club in the world. In the past you'd look at clubs like United, Real Madrid or AC Milan and wonder what it would be like to be there. Now, people look at Chelsea, and so much of that is down to Mourinho.'

The atmosphere has changed, as Lampard added, 'The build-up is much more relaxed. We used to have no music, no TV, no nothing. Now before a game we have it all. The night before a game is more relaxed, the pre-match meals are more relaxed.'

That was evident in the rich warmth Mourinho, displayed as he embraced his players following the Carling Cup semi-final victory over Manchester United at Old Trafford in 2005. Much has been made of the lack of dissent within Chelsea's squad from those players who have been 'rotated.' Largely that has to do, as Mourinho himself offers, with their hunger for success. They want trophies.

Tiago was Mourinho's fourth purchase in the flurry of comings and goings following the manager's appointment 'In Portugal everyone admired Mourinho,' Tiago says, 'because he won everything. In Portugal and in Europe. He's a coach who, I think, every player wants to work with.'

But why is he so effective? 'I don't know,' Tiago says. After a pause he adds, 'I think he's very clever. He works fantastically hard, not just him but all his staff. They are fantastic people – and the players know exactly what they have to do.'

Abramovich made up his mind he wanted Mourinho when he inspected the AC Milan trophy room and was taken aback by all the silverware. He came to the conclusion that Mourinho had won so much in just two years, compared to Claudio Ranieri's record over his entire career, let alone his four trophy-less years at the Bridge. Abramovich and Mourinho talked on the Russian billionaire's yacht, 'Le Grand Bleu', moored at St Tropez.

Mourinho immediately stamped his personality on Chelsea, as he was not interested spending fortunes on stars such as Ronaldinho, Roberto Carlos or David Beckham.

Whereas Ranieri recommended only three new players, Mourinho wanted four or five. Ranieri put forward a short list of new players: a striker, a central midfield player and centre half. Ranieri suggested Gerrard for the midfield berth; Fernando Morientes of Real Madrid, Didier Drogba from Marseille or Samuel Eto'o from Majorca as the new striker; and after his first choice, Walter Samuel signed for Real, a number of alternatives were suggested for central defence.

Mourinho wanted three of his Porto stars – Paulo Ferreira, midfielder Costinha and playmaker Deco – Tiago, and wouldn't have said no to Gerrard if he could be prised from Liverpool. Ranieri did not want to be too hasty in offloading players such as Jesper Gronkjaer, while Mourinho kicked out a dozen of the Italian's squad. Mourinho shared Peter Kenyon's conviction that Chelsea were vastly over-staffed. Melchiot, Petit, Stanic and Bogarde came to the end of their contracts and they were free to go; Hasselbaink and Desailly with a year left could also go on free transfers, and if they could not fix themselves up with clubs there was no place for them in the first team. Gronkjaer attracted a host of clubs including Birmingham and was sold off at a reasonable price. Others on loan such as Zenden at Boro and Carlton Cole at Charlton were also available. Zenden's move would become permanent, while Cole switched loans to Villa. Chelsea were looking to recoup some of the fees paid out for Argentina internationals Crespo and Veron.

But Mourinho would have to revise his targets with Deco signing for Barcelona. Porto midfielder Costinha also expressed a desire to follow Mourinho. 'I still have two years left on my contract at Porto but of course I'd love to go with Mourinho,' he said. 'I know if I go I will have more success.'

Mourinho arrived with his family at Heathrow on 1 June. Mourinho's contract was worth 6m euros (£4.1m) a year plus 1.5m euros (£1m) in bonuses triggered if he repeats the success he enjoyed at Porto in winning the championship and the Champions League. Kenyon negotiated a compensation package for Mourinho and his back room team of 2.5m euros (£1.75m). Chelsea poured money into Porto's academy to help them spot and coach players and, in return, get preferential treatment if they want to bring Portuguese youngsters to Stamford Bridge.

The most important of Mourinho's back room team is his assistant Baltemar Brito. The Brazilian has known Mourinho since the Portuguese was a teenager. Having left his homeland to play in Europe towards the end of his career, Brito played under Mourinho's father Felix at the small northern Portuguese club Rio Ave. A centre-half who acted as the on-pitch lieutenant of Mourinho senior, Brito helped Rio Ave to the final of the 1984 Portuguese Cup and became a close family friend. But it is to Jose Mourinho's wife, Tami, that Brito owes the progression from friend to Champions League-winning coach. Brito is aware of his debt to Mrs Mourinho, referring to her as his 'madrinha', or godmother, in recognition of her influence on his career.

After leaving Benfica in October 2000, Mourinho headed for the more modest side Uniao Leiria. Tami reminded her husband of the commanding personality of Brito, and Mourinho appointed him as his right-hand man.

Porto's fitness trainer, Rui Faria, is another key part of Team Mourinho. Born in the central Portuguese town of Barcelos, Faria was, like Mourinho, a graduate in physical education who had never played football of any distinction. He met Mourinho at a seminar day at Barcelona's Nou Camp, where Mourinho was working at the time as Louis van Gaal's assistant. Mourinho was impressed and stayed in touch, and when he took the job at Uniao Leiria in April 2001 he appointed Faria fitness coach and video analyst. Uniao Leiria struggled to attract 2,000 fans to its home games. But three years later Mourinho was in charge of a Champions League-winning team. No modern-day coach had achieved it at such a young age, or on Porto's meagre budget.

In his two full seasons in charge of Porto, the team won all but one of the six serious competitions they entered – two Portuguese titles, one UEFA Cup, one European Cup, one Portuguese Cup – and lost only two matches of consequence: the Portuguese Cup final and the one-off European Super Cup against Milan. Yet, in each of his close seasons he sold their most valuable player – centre-half Jorge Andrade to Deportivo La Coruna in 2002, and striker Helder Postiga to Tottenham Hotspur in 2003. The final ninety minutes with Porto reflected well on Mourinho, who made two contentious selections: Brazilian teenager Carlos Alberto started ahead of Benni McCarthy, Porto's leading scorer and conqueror of United. Alberto scored the first goal. And Pedro Mendes was picked ahead of Dmitri Alenitchev, who came on to set up the second goal and to score the third.

Mourinho picked his team for the final weeks beforehand. 'I decided the line-up a month ago,' he revealed. 'I first had the idea when Porto played Coruna [in the semi-final] and I saw Monaco in Chelsea. I was very clear about it. I was also clear that if we were not winning at half-time, I would put on McCarthy instead of Pedro Mendes, pushing Carlos Alberto back. But we scored and then had the chance to play in the style we prefer. I told Alenitchev to be the most attacking part of my midfield diamond and we mustn't lose the diamond shape. If you play in a perfect diamond, you control the match.'

Mourinho enjoys role reversal games, swapping places with his players and sometimes carrying out their orders while they act as manager. That's what happened to former Manchester United star Karel Poborsky when he told Mourinho – then in charge of Benfica – what position he wanted to play. Mourinho, who saw Poborsky as a winger, called him in and said, 'Right, you're the boss, why do you want to be playmaker?' He listened, let Poborsky pick his own place in the next match and took him off after half an hour. Poborsky says, 'Mourinho then told me, "Right, I'm the manager again. I gave you the chance to prove you were right and you proved nothing. You will play where I tell you from now on, and if you do not want to, you'll play in the reserves.'" Porto scout Gil Rui Barros says, 'I have never known a manager prepare his training sessions so thoroughly. Like Zidane with a ball at his feet, Mourinho has this thing that cannot be taught. He is the Zidane of managers.'

Mourinho's special attributes attracted the attention of English clubs even before FC Porto's European Cup victory. He was wooed by Liverpool in the spring but demurred. Five years ago Sir Bobby Robson asked him to join the staff at Newcastle United with a pledge that within two years he would be head coach. Mourinho declined. Spurs had made inquiries through intermediaries regarding their then vacant manager's job. 'It was in December or January,' said Mourinho. 'There was a contact but not direct. I was not interested at that time, I do not like to leave clubs in the middle of the season, so I thought, at that time, no chance.'

Mourinho, a deeply religious man, was struck by tragedy when his sister died in a diabetic coma during his spell with Barcelona. The experience reinforced his strong bonds with wife Tami, his nine-year-old daughter, Mathilde, and his son Jose, six. It was to see them that he left the scene of Porto's triumph so hurriedly – on the way to Chelsea.

Mourinho's uncle Mario Ledo owned a sardine cannery and grew rich under dictator Antonio de Oliveira Salazar's regime. Ledo died in 1972 and Salazar was later ousted leaving Mourinho's family on the wrong side of the political divide.

The canning factories were confiscated and Jose and his sister Teresa moved with Felix and mum Maria to a more modest home. He never talks of Ledo, whose death badly affected him as a nine-year-old.

Teresa died in 1997, aged 37. The official explanation was her diabetes. But others believe the drugs she began using after her marriage broke up caused the infection that killed her. Mourinho refuses to discuss it.

Before every kick-off, he kisses a photograph of his two children, and a crucifix.

PART ONE:
THE FIRST SEASON

The Premiership

'LET'S HAVE SOME FUN.'

Jose Mourinho in his first programme notes.

JOSE MOURINHO DELIVERS a message of intent at his unveiling at Stamford Bridge. 'We have top players at Chelsea,' he says. 'And, I'm sorry if I sound arrogant, we have a top manager as well. I don't want to be compared with coaches from the past, nor do I want to be viewed as the face of young managers in the game. I have won the Champions League. I'm not one who comes straight out of the bottle. I'm a special one. I am a winner because I'm good at what I do and because I am surrounded by people who think the same.'

The club's chief executive Peter Kenyon admits, 'I don't think we'll need to work on his confidence! He has been charged with being arrogant, but I don't think he is. He's very confident and self-assured and thoughtful about what he does. He's deliberate and has a gameplan.'

Mourinho adds, 'I want to win. Over the last two years I've had the taste. As a manager you want to feel the biggest success you can achieve. I want to keep this taste. I don't want to lose it. I don't want to get to 2010 or 2012 with just the same titles I have now. I want more. The people here have the same ambitions and mentality. We shouldn't be afraid to say, 'I want to win.'

'I accept that if I don't win this year it will be a failure. If I am sacked, I can always find another job. But I have not come here to give myself nightmares. I have come here to sleep well.'

Mourinho also responds to sniping from the outgoing coach Claudio Ranieri. 'I didn't like what he said about the Portuguese league being an easy one to win. I prefer to use my head and not react to other people's opinions. But what I suggest is that if someone is Mr Ranieri's friend, or has contact with him, you should explain to him that if a team is to win the UEFA Cup or the Champions League, it has to play clubs from other countries. I didn't win the UEFA Cup and the Champions League playing 20 Portuguese teams. I played and beat players and clubs from his country Italy, from England and Spain. Porto beat everyone in Europe. What has Ranieri won in 20 years? The Spanish Cup. I could say things like Ranieri has been in football for 20 years and the only thing he has won is the Spanish Cup. I could say that. I don't like to, but I could.'

Then Mourinho turns his attention to Sir Alex Ferguson, Arséne Wenger and Sven-Goran Eriksson.

After Porto had beaten Manchester United in the Champions League in Portugal, Ferguson said the opposition were divers. 'Ferguson had a reaction – something out of nothing,' says Mourinho. 'But I felt my players were big enough to cope with that type of pressure. I had to show them I was not afraid of him and that their boss was ready for a fight. After the second game at Old Trafford he came to the dressing room and congratulated me. And I have respect for such important people. I have not come here specifically to fight. I have come here to win. But at the right moment, if I feel my players, my group and my club are in a situation where they need my help, it's like family. And they will get it.'

Arsenal? 'Their manager is one of the best in the world. As for any weaknesses in his side, how can you identify weakness in an historic team? I need to learn about him and his side. In Portugal I could smell the changes managers would make at half-time. So I now need to look at Wenger and his players and discover their philosophy and playing style. That is why my scouts will watch his stars at Euro 2004 and then again in pre-season friendlies. When you go to war you have to know the opposition's strengths and weaknesses.'

As for Eriksson, Chelsea's first choice to replace Ranieri, Mourinho shrugs his shoulders. 'It is only natural they went for him. Mr Eriksson is a manager with a lot of prestige in the world. He also had a close relationship with Chelsea and, because of that, he was their number one choice. I don't mind ... because now I'm the man.'

Finally, Mourinho speaks of Roman Abramovich and the suspicion he will be difficult to control. 'I don't have to control Roman Abramovich – he has to control me! But, as in any business, you have to communicate with the top man. I spent two days with him on his yacht and he never once mentioned what he expected from me. Instead I gave him a four-page document about how I work and what I am. He is the owner and the first person in the club. But what I need to do I have already done. I have established clearly what my position is and my functions in the club.'

Claudio Ranieri was loved at Stamford Bridge and there was anger at his treatment. But he had won nothing of real consequence in nearly two decades in management; Mourinho has won the UEFA Cup, Portugal's league and cup double and the European Cup in two coruscating seasons at Porto. But Mourinho's mentor Sir Bobby Robson is concerned about his move to English football. 'The fact is Jose is coming into an area he doesn't know. He won't find the Premiership anything like the Portuguese league. He is joining the big boys and the big teams, where every game is a potential blip. In Portugal, if you can defeat Benfica and Sporting home and away, you are likely to win the title. What he has done on five or six occasions in European competition over the last two seasons is beat the big teams. He has to do that 38 times in the league.' Sir Bobby adds, 'I never thought of him as being a coach. I always felt his vocation would be in education because he had been a PE teacher.'

Mourinho responds diplomatically, showing his deep affection for Robson, 'I still see Sir Bobby as a father to me. My early times with Bobby were really important, and the way he put faith in me gave me confidence and taught me to be strong in believing myself. Tactically and dealing with players I could not ask for a better teacher, and I could not have learned from anyone better. It was an experience that was invaluable and I still telephone and talk to him now. He is a leader to me and I will go on respecting him as a great manager. He is always close to the players and that is something as a manager you must always be. They are your blood and the most important thing of all. They have to respect you and that is something that I learned form Bobby in the way they respect him and will always play for him. A little something from everything I achieve will always be dedicated to him.'

Mourinho prepared for his new job by sending a code of conduct to each of his stars. Porto's players were handed the same document and they responded. Gone are the days of late-night partying, weekend trips abroad and snubbing the press. Under the new regime all players must stick strictly to the rules or faces heavy fines or even suspension.

Split into seven sections, the rulebook states how players should behave with each other and the public – and the punishments they face if they break those rules. Players will be fined £250 for being 15 minutes late, with a further £500 penalty for the second quarter of an hour. Any later arrivals will mean a fine decided personally by Mourinho as he attempts to organise the training system right down to the smallest detail. Celestine Babayaro, notorious for his poor punctuality, arrives early for pre-season work!

At a time when the image of footballers off the field is under scrutiny, Mourinho has devised a clause to cover behaviour away from the club. 'Players must know that they're role models for children and adults, and they must always have an ethical and correct social behaviour. Players are not allowed to be away from their residence after oo.oopm. On the night before a resting day/free day, players are allowed to be away from their residence till 2.ooam.'

The rulebook says, 'Player misconduct towards technical staff, medical staff, kit staff and press staff will not be tolerated. Players' misconduct towards each other, be it in training sessions, match days, travelling or in the club's installation, will not be tolerated and will be considered a serious offence. All misconducts will be analysed by an executive director and the manager resulting, if appropriate, in a financial penalty and/or suspension by the club. Players who miss the appointments made by the medical department are subject to penalty fees and a disciplinary process. Direct red cards will be judged by the manager and the team captain. Disciplinary action will be taken if appropriate.'

Snacking before matches and ordering food and drink on room service during away trips is out. The code of conduct continues, 'Smoking and alcohol drinking is not allowed in the rooms. The medical department is responsible for choosing the meal menu. The players are allowed to choose or ask for a different pre-match meal according to their culture and their habits. Players have absolute duty to maintain a lifestyle that protects their capacity play to the best of their ability. This requires that they follow healthy diet, drink alcohol in moderation, avoid drugs and ensure that they have enough sleep. Injured players, foreign or not, may only leave the city or the country if permitted by the medical department and the manager.'

Mourinho calls for players not involved in Euro 2004 to attend Stamford Bridge on the first Monday of pre-season training at 8.15am. Hernan Crespo is the one player who does not show up. When Crespo arrives on Wednesday he is told decisively what his options are. Mourinho says publicly, 'We spoke in a very open way about whether he can find the motivation or the happiness for himself and his family to stay. For me, the player's desire is crucial. I told Hernan about the style, the quality of players I want, and the motivation. I was upset that he was not at our breakfast. You have always to be there – if the plane is full from Argentina, you come by bus. You can call. There is always a solution. He gave me excuses – some I could accept.'

Mourinho says he finds empathy from day one in Adrian Mutu, and that Eidur Gudjohnsen is a better player and a more willing enthusiast than he expected. He speaks at length about Mateja

Kezman, who lives the family life Mourinho admires, and who on the pitch represents his belief that 'modern' football demands that you defend from the front. And he speaks longingly about Didier Drogba, the Ivory Coast striker, who Olympique Marseille insist is not for sale, even at Chelsea prices.

Outcome: Mutu stays, but ends up being kicked out after a failed drugs test; Crespo is let go on loan to AC Milan; Seba Veron is similarly released on loan back to Italy; and Chelsea successfully pursue Drogba for a record transfer of £24m.

Marcel Desailly also leaves, Jimmy Floyd Hasselbaink departs to Middlesbrough, Mario Melchiot to Birmingham City, and Mario Stanic retires with a knee injury, all in the first week. Boudewijn Zenden, Jesper Gronkjaer, Emmanuel Petit and Winston Bogarde also depart.

Scott Parker talks positively about battling for his place in central midfield. 'I came to Chelsea to improve myself. I know it's a big task to get into the side in my best position in central midfield because Frank is a good player and Claude is as well. I want to kick on and establish myself as a Chelsea player, and fortunately Chelsea squashed the rumours that I would be one of those moving on pretty early in the summer. Every day there are rumours around this place, but that's the way it is going to be with such a big club.'

From Carlo Cudicini, the goalkeeper facing competition from the young Czech, Petr Cech, there is the acknowledgement that 'the challenge will be on the pitch, not in the contract' and the early indication is that goalkeepers are to be more involved in the whole group, not trained apart.

From Gudjohnsen there is the comment – enjoyed by Mourinho – that every movement, every moment, of the training sessions is controlled and organised. 'I read that Eidur said my training lasted exactly 90 minutes, and that the work and the rest were timed to the last stretch on the last stroke of 90 minutes,' muses the coach.

Frank Lampard's first meeting with the new boss is etched on his mind. Mourinho stared into his eyes and asked him, 'Are you a winner?' Lampard recalls, 'It was a strange scene, but it felt right and walking out we all thought, 'We're going to win something this season.' In a way he asks us that question every day. There is never a moment when you are allowed to relax. He'll have a joke, but you know with him the only thing that matters is winning and that has rubbed off on everyone.'

So does Mourinho genuinely believe Chelsea can win the Premiership in his first season in charge? 'Yes, I do,' he replies prior to the new season's opening game with Manchester United. 'One hundred per cent. I have no doubts that we can.'

As Mourinho prepares for the first match of the season, the issue that Sir Alex Ferguson refused to shake hands when Porto beat United in last year's Champions League is put to him. Not so, according to Mourinho! It suited the media to suggest bad blood, but he stresses, 'I have no problems with him. He complained about certain things in Porto, but he shook my hand after the match, and at Old Trafford he came to the dressing room to do it. I have respect for every manager when they have respect for me.'

The opening Premiership encounter will be 'entirely different' to the last time the two managers met in the Champions League, Mourinho insists. 'There is no comparison between a league match and a knockout competition. Also, my players at Chelsea are completely different – with the exception of Ferreira and Carvalho – from the ones I had at Porto, and the way we play here at the moment is different. Manchester United will also be different. When we played them last season it was at a time when they weren't feeling good. They weren't playing well. This season we have them in the opening game, and at the start everybody feels good and ready.'

Peter Kenyon, who was chief executive at Old Trafford before being lured to Stamford Bridge, has worked with both Ferguson and Mourinho, and he believes Chelsea's new manager can build dynastic success in the same single-minded way as the Scot has done at Manchester United. Mourinho responds in typical fashion, 'I don't want to be compared with other people. I am what I am, I've done what I've done, and I will try to do well again in the future. But I know that one day, instead of being a champion at the end of the season, I'll get the sack. These things happen in football. I don't think I'm the best in the world when I win, and I don't think I'm the worst when I lose. I'm just me.' And the showdown with Manchester United? 'If we win, we are not champions, and if we lose, we are not out of the fight. It is just one match, no more important than any other.'

The mind games are under way from the start. 'When Jose Mourinho goes to bed at night,' remarks an onlooker from Manchester United, 'his tongue gives a round of applause.' Ferguson says, 'Mourinho won the European Cup last season and the UEFA Cup the year before that, which is a great feat. You can't dismiss that sort of record. I'm sure we'll have a glass of wine together after the game.'

The United manager is invited to comment on how Mourinho has been talking himself up. 'Ach,' shrugs Ferguson. 'We'll just have to see how that develops. The personal aspect doesn't come into my thoughts. I'm more interested about new players coming into other clubs than new managers. Over the years we've had a great record at Stamford Bridge and we've probably been favourites most times, but Chelsea were second in the league last year and they've bought eight new players this year – big, international players – so it's not going to be easy.'

Normally, Ferguson would relish starting a campaign with such a big game. 'Not this season,' he says. 'Not with the injuries we've got. I'd rather have played someone else. You don't want to be three points behind one of your main rivals on the first day of the season.'

SATURDAY, 15 AUGUST

MANCHESTER UNITED 0, CHELSEA 1

Jose Mourinho offers Sir Alex Ferguson a glass of Chelsea's cheapest plonk after sending the Manchester United boss to his first opening weekend defeat in eight years. Gudjohnsen's first-half strike seals the points. Mourinho and Fergie shake hands and then share a bottle of Argentinean Shiraz in the manager's office.

But even as he admits his side are fortunate to start their campaign with a win, Mourinho is happy with the way his team are coming together. Mourinho says, 'Silvestre said we didn't have enough time to create a big team spirit – and he was wrong. I could have told him that my players have been fantastic from the first day and that mentally we are a team. When you consider we've only been together for a month it is great that we showed we have created this spirit and want to fight together.

'I don't think United deserved to lose. They controlled the game and made us change the way we played from what we wanted. But everybody gave one hundred per cent and showed the character we need and didn't allow them many chances at all.'

Fergie moans about Gudjohnsen's 'sloppy' winner and vows to step up his search for a striker after his injury-depleted side fail to test Cech. The United boss says, 'I didn't need him [Mourinho] to tell me we were unlucky. In a game like that you've got to make one of your chances count.'

The single goal comes with barely a quarter of an hour gone; yet Chelsea are already aiming to play on the break by then. 'Sometimes you have to play a little different to how you would like,' says Mourinho. 'We did not play better quality football because of our opponents. Sometimes football is beautiful because of competitiveness and organisation. Defensively we played fantastically with unbelievable team spirit. United pushed us back and I had to control the game.'

Ferguson is unsurprised by Chelsea's approach. 'I expected them to defend because of the way Porto played when they went 1–0 up against us,' he says. The goal comes when Geremi beats a sluggish Quinton Fortune to the ball, and Didier Drogba rises high to redirect a diagonal pass into the space behind United's defence. Howard's reaction lacks conviction, allowing Gudjohnsen to flick the ball goalwards. Not even Roy Keane's despairing sliding intervention can stop the ball crossing the line.

Eager to protect Gudjohnsen's early goal, Chelsea and their coach are consumed with caution. Petr Cech resorts to time wasting as

United's siege intensifies. One of Euro 2004's most impressive stoppers Ricardo Carvalho is introduced into midfield to kill off the match. Chelsea's leading contributors are two defensive midfielders: the outstanding Claude Makelele and the debut-making Russian Alexei Smertin. This pair give Chelsea the midfield steel that United, for all their pressure, cannot overcome.

As well as a full complement of points, Chelsea fans will also take heart from Cech's assured display. Tall and mobile, the Czech Republic international looks comfortable whether collecting crosses or dealing with shots. Ferreira endures one or two problems with Giggs but still exudes promise. Drogba plays an important part in Gudjohnsen's goal, confirming his aerial strength, but clearly requires time to pick up the pace and physical demands of the Premiership.

> **Team**
>
> Cech, Ferreira, Gallas, Terry, Bridge, Geremi (Carvalho), Makelele, Lampard, Smertin, Drogba (Kezman), Gudjohnsen (Parker).

So early in the campaign Arsenal's 4–1 rout of Everton bears overtones of the sweeping verve that carried the double to Highbury in 1998 and 2002. Arsenal's impressive win at Everton is without question the result of the opening weekend of the Premiership season. Alan Hansen writes in his *Telegraph* column: 'The victory was a clear message that said "Move over Manchester United" and also showed Chelsea that, whatever they spend on new players, Arsenal will continue to pulverise their opponents. Arsenal have yet to take United's mantle as the dominant force in English football, however, despite going through an entire league season without defeat last year. United's success over the last five years entitles them to that distinction and Arsenal have to overcome the obstacles faced by Sir Alex Ferguson's team if they want to become the undisputed top team.

'Four or five years ago, United's midfield of Paul Scholes, Ryan Giggs, David Beckham and Roy Keane would frighten anybody.

Nowadays, opponents will look at United's team sheet and fancy their chances. That is why I believe United will struggle to regain the title this year. Arsenal are beating them on the pitch and Chelsea are beating them off it, in the transfer market. I can only see the title being contested by Arsenal and Chelsea, with United probably having to be content with third place.

SATURDAY, 21 AUGUST 2004

BIRMINGHAM CITY 0, CHELSEA 1

Mourinho hails the team spirit that he feels can propel Chelsea to the title. 'It was amazing; I have never known anything like it before. The players who weren't involved were all calling into the dressing room on their mobile phones encouraging and cheering on the players who started the game. Perhaps that is normal for you in England but it is unheard of where I come from and it's a sign that we have a fantastic spirit and determination here.'

This is Joe Cole's day from the moment he is called on just after the hour mark and he delivers with style. Cole's entrance comes after Steve Bruce's five-man midfield has strangled the life out of Chelsea. The best chances fall to Julian Gray, but he cannons his first shot off Cech's right-hand post. Mourinho has no option but to make changes at the break, dragging off Smertin and Gudjohnsen and replacing them with Tiago and Kezman.

Cole then emerges and is told to play behind Drogba and Kezman. He flits out to the left, takes a pass from the otherwise unimpressive Lampard and makes tracks towards Maik Taylor's goal. His shooting from range isn't normally enough to trouble any keeper, but this time he finds the target with a deflection off Taylor's leg.

Mourinho blasts Robbie Savage for an elbow attack on Kezman that floors the striker ten minutes from the end. 'If an elbow situation happens in my country, or in Spain or Italy, then we accept it as part of our culture. But when I see it over here in England I am shocked and surprised as well as angry. England and the English people are the kings of fair play and that's why so many people love your game.

So when I saw that blond player elbow Kezman, sure, I was upset, but also shocked. I hope that you see it on film and that a disciplinary panel will deal with it.'

Bruce is gutted. 'We've been kicked in the teeth. But if you don't take four or five glorious opportunities that fall to you, you know you are going to get punished. We matched Chelsea in virtually every department, but we've wasted our chances... and they've taken the one that fell their way. Chelsea are a hard-working side, but if you look at Mourinho's team – and at his Porto team last season – they don't look remotely interested in entertaining. But what will he care? He's got six points out of six and we are left to lick our wounds.'

Team

Cech, Ferreira, Terry, Carvalho, Bridge, Geremi (Cole),
Makelele, Lampard, Smertin (Tiago), Drogba, Gudjohnsen (Kezman).

Chelsea sit joint top of the Premiership with Arsenal after winning the first two games. But, while the reigning champions have scored nine times in two games, Chelsea have eked out two 1–0 wins based on defensive solidity and organisation. It is a comparison Mourinho believes is unfair. He wants his team to play 'beautiful' football, but first he wants to win – and he reckons teams from this country, including Arsenal and the national side, have not enjoyed international success in recent years simply because they do not defend well enough. 'Football people in England should stop and ask yourselves for what reason English football has not been successful abroad. Spanish, Italian and Portuguese clubs have all won UEFA competitions, but England can't do it. You have to think about the reason the English national team has a top manager and top players and goes to the European Championship and World Cup and can't win. England has wonderful football but when you go outside this country they cannot do it. Manchester United was the last one when they won the Champions League in 1999. Why is that? You have to think about it because it is not normal. My philosophy is the philosophy which gave me six titles at Porto in two years. To win.'

Mourinho says his side should not be compared with the team Wenger has been nurturing since 1996. 'When I have a boy of seven years of age and when I have a young human being of seven weeks, the boy of seven years can run, jump, speak, communicate: you can see what he is. After seven weeks, when I had my daughter and boy, you just take care of them and try to create conditions for the little baby to grow. So you want to compare a team of seven years with the same manager, with the same spine year after year, with a team with 50 per cent new players, a new manager, new everything? You should compare the first two months of Mr Wenger in English football with my first two months. At the moment there are two teams – one is from the moon and one is from hell, but both have six points.'

TUESDAY, 24 AUGUST 2004
CRYSTAL PALACE 0, CHELSEA 2

Didier Drogba's first Premiership strike and a thumping clincher from Tiago make it three wins and three clean sheets out of three for Mourinho. In front of Sven-Goran Eriksson at Selhurst Park, Cole mounts a persuasive case for playing a major part in the World Cup campaign. He is the catalyst for a display that suggests the new-look Blues are beginning to take shape. He is a non-stop menace, liberated by a coach who wants to test out his impish skills.

Mourinho takes a leaf out of the Tinkerman's book with five changes, including full debuts for Tiago and Kezman. Danny Granville is the only survivor of the last Premiership clash between the sides, a 6–2 Chelsea win at Stamford Bridge six years ago, except then he was playing for the Blues. And he does his old side a favour when unmarked he heads wide of the gaping target from ten yards. It is a brief interruption as Chelsea take up the reins again and Cole draws a fine diving save from Julian Speroni after an instinctive give-and-go with Kezman.

But Chelsea are in front after 27 minutes. Kezman threads through for Babayaro, replacing the injured Bridge, to deliver a cross that begs for the powerful downward finish from the Drogba. Seventeen minutes from the end Tiago puts the seal on his personal display as he collects from Drogba and drills a fine shot into the corner.

Team

Cech, Ferreira, Gallas, Terry, Babayaro, Makelele, Lampard, Tiago, Cole (Geremi), Drogba (Gudjohnsen), Kezman (Mutu).

Mourinho says he plans to turn Lampard into the best midfielder in Europe. He missed UEFA's gala awards ceremony in Monaco to work with Lampard and his team-mates ahead of the home clash against Southampton. At those awards, Porto midfielder Deco was handed the Champions League Player of the Year award. Mourinho arranges for his own award for winning the Champions League to be given to him at Chelsea's home European clash against his old club. He targets the next Player of the Year award for Lampard. 'I want to change Frank Lampard as a player. I want to make him a better one. I want him to win the same trophy that Deco won on Thursday night. How can I achieve this? By winning, because Deco is the same player that he was two years ago. The only reason he won on Thursday was because he is a European Champion. Frank will be the same player but he will be adapted to a different philosophy.

'At the moment we do not have Arjen Robben or Damien Duff in the team wide on the left, but when they are in the team that will make it easier for him. Frank was involved in four of the six passing channels against Crystal Palace on Tuesday night. He was the player most in the opponent's final third coming from behind. And, with Tiago, he ran the most – 11 kilometres. In the last 15 minutes of the game when everybody's level was going down, he ran more than he did before.'

SUNDAY, 29 AUGUST 2004
CHELSEA 2, SOUTHAMPTON 1

They may not quite have the look of champions in waiting, but Chelsea beat Southampton more convincingly than the score-line suggests to make their best start to a season in the top flight. 'You can't do better than take 12 points from your first four games,' says assistant coach Steve Clarke. Chelsea should be three or four ahead by half-time, despite falling a goal behind to a wonderful strike from James Beattie within 12 seconds of kick-off. After equalising through a Beattie own-goal and then taking the lead with a Lampard penalty, Chelsea fail to kill off a Saints side who rarely threaten.

Wayward finishing, outstanding goalkeeping and goal-line clearances keep Chelsea down to a one-goal winning margin for the third weekend running. 'Missing chances is not a concern while we are winning games – it might be if we were losing,' adds Clarke.

Yet an unlikely upset looks briefly possible when Chelsea kick off and Cole's wayward pass sits up invitingly for Beattie to hit a beautiful volley that dips over the arching body of Cech from 25 yards. Gudjohnsen heads wide from close range, Drogba has a shot blocked by Antti Niemi and Lampard thumps a drive over the bar, all inside the opening ten minutes. Then Lampard swings in a corner, Gudjohnsen flicks the ball with a heel and it flies off Beattie's hip on to the crossbar and down over the line despite Anders Svensson's efforts to clear.

Svensson is in action again, clearing a header from the impressive Tiago off the line, but Chelsea soon have the decisive goal. Lampard swings in another corner and Claus Lundekvam handles under pressure from Drogba. Southampton argue for a push and are still unhappy after Lampard scores the resulting penalty, claiming he touches the ball twice.

The second half is less one-sided, although Niemi is still the busier keeper. 'That was probably our best performance so far this season,' says Lampard. 'We really played in the manner we want. We had a cutting edge in the box and, with better finishing, could have won by four or five. We've had a tough start to the season and won them all. We know Arsenal have been very good but we'll do our utmost to challenge them all the way.'

> **Team**
>
> Cech, Ferreira, Carvalho, Terry, Bridge, Makelele (Geremi), Tiago, Lampard, Cole (Duff), Gudjohnsen (Kezman), Drogba.

Mourinho says that what happens to him in football is second to his relationship with God. 'I'm scared of God. I'm a religious man, although I don't practise religion by going to church every day. I believe what I believe. There are certain things in this life that we cannot control. The first thing in my life is to have the people I love healthy and happy. I have no fear of losing, no fear of the critics. It is important to do your best, wake up every day with good ambition and go home to sleep well knowing you have done everything.'

The Premiership season takes a break with Chelsea losing 19 players to international duty, leaving Mourinho to work with only three first-team squad players and the injured Carlo Cudicini. 'It's more than frustrating,' he says after running through a series of videos and discussing tactics with his re-assembled squad. 'You can do nothing to improve your team. He adds, 'I told them the only chance we have at Aston Villa is to forget the internationals and next Tuesday's Champions League. Aston Villa are too difficult to be thinking of other things.'

SUNDAY, 12 SEPTEMBER 2004

ASTON VILLA 0, CHELSEA 0

Merely ending Chelsea's 100 per cent record is an achievement for Villa. Huth, Duff, Parker, Bridge, Johnson and Geremi are not even required on the bench to emphasise the strength of Chelsea's squad compared to Villa. David O'Leary changes his team, aping Chelsea's formation and thus curbing his wide players, Nolberto Solano and Gareth Barry. O'Leary says the changes are made with victory in mind but they seem primarily designed to stymie Chelsea.

The score-line suggests it works, but O'Leary is helped by Mourinho's refusal to involve Duff. Yet even without the width he offers, Chelsea have chances enough to win. In the opening half flowing moves create opportunities for Cole, who miskicks, and Drogba, who hits the bar.

Chelsea dominate after half-time, but Mourinho withdraws Cole and the link between midfield and attack is lost. Darius Vassell wastes a chance to put Villa ahead before Chelsea revive and Drogba is robbed of a penalty when felled by Ulises de la Cruz and is ludicrously cautioned for 'diving' by Rob Styles. An incandescent Mourinho justifiably criticises refereeing standards before claiming, 'It would have been two penalties in some countries. It was ridiculous.' Four wins and a draw is an excellent start to the season, but it still leaves Chelsea behind Arsenal who record their fifth straight victory.

> **Team**
> Cech, Ferreira, Carvalho, Terry, Babayaro, Makelele, Tiago (Smertin), Lampard, Cole (Mutu), Kezman (Gudjohnsen), Drogba.

Later Styles rescinds the yellow card shown to Drogba after watching video replays of the incident. Makelele announces his retirement from international football to concentrate on his club career. 'I think that a player like me cannot afford to answer international calls if he is not going to play. I shall be 33 in 2006. My future is with Chelsea.'

MONDAY, 20 SEPTEMBER 2004
CHELSEA 0, TOTTENHAM HOTSPUR 0

Mourinho feels cheated by an opposition who come solely to achieve a stalemate. Ledley King is the game's pivotal figure and he never looks like being caught as he marshals his side's defences. So Chelsea fail to capitalise on Arsenal's draw against Bolton the day before, and the gap at the top remains two points.

Mourinho is furious. Not with his players, who, for the second successive Premiership match, do not score, but with Jacques Santini, his team and their alleged time wasting. 'I think it is frustrating for me, the players, for every Chelsea supporter and for every football supporter. Because people are not paying money to see one team play and for another to keep falling down, kicking balls away, sending for the medical department and spending five minutes to change players. My team played fantastic football. They may as well have put the team bus in front of the goal.' Mourinho ends the match with four strikers – something he says he would never normally do. Santini is unrepentant. 'They have big international players, and that obliged my young team to defend.'

Chelsea extend their unbeaten run against Spurs to 29 league games, but that matters little in the context of this Premiership season. They need the three points. It is almost none. Cech pulls off the save of the match in pushing away Robbie Keane's header in the second half, although Gudjohnsen also strikes the base of the post, and Paul Robinson reacts smartly to dig out Lampard's fierce free-kick.

It is Lampard's 114th consecutive Premiership match – a new record – but he figures little. Chelsea only really start to fire in the final 20 minutes once Duff comes on and offers width. There are five minutes of added time at the end. 'There should have been 15,' says Mourinho.

Team

Cech, Ferreira, Carvalho, Terry, Bridge (Smertin), Makelele, Tiago (Kezman), Lampard, Cole (Duff), Drogba, Gudjohnsen.

SUNDAY, 26 SEPTEMBER 2004

MIDDLESBROUGH 0, CHELSEA 1

Before kick-off a minute's silence is immaculately observed in memory of local legend Brian Clough, born just a mile from Boro's former home, Ayresome Park. Clough scored a phenomenal 204 goals in 222 league and cup games for the club.

Mourinho's pre-match media conference is dominated by his view that he and his side have superseded Sir Alex Ferguson and

Manchester United as the ones most in football love to hate. Chelsea, however, might just win a few friends if they can replicate more performances like this and add a few goals for good measure. Chelsea only have Drogba's 81st-minute goal to show for their overwhelming superiority.

Mourinho concedes the paucity of goals is a cause for concern: just seven in as many Premiership matches. He complains that 'the knives always go in Chelsea's direction and the flowers in the other direction'. But he adds, 'One day a team will be unlucky: we will score from every situation and win 4–0 or 5–0. We had a lot of chances to score and the only surprise was that we scored so late.'

The goal comes when Lampard pulls a free-kick into the middle for Drogba to crack a right-footed effort from 15 yards that Mark Schwarzer can only help into the net.

The home side are not helped by the loss of Jimmy-Floyd Hasselbaink for ten minutes after sustaining a bloody head wound resulting from a dangerously high boot from Terry. While Hasselbaink receives stitches, Drogba and Duff, making his first start, both threaten and Smertin smacks a shot that Schwarzer parries. Moments later Boro are dealt another blow when Ray Parlour is carried off with a gashed knee after a jarring duel with Gallas. When Hasselbaink emerges for the second half, he is ordered to change his blood-caked shirt. With no ready-made replacement to hand, he sports injured defender Ugo Ehiogu's shirt. Steve McClaren admits, 'We lost Chris Riggott and Szilard Nemeth before the game. We lost Ray and Jimmy for a while. We didn't have another number 18 shirt for Jimmy. We didn't have enough of anything.'

> **Team**
> Cech, Ferreira, Carvalho, Terry, Gallas, Smertin (Tiago), Makelele, Lampard, Duff (Huth), Gudjohnsen (Kezman), Drogba.

Mourinho's side is taking shape. Lampard, Terry, Makelele and new signings Cech, Ferreira and Drogba have started every game. Gudjohnsen has started seven and come on as a substitute in the other two. Gudjohnsen has failed to recapture the form of the 2001-02 season when he scored 23 goals, but Mourinho has taken to him from the outset. The 26-year-old is an intelligent footballer whose excellent movement and touch creates space for his colleagues – rare attributes that were rewarded in the summer with a new £55,000-a-week contract.

With the strikers and back five largely picking themselves, the fiercest competition has been in midfield, with Cole, Duff, Tiago and Smertin sharing the remaining two places alongside Makelele and Lampard.

Cole has impressed at the head of the diamond until Duff's return from a shoulder injury reduced his workload, while Tiago and Smertin have started four games each on the right of a deeper midfield three. Smertin's emergence is surprising, though fully justified, but more of a shock is the disappearance of Scott Parker, who this time a year ago was among the most impressive performers in the Premiership.

The reigning PFA Young Player of the Year has played just eight minutes and only made the substitutes' bench on one other occasion. Parker's career appears to be going nowhere. The only experienced players further from the first-team than Parker are Glen Johnson and Carlo Cudicini. But 20-year-old Johnson has time on his side, while Cudicini, who returned to the bench for the Champions League victory over Porto, has been out for much of the season with an elbow injury and would walk into any other Premiership team.

Gallas reveals that Mourinho began his Chelsea tenure by telling his players their standards were not good enough. 'I think the atmosphere is very good, like it was last season. But Mourinho said at the start, "There are a lot of good players at this club, a lot of international players, but you haven't won anything. With this team we must do it." And that is true. This season is our season and everybody feels the same. We know it will be difficult because we know Arsenal are very strong and there's Manchester United, but we want to win all the games. Everybody is fighting on the pitch together and that's important. We play with our hearts.'

Lampard says the studious attention to detail that characterises the new regime means the team expect to win every game they play. That is the biggest change under Mourinho. Lampard says, 'The most important change is that the mental attitude now is: win, win, win. At times it wasn't like that last season. Now the accent is on winning every game we play – and every competition we're in.'

Lampard adds, 'In training, virtually everything we do is intended to replicate a match situation. That has helped the players technically and made us more tactically aware. The work we do with a ball, day in, day out, is the foundation of the team's strength. We're not conceding goals and look strong and solid because we hammer away at getting it right every day in training. The organisation is becoming ingrained. It's not that we've just got the one way of playing, but if we do change we really do know what we're doing because it has been mapped out beforehand. In the build-up to the game the manager will have prepared us for every possibility. He'll say, "If this happens, we might change to this." It's never off-the-cuff, as it was under Ranieri, it's always something that has been pre-planned.'

Is Mourinho happy winning 1–0? 'Of course he is. We all are,' says Lampard. 'The manager does like to play good football; he's not one of those who wants to defend, content to play unattractive football and nick a result. He'd be happier, obviously, winning 3–0, but 1–0 will do as well.'

Last season was easily Lampard's best. This time his football has improved again. 'The manager is great at giving individuals confidence. In my case, I'm taking free-kicks and corners, which I was never entrusted with before. He has given me that responsibility; it's something I've added to my game and it has made me believe in myself even more. He is bringing the best out of me. What I haven't got is as many goals, and that's something that bothers me because I think like a striker – if I haven't scored I'm not happy, however well I've played. I do need to get among the goals again. I've got one for Chelsea and one for England, which isn't enough.'

Chelsea's next opponents are Liverpool. 'We're ahead of them in the league, but they are making progress under their new manager,' says Lampard. 'It's usually a tight game, and last season they beat us 1–0 at our place. We can't allow that to happen again. The way Arsenal set the pace these days, you can't afford to lose many, and we need to keep winning.'

SUNDAY, 3 OCTOBER 2004

CHELSEA 1, LIVERPOOL 0

Joe Cole scores the winning goal and leaves with a bottle of champagne from Sky as their man of the match, but also with a stinging reproach from his boss. Mourinho accuses Cole of neglecting his defensive duties after the goal and hints that the England international finishes the game playing to the gallery, which includes Sven-Goran Eriksson, rather than for the team.

But Cole catches the eye with the neat finish he applies to Lampard's free-kick and the invention he brings as an auxiliary striker after coming on in the first half for Drogba. Mourinho, though, says Cole's display is 'not good enough' from the moment he finds Liverpool's net. 'Joe Cole scored a goal; that's very important. He gave us good dynamic and played really well in terms of that attacking dynamic. When he scored the goal the game finished for him. After that I need 11 players for my defensive organisation and I had just ten.'

Cole responds by saying, 'The boss has no axe to grind against me. He just wants to make me a better player. I will sit down with him and talk to him and listen to whatever he has to say. He's a fantastic manager.'

Mourinho also hits back at critics who have lambasted his team's four 1–0 wins. 'It is not fair. I think they should criticise the teams playing against us. Against Tottenham we created the chances and they did not have a shot. Liverpool came here with just Cisse up front and I think had one shot and Middlesbrough had one up front. But it is fair to say we should score more goals. Today we played for an hour with just Eidur as a pure striker. He is a good target. Duff is playing fantastic. The midfield is working very well and defensively we are playing great. So Arsenal are playing beautifully and we are playing not so good and not scoring many goals and we are just two points behind them – so in one weekend it can all change.'

With Drogba forced off through injury after 38 minutes and Kezman not on the bench, Cole is brought onto the right flank. He makes an immediate impact, setting Ferreira free down the line to cut inside and produce a pinpoint cross only for Lampard to send his diving header well wide.

Cole then hits the side netting before striking a half-volley from the edge of the area that Chris Kirkland manages to take the pace off before Harry Kewell heads off the line. But in what appears an expertly planned routine Lampard plays a delightful low free-kick for Cole to burst ahead of his marker and clip the ball first time past Kirkland.

Cech has to make an important late save from Steve Finnan, while Gudjohnsen and Cole also come close in the final stages. But once again it is 'one-nil to the Chelsea'.

> **Team**
> Cech, Ferreira, Terry, Carvalho, Gallas, Makelele, Smertin (Tiago), Lampard, Duff (Geremi), Drogba (Cole), Gudjohnsen.

Just eight goals in as many league games does not seem to compare favourably with Arsenal's 26. But Opta Index statisticians reveal Chelsea have had more shots than the Gunners and Manchester United. Chelsea have had 111 shots in the league compared to United's 102 and Arsenal's 101. Chelsea's goalscoring chances are hit by the news that Drogba needs minor surgery on the groin injury that forced him to limp off against Liverpool. And Adrian Mutu reveals a dispute with the coach. Mourinho claims Mutu has been injured and cannot play for Romania. But Mutu insists he is fit and flies out to face the Czech Republic. Mutu storms, 'I am in an open conflict with Mourinho who forbade me to go to my national team and said I was injured. It is not true – I have been in good condition for five days and he knew that. I don't care about being fined. I want everyone to know that the national team is the most important thing for me. Mourinho has promised me that I would play in the first team for some games. Then I wasn't even in the squad and I don't understand why. Probably the only solution, even if I don't want it, is to find another team.'

SATURDAY, 16 OCTOBER 2004
MANCHESTER CITY 1, CHELSEA 0

Mourinho's unbeaten record ends in a flurry of frustrated continental-style arm waving at the City of Manchester Stadium. After guiding his men through eight Premiership games without losing, he finally looks hot under the collar as a first-half Nicolas Anelka penalty brings the curtain down on the impressive start.

On a day when Arsenal are the only winners in the title race, Mourinho has to swallow defeat against a revved-up City side who deserve their win for a collective effort that leaves Chelsea for once unable to conjure a spark of magic.

The game is just ten minutes old when controversy strikes – leaving Chelsea a goal down and lucky to survive with 11 men. An easy-looking take for Gallas close to the halfway line suddenly turns into a nightmare as the defender slips on the greasy surface, presenting the ball straight to Paul Bosvelt. The Dutchman launches a long ball forward triggering a chase between Anelka and Ferreira, who grapples the Frenchman to the ground as they both surge into the area. Referee Howard Webb instantly awards a penalty but enrages Kevin Keegan by producing only a yellow card to punish Ferreira when, as last man, he should be sent off. A furious Keegan remonstrates with the fourth official before and after Anelka coolly sends Cech the wrong way with his penalty.

With Mourinho becoming more agitated at perceived each mistake, City fans have fun at his expense by mimicking his gestures as he waves his arms in exasperation. Having replaced Gallas with Bridge at the break, Mourinho then gambles by sending on Cole for Tiago with just over an hour gone. Despite Chelsea's escalating threat, City remain unruffled on the pitch even if Keegan's nerves are fraying.

This first defeat for Mourinho's side sees them drop five points behind Arséne Wenger's spectacular team. John Terry says, 'We want to win the title this season. But Arsenal are five points ahead of us now. A gap has started to form already and we simply cannot afford to let that gap get any bigger. We have had some great performances so far this season. But they go out the window when you suffer a defeat like this.'

On a day when Jimmy-Floyd Hasselbaink smashes in a hat-trick, the wisdom of selling the Dutchman has to come into question. Terry adds, 'We are getting chances but also getting caught offside too many times for my liking. We need to be more clinical, like Arsenal. When they get a chance they take it.'

Mourinho blames the international break. 'After the last two international breaks we have drawn with Aston Villa and now lost against Manchester City. Players go away for their internationals and managers have different ways of treating them. They come back in different conditions. Some play two games; some do not play at all. It is not an excuse but an important fact.'

Team

Cech, Ferreira, Terry, Carvalho (Geremi), Gallas (Bridge), Tiago (Cole), Lampard, Makelele, Duff, Kezman, Gudjohnsen.

Adrian Mutu's situation at the club becomes even more tenuous with the news that he has failed a drugs test. Mutu says he was tempted into taking drugs by the belief it would improve his sex life. The 25-year-old striker insists, 'I am not hooked on drugs. I categorically deny this. The only reason I took what I took was because I wanted to improve my sexual performance. It may be funny but it is true. I did not take cocaine. I took something to make me feel good.'

The Romanian, who joined Chelsea from Parma in August 2003, has had little impact on the team since falling out of favour with Claudio Ranieri in the second half of last season. Mutu has managed only two brief substitute appearances under Mourinho and claims that even before his failed drugs test he had come close to physically assaulting his new coach during a row. 'I have to admit that in the heat of our confrontation I did actually threaten Mourinho about what would happen if he ever went to Romania. In a moment of total madness I almost hit him too. But now I am calmer and I must say I have nothing against the coach.'

Chelsea refuse to comment but Gordon Taylor, the chief executive of the PFA, says, 'I have been in contact with the player but it would be wrong to say what he thinks. It's a matter of some concern because any action will apply internationally as well.'

Andrea Pretti, one of Mutu's representatives, adds, 'We are awaiting the counter-analysis. We don't think it will take long for things to happen, possibly a couple of days. You can imagine how the player feels. He already had technical problems at Chelsea and now this has just made it even worse. Until this situation is cleared up his future will is secondary.'

Mutu has four advisers, all apparently representing him. All are quoted in the press and all adapt different strategies in representing their client. The most famous, former Tottenham and Romania defender Gheorghe Popescu, arrives at Heathrow airport with another of Mutu's agents, Victor Becali. Before attending a meeting with Chelsea chief executive Peter Kenyon, Popescu confirms that Mutu will not be requesting the all-important B sample. 'I told him not to ask for the second sample so as not to prolong his agony.'

Mutu's fourth agent, Victor's brother Ion Becali, disowns his client in an extraordinary outburst live on Romanian television. Becali says, 'I found out about the drugs test last Tuesday. Jose Mourinho was a gentleman and called me up to tell me. I was very unhappy with Mutu when I told him about the test. I cannot protect him any more. Twice in the past I have wanted to break our contract because I was fed up with his attitude. He told me he had been given an illegal drug at a party. I know he has attended many, many parties like this. I think he wanted to copy David Beckham. But he was a very bad copy. Beckham is very professional.'

It emerges that Mutu was deliberately targeted by the doping authorities at the request of his manager. Gordon Taylor announces, 'Mutu's accepted that he did test positive for cocaine, and so we've got to deal with it under the social drugs procedure that we have in line with the FA. If the player accepts he is guilty and is prepared to undertake rehabilitation, to be checked regularly, to be clean, there is great sympathy towards the player.'

Mark Bosnich, also drug-tested at the request of the club, was sacked in 2003. If Chelsea sack Mutu, it would mean writing off the £15.8m they paid for him a year ago. 'Bearing in mind that investment, they've as much interest in getting the player back on track as the player has himself,' Taylor suggests.

Mourinho admits that it was a mistake for Chelsea to have bought Mutu and says he would have burrowed deeper into a player's lifestyle before signing him. 'When you spend big money with a player, you can't bet; you must be sure what you are buying,' Mourinho says. 'But sometimes you make mistakes. The best way is to analyse them in training because you cannot follow 16 hours a day outside. When you see a player committed, concentrated, strong, ready to do complex exercises, for sure his life outside football is good. When you see a player is tired, finds it difficult to concentrate, one day is very happy, another day is lonely and quiet, then you put the question mark and think, perhaps ...'

Chelsea decide to sack Mutu but reserve the right to claim compensation if he is not banned by the FA and is given a second chance in the Premiership or at a top club in Europe. 'We want to make clear that Chelsea has a zero-tolerance policy towards drugs,' a club statement says. 'This applies to both performance-enhancing drugs and so-called recreational drugs. They have no place at our club or in sport. In coming to a decision on this case, Chelsea believed the club's social responsibility to its fans, players, employees and other stakeholders in football regarding drugs was more important than the major financial considerations to the company.'

Mutu is charged and suspended by the FA. Kenyon defends the club's decision to 'target-test' Mutu and then sack him on grounds of gross misconduct. Gordon Taylor accuses the club of target-testing Mutu 'with a view to getting rid of him'.

Mourinho reveals he confronted Mutu over suspicions the player was using cocaine just days after joining Chelsea. 'When I met him on his first day in the pre-season in July and he was with his two agents Mr Becali and Mr Popescu I told all three, "I have information that you are on cocaine." All three were laughing, denying, saying this was a lot of lies about Adrian. After that I did not speak with them again because they denied the situation. For a long period we saw now and again strange behaviour. Arriving late a few times, not coming in to train other times. A doctor visiting his house and the apparent reason was just headaches. Injured when nobody knows how it happened – for example he was on the bench and did not play against Paris, yet the next day he was injured. We spoke about it. Is he pushing us to let him go in December? Is he doing this to get into a conflict with me [so I] say I don't want this player here? Or is he involved in other things? We began to question and the club doctor, because he has some experience that we do not have, was analysing with different eyes and he arrived at the decision that, maybe, yes. I would never sign him again. Not just because of the drug, but because he called me a liar.'

It is the first verbal attack from Chelsea as the battle lines are drawn ahead of a costly legal process. The club engages Jonathan Taylor, head of Hammonds' sports law group, with the FA appointing as prosecuting counsel Mark Gay, a board member of the British Association for Sport and Law. As well as representation from the PFA, Mutu's advisers are in advanced negotiations with Nick Bitel to act as defence counsel. The Culture, Media and Sport select committee called Bitel as an expert witness in its formulation of a drugs in sport report, and his testimony supports the FA's allowance in its rules for a divergence in the considerations of recreational and performance-enhancing drugs. This, along with Mutu's willingness to undergo a programme of rehabilitation forms the basis of Mutu's defence.

It is not, however, a discrepancy Mourinho appreciates. 'Recreational drugs are private life but football players, especially the pros of the big teams, they have a very, very big responsibility. The club bought [Mutu] to be ready to play football and in this moment he will be out of competition for a long period. The first one to break the relation was the player so he cannot complain.'

Mutu responds, 'Chelsea have destroyed me – I don't know what I am going to do. I am shocked and surprised by their decision. I didn't expect them to pay me while I was suspended but I never thought they would sack me either. Why didn't they wait to do this? Now my career is in ruins. I might as well walk away from football. What is there left for me?'

Peter Kenyon claims the player ignored their efforts to help him with his drug problem. Kenyon says, 'Players are given ample support these days and we fully support the PFA. But the same support was there for Adrian Mutu. He chose to ignore it, to lie, and as a consequence of that the rules are quite simple. To suggest there was no support and that we hung him out to dry because we wanted to get rid of him is absolute rubbish. We could have come to the decision in the summer, to move Mutu out and get a transfer fee for him. But we embraced him and wanted him to be very much part of our squad.'

Kenyon adds that Chelsea would dish out the same treatment to any player who fails a drug test. He claims both Mutu's contract and the FA's guidelines give Chelsea the right to sack their player, even before he has been through the FA disciplinary procedure.

SATURDAY, 23 OCTOBER 2004
CHELSEA 4, BLACKBURN ROVERS 0

Eidur Gudjohnsen produces a sublime hat-trick to hand Abramovich an early 38th birthday present. Chelsea's league goal tally increases by 50 per cent! This is the response to those who say Chelsea do not possess the attacking power to keep pace with champions Arsenal. Gudjohnsen says, 'I think we've been threatening to score a few goals in a match. We've been playing well, creating a lot of chances and it is just a matter of putting those chances away. Today we did that, plus the fact that we got another clean sheet, which is also fantastic. I've scored two goals for Chelsea on quite a few occasions but never a hat-trick. It's very pleasing and something I'll treasure.' Duff completes the rout with the fourth goal against his old team.

Mourinho gives Scott Parker and Glen Johnson their first starts under his reign. But with Parker sitting in front of the back four and Gudjohnsen as the only recognised striker, this does not look like a day for spectacular, free-flowing football. However, when Chelsea break, Duff and Smertin produce enough width to cause Rovers major problems.

After a Paul Dickov penalty appeal is waved away by referee Graham Poll, Chelsea seize their chance with two strikes in a minute. Cole's fantastic touch supplies the first in the 37th minute when he picks up a short Parker ball 35 yards out and chips a pass into Gudjohnsen's run a few yards from goal. With more shin than boot Gudjohnsen angles the ball past Brad Friedel. Seconds later another long ball – this time from Lampard – has the same timing and precision to give Gudjohnsen the chance to volley in.

Gudjohnsen's commitment pays off in the 50th minute when a surging run tempts Craig Short to bring him down just inside the box for a clear penalty. Gudjohnsen gleefully slots away his hat-trick.

At times Parker's desire gets the better of him – he picks up a needless booking for a rant at Poll – and much of his work is over-ambitious. But his presence at the base of midfield releases Lampard. Arjen Robben comes off the bench for a devastating 26 minutes, eight months after Chelsea agreed a deal with PSV Eindhoven. Mourinho says, 'I think our fans can now see what a blow it has been to have him out all this time. He is really important for us and we have been counting down the days until he was finally ready to play because he's one of the best in the world. He has super speed but he's not the type of player who has pace but lacks vision or the final ball. When he gets into position he chooses well when to pass, when to cross or when to shoot. He created a lot of chances for our strikers during his time on the pitch and I don't see why he couldn't play at the same time as Damien Duff.'

It is Duff who completes the scoring in the 74th minute. Mourinho adds, 'It was a good day for us after a difficult week. It was important for Eidur's confidence that he got the hat-trick. Now I can watch the Manchester United – Arsenal game with a smile. If United win we close the gap and if Arsenal win we distance ourselves from United. I still hope it's a draw, though.'

Team

Cech, Johnson, Carvalho, Terry, Bridge, Parker, Lampard, Smertin (Tiago), Duff, Cole (Robben), Gudjohnsen (Kezman).

Arsenal go down to a contentious and significant 2–0 defeat to Manchester United that reduces their lead to just two points. Everton, who visit Chelsea in two weeks, and who were many experts' tips for potential relegation, are surprisingly just a point further behind.

After his impressive display against Blackburn, Robben reveals he could well have ended up at Chelsea's big rivals Manchester United. United moved for the winger first, only for Chelsea to act decisively when Old Trafford negotiations stalled. Robben says he has no regrets. 'There was some interest from Manchester United. I went there but the second step is that the clubs have to come to a deal. They didn't. Chelsea were very quick and gave me the feeling that they wanted to get me. It wasn't a difficult decision because that gave me a lot of confidence. I had a meeting with four people, including Peter Kenyon and Claudio Ranieri. It was a good meeting.'

The subsequent managerial upheaval did not worry Robben. 'That wasn't a problem as I had that before at Eindhoven. When I was signed there, it wasn't long before Guus Hiddink came to the club. At Chelsea I knew Mr Mourinho was a good coach. I have a lot of confidence in him as a trainer. I can learn a lot from him. The only thing you have to do as a player is show what your qualities are, then it doesn't matter which manager is there.'

Good judges in Dutch football, such as the outstanding former Holland midfielder Wim van Hanegem, believe that ultimately

Robben's best position will be as a classic 'number 10', playing behind and around the main striker. As a child and in some of his teenage years he played that role before moving to the left wing when he became a professional. At PSV Hiddink pointed out to Robben a negative aspect to his game, one that has continued to dog him since Euro 2004 – a reputation as a player who goes to ground far too easily. But Robben feels that his style of play makes it inevitable that he will fall regularly. 'That's always the case when you are a fast player and you go past people. If they just touch you a little, sometimes you are out of balance. I know I'm not a diver. For me it's not a problem, but I know people call me that and I have to be aware.'

Adrian Mutu is suspended from football for seven months and fined £20,000 following the FA's disciplinary hearing. Mutu's ban is conditional on him successfully completing a period of rehabilitation and is backdated to start on 25 October. That means the suspension concludes on 18 May.

Peter Kenyon criticises the seven-month ban claiming the FA have been too lenient. In a statement Kenyon says, 'Chelsea are extremely disappointed with today's verdict. We believe it is far too lenient and sends out the wrong message about drugs in football. It is also indicative of a lack of direction within the FA at this time. As a club we can only take the action that we believe is right for Chelsea. However, the FA have a much wider responsibility to look after the interests of the game as a whole and, in this case, we believe it has shown itself to be weak over the issue of drugs.'

Gordon Taylor reveals the striker's thoughts after the hearing. 'Adrian admitted the charge from the beginning and accepted his responsibility,' declares Taylor, with Mutu standing just behind him. 'He is sorry for the problems that have been caused and he very soon wants to restore his good name in the international football world and particularly in his homeland of Romania. He is now looking forward to getting his career back on track in top-class football after next May.'

Mutu apologises to Chelsea's fans, blaming injury problems and loneliness for his 'mistakes' – but he insists he never tried to cheat. 'I am still disappointed with myself but now, because I know what I'm going to do and know what the ban is, I can breathe easier. I needed help and expected Chelsea to help me and I think he [Kenyon] wasn't so fair. They terminated my contract before the FA made a decision. In Tony Adams and Paul Merson's cases they were being helped by the club and that means a lot for a player.

'I first took the drug in February. I didn't want to cheat on football. I had been injured in that time and because I was very sad that night I got drunk. I don't drink usually so it's easy for me to get drunk. I made a mistake and I know that now and I am very sorry about this. I know I have disappointed them [the fans]. I wish them all the best, and I wish to see Chelsea at a good level and come back to Stamford Bridge and play against Chelsea. I've made a mistake and I am sorry. Who doesn't make mistakes in this life?'

Mutu fires his agents and signs a new deal with an Italian management company led by Alessandro Moggi, son of Juventus managing director Luciano Moggi. And he fires a parting shot at Mourinho. 'I am sure Mourinho didn't notice that I had a busy private life because he simply didn't care about me. My problem with him was to do with the national team. I will always have a problem with a coach who doesn't let me play for my national team. As a coach Mourinho is very good, but as a person I have a big question mark about him.'

SATURDAY, 30 OCTOBER 2004
WEST BROMWICH ALBION 1, CHELSEA 4

Mourinho repeats his claim that Chelsea are statistically the best team in England after their second successive four-goal Premiership win sends them level on points with Arsenal, who are surprisingly held to a draw by Southampton. 'Our first-half display was our worst performance this season,' says Mourinho. But it got much better in the second half and the substitutions worked. With the other results it was a fantastic day for Chelsea. That is the beauty of the game in

England – if I was five or six points ahead in Portugal, the title would be over. Over 14 matches in all competitions we have a better statistical record than Arsenal because we have won 12 and drawn two, while they have won 10 and four draws – now that gap has widened. I would say they have just been better than us in the Premiership.'

Chelsea break the deadlock late in the first half when Terry dives to guide a looping Lampard delivery across the face of goal. Albion freeze and Gallas volleys home a rare strike. Mourinho is still not happy and hauls off Cole and Bridge. Robben spices up the attack and, within two minutes, sees a shot drift wide. Gudjohnsen makes it 2–0, heading home Duff's 51st-minute cross. Albion give themselves hope when Zoltan Gera lashes the ball into the net. But their hopes are short-lived as Lampard runs 70 yards and releases Duff, who clips his shot over Russell Hoult and inside the far post. Lampard then makes it four in the 81st minute with a stunning strike.

With eight goals in two Premiership games and a five-point deficit on the Gunners wiped out, the table has a different complexion. Yet Lampard, the driving force behind this impressive victory, admits he feared the worst at Arsenal's record-breaking start to the season. 'It's nice to see Arsenal are human after all,' says Lampard. 'They have been unbelievable this season and they almost didn't seem human when they were winning every week. Arsenal have been phenomenal and everyone has been talking about how well they have played, but points are all that matters. We have come back at them and that is how a football season works. They have conceded a few points and now we need to make sure we keep our own results going. We have been accused of being boring but, in the second half, we were strutting about.'

Robben catches the eye with his ability to switch wings, track back and run at people. Mourinho says, 'He brings something different to the team. He was fantastic and always dangerous every time he had the ball.'

Team

Cech, Ferreira, Terry, Gallas, Bridge (Carvalho), Smertin, Makelele, Lampard (Tiago), Cole (Robben), Gudjohnsen, Duff.

Following an impressive 1–0 win in Moscow to romp through to the knock-out stages of the Champions League with two games to spare, Chelsea now have the advantage of concentrating on the title, with Arsenal wobbling and United uncharacteristically inconsistent in Europe. Mourinho says, 'We've put pressure on ourselves as we've not asked for time. We said from the beginning that we want to win every game and to be one of the best teams in Europe. Of course next season my team will be better and in two seasons even better, but at the moment we're fighting for results and coping well with the pressure. We can achieve something big this season.'

Arsenal's blip raises expectations of the title coming to Stamford Bridge for the first time in 50 years, but Mourinho tells his players to concentrate on themselves. He says, 'We can't think about Arsenal. We have to win our own matches and see what they do. They cannot win every match but will not lose points every weekend. Maybe tomorrow they will lose points or they will return with a victory at Crystal Palace, but we must make sure we win our game and stay on top of the league. We've lost one game to Manchester City, but after that won five consecutive games, which is very important. You have to show you're strong enough for the fight.'

SATURDAY, 6 NOVEMBER 2004
CHELSEA 1, EVERTON 0

Robben tells his team-mates in a pep-talk before the game to play so well that Arsenal will 'shit in their pants'. Mourinho likes a player to address the team in the dressing room prior to kick-off and it works. Robben declares, 'I kept it simple and said, "Let's continue what we have been doing. Arsenal are playing after us today so let's pressure them, make it hard for them."' Robben's gloriously spectacular second-half strike on his first Premiership start ends the only unbeaten away record in the Premiership, and Arsenal are later held to a 1–1 draw at Crystal Palace.

Chelsea rotate their team with Johnson, Gallas and Parker giving way to Ferreira, Babayaro and Tiago. Makelele and Tiago spend the first half trying in vain to wriggle out of Everton's midfield straitjacket. Kezman replaces Tiago, but his settling-in period is proving long and laboured, and it is not until 20 minutes from time that Nigel Martyn is exposed, only for Gudjohnsen to waste a Terry knockdown.

Kezman's appearance at least galvanises Gudjohnsen and it is his superb turn and floated pass that leads to the breakthrough. Robben dashes clear and not even David Weir's desperate tug can prevent the tricky winger from lifting a delicate lob over Martyn. Tim Cahill's unchallenged header late on is a notch short of the power needed to beat Cech, who is proving the shrewdest of all Chelsea's purchases.

Robben acquires a new nickname, 'The Catalyst', because of his ability to turn games around after coming off the bench. There is an expectant buzz from the crowd whenever he is in possession and he comes desperately close to scoring a magnificent goal midway through the first half when he chips the ball cleverly over Weir's head, then lets fly from the edge of the D. But Martyn brings off a top-class save.

Mourinho acknowledges Everton's performance. 'They have players who are strong, experienced and were good defensively. But we kept the faith, and when Arjen scored we were able to change our organisation and come away with the points. I told the players at half-time if we want to be champions, we have to play like champions – we have to play risky. The alternative was to stay comfortable and enjoy life but, if we play that way, there will be no trophies for us at the end of the season. At the end it felt like a cup final in the dressing room. That is how it must be for the rest of the season.'

Robben, on the mark at CSKA Moscow in midweek, adds, 'It was nice for me to score again but it's been a great week for the team. I can tell you now that we aren't going to win all the games until the end of the season. We will lose and that's all part of the game. But you have to try to win all the prizes. That's how it should be. The Premiership is much tougher than the Dutch league, with big games every week, but I am ready for the physical challenge. I came here to win championships and believe I can do that with Chelsea.'

Everton boss David Moyes says, 'I thought we could hold out but Robben proved the difference. If I had £12m, I would buy a player like that. But the fact is if you can't shop at Armani, you have to shop at Marks and Spencer.'

Team

Cech, Ferreira, Carvalho, Terry, Babayaro, Tiago (Kezman), Makelele, Lampard, Duff (Huth), Gudjohnsen (Geremi), Robben.

Mourinho dismisses speculation linking him with a January move for Real Betis winger Joaquin and Tottenham's Jermain Defoe. He is adamant that his 23-man squad is strong enough to cope with the dual demands of the Premiership and Champions League and has no plans to replace Adrian Mutu. Mourinho says, 'I don't need any more strikers or any other players in January. Duff and Robben are playing well and linking together. We don't have a pure outside-right player, but have two left-footed players who can play together. Eidur Gudjohnsen did a very good job at the start of the season. If everybody is fit I have a lot of options.'

But while he is happy with the team, Mourinho calls on Chelsea fans to be more vocal. He tells Chelsea TV, 'When I can hear 2,000 Everton fans behind me and 35,000 Chelsea fans not being too enthusiastic, I feel we need more.' He also says he wants his long-term future to be at Stamford Bridge. 'I'm so happy with English football, my players and the people that surround me at the club that I want to be here at Chelsea for many, many years.'

John Terry also shows his commitment to the club by signing a new five-year contract just 18 months after putting pen to paper on his last deal. 'I want to be here for the rest of my career,' he says. 'The manager is a key figure. He's made me club captain and I want to stay here and play for him.'

Mourinho looks for an English solution when it comes to strengthening his squad. He believes it is crucial for the development of the team to keep the core of his side as English as possible, and only 'crazy' fees will stop him from scouring the country for new talent in the future. Mourinho says, 'John signing a new deal for us was crucial. It was very important to keep the core of the team English, with players of a strong mentality. We must only go abroad to buy what we don't have here. If you don't have a special player for a special position in the English market you have to look abroad. But the most important thing is to try and look for English players first. But sometimes the fees are crazy amounts, so we have to look elsewhere.'

Next up for Mourinho's table-toppers are local rivals Fulham at Craven Cottage, while Arsenal face a high noon showdown at Tottenham. Mourinho taunts Arsenal by insisting Chelsea are so far ahead of the rest that they will win the Premiership two weeks before the end of the season. Mourinho has only been top for seven days but is determined to stay there for the long haul. He says, 'Just ten minutes ago I was driving down the King's Road with one of my assistants and he said that on 14 May it will be crazy because that's the final day of the season. But I said maybe we should do it two weeks earlier and celebrate then.'

SATURDAY, 13 NOVEMBER 2004

FULHAM 1, CHELSEA 4

Arsenal win 5–4 at the Lane in the midday kick-off, but Chelsea respond in style to restore their two-point lead with another Robben-inspired performance. Mourinho chooses a Chelsea side almost unrecognisable from the team that beat Newcastle in the Carling Cup in the week, making seven changes.

Chelsea take a deserved lead through a fantastic Lampard free-kick into the right corner from almost 30 yards. Fulham simply cannot get a foothold in the match and, after Papa Bouba Diop has made a great last-ditch clearance following Terry's header across goal, the home side are lucky not to concede a penalty. Robben feeds Lampard on the edge of the box after 36 minutes, and the England midfielder's shot hits Zeshan Rehman's raised arm, but referee Uriah Rennie waves play on. Lampard is again unfortunate in first-half stoppage time. Although he appears to be tripped in the area by Moritz Volz, he is booked for diving.

Fulham produce a stunning equaliser on 57 minutes – and it has to be to beat Cech. Terry's headed clearance drops to Diop 30 yards out, and the Senegalese midfielder's vicious volley shoots into Cech's right-hand corner for a memorable first club goal.

But Chelsea regain the lead two minutes later as Robben shows wonderful footwork to elude Zat Knight, Rehman and Mark Pembridge before firing in with his left foot from 15 yards. That proves the catalyst as Gallas seizes on a Diop miskick and heads in from three yards at the far post. Chelsea then seal it with a delightful fourth goal nine minutes from time. Tiago feeds Robben down the left, and the winger's marvellous back-heel gives the Portuguese player time and space to arrow a 16-yard shot into the right corner.

Once again Robben is the difference, with arguably his best performance so far. He takes the match to Fulham, sets up the fourth goal and tops his display with one of the goals of the season. So was it Ranieri, or was it Kenyon who snatched Robben away from Manchester United? 'If it was Mr Ranieri, then congratulations, thank you very much,' muses Mourinho. 'If it was Peter Kenyon or Mr Abramovich, then I say perhaps they should both become managers, because they know a lot about players.'

Chelsea's goal difference is closing in on Arsenal's, and Mourinho taunts Arsenal's defence for conceding four times at Spurs. 'I didn't see Arsenal's game, but 5–4 is a joke result. It is not a real football result; it was like a hockey match. For a team to give away four or five goals, the defenders must be a disgrace. I often play three versus three in training and if the score gets to 5–4 then I send the players to the dressing room and stop the game! They are obviously not doing their job properly and it is no point going on with it – and that's just in a three-a-side game. In a true game I cannot believe the defenders are doing their job properly at all and as a manager this would be a nightmare. Some people may go away thinking it was the best game they had ever seen but as a manager how could you be happy?' While the Gunners have conceded four goals in one game, Chelsea have conceded just four Premiership goals all season.

Mourinho adds, 'I do not think I am vain or arrogant but I believe that now we are top of the table Chelsea can go on to win the championship. I don't say this just for the sake of it – I say it because I truly believe we are good enough to win the title. This was a big test for us and we had the answer. We showed we could handle the pressure. I still remain convinced that we can become the champions.'

Once again preparation is meticulous. Robben says, 'Before every single match you are given a full dossier on your direct opponent – not the team but the precise man you will be playing against. For example, my direct opponent against Fulham was around two metres tall and the coach wanted me to know that in advance and prepare for it.' Terry reveals that the derby status of the game was explained in no uncertain terms to all the new players. 'Before the game we made sure that everyone in that dressing room knew exactly what games between Chelsea and Fulham mean. The rivalry between the clubs and the history of the fixture is very important to our supporters and to get the result against our neighbours that puts us back on top of the league is even better.'

Team

Cech, Ferreira, Terry, Carvalho, Gallas, Lampard, Makelele, Smertin (Tiago), Duff (Kezman), Robben, Gudjohnsen.

The search to replace Mutu takes Roman Abramovich, accompanied by Kenyon, to the Ajax Amsterdam Arena at the weekend to watch Feyenoord starlet Salomon Kalou. The Ivory Coast-born striker has hit an impressive nine goals in 12 games in the Eredivisie – flourishing under the tutelage of Ruud Gullit. The 19-year-old has a quiet game in the 1–1 draw with Ajax but is earmarked for great things at the De Kuip Stadion.

Valeri Bojinov has caught the eye of Mourinho with eight Serie A goals for Lecce. The 18-year-old is just one goal behind Andriy Shevchenko, Inter's Brazilian ace Adriano and Roma hitman Vincenzo

Montella. Mourinho sends assistant Steve Clarke to watch the Bulgarian international in action against Juventus and Siena. Arsenal, Barcelona, Marseille and Borussia Dortmund are also chasing Bojinov.

Mourinho says he is delighted with how quickly the team have gelled. 'It was the big question mark. I'll never forget a word I had with Mario Stanic. He left the club but he was with me on the first day and said something like, "A lot of people have arrived in England and they adapt to the English reality of football. But I know that your methods and your philosophy and your way of thinking are very special. Don't ever change, even if it takes time, don't change." I'll never forget what he said. So it was a question for me whether the players could adapt. I followed an Italian manager, and it cannot be easy when you follow a manager who thinks very differently.

'At the moment I feel we are a very strong team defensively. I don't say we are a defensive team. I say we are a strong team in defensive terms, but at the same time lacking sufficient fluidity in attack, because that will take time to come. But we play very good football at times. The only thing I would like is to have more control of the game in terms of possession. In five years I have never had a match where my team has had less possession than the opponents. Never, never. We could play Real Madrid, we could play Deportivo La Coruna, even Manchester United; we always had a bigger percentage. Again, that takes time, but the team is going in the right direction.

'We must think more about our football and not play by instinct. When you play another team with the same qualities as you, normally the better one wins. But when you play against other teams who can stop during the game and think collectively, it becomes much more difficult. You see how Spanish, Italians, Portuguese play football? I don't say that they are perfect. English football has a few things to learn from them in the same way they have a lot of things to learn from English football. I have a lot to learn from English football and am completely open to good influences. But I also have things to give. The lines of communication between me and my players are wide open and the intention is to improve the whole team by each one of us giving our best. I believe it can make us a strong team. I cannot say we will win the Champions League or the Premiership, but I know that we can do it. Real Madrid have a group of stars and they have a group of young boys who are not ready to cope with that pressure and that quality. What is missing is what I call low-profile players. For example, in my team I love to have Geremi on the bench because he's a low-profile player who is ready to help, to fight for the team, to do the job I want him to do. If I need him to play right-back, he can play right-back. If I need him to play right-winger, he can play right-winger. If I need him to pick up a man and mark him out of the game, he does it.'

SATURDAY, 20 NOVEMBER 2004

CHELSEA 2, BOLTON WANDERERS 2

Never before in his managerial career can Mourinho recall losing a two-goal lead. 'No, no, no, never. Never, never, never,' he insists. A club record ninth successive victory in all competitions is snatched away by the set-piece specialists who earn a draw from two free-kicks, the second three minutes from the end.

The noisiest roar of the afternoon greets the news that Arsenal have mysteriously failed to see off West Bromwich Albion at Highbury, but that is eventually followed by 40,000 groans at Bolton's equaliser. The surprise bulletin on Arsenal's latest lapse arrives well before the finish at Stamford Bridge, where traffic and transport chaos delay the kick-off by 30 minutes.

Duff makes a blistering start after all the delays, scoring after 36 seconds. Robben feeds Lampard for a shrewd through-pass to Duff, just about onside. His first touch seems to have taken the ball too wide, but he uses the wet surface to slide forward and knock the ball into the empty net from an angle. A goal right at the start of the second half by Tiago seems to have extended Chelsea's advantage at the head of the table to four points, but Kevin Davies and then Rahdi Jaidi do Arsenal a huge favour.

A measure of Bolton's effectiveness is that they have met last season's top five Premiership teams and remained unbeaten. Sam Allardyce rightly praises the 'resilience, belief and team spirit' that keeps them in contention, while admitting, 'We've nicked a point.'

Mourinho is dignified in his disappointment. 'I don't think many people like the way Bolton play, but they're effective and dangerous. It was a bad result because we want to win every game. Yet we have to be fair. It is very difficult to play against them. Bolton can beat everybody because they create danger from nothing. It is a style I don't like – but we have to give them credit. I'm happy we only have to play them once more.'

Mourinho describes how Bolton attack as 'ugly', but confesses his team had no answer to the aerial bombardment. That is despite spending 20 minutes before kick-off going through a video of Bolton's set-pieces with his players.

But for a long time the only scare for the home side is self-inflicted, Carvalho almost turning the ball into his own net as it bounces awkwardly at him from a free-kick by Bruno N'Gotty. Bolton hold out until the interval, only to be undone again two minutes after it. In the home side's first attack of the second half, Duff controls Robben's corner from the right and lays it back to him for a cross that Tiago meets with a vicious low volley.

But Bolton's self-belief has been boosted by their unexpectedly good results and a set-piece soon revives them and their supporters, who have been complaining about the £40 admission price. Speed swings in a free-kick that evades Cech, and Davies heads it past him off the shoulder of Jaidi. It is only the second Premiership goal Mourinho's team have conceded on the ground all season and the first in almost three months.

Chelsea have chances to extend their lead, but Jussi Jaaskelainen beats away Lampard's fierce drive, Gallas's shot from the rebound painfully strikes a defender, and Gudjohnsen's effort from a corner is held by the keeper on the line at the second attempt. Gudjohnsen then strikes the crossbar, and the sucker punch comes three minutes from time when N'Gotty pumps another free-kick forward and Jaidi latches on to Davies' knockdown to shoot past Cech. Having scored at Highbury in another 2–2 draw earlier this season, the Tunisian has been as even-handed in the championship race as the rest of his side.

Despite Cech flapping for the first goal, Mourinho insists, 'I have no criticism of my players. We're top of the league. My confidence doesn't change; my happiness with the players doesn't change. I never speak about my players when they make big mistakes. I never consider one player individually guilty for a defeat; if anyone is guilty, it's the manager. Petr will face Charlton with my confidence.'

Team

Cech, Ferreira, Carvalho, Terry, Gallas, Tiago, Lampard, Makelele, Duff (Kezman), Gudjohnsen (Johnson), Robben.

Charlton call an end to their simmering feud with Chelsea ahead of their match at The Valley. First there was the row over the Stamford Bridge 'beach' a couple of years ago when the Premier League fined Chelsea £5,000 for failing to inform Charlton about the state of the surface. The Addicks felt less bruised about the outcome of the Scott Parker stand-off a year later, their first confrontation with the Abramovich regime. While unhappy that their star player had pushed too hard for a move and suspicious about the advice Parker was getting, the basic £10m fee Charlton eventually agreed was good business.

Part of the midfielder's deal included provision for striker Carlton Cole to stay for a second season on loan with Charlton. When he chose not to stay in the summer another row blew up. Chelsea loaned Cole to Villa instead, and when the Stamford Bridge club could not offer Charlton an acceptable alternative, Valley lawyers combed the small print of their contracts. The Premier League again were called in but the clubs managed to settle things on their own and Chelsea paid an undisclosed but significant compensation fee.

Prompted by back page headlines in three national papers, Mourinho rules out a move for Tottenham's Jermain Defoe in the

January transfer window. Mourinho says, 'It is completely untrue. Not because I don't like the player – I like him. He is a very good young player but we are not interested.'

Arséne Wenger says he believes Chelsea will make a fresh move for Steven Gerrard at some point. Gerrard was close to a £25m switch in the summer but made a massive U-turn and pledged his future to the Merseysiders. Wenger says, 'Chelsea get who they want sooner or later, so it might be only a temporary decision. But I am not jealous of their money. I find it exciting to fight a team with much bigger potential, financially.'

The Gunners' loss of form has coincided with an injury to Sol Campbell, but Mourinho says, 'Arsenal, Chelsea and Manchester United all have big squads, which offer solutions to all the problems that come up. So there should be no excuses. Ourselves, Arsenal and United have all had injury problems, but ones we can cope with.'

SATURDAY, 27 NOVEMBER 2004

CHARLTON ATHLETIC 0, CHELSEA 4

John Terry and Frank Lampard are once again the driving force behind another Chelsea victory. Terry's second-half goals, separated by just three minutes, are a testament to his determination to get forward, as well as marshal the meanest defence in the top flight. While Lampard gives a performance that is a fitting tribute to his grandfather who passed away the day before.

Another lightning start sees Duff on the scoresheet after 229 seconds. Gudjohnsen gets the ball deep and flicks it hard and low into Duff's path. The Irishman sweeps past Paul Konchesky and arrogantly pokes the ball into the far corner of Dean Kiely's goal.

The only blemish in a near-perfect first half comes when Carvalho plants a diving header on to his own post. But Mourinho is far from happy with just a one-goal interval lead and lets his team know it.

Charlton's hopes go into decline within five minutes of the restart as Terry stages his scoring spree. First he bustles in with a header from Duff's looping corner, which bounces just in front of Kiely giving him little chance. Then he taps in after another Duff corner is headed back across goal and Radostin Kishishev can only clear the ball to the Chelsea captain.

Just before being replaced by Drogba, Gudjohnsen holds himself onside just long enough to score the fourth after a stunning low pass from Lampard leaves him the simple task of tapping past Kiely.

A year ago Alan Curbishley's side gave Ranieri's title pretenders a harsh lesson as they beat the Blues 4–2 on Boxing Day. But Mourinho's Chelsea are a different class and the efficiency of their victory echoes around the dressing rooms of Highbury and Old Trafford.

Team

Cech, Ferreira, Carvalho, Terry, Gallas, Tiago, Makelele, Lampard, Duff (Geremi), Robben (Babayaro), Gudjohnsen (Drogba).

Arsenal lose 2–1 at Anfield, leaving them five points behind Chelsea in a remarkable turnaround at the top of the table. Their hopes of retaining the title are dealt a further blow when Vieira is ruled out of the crucial showdown with Chelsea at Highbury after receiving his fifth caution of the season. Vieira says, 'When we are going through a difficult time like this, I have a big part to play and I will try my best. As a team we have to improve. It is up to us. If we really want it, we are going to do it. The quality and the hunger to keep the title is there. We know what we have to do.' With Brazilians Gilberto Silva and Edu injured, Wenger has no option but to field an inexperienced central midfield duo of Mathieu Flamini and Francesc Fabregas against the league leaders. After just one win and four draws in the last six Premiership games, Arsenal desperately need the win against Chelsea to revive their title challenge. Vieira adds, 'We know we played better at the start of the season. We need maybe a bit of togetherness to help us win the games. Three or four years ago maybe we would have won the game at Liverpool. We are disappointed because we wanted to start winning again.'

But first up for Chelsea are Newcastle under new manager Graeme Souness. The Scot believes fans will look back in future years and acclaim Mourinho's Chelsea for their starring role in a golden era in the game's history. As a player Souness was a hugely influential figure during Liverpool's golden era. 'People often talk to me about the good old days, but in 20 years' time what we are doing today will be considered the good old days. In my opinion these are the glory days and as a manager it's a privilege to be involved. In years to come I think they'll be saying, "D'you remember the great Chelsea and Arsenal teams at the start of the century?"

'It's easy to be dismissive of Chelsea's success and say they've achieved this and that simply because of the money they have,' adds Souness. 'But the manager still has to do the job. He has to sign the right players, pick the right team and get them to win consistently. He's done all that in my opinion with some style. You also have to say that he has an outstanding pedigree. You don't win the Champions League and the UEFA Cup without talent and without making the right decisions. But what I've learned is that no manager gets everything right. Yes, you enjoy the highs, but there are lots of lows too. That's the price on the ticket. There's a great sense of responsibility when you're the manager.'

SATURDAY, 4 DECEMBER 2004
CHELSEA 4, NEWCASTLE UNITED 0

Chelsea consolidate their position at the top with four second-half goals. Drogba stands in front of the adoring Chelsea faithful bellowing 'I'm back!' in celebration of his superb strike. The curse that normally comes with both the Player and Manager of the Month awards is lifted as both Mourinho and Robben receive their accolades before kick-off and again make their own special contributions. The deepest joy, though, is reserved for Mateja Kezman's first league goal: an absolutely delightful chip from the spot.

Lampard breaks Newcastle's resistance with the opener in the 63rd minute, and substitute Drogba adds the vital second five minutes later before Robben and Kezman wrap up the points with two goals in the final minutes. Unchanged from the team that thumped Charlton, Chelsea have a Terry header correctly ruled out for offside early on. In a lively opening Cech brilliantly pushes aside a Laurent Robert free-kick from 25 yards, while Craig Bellamy should put the visitors in front when Dyer carves open the Chelsea defence with a perfect through-ball. Once again Cech thwarts his man and Chelsea escape again when the ball runs loose to Robert from the keeper but the Newcastle winger sends his effort wide.

Gudjohnsen is then left in the clear with just Shay Given to beat after a defensive mix-up, but the Icelandic striker shoots wide with the goal at his mercy. Mourinho replaces him with Drogba at the interval. Robert brings another excellent save from Cech from a free-kick before Lampard makes no mistake from six yards after latching on to a Drogba knockdown.

Five minutes later roles are reversed as Drogba runs on to Lampard's crafted long ball and beats Given with a clever left-footed shot inside the right-hand post. Chelsea are now irresistible and, after Kezman hits the post, Robben wraps up the points after weaving his way into the area. And there is still time for Kezman to break his Premiership duck from the penalty-spot in stoppage time after Given brings down Duff.

'For the last three or four months I've been unlucky,' insists Kezman. 'I hit the post again today but all the players have helped me with my confidence. I know all the lads were behind me, so you can try anything. I worked hard every day to get to this moment. I've played more than 1,000 minutes this season and had only scored one goal in the Carling Cup, so it has been very difficult. Goals are my life. That's me. Without goals I have a difficult life. When you have scored 20 or 30 goals every year for the past seven or eight years and then go three months with just one, it is very hard. You could see our spirit after I scored. Every single player came to me. That was fantastic and that is our strength this season. That is how we can be champions.'

It is the fifth time in seven Premiership games that Chelsea have scored four times. Newcastle, like Blackburn, West Brom, Fulham and Charlton before them, are simply blown apart. Chelsea are now

33–1 for a clean sweep of the Premiership, the FA Cup, the Carling Cup and the Champions League.

> **Team**
>
> Cech, Ferreira, Terry, Carvalho, Gallas (Bridge), Tiago (Kezman), Makelele, Lampard, Robben, Gudjohnsen (Drogba), Duff.

Both Arsenal and Manchester United win 3–0 at home later in the afternoon and Sir Alex Ferguson says he expects Chelsea to slip up in the title race. 'Chelsea will have a blip. They will lose games. It's then a case of how their players react which will be important. Arsenal and ourselves have got that experience. We have seen title challenges be over by March. Chelsea don't have the experience of winning when it really matters.'

Contractors move in to relay the pitch at Stamford Bridge, which should be ready for their next home game against Norwich in 12 days' time. The surface has deteriorated severely and the win against Newcastle was played in particularly difficult conditions.

Chelsea warm up for the title showdown at Arsenal with a Champions League defeat at Porto. 'Every defeat hurts and we're used to winning,' says Terry. 'It doesn't change the group but we wanted to win the game. We don't like losing games and picked a strong team to win it. We're all angry after defeats, including the manager, but we can see the bigger picture. We've got a more important game on Sunday.'

Claudio Ranieri will be in the stands to watch his old side for the first time since being sacked. 'Italian television have asked me to be the commentator for this match and I plan to go to the game,' he says. 'I won't see anyone at Chelsea but plan to go straight to the stadium. I've had no contact since I left the club and am a very reserved man. If they don't want to see me that's fine and I'm happy with the way things have turned out. I don't want to disturb anybody and will just watch the match and see some old friends.'

Having led Chelsea to second place in the Premiership and the Champions League semi-finals last season, Ranieri is convinced they can go one better this time around. 'Chelsea must be one of the favourites for the Champions League because Mourinho has won it before and my players had a good experience last year. It's possible for them to win the Champions League and the Premiership. Why not? Chelsea are very strong. We did a very good job last year putting the foundations in place and they're continuing to progress.'

Chelsea's dramatic victory in last season's Champions League quarter-final may have been the high water mark of Ranieri's reign but that should not detract from its significance after 17 games without a win over their London rivals. Ranieri adds, 'I was very happy Chelsea got Drogba because in my last meeting with Abramovich in Milan I said he should sign him. He wanted to know my ideas for new players, and I said Drogba, another central defender and Steven Gerrard. It was my idea to sign Robben and I met him in Eindhoven. I'd watched a lot of videos of him and was very impressed. I'm not surprised by his success and when I met him I was sure straight away. I told him he could play on the left, on the right and he could swap with Damien Duff. I knew very well they could play together.'

Robben reveals he feared he had testicular cancer at the beginning of the year. He needed an operation to remove a lump – and then faced an agonising wait while tests were done. 'I was very scared – it was a very difficult time. I found a little lump and went to the doctor. He told me I needed an operation. I then had to wait for the results and I didn't know if it was going to be good or bad news. The waiting was terrible for a few days. I didn't know what was going to happen to me. It was a horrible wait. Then I heard the news was good and it was a massive relief. At that time football was no longer important – the most important thing is to be healthy and for your family to be healthy. It's good to talk about it and put it out in the public domain. Why would you be embarrassed about it? It can happen to any man at any time and can lead to terrible consequences.'

Arséne Wenger sends his stars to the bowling alley to ease the pressure ahead of the game. While Mourinho was pushing his stars through a gruelling training session, Arsenal's first-team squad enjoyed skittles for three hours. The Arsenal manager insists his side are back to top form after crucial wins over Birmingham and Rosenborg – and will prove it with a victory at Highbury, even without the suspended Vieira. 'We just want to win,' says Wenger. 'I don't think their fans will laugh when they lose the game. We are ready. We have won two games since last week. We have the talent and the spirit and we believe we will do it. We're looking forward to the game.'

But Mourinho sees things differently. 'At the end of the game Chelsea will be top of the league. So it's not a question of whether this game can decide a change of positions. It's not a case that because of this game Arsenal could go top and Chelsea go second. The only question left is: two points difference, five points difference or eight points difference? And I tell you eight points difference is a lot. If we win, it is significant. If we draw, it's five points; if we lose, it's two points. But our next two matches are at home against Norwich and Aston Villa. So it's significant if we win.'

Wenger is sure the neutrals are behind Arsenal because Chelsea are backed by Abramovich. He says, 'I am surprised that more people are not behind us because we have less money than Manchester United and Chelsea, with whom we are direct competition. We have 30-times less investment capacity.'

But Mourinho ridicules that notion, 'When Thierry Henry signed for Arsenal was that for free? Did Juventus give him to Arsenal? When Vieira came here was that on loan? Did they rent him for £100,000? Was Reyes free from Sevilla? That surprises me, the fact that Sevilla made Reyes a Christmas gift. Ha! How much have I spent at Chelsea? Sometimes you confuse things by saying how much Chelsea have spent. We don't spend too much – maybe Man United spend more than me.'

Mourinho has splashed £70m of Abramovich's money on five players in his short time in charge, and, even though Wenger has laid out £95m, his net expenditure is just £9m in eight years. Wenger hits back, 'Of course we've spent. I didn't say we hadn't. I don't feel we're poor. But if I ask who has the biggest financial potential, Chelsea or Arsenal, what would you say? Arsenal? I don't think so. We bought

Thierry Henry with the money we generated from Nicolas Anelka – less than half of it. We bought Patrick Vieira for £3.5m at that time so you cannot say that was a big investment. It forces you to be a little bit more creative.'

Mourinho says that Vieira's suspension will be a big blow to Arsenal, but he points to the fact that Arsenal's magnificent, free-scoring run at the start of the season came without the Frenchman, who was recovering from injury. He says, 'They will miss him. The same way that I would miss John Terry if he was not involved in the game. And, to be fair the best period of the season they have had was at the beginning when they beat everybody scoring four and five. And Patrick was not there. It looks a contradiction because Patrick is a fantastic player. But it's reality. They didn't miss him in that period. I think they have a lot of potential. Their young players are good. Flamini is good, Fabregas is good, Robert Pires can play in the middle as he is top quality and has a lot of experience. So I think they have an answer and I think they have a great side.'

Mourinho adds that he has used Kezman in training as a double for Thierry Henry. The coach explains, 'Henry is one of the best strikers in the world; there's no doubt about it. What he has done in English football in recent years speaks for itself. He's a threat; he can score. You have to try to control his movement, but not just his movement but what the team tries to create for him. We've studied the movements he makes on the pitch and for the last two days we have tried on the training ground to practise our defensive movements in relation to Thierry's attacking movements. Kezman took on the role of Henry, and now I think we are ready to fight him.'

Mourinho also points out that he has not lost a big game in his entire career. In two and a half seasons with Porto Mourinho was unbeaten in games against major rivals Benfica and Sporting Lisbon. So far this season Chelsea have already beaten Liverpool and Manchester United. 'In 12 or 13 big games with Porto, classics as we call them in Portugal, we never lost. I've got a very good record in important matches and have every confidence in my team.'

SUNDAY, 12 DECEMBER 2004
ARSENAL 2, CHELSEA 2

A global television audience of 600 million watches events underline the growing interest in Chelsea's attempt to oust their London rivals as Premiership champions. The players demonstrate how a tense, competitive fixture can be spectacularly entertaining and still promote its finer virtues.

One of only four Englishmen in the starting line-ups, Terry's leadership is as important as the contributions from more glamorous names. But Mourinho is angry Thierry Henry's quickly taken 29th-minute free-kick is allowed to stand, even though referee Graham Poll has not blown his whistle and Cech is still busy lining up his defensive wall. Mourinho is grateful for a late let-off as Henry misses a glorious 77th-minute chance to wrap up victory for the Gunners, who are still left trailing leaders Chelsea by five points.

Mourinho says, 'I don't want to talk too much about it otherwise I will have to go before the FA, spend time in the stands and it might cost me money I would rather spend on Christmas presents. But I am more than unhappy. Unhappy is a nice word and I cannot say the word which is in my heart and soul. Because I cannot forget Arsenal's second goal I don't think it was a fair result. But my players gave a big performance and the result keeps the distance between us and the other teams. The game had a dark moment and it's difficult to forget that. The way both teams fought and performed made the result fair but Chelsea scored two goals and Arsenal only scored one.'

Henry responds, 'The referee asked me, "Do you want to wait for the whistle and for the players to go back ten yards?" He said, "You can have a go," and I was just waiting for Eidur Gudjohnsen to move out of the way.' Poll adds, 'The whistle doesn't need to be blown. I asked Henry, "Do you want a wall?" He said, "Can I take it, please?" He was very polite, and I said, "Yes". I gave the signal for him to take it and he did.'

Mourinho claims that a leading referee – it was, by coincidence,

Poll – visited the Chelsea training ground in the close season to clarify some of the rules. 'One of the things he explained to us was free-kicks – walls, distance, whistle – everything was clear,' says the Chelsea manager. Henry scored in similar circumstances against Aston Villa last season and Ian Harte once did the same to net for Leeds against Arsenal.

Terry is furious with his team-mates for the lapse in concentration, and gives Cech a serious dressing down. 'We have worked on that. I wasn't trying to dig him out. We made someone face Petr so he can direct the wall, and the others the play, so they can see what is going on. We didn't do that so it was disappointing.'

Later Cech tells a Czech newspaper, 'Maybe he's [Poll] an Arsenal fan or it was just a failure. We were able to win the game but the referee scored a goal for Arsenal and that was earth-shattering. It's not acceptable. Referee Poll has cheated us. He clearly showed he will give a whistle. We prepare ourselves for these situations. We had seen this in our preparation. Henry is very quick thinking and he tries it. He tried it recently in the Champions League. That's why Eidur Gudjohnsen was directly stood in front of the ball. Eidur asked the referee three times whether he gives a whistle first. Graham Poll ordered him to get away from the ball. Eidur asked him if would give a whistle and he said he would, but there was nothing.'

Gudjohnsen claims Poll helped Henry so much that it was like watching a training ground routine. He says, 'We asked the referee to blow the whistle and he told one of our players what he was going to do. I saw in Henry's reaction that he didn't want the whistle and in the end it looked like a set-piece from the training ground, where one player stands in front of the ball and just jumps out of the way. Sometimes they go for you and sometimes they go against, but luckily Arsenal didn't gain any points on us because of something like that.'

Henry sets the tone for a pulsating contest when he scores within 75 seconds. Cesc Fabregas picks out Henry with a great ball forward, and his nod-off allows Jose Antonio Reyes time to find the striker once again with Chelsea unaccountably standing off. Henry controls with his right foot before spinning to arrow home with his left.

Manuel Almunia, given the nod ahead of Jens Lehmann once more, and who looks far more confident throughout, shows his quality with a flying leap to turn aside Lampard's rocket. Yet when Robben swings in the resulting corner, Sol Campbell is inadvertently blocked by Henry to allow Terry a free header.

On the half-hour Robert Pires earns a free-kick after tangling with Terry and Makelele. Poll stands over the ball with Henry and Gudjohnsen refuses to retreat. But Poll gives the nod and Henry beats the unprepared Cech with a deflection off Tiago's shoulder. Chelsea are furious but the goal is legitimate.

Mourinho's interval switch, with Drogba and Bridge coming on, leaves Arsenal trying to work out their marking duties. Within 35 seconds of the restart, Lampard delivers a free-kick from the left, Gallas outjumps Ashley Cole and nods down into the six-yard box for Gudjohnsen to loop the ball in with a stooping header.

Chelsea take control, and for a while they seem set to score with every free-kick or corner they launch into the box. Lampard is disgusted with himself for failing to hit the target from six yards. Then Almunia does just enough to divert Robben's shot wide after a wonderful dribble past three defenders.

But it is Arsenal who squander the best chance, with Henry the guilty party. Mathieu Flamini's energy and Fabregas's vision put Pires into space on the right, he pulls back but Henry's outstretched left foot can only fire into the North Bank.

The hugs between Terry and Henry at the end are proof of mutual respect. Henry, though, has shown why Abramovich waved a £50m cheque in front of Arsenal vice-chairman David Dein for his services a year earlier. Even without Henry, Chelsea remain favourites to lift the league crown. With him, it would be no contest. Arsenal are left in third place behind Everton, but the Merseysiders are punching well above their weight.

To twice come from behind against the champions at Highbury says something about Chelsea's character. 'I thought my players were fantastic after Arsenal's second goal,' says Mourinho. 'They kept cool, remained in control and gave proof of their strong mental state. When a strange thing has happened, players can lose control. But after Arsenal's second goal – if you can call it a goal – my players were fantastic. We cannot promise anything yet as we don't know. Maybe we'll finish second or third, but maybe we will finish first.'

For Terry, nothing less than first will do. 'We have been too close too often and I am fed up with it now. I want to win something this year. The Premiership would be fantastic, and we showed in the Carling Cup that we are in every competition to go and to win everything we are in. You could see that by the determination of all the lads. We have great experience in the side and we want to go that extra length and go and win the Premiership. We have an edge over them now – and we showed that when we were 2–1 down against a side who have been so great for so many years.'

Team

Cech, Ferreira, Carvalho (Drogba), Terry, Gallas, Duff, Tiago (Bridge), Makelele, Lampard, Robben, Gudjohnsen (Parker).

During the match yobs singled out Vieira, who was watching from the stands, for sickening racial abuse. Anti-racism group 'Kick It Out' demand action. Spokesman Leon Mann says, 'Their chants were racially offensive, but I am sure there are Chelsea supporters who were disgusted. The problem is a minority can become vocal and give the club a bad name. I'd urge supporters to come forward and ensure these morons get what they deserve. I'll be in contact with the clubs to ensure these people are punished. We have a good relationship with both clubs who've done a lot of anti-racism work. And I will ask Arsenal to see if they can highlight the incident on CCTV cameras and see if Sky Sports footage picked it up.' An FA spokesman says, 'We have not had any complaints regarding any racist chanting. But we would be prepared to investigate if there were any complaints.'

Cech continues to talk about his anger over the Henry goal suggesting Poll must be suffering 'an uneasy conscience'. But former Premier League referees' chief Philip Don says, 'The referee does not have to blow the whistle to restart the game – it can be the voice, the hand, the arm or the nod of the head.'

Jermain Defoe urges Tottenham to sign Joe Cole, who is now a peripheral figure in Mourinho's squad. 'Joe would fit in well down here,' says Defoe. 'He can play on the left, on the right or behind the front two. He is such a good player. Hopefully he will come to Tottenham.' But Cole is determined to stick it out until the end of the season even though he has not started a Premiership game since the win at West Brom in October and has even failed to make the substitutes' bench in recent weeks. Mourinho insists, 'He is ready to fight for a place here and, in fact, that's the same feeling that I have. We have had a conversation and I said, "No chance of leaving. Don't think about it because I need everybody." It's just a question of getting a chance. I've told him he's a good player, he works well and has a lot of ambition but at this moment the team is winning, playing very well and I'd be stupid to change it too much.'

Sir Alex Ferguson switches his psychological attack to Chelsea. He says, 'Chelsea? They will find it difficult coming north to get points. Without doubt, Chelsea are the new force. Yet their form is not much different from last season. If you look at the last few seasons, Chelsea have always been up there at this time. It is when they come up north you will see. They have got to go to Liverpool and Everton. It's different after New Year – different pressures, you see. I always think the league starts on New Year's Day.'

Mateja Kezman says he considered walking out on Chelsea shortly after joining the club, depressed at failing to hold down a regular place in the side. Only a heart-to-heart with Mourinho prevented his premature departure. Kezman says, 'On more than one occasion I just wanted to drive to the airport and jump on the first plane home. My wife and I were struggling desperately with the situation. I even remember saying to myself, "If this doesn't change by January, I will have to find myself a new club." I had to tell him how I was feeling. It is not in my nature to keep quiet. I knew if I was burdened by unhappiness it would eventually go terribly wrong for me on the pitch. I wasn't frightened to approach Mourinho. We talk a lot anyway, so I didn't find it too difficult to have showdown talks with him. I'm pleased to say he immediately calmed me down and said, "Don't worry, it will work out. I have immense confidence in your ability as a striker." I assured Mourinho that I had not come to Chelsea for the money. I know other players love the money and big contracts, but for me the football is far more important.'

Kezman adds he feared he would go broke in the opening weeks. He says, 'We initially hired an apartment in Kensington which is extremely close to Harrods. I thought I would go bankrupt. My wife seemed to think there was only one shop in London so she went shopping at Harrods all the time. Fortunately we have now bought our own place: a house which needed a few things doing to it. Nevertheless we feel at home there.'

He adds, 'There are a lot of similarities between me and the manager. Mourinho is a very emotional man. He is passionate about everything he does. He has what I call a proper Portuguese mentality, one that is very similar to a Serbian. Mourinho is arrogant, but in a way you respect. And if we want to be the best and win big trophies, it's vital the manager comes across as a winner. Mourinho makes sure he does. All the time he is telling us we are going to win all the big trophies this season. He emphasises the point so often that the players now believe they are born winners. Honestly, we actually believe we are going to win the league and the Champions League. I think Mourinho has brainwashed all of us. I rate him among the best coaches in the world. He is unbelievable when it comes to analysing games and putting players in the right frame of mind to maximise their effectiveness. No matter who we play, Mourinho always knows every minor detail about that team. Believe me, he is as sharp as a knife. Nothing eludes him.'

Kezman reveals the human side of Abramovich, who hangs around the dressing room cracking terrible jokes. 'I have been so surprised by the incredible atmosphere among the squad players. A lot of that is down to Mr Abramovich. He comes down to the dressing room after every game. He talks to us individually and he shows his warm character. Believe it or not he is actually a very funny man. He cracks jokes every time he comes in. He makes us laugh because most of them are lousy. I think people see him as the big untouchable businessman, but he is a wonderful guy.'

Mourinho must make at least one change for the next game against Norwich, with Bridge replacing Carvalho. The Portuguese centre-back will be out for two to three weeks with a broken toe and, with Robert Huth still injured, Gallas moves to partner Terry at the heart of the defence.

SATURDAY, 18 DECEMBER 2004
CHELSEA 4, NORWICH CITY 0

Chelsea ensure they will be top at Christmas, with a performance of speed and finesse that swamps the visitors and has the game safe by half-time. 'It was pure counter-attacking football,' says Mourinho. 'We had good dynamics and speed and took up good positions. In fact we could have scored just the one in the first half and three in the second, because we were scoring from counter-attacking. The present system with Arjen Robben in the team suits my players' qualities and we can control the game.'

Mourinho pays Norwich the dubious compliment of fielding what has come to be regarded as his strongest team. Norwich settle quicker and for a time look as though they can give Chelsea a test. But Thomas Helveg and Gary Doherty hand Chelsea a comfortable two-goal lead. The first blunder comes in the 10th minute when Helveg's attempt at a backpass goes straight to Duff. The Irishman storms forward and curls a low shot into the net.

Norwich then suffer another blow when striker Mathias Svensson limps off after falling badly and twisting a medial ligament. He is replaced by Leon McKenzie, who is lucky to avoid giving away a penalty when he clearly punches the ball in his own area. But Chelsea do not have to wait long for a second goal and it is Doherty who obliges in the 34th minute. The former Spurs defender crazily flicks the ball out of his area to Robben, and the Dutchman's square pass sets up Lampard to power a stunning shot into the top left-hand corner. John Terry's programme notes prove prophetic as he jokes that he will have to buy Lampard some vaseline to rub on his chapped lips for Christmas as the midfielder kisses the badge on his shirt so often.

A minute from the break, Robben drifts in from the right flank and finds Lampard in the box who flicks the ball to Tiago. The Portuguese player's back-heel falls to Robben, who completes the sorcery with a ferocious smack that gives Rob Green no chance.

Asked what could stop Chelsea winning the league, Mourinho shrugs and says, 'A better team than us. At the moment nobody is better than us, but you never know. If we keep our present mental and tactical strength, I think nobody can stop us. We have to lose matches in the second half of the season but at this moment no one is better than us. In the future, I don't know. Maybe Arsenal or Manchester United can jump to a different level or maybe we can slide into a lower level. We could have injuries and players could lose form, but at this moment my confidence of winning the league is big.'

Team

Cech, Ferreira, Gallas, Terry, Bridge, Tiago (Parker), Makelele, Lampard, Duff, Gudjohnsen (Drogba), Robben (Kezman).

Sol Campbell's stunning late strike at Portsmouth lifts Arsenal back within five points, and Arséne Wenger warns Mourinho that Chelsea are not unstoppable. 'We are back in the race,' says Wenger. 'We are very hungry and we have talent and the ingredients to make the race interesting.'

Celestine Babayaro turns down loan moves to Crystal Palace, Middlesbrough and West Brom to fight for his place. The Nigeria left-back has made just one Premiership start under Mourinho, but is hopeful of extending his stay at the club he joined seven years ago. Babayaro is Chelsea's longest serving player and wants a new contract when his current deal expires in the summer.

There is bad news for Scott Parker who will be out for several weeks. An X-ray shows a broken metatarsal bone in his foot. The player admits he may have caused some of the damage himself. 'I went for a one-two with Damien Duff but the pitch was poor and my foot buckled and I heard something pop. I went straight over to the physio when we scored and the manager wanted me to come off, but I just wanted to carry on and impress. It just made things worse.'

Mourinho responds to Sir Alex Ferguson's suggestion that Chelsea will drop points when they have to play up north by saying, 'I know that Manchester United will lose points in the south – because they already have done. They lost three points at Stamford Bridge, three points at Portsmouth and two at Fulham. For sure, they have a problem in the south. We will have to wait and see whether we have a problem up north.'

With the busy and vital Christmas period up next and the transfer window after that, Frank Lampard insists the squad is in perfect shape. 'You are always wanting to strengthen the squad but we have a really steady ship at Chelsea and we're going well.' After a session at the club's new training ground in the Surrey countryside, Mourinho says the chequebook will not be coming out more than once, and only then because of the injury to Parker. 'Scott has been important for us over the last two months and was becoming a regular. I don't need a top, top player. Forget Joaquin, forget Defoe, forget all the other names you could speak about. If we do something it will just be a player to help us. Anyway, to get better midfield players than we have got already, I wouldn't know where to find them.'

But with four matches in the next ten days, starting at home to Aston Villa, and with Carvalho, Huth and Babayaro all on the injury list, Mourinho knows he needs his whole squad to be ready. 'January and February are months when I need everybody and I have only 16 outfield players fit. I cannot give the players days off. Everyone is selected,' he says. The only concession to the Christmas holiday is letting his players start training on Christmas Day a few hours later than usual.

But David O'Leary's troubles put Mourinho's situation in perspective. He is struggling to fill his side's bench, as his squad is decimated by injuries and he is unable to field Carlton Cole because of his loan deal with Chelsea. O'Leary says, 'I have got 14 fit players and two goalkeepers. It doesn't give you a lot of options.'

SUNDAY, 26 DECEMBER 2004
CHELSEA 1, ASTON VILLA 0

Damien Duff's goal is enough to beat Villa and Mourinho insists he is more than happy to grind out 1–0 wins for the rest of the season if it means winning the Premiership. 'It is not our target to be winter champions,' he says. 'The aim is for us to be champions at the end of the season. At the moment we have a five-point advantage and this result was important to keep that distance. This result puts us in a comfortable situation and the question now is simply whether our lead goes up to eight points or down to two. The fans believe we can win the title and they understand that when you are playing to be champions you cannot afford to lose points in stupid circumstances. Everyone speaks of all the 4–0 wins we have had lately but the clean sheets we have achieved are just as important. The aim is always to play good football, score early and win easily. But when you get to 75 minutes with the score still at 1–0 it becomes a case of rolling up our sleeves, playing with our hearts and fighting to keep the lead. Today we have done that.'

O'Leary insists, 'The goal aside, it was an even game. It was never our intention to just come here and defend. It was all I could do to name five on the bench today and there is always the chance that you can come here and get a drubbing. But I didn't want to sit back and wait to get hammered. We gave it a go and Chelsea were pretty nervous towards the end of that game.'

For the sixth time in his last nine games Duff opens the scoring to set his team on the road to victory. On the half-hour a Villa attack breaks down just inside the Chelsea penalty area and Lampard's pass immediately feeds Robben for a run from inside his own half. Villa's defence backs off the advancing Dutchman and, as Gareth Barry comes inside to cover, Robben slips the ball out to Duff, who cuts inside Liam Ridgewell and beats Thomas Sorensen with a low shot inside his near post. It is a goal that has been coming for some time. Terry has already headed just over from Lampard's deep free-kick and another Duff left-footer has grazed the far post. Yet Villa stick to their gameplan and refuse to blindly chase the game as they seek to deny Chelsea their first Boxing Day victory since 1999.

Petr Cech says, 'It fills me with so much confidence playing behind such great defenders as John Terry, Ricardo Carvalho and William Gallas. They make life so much easier for us, because we all know that if we score one goal, that is often enough. We win 1-0, the game is finished and we have another three points.'

> **Team**
> Cech, Ferreira, Gallas, Terry, Bridge, Tiago, Makelele, Lampard, Duff (Smertin), Robben (Johnson), Gudjohnsen (Drogba).

Thierry Henry hits his 20th goal of the season in Arsenal's 2–0 win over Fulham at Highbury, lifting him up to joint second alongside Ian Wright in the all-time list of Arsenal's league scorers with 128. He says, 'I didn't care what Chelsea did. We only need to think about what we need to do. If we didn't believe we could catch them we might as well give up now and go home. We have to believe we can do it. I didn't ask for their result after the game, we just concentrate on our job.' Wenger also insists his side are not worried about Chelsea, 'There is so much time to go that what is most important is we focus on our quality. We don't have to worry about anyone else. If we win our games then I'm ready to count at the end of the season. It's too far away to even speculate about a slip by Chelsea. I do not worry about results of other teams. What can we change about them? Nothing.'

Mourinho is named as coach of a 2004 fantasy team by French sports daily *L'Equipe*. He ends a magical year with his Chelsea side on top of the Premiership after winning the Champions League and the Portuguese title with former club Porto. Two Chelsea players – central defenders John Terry and Ricardo Carvalho – are also named in the team.

Mourinho's first taste of the English festive football calendar is not to his liking. 'I understand Boxing Day is an important day for your football culture and I accept that we have to play on 26 December,' he says. 'But it makes no sense to play again on the 28th. And if some important players get injuries during these matches then we really have to think about this programme. The fact is we have just 24 hours after the Villa game to train and travel to Portsmouth for our next match. I know it is the same for every other team and we must all play under the same circumstances. But to have just one day's rest makes the circumstances so difficult. Speak with the specialists in energetic systems, the biochemists and the physiologists and they will all tell you that it is completely impossible for a player to recover from a Premiership game in 24 hours.'

He already faces a defensive headache as William Gallas has picked up a hamstring strain during the Villa victory. With Huth crocked and Carvalho not one hundred per cent, Mourinho has few options. 'Maybe we will see a lot of goals on the 28th but that will not be because the teams are good but because the players will be broken by the physical intensity.'

Smertin, who spent last season on loan at Fratton Park, warns they must keep Patrik Berger and Aiyegbeni Yakubu quiet if they want to beat Pompey. The Russian midfielder says, 'It is going to be something special for me to go back there. I like Portsmouth's supporters because they are very loyal and they like me as well. Portsmouth play with a big spirit. Yakubu is a great player and very strong. He is hungry and motivated. Their best player is Patrik Berger. He is very dangerous and we have to watch him.'

TUESDAY, 28 DECEMBER 2004

PORTSMOUTH 0, CHELSEA 2

Mourinho is full of praise for the way Chelsea hold off a pumped-up Pompey, who give them the run-around for 45 minutes. 'Portsmouth made it very difficult for us and showed why they had beaten Manchester United at home and were unlucky against Arsenal.

But we got ourselves in a good position after half-time. It is a really big victory for us.

'I told my players at half-time this was not a day to dribble or play wonderful possession football. But it was a day to show how to be champions – which we did. Only top players can fight like we did today. From a mental point of view we have overcome a great obstacle by winning at Christmas. Six points out of six shows we do not have a jinx. There are still some hard tests ahead but my players have shown they have the desire to win the title and they know they have the ability.'

Mourinho is unhappy on two accounts. 'Yes, you can play two games in two or three days but it is still not correct. You can smoke three boxes of cigars and still be alive but that doesn't mean it's right or healthy.' He is also upset that the Gunners have an extra day's rest over the busy holiday period before facing Newcastle. 'They always seem to have two or three days' rest in which to recover,' he says. 'Perhaps it's something to do with the TV schedule. All my players are tired – especially John Terry. He has had to play two big games one after the other but at least he has a few days to get ready for Liverpool on Saturday.'

Robben celebrates the opener by whipping off his shirt and is booked and substituted all within two minutes. He laughs all the way to the dugout, pausing only to shake hands with referee Alan Wiley. An added-time goal from substitute Joe Cole confirms an eight-point lead at the top of the Premiership. Robben's eighth strike could well be seen in retrospect as one of the defining moments of the campaign. With just 11 minutes remaining, a move involving Cole, Duff and Gudjohnsen ends with Robben having a clear shooting chance on the right of the box. He strikes it well enough, but a deflection off Matthew Taylor makes sure Shaka Hislop is finally beaten.

Cole comes off the bench to add spark, invention and the killer second goal, which he drives home from the edge of the area. 'We just seem like a machine at the moment,' says Cole. 'I can imagine that what we were saying about Arsenal last year is exactly what they're saying about us now. What we've done defensively is amazing. The strikers and midfielders have been grabbing the limelight but if you look at the back five with the goalkeeper, and no matter who comes in, it's the same story. That's fantastic. Petr is looking like the best keeper in the world. The big man is keeping Carlo Cudicini out and we all know what Carlo can do, so to have two of them can be the difference in the title race. The one thing we have to avoid is complacency and as long as we steer clear of that I don't think we will have a blip.'

The Chelsea celebrations are tinged with relief, as they hardly look potential champions for the first 45 minutes. Pompey come at them with the sort of passion and non-stop aggression that has seen them beat Manchester United and almost hold Arsenal at Fratton Park. Cech somehow gets a hand to a magnificently struck 30-yard swerver from Nigel Quashie. Half-time brings an abrupt change – just as it did against Fulham, Newcastle and Arsenal. Pushing up much further than they did in the first half, Chelsea play Pompey at their own game and pressure them out of possession.

Glen Johnson sees his header from Robben's corner scrambled off the line before Gudjohnsen, who has replaced Drogba, flicks the loose ball over. Hislop denies Gudjohnsen only with a well-timed save at his feet after good work by Robben. But with time running out Robben once again inspires his team to victory.

Didier Drogba's uninspiring comeback is the downside of the win. Mourinho says, 'We know we have to be patient with Drogba. Steve Clarke had the same operation in his career and says it might feel like it is better but often it is not completely and you need more time. We will try to give him this.'

Since their lone league reverse at Manchester City, the team have dropped just four points out of 33, with Cech and his backline amassing 14 clean sheets in 20 Premiership outings. Although Mourinho admits it will be impossible to have a more 'perfect' year personally than 2004, his new club still have every target in front of them. Mourinho says, 'It was a good year for the club – but they didn't win anything and in 2005 we have to start bringing titles to the club. Unless we go and win trophies, what we've done so far will mean nothing. We have to be top still in May to win the trophy and the Premiership is the trophy we really want.'

Portsmouth coach Joe Jordan says, 'It was terrible to lose to Chelsea after playing so well, but at the end of the game you had to acknowledge you had been up against something special, something you don't encounter so often these days. Chelsea have great talent and resources, but you have to admit they have something else, something put there by Jose Mourinho.'

Team

Cech, Johnson, Terry, Gallas, Ferreira, Makelele, Smertin (Cole), Lampard, Duff, Robben (Geremi), Drogba (Gudjohnsen).

Manchester United make it seven wins and a draw from eight games with victory at Villa, but still can't close their nine-point deficit on Chelsea. 'We are getting in and around the teams behind Chelsea now,' says Sir Alex Ferguson. 'It's getting to Chelsea themselves that is the problem. They are on a great run but we know that when they stumble, as long as we have kept our consistency going, we will go very, very close. All we can do is maintain our form. If we keep playing the way we are playing, we will get our rewards.' Arsenal also maintain their challenge with Patrick Vieira's 20-metre volley enough to give them a 1–0 win at Newcastle.

CSKA Moscow, the Russian club Abramovich sponsors, are reported to have rejected a move by Chelsea to sign Czech international midfielder Jiri Jarosik. Jarosik joined the club in the summer of 2003 for a then Russian record of £2m and faced Chelsea in the Champions League. Chelsea see him as a short-term solution to their injury troubles.

Mourinho is relatively busy wheeling and dealing as he allows Celestine Babayaro to be sold to Newcastle for £1m, with speculation that Toon defender Olivier Bernard will end up at Stamford Bridge. Newcastle United record their thanks to everybody involved at Chelsea for their cooperation and goodwill. Babayaro won the FA Cup, League Cup, Charity Shield and European Super Cup during his time in London, but has increasingly found himself in the wilderness since Abramovich's millions allowed first Ranieri and then Mourinho to invest heavily in new talent. He played 197 times for Chelsea.

Mourinho comments, 'It was a decision made in the interests of the player, not for us. It was not a selfish decision by me or the club. It was a decision taken in relation to the player's future and the best for his career. We had several offers for him but none like the one from Newcastle. Their offer gives him a fantastic future. We will miss him both as a player and a person. Our decision to cooperate with him was, I think, very fair. They are a big club and they play for big things.'

Birmingham cancel Mikael Forssell's loan contract. The Finnish international was signed on loan for a second season but a serious knee injury ruled him out for almost the entire season. City execute a get-out clause in the loan agreement and Forssell returns to London to undergo rehabilitation on the injury following an operation.

Mourinho describes John Terry as 'the best central defender in the world'. 'Since the first minute I arrived here he's played at the same level. Not up and down, no mistakes. Not more committed against Man United and less concentration against West Bromwich. It's not like he prefers to play against tall and strong strikers and has it difficult against fast ones. For him every game is the same, every opponent is the same, the level of his performance is the same. He leads the team. He is an important voice on the pitch, where I'm not. He's absolutely amazing.'

Terry is a key influence within the team, both on the field and in the dressing room where he often gives fiery speeches ahead of games. Mourinho adds, 'In some clubs the captain is the captain of the manager. In other clubs he's the captain of the players. In another club he's the captain of the club because he's been at the club for ten years. John Terry is everything here.'

Mourinho is also clear in his admiration for Lampard. 'Frank is improving every day. Like Steven Gerrard he is one of the best in the world. It's difficult to say who is the best because some midfield players are more defensive, some more offensive. I would say Frank Lampard and Steven Gerrard can both do things. They are great players.'

Gerrard remains top of Mourinho's wanted list, but Liverpool manager Rafael Benitez says, 'If we play well and win I'm sure Steven will think we can beat any team in the Premiership. I want him to stay and he knows that.'

Chelsea are 15 points ahead of sixth-placed Liverpool going into their match at Anfield. Yet Benitez insists his team can win. 'We are a better side since Chelsea beat us 1–0 at Stamford Bridge in October. We have a better mentality and we possess more confidence. It is true that Chelsea have the strongest squad in the Premiership and they have a lot of very good players. But I also believe we are capable of beating them. They have spent a lot of money over the last two or three years on players, but that doesn't worry me particularly. When I was at Valencia it was a similar situation, because Real Madrid and Barcelona had more money yet we still won the title.'

SATURDAY, 1 JANUARY 2005
LIVERPOOL 0, CHELSEA 1

Chelsea's victory is steeped in good fortune as Liverpool dominate and the referee misses a certain penalty. And, like at Portsmouth, the breakthrough comes from a deflected shot. Chelsea have to get back to attacking in a fluent fashion. Gudjohnsen is off colour, while Drogba has still to regain his confidence and power. Chelsea count on the excellent Cech, whose uncanny reflexes enable him to pull off a close-range save when Tiago smashes the ball against Antonio Nunez.

Mourinho takes pride in his side's resilience in the north, which Sir Alex Ferguson had put into question. 'I am proud of my players,' says Mourinho. 'We needed some luck, but luck has a habit of turning up for the champions at the right times and at the right places. We have proved to Manchester United and Arsenal that they will have to really fight for this title, but I think it will now be very difficult for them to catch us. I feel sorry for Liverpool. I didn't see the handball they claimed against Tiago, but sometimes these things go for you – that is football. My players fought and fought and in the end they deserved some luck. But I felt Liverpool also played very well and a draw would have been a fair result.'

Cole follows up his goal at Portsmouth on Boxing Day by crashing home a late winner. Much of Chelsea's first-half struggle hinges on the way John Arne Riise exposes Glen Johnson. But with 76 minutes gone Mourinho sends on Cole for Duff – and is rewarded almost instantly. Robben's corner is headed towards the edge of the box by Johnson, and Cole fires home a low shot that heightens an already rampant sense of injustice fuelled by referee Mike Riley's decision to reject two justified penalty appeals from Liverpool. Undaunted, Chelsea hold out to the end.

Having broken the ankle of local favourite Xabi Alonso with a foul, Lampard has a quiet game. He also earns a one-match ban by picking up his fifth booking of the season for the challenge. He says, 'Me missing one game is nothing compared to Xabi being out for so long. I never intended to hurt him. Obviously, I will say I'm sorry for what happened.'

There is no doubt that Liverpool should have a penalty when Tiago palms the ball from the head of Nunez, and probably another when Makelele bundles over Florent Sinama-Pongolle. Benitez says Cech is Chelsea's finest player. He makes an outstanding save one-on-one from Djimi Traore in the 15th minute, another from Nunez after 42 minutes and pushes a Gerrard free-kick away with four minutes remaining.

Robben should score after springing the offside trap in the 18th minute, but hesitates, cuts inside and is charged down by Jerzy Dudek. Gudjohnsen should also be quicker to a 50th-minute Duff cross.

But this is a day for defenders as the Blues complete their first league double over Liverpool for 85 years. Benitez snaps, 'We lost the game because of two things – the injury to Xabi Alonso, who we have now lost for five or six weeks, and the referee's failure to award us a penalty.' Jamie Carragher also raps the ref. 'He has got it wrong in the two big games he has refereed this season and those two decisions could prove the difference between Arsenal or Chelsea winning the league,' he says. Riley gave Wayne Rooney a hotly disputed penalty in the Manchester United v Arsenal showdown ten weeks earlier that helped end the Gunners' unbeaten 49-match record. Carragher adds, 'If Arsenal had got the right decision at Old Trafford, who knows what might have happened then? Top games need top refs. And with those mistakes the FA have to ask whether this referee should be up there. He was in a great position to see what happened in our game. He was putting his whistle into his mouth and I don't know if he lost his nerve or what.' Even Claude Makelele admits, 'It was a penalty.'

Team

Cech, Ferreira, Terry, Gallas, Johnson, Lampard, Makelele, Tiago, Duff (Cole), Gudjohnsen (Drogba), Robben (Kezman).

Arsenal and Manchester United both win later in the day to keep up their challenges, but Chelsea are on course to beat United's 91-point Premier League record. Czech international Jiri Jarosik signs for the club and says, 'I am delighted. It is the greatest chance of my life.'

Chelsea's interest in Rio Ferdinand prompts Manchester United to consider opening new contract talks with the defender to keep him at Old Trafford until 2010. Abramovich, who has long been an admirer of the England star, is reported to be preparing a £6m-a-year deal to lure him to Stamford Bridge in the summer. Ferguson tells his club they must move now to prevent Ferdinand leaving, even though he still has two and a half years left on his £70,000-a-week contract. The prospect of linking Ferdinand with Terry could make Chelsea an even more formidable force.

Steve McClaren, boss of Chelsea's next opponents Middlesbrough, believes Chelsea have to keep John Terry fit to maintain their charge. 'I worked closely with John at Euro 2004 and he impressed me immensely' says McClaren. 'But if Chelsea lose Terry or Frank Lampard it will hit them hard. They are Chelsea through and through – talk about the heartbeat and core of a club. They were that last season and have matured and developed since.

Chelsea are going well but if they lost one of those two it would hurt. Their key players are Terry, Lampard, Makelele, Duff and Robben. If they get injuries it could change.'

TUESDAY, 4 JANUARY 2005
CHELSEA 2, MIDDLESBROUGH 0

Didier Drogba's double sends Chelsea seven points clear as title rivals Arsenal and Manchester United both slip up at home. Drogba signals his return to sharpness with blistering strikes in the 14th and 17th minutes.

Already favourites, the leaders are installed as champions-elect by Sir Alex Ferguson. 'Chelsea can only throw it away,' the Manchester United manager says after his team's 0–0 draw at home to Tottenham Hotspur. At Highbury, after a 1–1 draw against Manchester City, Wenger is a little more defiant. 'To give up and say they have won the title would be criminal and totally unprofessional.'

From the moment Drogba latches on to Lampard's pass to slip the ball past Mark Schwarzer, there is only ever going to be one outcome. Drogba then uses his head to connect with Lampard's free-kick and beat Schwarzer again. On both occasions the Ivory Coast star shakes off marker Gareth Southgate. Little wonder Mourinho made little effort to keep Jimmy-Floyd Hasselbaink. The former Blues goalscorer is presented with a commemorative medal by one-time strike partner Eidur Gudjohnsen before the game, marking his four seasons at Stamford Bridge. But that is all he has to show for a fruitless first return.

Cole, making his first Premiership start since October in place of Tiago, is lively, while Alexei Smertin does not look out of place as a makeshift left-back. When Smertin succumbs to illness, Johnson takes his place. No matter how Mourinho shuffles his pack, he always seems to come up with a winning hand.

Schwarzer twice spills low shots from Robben with no one on hand to convert the follow-up, and Duff sends another drive tantalisingly across the face of goal. Drogba pulls a huge Cech clearance out of the sky but his shot on the turn is straight at Schwarzer. And Duff rattles the bar with a fierce 57th-minute left-footer. Even Ferreira has a go, racing on to Lampard's pass but scooping his shot just over. Lampard has another shot blocked by Schwarzer, but the best move of the game comes in the closing minutes when he shoots just wide after an irresistible move of 20 passes.

The only blemish is Robben's fifth yellow card, which rules him out of the first leg of the Carling Cup semi-final with Manchester United. It takes McClaren around an hour after close of play to emerge from the dressing room to share his thoughts on the pummelling his side have taken. McClaren has no complaints about his team. He is pleased with them for 'not folding'. If the manager of the sixth-placed side in the Premiership will settle for a two-goal defeat by Chelsea, then you shudder at what those below him will accept.

Team

Cech, Ferreira, Gallas, Terry, Smertin (Johnson), Cole (Tiago), Makelele, Lampard, Duff, Robben, Drogba (Kezman).

Jiri Jarosik reveals he would have been caught up in the tsunami disaster had he not cancelled a holiday in Asia for talks with Chelsea. 'I was set to go on a break to Sri Lanka over the Christmas period but because of the transfer negotiations I cancelled the trip. Someone up there must love me.' Jarosik was initially thought to have moved on a six-month loan, before details of his improved contract emerged and a fee of £2.5m. The versatile schemer has been likened in style to Patrick Vieira and will provide cover in central midfield with Parker sidelined by a broken foot.

Jarosik stresses that it was Blues manager Jose Mourinho, not Abramovich, who was the driving force behind his move. 'Mr Mourinho was the one who wanted me to join and that was important. He told me he wasn't interested in signing a stuck-up superstar but wanted an experienced and hard-working player. He told me I had a chance to get into the team straight away.'

CSKA coach Valeri Gazzayev is infuriated by Jarosik's departure, maintaining a stony silence, but privately asking friends how the club can have let it happen. The answer, as with many Moscow mysteries, lies with Abramovich, close friend of CSKA president Yevgeny Giner, and his oil company Sibneft, bankroller of the entire club.

Mourinho has used Geremi as an example of a faithful squad player, but now the Cameroon international wants to leave to find first-team football. The £6.9m buy from Real Madrid urges Boro to re-sign him after his 33-game loan spell there in 2002-03. Geremi says, 'I'm not satisfied at Chelsea because I am not playing. Mourinho is not giving me opportunities and I do not like being on the bench. I would prefer to leave and the option of Middlesbrough is excellent, because I have great memories of my stay there.' Geremi is the first player to demand a move and says he preferred life under Claudio Ranieri. 'Mourinho is a good coach but makes few changes,' he says. 'Ranieri made more rotations than Mourinho. This way the players were more satisfied. I am good enough to play in the Premier League and I have demonstrated it in the last two seasons – but in this one I cannot. I don't regret coming to England because in my time here I have learned a lot. But I want to play.'

Steve Clarke says none of Mourinho's squad will be leaving, and that includes the unhappy Geremi and defender Robert Huth, who is interesting Bayern Munich. Chelsea agree a £10m fee with Feyenoord for their 19-year-old striker Salomon Kalou. The Ivory Coast-born marksman will not move to Stamford Bridge until the summer because he must wait at least three months to obtain the Dutch passport vital to his involvement in English football. Arsenal are monitoring Kalou's progress and hope to snatch the player over the delay with his passport. Kalou is widely regarded as the most talented young striker in European football, and his all-round game has been compared to Thierry Henry's. Holland boss Marco van Basten has almost guaranteed Kalou a place in the national side when he attains his passport.

Adrian Mutu signs a five-year contract with Juventus and could even play for Italy's Serie A giants in the Champions League final against his former club as his seven-month ban ends a week before it on 18 May. Juventus announce Mutu's signature as a free transfer as he is technically a free agent, but Chelsea demand a transfer fee to offset the loss of an asset valued at £13.7m. The club still hold the player's registration and it will not be released until after his claim for wrongful dismissal is heard by the Premier League. If they fail to extract a transfer fee from Juventus, Chelsea could pursue compensation through the courts. A senior Chelsea source says, 'Our position hasn't changed one iota. We definitely feel we deserve some compensation from the player or his new club. You don't just wave goodbye to a £13m asset.'

Martin Jol, whose Spurs team Chelsea face next, says he believes Robben can become the best player in the world. The Dutchman says, 'Johan Cruyff is a huge phenomenon in Holland. I said three years ago that Robben is a small phenomenon but he will be big – very big. In England you don't understand how big Cruyff is. So when I say Robben is a small phenomenon, it is a big compliment. In Holland we all think Arjen is the best winger in Europe. When I argue Johan is the best player ever, I'm told it was George Best. I appreciate that but Johan Cruyff played for 18 years and, although George Best was unbelievable, he only played seven or eight years. There is a big difference. But Robben can do the same. Even at 16 when he broke into the Groningen first team he was playing as well then as he does now. When Robben played against my teams in Holland, he always punished us. If we went 1–0 up, he would get it back. I never had any success against him at all. The argument went that maybe he could take on and beat five or six players in the Dutch League but he could never do the same in England. But here he is doing exactly that.'

SATURDAY, 15 JANUARY 2005
TOTTENHAM HOTSPUR 0, CHELSEA 2

Thanks to a double from Frank Lampard, Chelsea become the first Premiership side to keep six consecutive clean sheets while winning every game. Sitting in for Mourinho, Steve Clarke says, 'It was a difficult game for us, so obviously the celebrations at the end told you how much it meant to us as a club. I don't think there is a better midfielder than Frank Lampard. He's been very consistent in his performances and England are lucky to have Frank and Steven Gerrard available for central midfield. He showed his quality when he took the penalty as there was a lot of pressure on him and he also showed great energy to get there for Eidur Gudjohnsen's cut-back in the last minute.'

Lampard snaps back at a spectator dishing out abuse as he walks off for half-time. His crime is to have converted a disputed first-half penalty. Alexei Smertin goes down over Ledley King's outstretched leg prompting vehement Spurs protests. But Lampard coolly smacks home the spot-kick. Tottenham's decision to replay the incident in super slo-mo on the giant video screen is regrettable, and the normally placid Lampard reacts to some fairly vicious abuse as he leaves the pitch for the interval.

Earlier, Robben is clearly nudged by Noe Pamarot as he scampers into the penalty area in familiar style. 'I thought that was a penalty, the one before was a penalty, plus another one we should have had in the second half,' says Clarke. The fourth official signals four injury-time minutes, before Lampard finally ends Spurs' stubborn resistance and gives the score-line a gloss that is harsh on hard-working Tottenham. But this is Chelsea's 14th match unbeaten and it is 601 minutes since Cech conceded – a statistic that is testimony not only to the Czech's prowess but to the defensive qualities of the entire squad. No other central defensive pairing enjoys the sort of cover given by Makelele.

A parry from Jermain Defoe's deflected shot is all that Cech needs to do to extend his run beyond the nine-hour mark. Smertin comes closest to beating his own keeper with a wild miskick that misses the far post by inches at a Tottenham set-piece.

Jol insists the penalty should not have been given. 'I can see why the referee gave it from his angle. But when you see it from a different view Alexei Smertin stamps on Ledley King's foot. He was running very fast and maybe I would have fallen over too – but I am

48 years old. It was a shame as at that time we were the better team. I said after the Manchester United game these things even out, but I am having second thoughts on that.'

Pamarot is also incensed. 'There were many Chelsea players diving during the game,' he says. 'I don't think anyone thought it was a penalty – except for the referee. But it was not just the penalty, Robben was doing it as well and I don't think it's fair. He is great player, but he was diving all the time, so you can understand the fans being angry about it.'

The key flashpoint in Pamarot's row with Robben is a first-half penalty claim before the Smertin incident. Robben falls inside the area under pressure from the Frenchman. Heated words are then exchanged between the two players.

Despite scoring both goals, Lampard says it is his team's defence that should be praised. 'William Gallas and JT give us a lot of confidence at the back. They are fantastic together. A lot has been said about John and rightly so because he has been fantastic. But he and William complement each other so well. John's all-round defensive game is brilliant, and with William's pace next to him they are a very difficult pair for any team to play against. Add to that the fact they have a great goalkeeper behind them. I can't speak highly enough of all of them. They have been superb all season.'

Lampard revels in the frustration he knows Chelsea's pursuers must be feeling from his experience of never quite being able to catch Arsenal a year ago. 'Arsenal set the standard last year by playing the way they did. It's not nice when you keep getting good results and they keep getting good results too. And then eventually you slip up and they still get a good result. That's what it was like when we were chasing Arsenal last season. But we are the ones that have been doing that recently, leading from the front, and that has to continue if we are going to win the league. We know that. And with the spirit we have got and the confidence we have got, there's no reason it can't continue. There's a lot of spirit round here. We celebrate every game we win because we know how important each game is and this one at Spurs felt special.'

Even Joe Cole has shed his reputation for failing to track back. As a second-half substitute, he makes three important tackles, each visibly applauded from the bench by Mourinho. 'I think we took a big step towards winning the title today,' says Cole. 'You could see afterwards that the boys were loving the result. It was hard-fought, but we deserved it again. The close games are the ones that taste best. They are the great victories. The boss asked me to come on and make sure I kept it tight. I could do that and it was good. The result puts the pressure on Arsenal. We know how it feels from last year, when they just kept on winning. It's up to them to keep getting the right results.'

Clarke's message to Chelsea's rivals is the bleakest of all. 'Other people talk about us having a blip. Well, maybe we have had our poor run already when we drew either side of our defeat to Manchester City. Maybe we've had our blip already.'

Team

Cech, Johnson, Gallas, Terry, Ferreira, Smertin (Jarosik), Makelele, Lampard, Duff (Cole), Drogba (Gudjohnsen), Robben.

In the evening Arsenal lose 1–0 at Bolton to extend Chelsea's lead to a formidable ten points plus a vastly superior goal difference. United lie a further point behind after winning at Anfield.

The Gunners overcame a nine-point deficit to beat Manchester United to the title in 1998, but, just as in April 2003 when Arsenal blew a two-goal lead to draw 2–2, the Reebok Stadium has become the graveyard of their title aspirations.

What is most shocking about Arsenal's third defeat of the season is the resigned way they seem to accept it. It is hard to believe that these Gunners are the same team hailed as 'The Invincibles' just three short months ago when they went a record 49 games unbeaten. Wenger reflects, 'Chelsea are a strong team and they have a lot of experience in different departments of the team. But it would be an easy excuse to say that we lost to Bolton because we are young. Chelsea have improved each year and they have bought great players like Drogba, like Robben, like Tiago, like Carvalho, like Paulo Ferreira, like Cech and that makes the difference. But that does not irritate me that they can improve their team because they have the money. It does present us with a problem, but their money does not mean that we have to lose to Bolton. It's not Chelsea's fault or their money, it's down to us.'

Mourinho combines a scouting mission to check on Champions League opponents Barcelona with the chance to run the rule over Barca's brilliant Brazilian Ronaldinho. Ronaldinho would cost a cool £60m. The door is open for an offer after the Brazilian said only last month, 'Any great player would want to be part of the sensational Chelsea team. They are amazing and I can see myself living in London one day.'

Sir Alex Ferguson warns Mourinho would be 'foolish' to think the title will be Chelsea's if they can stretch their lead. 'In the past Newcastle were 12 points clear, we threw a 12-point lead away once, and Blackburn almost threw a 13-point lead away. So we know it can happen. Chelsea would be foolish to think it could not. If they hit a blip, the key is how they recover. Look what happened after Arsenal lost to us at Old Trafford. They dropped nine of their next fifteen points. Arsenal and ourselves have to hope that does happen to Chelsea. And the only thing you can do is be patient. I also think an injury to one of their important players: Frank Lampard or John Terry, maybe Arjen Robben or Damien Duff, would slow Chelsea down.'

Roy Keane backs his manager, convinced Chelsea may yet crumble under the weight of expectation. 'We've been in Chelsea's position before, but a lot of their players haven't had the experience of being there. That's why it is important to put them under pressure. They've answered all the questions so far but we'll see what happens from now.'

Mourinho says he is so relaxed that he no longer watches Arsenal and Manchester United and is amused by the escalating war of words between Sir Alex Ferguson and Arséne Wenger. 'They can say what they want,' he says. 'It doesn't interfere with what I think. There is no pressure at the top. The pressure's being second or third. When you lead you can forget about the other teams. I don't see Arsenal and Manchester United's matches on television; I'm not listening to the radio waiting for their results. If we win, then our job for that week is done.'

Didier Drogba hits back at critics branding him a waste of money with just nine goals in 22 games. 'People talk about my fee all the time,' he says. 'They don't call me Drogba, but the £24m man. When they look at me they are more wide-eyed about the price than my qualities. Despite the critics, I am satisfied with my first six months in England and I don't feel I am suffering because of the price tag.'

Abramovich faces formal legal action in a Swiss court. The European Bank for Reconstruction and Development (EBRD) – partly funded by the British taxpayer – says it is seeking to recover $17.4m (£9m) through proceedings in the Fribourg court against Abramovich and a colleague. Abramovich's side accuses the bank of 'negligence' and warns he might bring a defamation case if certain allegations against him are repeated by the EBRD. The Fribourg case centres on a loan apparently given to a Swiss oil trading company, Runicom SA, which was said to be controlled by Abramovich and Eugene Shvidler, chief executive of Russia's Sibneft oil company. A spokesman for Abramovich says suggestions that Chelsea assets are at risk are 'far-fetched'.

Mourinho wants to beat Liverpool to the signature of Scott Carson but Rafael Benitez plays upon the fact that the 19-year-old keeper might find an easier route into the first-team at Anfield as Cech is in such fine form. Mourinho tells Chelsea TV, 'We don't need another goalkeeper. We have a great group of keepers, but the reality is that we need the best players in the country, especially English ones. If a very young goalkeeper is available, we can think about it for the future of the club, instead of having Lenny Pidgeley as the [only] young goalkeeper. We could have both of them and maybe send one on loan.' Chelsea make a £450,000 bid but Leeds, desperate for money to pay their tax bill, prefer to sell Carson to Liverpool for £600,000. Chelsea are reluctant to increase their bid for an unproven youngster even though Cùdicini is set to leave in the summer.

With one eye on the upcoming Carling Cup semi-final second leg, Sir Alex Ferguson heaps unprecedented praise on Mourinho. 'Jose has done great since coming here,' he says. 'He has a confidence about him that has seeped into his team. He has got an assuredness and determination about them. He has been good for the Premiership. He has a wit and a humour about him. He comes across well and I get on OK with him. We had a spat last year but ...'

Chelsea pay £24.5m to end their sponsorship deal with kit-maker Umbro as they line up one of the biggest shirt contracts in world football. Umbro have supplied Chelsea since 1995. In 2001 the west London club signed a further ten-year deal with Umbro, which was worth around £50m. The contract will now end in June 2006, five years ahead of the original date. Umbro release a statement to the Stock Exchange saying the deal has been terminated by 'mutual agreement'. Peter Kenyon is busy securing a lucrative new sponsorship deal, rumoured to be with adidas, to fit the club's higher global profile. Manchester United currently have comfortably the biggest kit deal in British football. Kenyon, then at United, agreed a £300m 15-year contract with Nike in 2000 after also dispensing with the services of Umbro. Chelsea have already announced that their four-year £24m deal with shirt sponsors Emirates will end this season.

Chelsea may also have to write off a further £11m to offload Argentine striker Hernan Crespo. AC Milan, where he is currently on loan, want to sign him, but for just £5m. But Crespo is back on form in Serie A, blaming injuries and cultural differences for his failure to succeed in London. 'I just couldn't assimilate. The Italian way of playing suits me better than the English one, but it didn't have anything to do with that. I was happy enough with my scoring record.'

SATURDAY, 22 JANUARY 2005
CHELSEA 3, PORTSMOUTH 0

Didier Drogba's brace takes him to 11 for the season, overtaking Gudjohnsen as top scorer. But it is Robben who inspires this victory in the opening 39 minutes.

Robben says, 'With our defence we know when we score one goal we win. But we don't just want to win 1-0. We know everyone on the outside wants us to lose but that's not a pressure. I don't sense any pressure in our dressing room. We're playing with a lot of confidence and enjoy every minute of every match. To other people, it seems like we're unbeatable.'

Having resisted the temptation to go down after being fouled, Robben crosses for Drogba to score the first before hitting the target himself shortly afterwards, again staying on his feet as he stumbles past the keeper. Robben takes the opportunity to again refute diving insinuations. He says, 'If you saw the two moments, they were just two penalties and that's it. No diving. Today I kept my feet for the first goal and I went round the keeper for the second.'

Drogba scores his second, converting a free-kick won by Robben. The Dutchman is deservedly given a standing ovation when he is substituted late on.

There are changes in defence, with Bridge returning and Ferreira moving back to the right side. Cole is given a place in the midfield three for the third time in four home games. Portsmouth make early inroads, with Matthew Taylor's cross-shot saved by Cech, but Chelsea are untroubled and simply wait for their moment to pounce. That takes just 14 minutes, and referee Mike Riley intelligently ignores his assistant's well-intended flag for a foul on Robben as he speeds past Gary O'Neil. Robben rides the mistimed tackle and cuts the ball back invitingly for Drogba to sidefoot home from close range.

Six minutes later Chelsea have victory in their grasp as Lampard plays a skilfully weighted ball through for Robben to chase onto and the Dutchman skips around keeper Jamie Ashdown and clips the ball inside the post from a tight angle.

Portsmouth squander their only chance after Lampard's careless pass leaves Terry under pressure from Yakubu. The Nigeria international clips the ball past Terry and bears down on goal, but his shot rolls inches past the post with Cech beaten. That is as near as Portsmouth come to making a game of it. Two minutes later Robben is upended in full flight on the edge of the penalty area by David Unsworth, and Drogba strikes a fierce free-kick past Ashdown. Game over.

The second half is something of a procession, with Mourinho removing Drogba, Duff and Robben, but showing his strength in depth as Gudjohnsen, Kezman and Tiago come on. O'Neil strikes a 20-yard free-kick that Cech tips over, but it is Chelsea who come closer to scoring when Cole gets on the end of a cross and shoots straight at Ashdown.

Steve Clarke warns Arsenal and Manchester United that Chelsea will not get complacent. 'The first thing to do is to win the game and we put ourselves in a position to do that in the first 45 minutes when our performance was electric. It was an easier 45 minutes in the second half.

'It doesn't seem to be strange to be in this position. It seems to be what we deserve for the hard work we've put in this season. Obviously, after a game like that, you think we didn't look like losing that match but there will be difficult matches along the way. We're under no illusions. It's hard to see a danger at the moment. But we won't become complacent.'

Team

Cech, Ferreira, Gallas, Terry, Bridge, Lampard, Makelele, Cole, Robben (Kezman), Drogba (Gudjohnsen), Duff (Tiago).

Boro boss Steve McClaren has three bids for Geremi turned down but finally agrees a £3m deal with Chelsea, only for the midfielder to reject a three-and-a-half-year contract. While the media focus is on allegations of tapping up Ashley Cole and Steven Gerrard for summer deals, John Terry speaks out for Wayne Bridge. He says, 'Wayne's been fantastic all season. He's been in and out of the side but in particular the last five or six games he has been one of our best players. He had the same problem last summer when there was talk about Roberto Carlos coming here, but he came back for pre-season really sharp and he dealt with that. He knows he's up there with Ashley and Roberto so he'll deal with it the same way.' Terry is much liked within the dressing room for expressions of public support such as that. But in reality Bridge shares the same agent, Jonathan Barnett, as Cole, so would be under no illusions about his position at the club.

Mourinho is voted the best club coach in the world in 2004 by the International Football Federation of History and Statistics, finishing well ahead of Arséne Wenger and Didier Deschamps. He now plans to finish well ahead of Wenger and Sir Alex Ferguson in English football. Wenger enjoys a tribute night in his honour at The Savoy hosted by the Football Writers Association, only to discover the Premiership trophy draped in blue ribbons, although Arsenal are still technically the champions. Wenger gracefully accepts the explanation that sponsors Barclays colours are blue!

Mourinho responds to comments from Wenger claiming that Chelsea are merely an 'effective' team, who lack the flair of Arsenal. 'In the beginning we were called boring Chelsea,' says Mourinho. 'After that we couldn't score goals. After that we were top but would not be for long. After that, when Christmas arrives, we will lose matches. After that it is Boxing Day and Chelsea never win on Boxing Day. After that they said we cannot win in the North. After that they said if we lost the Carling Cup semi-final, the blip would start. If they really believed we are not strong enough to win this competition, they would not speak about us. They speak about us because they know we can win.'

Wenger missed out on signing Cech from French club Rennes and concedes he is a player who slipped through the Highbury net after they monitored his progress at previous club Sparta Prague.

At the Czech club he went over a thousand minutes before conceding a goal in any competition – attracting Arsenal's interest. Wenger says, 'We wanted to take him before he went to Rennes but we could not get a work permit. At the time he had not played the necessary amount of games for his national team.

'Yes, we missed out, but these things happen. He is not the only player we have missed out on. And when he moved to France we still had David Seaman and we had Jens Lehmann. But Cech is doing well and he is developing well. He has what you need to play in England.'

Chelsea's season continues serenely as they complete a Carling Cup semi-final victory over Manchester United and then beat Birmingham to reach the fifth round of the FA Cup. Next up is a league game with Blackburn, but before that Mourinho knows that one of Chelsea's closest challengers in the league will suffer a further setback with Arsenal set to take on United at Highbury. 'It's a good game for us,' says Mourinho.

Sol Campbell makes no secret of the win-or-bust scenario. 'Everyone at Arsenal has been waiting for this game. We're up for this one. We know we have to win. A draw does nothing for us – or them. Campbell winces at the transfer of Arsenal's 'invincible' tag to west London. 'We had that strength last season and now it's their turn. It's frustrating. Unless something dramatic happens it's hard to see Chelsea blowing it.'

Gary Neville is in agreement, 'Whoever loses from our game with Arsenal are going to find it very difficult to get back into the race, and it's hard enough to do that already. But there will be twists and turns left in the championship race. And I have a sneaking feeling the team that wins between us and Arsenal could put a lot of pressure on Chelsea.'

In the end it is United who take the points as they win another tasty encounter between the two 4–2. Wenger says, 'The championship is too far for us now,' and Arsenal suffer another blow as Sol Campbell sustains a serious ankle injury. Henry identifies Arsenal's lack of strength in depth as the main reason for their surrender of the Premiership crown. 'The turning point was when we lost the likes of Edu and Gilberto Silva and other players through injury,' he says. 'Without talking bad about anyone, look at our bench. Look at the bench of Manchester United, look at the bench of Chelsea.'

Mark Hughes, now in charge of Chelsea's next opponents Blackburn, was part of the Manchester United team that won the double in 1994 and went within a game of landing an unprecedented domestic treble. He feels it is easier for Chelsea to succeed as referees have made the game less physical by clamping down on tackling. 'That Manchester United side I was involved with was a fantastic side. It was a side for that era and we had to cope with the physical challenge in the first 20 minutes, half-hour of games. I don't think with the way games are refereed today that teams can do that any more and that makes it easier for the good teams.'

WEDNESDAY, 2 FEBRUARY 2005
BLACKBURN ROVERS 0, CHELSEA 1

After completing their hard-fought victory, Chelsea's players take a few seconds to comprehend Mourinho's tugging at his trademark grey overcoat; then they pull off their shirts and vests and hurl them to their travelling fans. 'This was not a football match,' Mourinho says afterwards, 'it was a fight'. So much for Sir Alex Ferguson's jibe that Chelsea would struggle in the North.

Robben scores the only goal after five minutes before Cech brilliantly saves Paul Dickov's penalty to help Chelsea open up an 11-point lead at the top. Cech sets a new Premiership record for not conceding a goal; it is now 781 minutes since he has been beaten, surpassing Peter Schmeichel's 1997 mark. Cech says, 'Schmeichel was one of my greatest idols. That is why I enjoy my record even more. I wish that my career would go on as successfully as Schmeichel's did.' He has not yet equalled his own personal record while at Sparta Prague.

But it is not all good news for Chelsea as Robben is forced off with an injury after just 12 minutes and sits on the bench with crutches beside him and a hospital appointment for X-rays and a scan the next morning on an injured foot.

Hughes' tactics were to unsettle Chelsea from the start, stationing combative South Africa captain Aaron Mokoena in front of the back four, with Robbie Savage at the heart of the team. Mokoena makes his intentions clear by trying to wrestle Lampard to the ground as they wait for a corner. Only five minutes have gone when Chelsea burst into the lead. Lampard spreads a long ball for Gudjohnsen to flick on to Robben, who turns Lucas Neill and unleashes an angled drive that dips under Brad Friedel. But then Robben tries to win possession to launch another attack, but Mokoena catches him late and the Dutchman limps off to be replaced by Cole.

Blackburn gain confidence from Robben's misfortune and in the 33rd minute Savage tumbles under a challenge from Ferreira and wins a penalty from Uriah Rennie. Dickov hits the penalty low to Cech's left but the giant goalkeeper flings himself across his goal to parry. Cech then hurls himself at the loose ball and takes a hefty kick in the ribs from Dickov, provoking one of many ugly scenes. Mourinho is furious and his mood is hardly improved when Dominic Matteo cuts Cole down right in front of the Chelsea bench.

When Dickov takes yet another slash at Cech a few minutes later, catching the keeper on the knee, Chelsea's players snap. Terry grabs the Scot by the throat and a melee erupts. The game is in danger of veering out of control with Savage charging around looking for trouble. After the interval Savage launches himself at Duff and Mokoena chops down Lampard. Terry gains a measure of revenge when he clatters into Dickov and is shown the yellow card. Dickov is finally booked for shoving Terry in the face. How it took so long is a mystery!

Despite getting his chance to impress as a replacement for Robben, Cole spends the match being chastised by Mourinho for drifting out of position, and the substitute is substituted with 11 minutes to go. It is so clearly a punishment that Cole does not bother to wait on the bench to watch the closing stages.

Mourinho accuses Blackburn of trying to kick his side off the pitch. 'I think they felt they couldn't beat us at football so they tried to beat us with a different kind of football,' he says. 'I'm not saying they tried to get players injured, but they were nasty, and they tried to intimidate our players. We gave a big answer here tonight; we showed we can deal with that tactic. We fought fantastically well, everyone battling for the same cause. The blond boy in the middle, yes, Robbie Savage, made 20 faults and no yellow card. It's difficult to control emotions. They were direct for every ball. They were aggressive, hard and nasty.'

Mourinho also alleges dirty tricks by Blackburn before the game. 'During the afternoon it rained only in this stadium – our kitman saw it – they tried everything. There must be a microclimate here. But we coped with the heavy pitch well and the Blackburn game left me confident about what we can do if we go to another stadium and face the same conditions. That is another sign that we can adjust to every situation.'

But Blackburn manager Mark Hughes is also incensed by Mourinho running on to the Ewood Park pitch at the final whistle to celebrate with his players, rather than shake his hand. 'I'm upset that the opposing manager was not gracious enough to shake my hand. Sometimes you have to be gracious in victory as well as in defeat. The best way to play them is to knock them down a peg or two and we did that. Chelsea know they have been very fortunate to leave here with three points. They are not the best team in the country – at least not on this showing.'

> **Team**
>
> Cech, Ferreira, Gallas, Terry, Bridge, Tiago, Makelele, Lampard, Duff, Gudjohnsen (Kezman), Robben (Cole (Jarosik)).

The tapping-up row over Ashley Cole rumbles on relentlessly. Arsenal vice-chairman David Dein says, 'We will see what the quality of the evidence is and take it from there. Ashley Cole is committed to Arsenal and under contract until 2007.' A Chelsea statement reads, 'The club has an established policy on stories linking it with players, whatever the circumstances. We have not commented in the past, do not intend to comment now, and will not do so in the future.' The Premier League say they will only launch an investigation if there is a complaint, which has so far not been forthcoming from Arsenal.

Ironically, Mourinho describes Cole as 'the best English defender' in an article in the Portuguese newspaper *A Bola*. Talking of his future transfer targets, Mourinho says, 'We'll buy two – one left-sided defender, because I only have one – and another player. The defender has to be good to join our squad. About the other, it has to be a great player. We are already scouting half a dozen of them, who are the best in the world, because only they have the ability to join a super, balanced squad like ours.'

Wenger maintains Cole will still sign a new contract at Highbury, 'I am one hundred per cent sure Ashley Cole will extend his contract as he is part of the bunch of players who are the core and heart of the team. Ashley said he is fed up with that story. He is completely committed to the club and he doesn't want to know about it.' Wenger calls on Chelsea to make a categorical denial that Mourinho and Kenyon attended a secret meeting with Cole. 'Before we complain, we must have evidence the meeting has happened but I don't know how so much assertive evidence comes out in a newspaper [if it is] just being invented. It looks to me like, yes, it has happened, although I don't know [for sure]'.

Cole himself says, 'Arsenal fans will want to know what's going on, but I'm signed here for two years and we have just got to see how it goes. I just to want to get back to playing football and trying to win the league.' Bookies William Hill offer even money Cole will be a Chelsea player by the first day of the next Premiership season.

Sheffield Wednesday complete the signing of Chelsea midfielder Craig Rocastle on a free transfer. The 23-year-old signs for two and a half years. Rocastle, who arrived at Stamford Bridge from Kingstonian in August 2002, has been on loan at Hibernian since August, making 14 appearances for the Scottish Premier League side.

Chelsea have major concerns about Robben after scans of his damaged foot are inconclusive due to the amount of swelling and bruising. Mourinho says, 'There are no conclusions for the moment. The only conclusion is big, big pain. Arjen cannot walk, he cannot put his foot on the floor and he is immobilised.'

Blackburn and Chelsea are charged by the FA with failing to ensure their players conduct themselves in an orderly fashion. The charge relates to a mass confrontation after Morten Gamst Pedersen tried to head the ball out of the hands of Cech. A number of other players on both sides joining the melee.

Mourinho, whose contract is worth more than £4m a year over four years, says he hopes to stay at Chelsea for a long time. 'I signed an extraterrestrial contract and the intention is here to sign a new one and ideally it would be from four to eight years. Improving the four-year one makes no sense, because I knew what I signed and I know that I'll abide by it. I'm happy with my conditions and I'm completely committed to the growth of the club in many different levels. I like English football a lot; I like to live in England a lot. Therefore I can't see myself anywhere else. I mentioned, it's true, that I'd like to coach in Italy and also the national squad, but I see this day as very far away.'

Next up for Chelsea are Manchester City, the only team to have beaten them in the league all season. City manager Kevin Keegan is fulsome in his praise for Mourinho. 'He was very gracious when we beat them at our place earlier in the season,' he says. 'What I find most remarkable is within weeks he turned a set of talented individuals into an exceptional team.'

But Chelsea will have to face City without Robben, who fears he has broken his foot again and could be out for the rest of the season. Whether it is a break or not, Robben is resigned to being sidelined for some weeks. He says, 'This is a disaster – everything was going so well. It is a massive blow and comes just at the moment when I was in top shape and very fit. But now it is worthless and I have to fight back for the second time this season.'

SUNDAY, 6 FEBRUARY 2005

CHELSEA 0, MANCHESTER CITY 0

Manchester City frustrate Chelsea again, with David James somehow keeping out Lampard's close-range volley in the last minute. Mourinho is in a prickly mood after seeing his side's lead at the top of the table cut to nine points. 'I prefer to say my players in finishing situations weren't lucky and they had in David James a goalkeeper who made incredible saves to get them the point,' he says. 'Only one team had chances to score goals, but we couldn't score and they fought a lot, defended a lot and had a good goalkeeper. They were lucky.'

Those comments do not sit comfortably with Keegan, who says, 'Jose has got to learn to give other teams credit. He has to be careful not to get frustrated and say things he will regret. This might be a big point for Chelsea because they could have lost. Chelsea will get a lot more of this before the end of the season. There's only Manchester United and Arsenal who will come here and take them on. It would have been a travesty after the work we put in if David James hadn't made that save. We had a plan and it worked.'

Chelsea miss the influence of striker Drogba and especially Robben. Early on Kezman almost creates an opening for himself when latching onto a poor headed clearance 25 yards out. But after knocking the ball past outstanding centre-back Richard Dunne, he then theatrically goes to ground, and can count himself fortunate not to be cautioned by referee Howard Webb.

Duff finds enough space on the left-hand side of the area to test James with a low drive. The keeper gets down well to parry and Kezman fails to turn in the loose ball from no more than a yard out.

The City goal is leading a charmed life, with Paul Bosvelt somehow scrambling Gallas' header off the line in the 38th minute. Just before the break the visitors then have a gilt-edged chance themselves when Shaun Wright-Phillips chases a long punt across field and turns Gallas, enabling him to pull the ball back across the six-yard box. Terry slips at the vital moment, handing Fowler a free header, but the former Liverpool striker sends his diving header wide.

In the second half Tiago replaces Jarosik, and Cole then comes on for Kezman, but Chelsea are still unable to beat James in the City goal for the second time this season. After the game Cech hails James as the best goalkeeper the team has faced in England. He says, 'David James saved his team and put in a great performance and was the only reason we didn't win the game.'

> **Team**
>
> Cech, Bridge, Ferreira, Terry, Gallas, Jarosik (Tiago), Makelele, Lampard, Kezman (Cole), Gudjohnsen, Duff.

Before the match the Premier League announced they had received a formal complaint from Arsenal and would convene a commission into the Cole tapping-up allegations. The hearing will take place before a three-man panel made up of a QC and two other commissioners.

Mourinho reacts with contempt for the Premier League's decision. 'I know nothing about it, I don't know and I don't want to know,' he says. 'I'm not a lawyer; I'm a football manager. What matters to me is to train to get the best results. When I win I am happy and when I don't I am not.'

The club issues a statement saying, 'Chelsea can confirm it has been in discussions with the Premier League over the last few days and we will be cooperating fully with the inquiry announced today. It would be inappropriate to make any further comment until the inquiry is completed.'

Terry and Bridge pull out of the England squad to face Holland through injury, but Lampard is picked for the game. Lampard also picks up the England Player of the Year trophy as voted for by fans on the FA's official website. Lampard picks up 40 per cent of the vote ahead of Wayne Rooney (16 per cent) and Steven Gerrard (10 per cent).

Chelsea's hopes of landing an unprecedented quadruple are dealt the biggest possible blow with confirmation that Robben has broken his foot. Once the initial swelling around the injury had subsided scans revealed a double break that could keep the Blues star sidelined for up to two months. Robben will miss the Carling Cup final and the first leg of the Champions League last-16 clash against Barcelona.

Physio Mike Banks says, 'One is a chip on the side of his foot, the other is a small break on the third metatarsal. But this is not the traditional metatarsal that has become so famous since the last World Cup and which has kept Scott Parker out for two months. The fractures are tiny and he could be playing next month.' Robben's injury is linked with the surprise announcement that doctor Neil

Frazer has quit after five years at Stamford Bridge. Frazer allegedly left following a string of clashes with Mourinho, who wanted Robben fit for the Carling Cup final.

Lampard argues that although Robben will be missed, Chelsea are far from being a one-man team. 'Of course we will miss Arjen,' he says. 'He has such great pace and he has given us so much since he's come into the team. People have made a massive thing of him though and we're far from a one-man team. We were pretty much top of the league before he played for us and we have got to carry on without him.'

Damien Duff shows that he could be the man to lift Chelsea in Robben's absence with a mesmeric performance against Portugal on his 50th cap for the Republic of Ireland. Mourinho witnesses the display as Duff inspires the Irish to a 1–0 win.

After the match Mourinho hugs Duff before seeing him into a black Mercedes to be whisked away to Dublin airport – along with Ferreira and Tiago – for a private jet back to London. Last September Mourinho attended the Republic of Ireland's World Cup qualifier against Cyprus in Dublin and left without even speaking to Duff. That upset the 25-year-old, who feared at that time that Mourinho did not want him, having seen Robben arrive at Chelsea. Against Portugal there is an edge to Duff's performance, and Mourinho, to his credit, has made Duff a better, harder, fitter player. Mourinho may not have had him in his plans when he arrived – there has been continued speculation over wingers such as Joaquin – but he has revised his opinion.

Mourinho stands to earn a £4.2m bonus if Chelsea win the quadruple. Winning the Premier League title will earn him a £1m bonus – double what Ranieri would have received – with more than £2m extra if he then wins the Champions League. Again that is double the bonus that would have been paid to Ranieri. In all the bonuses effectively add up to an extra year's salary for Mourinho, who will then be by far the highest paid football manager in the world.

Abramovich has been paying the players an extra £4,000 for every Premiership game they win, and £1,500 for a draw, on top of their lucrative salaries. Abramovich has also been handing over 50 per cent of all prize money from the Champions League to the players. Last season that meant the squad shared £3m – £200,000 each if they were in every squad. The players negotiated their deal when Abramovich bought Chelsea, but the system of payments per game has been dismantled by Mourinho, who does not agree with appearance money and has rolled it into lump-sum bonuses to be paid to the squad at the end of the season depending on what they win.

SATURDAY, 12 FEBRUARY 2005

EVERTON 0, CHELSEA 1

James Beattie helps make a difficult trip much easier with a senseless red card after just eight minutes as Chelsea record their ninth 1–0 win in the Premiership. Joe Cole provides in insight into the enormity of the victory. He says, 'People looked at us without Robben and Drogba and probably doubted us but we came to perform. This was a big win, as important as the ones at Spurs and Liverpool. You looked around the dressing room afterwards and you could see how determined everyone had been not to give Manchester United and Arsenal anything to bite on. Wherever we go to play – Manchester, Barcelona or Timbuktu – it doesn't matter to us. We feel we can win every match we play.'

Beattie's moment of madness costs Everton dear when he chases a long ball down the left with Gallas obstructing his run. First the striker pushes the Chelsea defender and then moments later he butts the back of his head. Beattie is defended by David Moyes, who says, 'I don't think it was a sending-off. First there was a push and then Beattie just runs into the back of him. The centre-half went down far too easily. I was a centre-half and I would have been embarrassed to have gone down like that. Not in a million years would John Terry have gone down in the same way.'

Beattie himself comments, 'We were chasing a ball into the corner and William Gallas was looking over his shoulder and blocking me off. He was stopping as we were running and I said to myself, "If you're going to stay in my way I'll go straight over you." Our heads barely touched. If I'd done it deliberately he'd have stayed down a long time.'

Everton's ten men put up a long, brave fight until a second-half Gudjohnsen tap-in breaks the deadlock. Chelsea return to their 4-3-3 formation, with Cole on the right and Duff on the left, and they dominate the early possession. Everton barely have a decent touch of the ball before they are reduced to ten men.

The home side's work-rate underlines their approach to the whole season, but they tire in the face of Chelsea's persistent attacks and eventually concede after 69 minutes. Ferreira's low cross fizzes into the box, Gallas hits the bar from close range and Gudjohnsen has a simple tap-in.

But it is Everton who apply the pressure towards the end, with Chelsea defending in depth as the crosses start to rain in. Mourinho responds by sending on extra defenders in Johnson for Tiago and Carvalho for Duff, while Jarosik has already replaced Cole to counter the aerial threat of Duncan Ferguson. Chelsea finish with six defenders in a line across their area and Everton even send goalkeeper Nigel Martyn up for set-pieces, but they cannot prevent another victory for Mourinho's men.

Gudjohnsen hails the win as 'massive'. He beams, 'I'm sure many people sitting at home were wishing us to drop points, but we bounced back from last Sunday. Nigel Martyn pulled off some fantastic saves but in the end we managed to get the goal and the points and that's what counts most at this stage of the season. We concentrate on our own results to begin with and then that puts the pressure back on Manchester United and Arsenal. This is a massive three points for us today.'

Mourinho leaves it up to Steve Clarke to give his version of events. Clarke says, 'It's a difficult place to come and we are delighted with the win. But I think the sending-off changed the game. The way it started, it looked as if it was going to be an open, entertaining match, which would have suited us. But once Beattie was sent off they shut up shop and it was down to us to try and break them down. At half-time we said to keep patient, to keep passing and to make the most of the extra man and then it would come. And we managed to edge it, although you have to say it could have been more as their keeper made some great saves.'

Team

Cech, Ferreira, Gallas, Terry, Bridge, Lampard, Makelele, Tiago (Johnson), Cole (Jarosik), Gudjohnsen, Duff (Carvalho).

After having more time to study replays of Beattie's red card, Moyes admits he was wrong. 'My first comments came immediately after the game and at that time I'd had the opportunity to see a quick rerun. Having had more time I believe I should set the record straight by conceding that Beattie's sending-off was correct.'

Manchester United beat Manchester City 2–0 for their 13th win in 15 league outings, but such form is immaterial with Chelsea's consistency. Sir Alex Ferguson brands the Premiership leaders 'lucky'. He says, 'Chelsea aren't playing as well as they have been and they've been lucky recently. There's no doubt they're getting all the breaks at the moment and we're not. I couldn't believe that sending-off at all. That was a real kick in the teeth for us.'

Gudjohnsen is arrested for alleged drink-driving after police spot him driving suspiciously. The 26-year-old is flagged down by police at 5.20 on Sunday morning after celebrating with team-mates. A breath test shows he is fractionally above the drink-drive limit. Traffic police drive him to Battersea police station where he is given a second breath test, which is said to hover on the limit of 35 micrograms of alcohol per 100 millilitres of blood. He is then given a blood test. The father of two is bailed after three hours in custody pending the result of the blood test. 'It is touch and go whether he will be charged,' a police source says. Gudjohnsen is also cautioned by Mourinho after being in breach of the club's 2am curfew.

There is no doubting Mourinho's admiration for Gudjohnsen, who he regards as an intelligent and versatile footballer. Gudjohnsen was the first Chelsea player to be handed an improved contract by Mourinho and is one of his trusted confidants, sitting on the players' committee with Makelele and Cudicini.

The quest for the Premiership is on hold for three weeks, but the squad face three cup ties in eight days. First Mourinho's men go to Newcastle in the FA Cup, from where they will flew direct to Barcelona for the Champions League last-16 clash three days later. Four days after that, Chelsea face Liverpool in the Carling Cup final at the Millennium Stadium.

Chelsea pull off a clean sweep of the Barclays awards for January. Mourinho is named Manager of the Month for four straight wins, Terry is Player of the Month, and there is a special merit award for Cech keeping ten clean sheets in a row.

Chelsea's Premiership break starts badly, with back-to-back defeats in the FA Cup and away to Barcelona in the Champions League. Patrick Vieira says it could derail Chelsea's season. Arsenal endured a similar test in 2004 when they lost their FA Cup semi-final to Manchester United and then crashed out of the Champions League to Chelsea three days later. 'We must wait and see how Chelsea respond,' says Vieira. 'They have lost a big game and there's still so many games for them to play – for us as well. There's still a really long way to go. We are a little bit behind but I don't think we're out of the title race.'

Chelsea are linked with a succession of transfer targets, from the usual suspects to Theo Walcott, a 15-year-old schoolboy winger, rated by one respected scout as the best of his age group in Europe. Chelsea are willing to pay £2m before he has even taken his GCSEs, but he turns down the riches on offer at Stamford Bridge. The boy already has an agent and a boot deal. The west London club lead a pack that includes Liverpool, Manchester United, Arsenal and Real Madrid. But the boy plans to commit to Southampton, where he has progressed through the academy.

A goalscorer tops Chelsea's list, with everyone from Michael Owen to European Footballer of the Year Andriy Shevchenko being linked with a move to Stamford Bridge. But the AC Milan and Ukraine striker stresses that he is not prepared to join Mourinho's foreign legion, even though he holds both coach and Abramovich in high regard.

Inter Milan's Brazilian Adriano is Mourinho's choice, but the Italian club have already turned down £50m from Real Madrid. Joaquin also remains a possibility. Mourinho says, 'He is a very good player and I admit there was contact. We asked and the other party replied. Nothing has been discarded with regard to him. We could try and sign him in June or December.' The 23-year-old winger remarks, 'I came close to joining Chelsea in January for £30m but the deal collapsed. I don't have a preference between them and Real Madrid but it would not be a problem living in London.' His dad, Aurelio Sanchez, who acts as the player's agent, insists the clubs have agreed a fee and the winger is ready for talks. Sanchez says, 'Chelsea are going to offer more than £20m for Joaquin and Betis president Manuel Ruiz de Lopera is convinced by that. Now they will have to convince Joaquin.'

Liverpool skipper Steven Gerrard or Lyon's highly rated Michael Essien are contenders for the midfield slot, while Mourinho dismisses the idea of signing Ronaldinho, 'Barcelona don't have to be worried about us coming in for Ronaldinho,' he says. We won't be back for him because we have totally different qualities. Ronaldinho could play in any team in the world – there's no manager so stupid as to say he wouldn't take him. But it's a policy of building a team. Our team is still forming and developing, in spite of the results we have achieved. It's not a team which has found its full potential.' With Ronaldinho beginning talks over a new contract at Barca, his agent has been talking up Chelsea's interest. But Mourinho adds, 'We know very well what we need to improve the squad but I'm very happy with what we have. I value the players who are already at Chelsea. We're not going to spend, spend, spend and buy and sell every year. The time must come for stability.'

Everton and Birmingham continue to be linked with a summer move for Scott Parker. Mikael Forssell meanwhile rejects a move back to Birmingham to fight for his place at Stamford Bridge, as he is 'looking forward to the chance to impress the right people'. Carlo Cudicini is lined up for a move to AC Milan. His agent Federico Pastorello says, 'It's not a good thing being on the bench after having been named the Premiership's best goalkeeper two consecutive times.' Arsenal and Manchester United are also interested.

Mourinho appoints the doctor who guided Kelly Holmes to her double Olympic success to help Chelsea win gold this season: Dr Bryan English from UK Athletics.

English played a key role in getting Holmes fit to win both the 800m and 1500m in Athens and his record of getting athletes back to fitness quickly is the reason Mourinho has got him on board.

Eidur Gudjohnsen discovers he will not be charged after his arrest for drink-driving, but Glen Johnson is banned after being found speeding at 112mph on a motorway with five friends packed into his car. He loses his licence for a month after answering a call to pick up pals whose car had broken down on the M25.

With Chelsea preparing for the Carling Cup final, Manchester United scrap through against Portsmouth to close the gap at the top to six points. But Arsenal's pursuit is dealt a blow when they are held 1–1 at Southampton. Chelsea end their testing week by getting back to winning ways and claiming their first bit of silverware in the Carling Cup final. Mourinho escapes any FA sanctions after being ordered out of the dugout during the match. It has been a feisty week of cup football before a return to the Premiership.

Mourinho vows not to change but promises there will be no repeat of the controversial 'silence' gesture. 'I know I cannot do that gesture in England. If I do it, the police come and put me in the dressing room and because I don't want to go to the dressing room again, I cannot do it. It is as simple as that – what I can do and what I can't do.'

Manchester United blow their chance to close the gap at the top to three points. Playing ahead of Chelsea, United are held to a 0–0 draw by ten-man Crystal Palace. So Chelsea's lead stays at a healthy five points, with Norwich away the first of two matches in hand to come.

SATURDAY, 5 MARCH 2005
NORWICH CITY 1, CHELSEA 3

Chelsea require two goals in seven second-half minutes from Kezman and Carvalho to silence relegation-haunted Norwich after Leon McKenzie dares to threaten an upset. In the end Chelsea merely underline their claim that the Premiership crown is theirs for the taking.

Mourinho deliberately chooses not to tell his players about United's earlier draw at Palace. 'We don't think about them – they think about us,' Mourinho says. 'I always like my players to be under pressure. Because Manchester United dropped points, it could influence my players in a negative way – so I did not want them to know.'

Mourinho adds that Robben may be able to return in the all-important Champions League second leg against Barcelona after more than a month out with a broken foot. 'He has a chance – maybe not to play 90 minutes – but he has a chance.'

Cole does everything possible in his man-of-the-match display against Norwich to prove Chelsea can survive without the Dutchman. Cole's performance, only the second time he has completed 90 Premiership minutes for Mourinho, is not just about his splendid goal. There is also a brilliant pass that Drogba contrives to miss, excellent movement and a growing awareness of when to perform the tricks and when to keep it simple. Mourinho says, 'Earlier in the season I saw Joe doing fantastic things but sometimes disappearing a bit from the game. But recently he's played very well. He was good in difficult circumstances in Barcelona, very good against Liverpool, and this was his most consistent performance. At the moment he's very confident, he's playing well, showing his talent and at the same time he's showing he is a team player, so I'm very happy.'

From the start the pressure is relentless. There are just seven minutes on the clock when Jason Shackell makes a heroic recovery to keep the champions-elect at bay after a lovely midfield move. Drogba drops deep to lay the ball back to Lampard, whose little chip over the top sends Duff clear with only Rob Green to beat. Duff dinks the ball towards goal and Chelsea's travelling fans let out a mighty roar, only to find it strangled in their throats as Shackell gets back superbly to head the ball off his line.

In the 12th minute Ferreira plays a tidy ball back to Lampard, whose shot dips viciously inches over the bar. From the next attack, Norwich crack. Makelele plays a through-pass to Cole, who is caught in possession and seems to have lost the ball as he crashes to the ground. But Cole jumps to his feet and is first to the loose ball. He strides on two paces and unleashes a left-foot shot that simply flies past Green.

True to form, Cole manages to waste one only half as difficult six minutes later and is then booked for a foolish tackle on Darren Huckerby.

But when McKenzie gets in front of Ferreira to head in a Huckerby cross – Norwich's first genuine chance of the match – it looks as though Chelsea have squandered two points. Cech's record run without conceding a goal finally ends at 1,025 Premiership minutes. Mourinho immediately springs into action, introducing Kezman and Gudjohnsen. He is instantly rewarded, with both substitutes involved in what proves to be the vital second. A Cole cross is deflected into Gudjohnsen's path, and he picks out Lampard with a half-volleyed forward pass. Lampard touches it past the keeper but it needs Kezman to guide it into the gaping net.

Carvalho grabs his first goal for the club, a header from a Lampard corner in the 79th minute, to end the contest.

If anything sums up Chelsea's iron grip on the Premiership it is the almost total lack of celebrations. Brief hugs and grasped hands sum up a team already focusing on the next task with mighty Barcelona. As Mourinho predicted, the Carling Cup triumph makes his men more relaxed and able to play with conviction.

Mourinho comments, 'I try to show the players every day, every match, my experience and my confidence, just by saying to them, "How can we be under pressure when we have a six-point advantage with a game in hand?" I try to motivate them by saying one weekend that we need eight victories, the next that we need seven. Now we need six.'

> **Team**
>
> Cech, Carvalho, Johnson, Ferreira, Terry, Cole, Duff (Jarosik), Lampard, Makelele, Tiago (Kezman), Drogba (Gudjohnsen).

Mourinho reveals the players dedicated their win at Norwich to Wayne Bridge, who will be out for ten months, missing much of the start of the next season, after breaking his ankle in the FA Cup loss at Newcastle. Already linked with one left back, Mourinho will need two.

Mourinho is fined £5,000 and warned about his future conduct by an FA disciplinary commission for accusing Manchester United players of diving following the Carling Cup semi-final first leg tie against Manchester United. Mourinho is so angry at being fined for his 'cheat and cheat' comment that he considers reducing his cooperation with the FA on England issues. He has welcomed Sammy Lee from the England coaching staff to the training ground and is uncertain whether to remain so accommodating after being punished for words which he says were misinterpreted. But he will not withhold players from Eriksson.

In back-to-back hearings Chelsea and Blackburn are fined over the brawl that marred the end of their Premiership clash. The Blues deny a charge of failing to ensure their players conduct themselves in an orderly fashion, while Blackburn admit the same charge. Chelsea are fined £15,000 and warned about their future conduct by the FA's disciplinary commission, while Rovers are given a £10,000 fine and a future conduct warning.

A goodwill mission is lined up for the next international break with Mourinho off to the Middle East to a soccer school in Israel with Jewish and Palestinian kids. He says, 'This invitation makes me feel very honoured. It will be my modest contribution to strengthening the ties of understanding and friendship between the two peoples, who, like myself, want peace.'

In a meeting with the Premier League's lawyers Denton Wilde Sapte, Peter Kenyon states that a meeting has taken place with himself, Ashley Cole, Cole's agent Jonathan Barnett, Jose Mourinho and Pini Zahavi. However, Chelsea refute Arsenal's claims that they approached the England international while also rebutting reports that they have opened provisional negotiations with Cole on a £90,000-per-week contract. Chelsea's testimony is that the player and his agent contacted Zahavi to request a meeting. Zahavi then arranged and paid for hire of the Royal Park Hotel's Green Room to hold the meeting, at which Cole and Barnett aired their frustrations at stuttering contract negotiations with Arsenal.

Nick Fitzpatrick, who is conducting the inquiry, requests telephone records of the relevant parties to help to decide who made the first approach. If Chelsea's claims are upheld by the inquiry, Cole will be in breach of the Premier League's rule K5, stating that, 'A contracted player, either by himself or by any person on his behalf, shall not either directly or indirectly make any approach [to a club with a view to negotiating a contract with that club] without having obtained the prior written consent of his club.' Cole would also be in breach of his contract with Arsenal. Chelsea face a charge under rule K3, which forbids unauthorised approaches for other clubs' players.

The Cole camp admit they asked to meet Zahavi as part of their strategy after contract talks with Arsenal turned sour. But Barnett declares, 'I am happy to confirm on the record that the accusations levelled at Ashley are entirely false. For it to be suggested that I cynically set up a meeting with Chelsea and dragged them to it almost against their will is ludicrous.' Cole is dropped to the bench by Arséne Wenger for Arsenal's FA Cup win at Bolton.

Mourinho gives evidence to the Premiership lawyers on the same day Cole turns up to present his side of the story. Mourinho backs up Kenyon's claim that Chelsea did not make an illegal approach. The Blues manager, like Kenyon, argues they merely attended out of curiosity, listened to what Cole and his agent had to say and then left. Mourinho insists Cole was not enticed to quit the Gunners and that no offers were made. In his evidence, Cole is adamant he never had any intention of discussing anything with Kenyon and Mourinho. He tells the inquiry he was having a meeting with Barnett in his office when Zahavi called and told them he wanted to talk at the nearby Royal Park Hotel.

Mourinho is reported to have said, 'I never dreamt I could consider signing you. You are already the best left-back in the world but I want to see it in your face that you want to play for us. Join us and you can win everything – the Champions League, the Premier League ... everything.' There are also strong hints that Cole was actually told he would be teaming up with Gerrard next season. Liverpool make it clear they are not lodging a complaint.

Bryan Robson, manager of Chelsea's next opponents West Brom, warns Mourinho and his players that they should keep quiet until they can back up their actions with more trophies. 'Chelsea have that tag of wind-up merchants and, until recently, they had not won anything for years. They seem to have done it to people from different walks of life, too – refs, officials, fans, players, journalists. If you win doubles and trebles you can talk about yourself a bit more. But they will be the first to fall flat on their faces if they do not get results.'

Mourinho attends a reception at The Butcher's Hook pub, opposite the ground, to mark the centenary of the club. Claudia Schiffer, Gordon Ramsay and Bernie Ecclestone add the glitz. The eatery held Chelsea's first board meeting, chaired by Gus Mears on 14 March 1905 – only this time there is Russian caviar on the menu.

Ken Bates says Claudio Ranieri's contribution to Chelsea's current success should be recognised. 'I was disappointed he wasn't invited on Monday night,' says Bates. 'I'm sure Claudia Schiffer, Bernie Ecclestone and Gordon Ramsay have made a significant contribution to Chelsea's history. They just haven't been given proper recognition by the Press. Ranieri is entitled to recognition for laying the foundations of what Chelsea have now. He should get credit for taking the team to an FA Cup final in 2002 and the semi-finals of the Champions League last season. It happens quite a lot in football that a manager walks into a club, takes over someone else's team and makes them better. I'm not knocking Jose Mourinho. He has changed tactics and the players praise him highly. He has played a part. But Claudio was always a long-term builder.'

TUESDAY, 15 MARCH 2005

CHELSEA 1, WEST BROMWICH ALBION 0

Mourinho collects an award from the League Managers Association but, facing charges from the FA over the Ashley Cole affair and UEFA following comments after the Champions League clash with Barcelona, he has the worried look of a man at the centre of several storms. When Drogba scores he rushes over to his manager insisting he joins in the celebrations.

One young fan holds aloft a homemade poster reading 'Mourinho Is Innocent'. It is hardly the flourish of the spectacular against Barcelona but Drogba's first-half clincher sends them 11 points clear with just nine games to go.

Steve Clarke says, 'Jose is only worried about winning trophies. We have one trophy already with the Carling Cup, we are through to the last eight of the Champions League and 11 points clear in the Premiership. We aim to add those two as well, so what more can we do? It's not won yet, but it's another big step on the way, with another three points. That's what we wanted before the game and that's what we got.'

Bryan Robson fumes that Geoff Horsfield had two 'goals' ruled out for offside. 'I'd like to see his second again. It looked perfectly good to me. I still don't know why it was disallowed.'

Terry marshals his defence impeccably and almost gets the home side off to the perfect start as he heads Duff's corner goalwards in the first minute. Gudjohnsen tries to deflect the ball in, but only succeeds in heading it wide.

Drogba should break the deadlock in the fifth minute but his shot on the turn from six yards is weak. Drogba then sends a free-kick by Lampard over the bar.

Cole causes all sorts of problems down the right flank and

provides two crosses that Drogba and Gudjohnsen fail to get on the end of. Soon after Duff is inches wide with a left-foot pile-driver from the edge of the box, which again Drogba just fails to convert with a cheeky flick. After Drogba fails with yet another chance, even he cannot miss Duff's inch-perfect cross in front of an open goal after 24 minutes. Lampard carves open the defence with a perfectly weighted pass and Duff sprints clear before delivering a low cross for Drogba.

Before half-time Cole sends Drogba clear again, and although he rounds keeper Russell Hoult the ball is cleared. In the last 12 minutes Drogba is guilty of two more glaring misses. First he heads wide from Cole's cross and then he blasts the ball over the bar from six yards.

Terry insists Chelsea are taking nothing for granted despite their commanding Premiership lead. 'It's not in the bag yet and there's still a long way to go. Manchester United are pushing us all the way, Arsenal are still there and all we can do is to keep winning our games and putting more pressure on them. We are a bit disappointed because we had the chances in the first half but three points was what we came for. It was hard to get the points against a team desperate to stay up.'

Team

Cech, Ferreira, Terry, Huth, Gallas, Cole (Kezman), Makelele, Lampard, Gudjohnsen (Jarosik), Duff (Smertin), Drogba.

Wayne Bridge reveals he has had plenty of well-wishers as he begins his recovery from his broken ankle. Bridge says, 'Mr Abramovich and Mr Mourinho plus most of the other players came to see me in hospital, which was great. Alan Shearer popped in, too. Everyone's been brilliant. So many people have tried to keep my spirits up. Since I've been out of hospital the lads have been round every day. I can't believe how much support I've had. I think they know how serious my injury is and they feel for me. They know I'm missing out on the rest of the season and they've promised to win the title for me. I personally think it's already in the bag and I can't wait to get my hands on my medal.'

Bridge explains the full horror of his pain. 'They had to wait for the swelling to go down before they operated. I had no idea what I had broken but it was even worse when they finally sat me down to tell me what had happened. I had broken two bones in my right ankle, ripped the ligaments and broken the fibula in my leg. By the time they came round to operating on me I was on morphine because the pain was so unbearable. The operation took two hours. I saw the boss and he told me to take a holiday for a few weeks so I can get my mind right for the work that will be needed.'

Despite all their disciplinary problems with Europe's governing body, Chelsea are in line to win the Fair Play League! The table is not merely determined by bookings and red cards. A UEFA spokesman says, 'Other factors are taken into account such as the behaviour of team officials towards the referee, the behaviour of the team and also the crowd behaviour.' The marks are only given to teams during Premiership matches, which is why Chelsea are top.

Mourinho chooses to concentrate on the next assignment against Palace rather than worry about drawing Bayern Munich in the Champions League quarter-finals. He says, 'This is a time to remember we have not won the league. Chelsea have not won it for 50 years and this Chelsea side hasn't won it yet in 2005. We want to win the league and we want to win it properly. It is over a year since Chelsea have lost at home and that includes all the time I have been here. Our home record is good but it can still be even better. There's five more home league games and we're aiming at two more Champions League home games, so we can go as high as 24 home wins in one season. I believe we can achieve this.'

SATURDAY, 19 MARCH 2005
CHELSEA 4, CRYSTAL PALACE 1

Spring is in the air, Robben is back, and on a scorching afternoon Mourinho sports a scarf! Joe Cole responds to the long-awaited return of Robben by inspiring Chelsea to a convincing victory as Mourinho's side take another major step towards the title.

Palace commit the cardinal sin of allowing Lampard far too much space outside the penalty box. Still 25 yards out from goal, he takes aim with 28 minutes gone and powers a superb drive into the corner of the net. Chelsea continue to threaten, with Johnson striking the side netting, Drogba volleying just wide and Lampard failing to make proper contact with a diving header. Palace make Chelsea pay for an uncharacteristic defensive lapse just before the break. Chelsea fail to deal with a weak, low corner from Wayne Routledge, with Lampard missing his kick at the near post. The ball speeds across the turf to Aki Riihilahti, whose shot from just six yards out deflects slightly off Carvalho and into the net.

Gabor Kiraly produces a fine reaction save to tip Drogba's overhead kick around the post, while Carvalho also heads narrowly wide. Andy Johnson scuffs his shot wide when presented with a clear opening from Gonzalo Sorondo's mishit cross-shot.

Cole has profited from Robben's injury-induced absence and his vital 54th-minute strike is proof of his renaissance. The midfielder scampers downfield as Chelsea counter-attack and, despite initially tripping over, he hauls himself to his feet and times his run perfectly to race onto Gudjohnsen's pass. Cole briefly weighs up his options before striking his shot into the far corner, leaving Kiraly helplessly rooted to the spot.

Mourinho initially turns to Tiago to shore up his midfield as Drogba comes off, but Robben is finally brought on with 17 minutes left. Significantly, it is Duff – not Cole – who makes way.

The Dutchman is immediately involved in the third goal, although there is little obvious danger until Kiraly's blunder allows Kezman's shot to slip through his grasp.

Robben almost scores himself in the closing stages, and Kezman rounds off the scoring from close range in the last minute after a scramble in the Palace penalty area.

Cole is man of the match and he can hardly contain himself as Chelsea remorselessly close in on the title. 'I'm just so excited,' he says. 'I can't stop looking at the fixture list and thinking if we win this game, this game and this game, then ... But it's important to check yourself and just think about winning the next game. I don't know whether it's the best form of my life, but it's certainly the most I've enjoyed my football as we're winning games week in and week out.'

Palace are left to reflect on Johnson's missed chance just before half-time. Iain Dowie says, 'With a 2–1 lead at half-time it would have been better, but Andrew has done well for us this season, so I'm not going to blame him for that miss. The score-line was probably harsh but you can't defend like we did for the second and fourth goals. We shouldn't have let Joe Cole get in there for their second goal. Manchester United, Arsenal and Chelsea are all good sides but Chelsea are capable of beating you in different ways. Now the other two have everything to do to catch them.'

Team

Cech, Ferreira, Terry, Carvalho, Johnson, Makelele, Cole, Lampard, Duff (Robben), Drogba (Tiago), Gudjohnsen (Kezman).

The board of the FA Premier League charges Chelsea, Jose Mourinho and Ashley Cole with breaches of their rules over the tapping-up affair.

An FA Premier League statement reads, 'The board will be asking for a formal response to these charges within 14 days and have begun the process of appointing a three-person independent commission, in accordance with their disciplinary procedures, to determine this matter.

'The board wish to state that they have so far received cooperation from Chelsea FC, Mr Mourinho and Mr Cole and expect this to continue.'

However, the statement adds, 'As licensed agents, Mr Jonathan Barnett and Mr Pini Zahavi do not fall within the jurisdiction of the FA Premier League for the purposes of this matter. The board will be forwarding information gathered during the inquiry to the Football Association with a view to considering whether further steps should be taken in relation to their actions.'

World Cup qualifiers mean another Premiership break but little rest for Chelsea's squad of international players. Joe Cole's sparkling club form convinces Sven-Goran Eriksson to start with him in England's game against Northern Ireland and the midfielder makes the vital breakthrough just after half-time and is inspirational throughout in a 4–0 win. Lampard completes the scoring with a shot that beats Maik Taylor after glancing off Colin Murdock.

'There are not many better central midfielders than Frank Lampard, I'm quite sure about that,' Eriksson says. 'I don't want to say he's the best in the world, as it's not fair, but I wouldn't change the four midfielders that I had there with anyone.'

Steven Gerrard uses the international break to stress his commitment to Liverpool. He says, 'I held a press conference last summer to say I was staying and the situation hasn't changed since then. There's no deal for me to go anywhere and I've not even been thinking about that. There has been a lot of rubbish written about me this season and it's getting ridiculous. There are people out there whom I've never even met assuming they know what I think.'

But the internationals bring bad news for Chelsea when Arjen Robben limps out of Holland's 2–0 win in Romania after setting up the opening goal for Phillip Cocu. 'It is difficult to say how many weeks I will be out, but it is clear that it is not good,' says Robben. Armenia and Bayern are out of the question in any case.'

Mourinho spends part of the international break in Tel Aviv, invited by former Israeli Prime Minister Shimon Peres. 'Coming here makes you realise that football is not the most important thing. My world of football is very different to theirs. Football has a magical power in social terms. I am happy to be able to use that power to help this cause. Professional football does not always set the best example. I admit and accept that. When I have finished with football there are many things in the world that will make me feel happy. This is one of them. From now on, if there is anything I can do to help, I will. If they want my support they can count on me.'

Mourinho takes presents from Chelsea and hands out medals to the youngsters. He joins in a game against Israel's five-a-side champions – a team from both Palestinian and Israeli backgrounds. 'The power we have to change the world through football cannot be ignored,' he tells them. He adds that he plans to retire from football management at the age of 55 after spending another ten years with Chelsea and three years in charge of his native Portugal.

Chelsea are dealt another major injury blow as Paulo Ferreira suffers a suspected fracture to his right foot during Portugal's World Cup qualifier against Slovakia. He is expected to miss the remainder of the season. Ferreira is immediately flown back to London by private jet for an assessment and scans. The injury leaves the squad severely stretched giving Johnson his big chance, but Mourinho only has five fit defenders and no cover at all for the full-back positions. Terry has a sore back while Carvalho has only just recovered from a broken toe.

Reports in Portugal claim Mourinho may consider walking out on Chelsea at the end of the season. Chelsea immediately dismiss the story – which started on the privately owned Portuguese SIC television station – as nothing more than an April Fool.

But the station has a close relationship with the Chelsea manager, who is due to start presenting his own chat show on the channel in May. The reports claim Mourinho was angered by Chelsea's refusal to appeal over the two-match touchline ban handed to him by UEFA for comments about the referee in Chelsea's Champions League tie with Barcelona.

Mourinho, the reports claim, took his own legal advice – contacting lawyer Jean-Louis Dupont, who handled the Jean-Marc Bosman case – and was told any appeal against the ban would succeed. It is claimed that Mourinho held meetings with Kenyon and complained about the stance taken by club chairman Bruce Buck, a lawyer himself, who counselled against any appeal. Mourinho, so the reports claim, said that Chelsea should stick together more over the issue.

Sources in Portugal confirm there is truth in the reports that he was beside himself with rage over the UEFA ruling and Chelsea's reaction.

SATURDAY, 2 APRIL 2005

SOUTHAMPTON 1, CHELSEA 3

On the surface it is business as normal for Mourinho as Chelsea outclass Southampton on their home turf, where they have not lost since September. But with the dust still settling on his UEFA ban Mourinho dodges the post-match media conference and beats a hasty retreat to the team bus.

Chelsea appear to be saving themselves for the Champions League clash with Bayern Munich as they play well within themselves. A dubious free-kick goes Chelsea's way and Lampard's thumping effort takes an outrageous deflection off Rory Delap on the end of the wall to confound Antti Niemi. Home fans are not enamoured with some of Mark Halsey's decisions, and when he gives Chelsea another free-kick after what looks like a good challenge by Nigel Quashie on Gallas, they chant 'have you bought the referee'.

In the 39th minute Johnson's penetrating run past a series of half-hearted challenges ends with a subtle pull-back for Gudjohnsen to drill past Niemi for 2–0.

Kevin Phillips gives the Saints hope just three minutes after coming on when he fires a left-foot shot from Delap's cross past Cech after a lapse from Gudjohnsen.

But with eight minutes left Chelsea unfurl the kind of smooth passing move that is the hallmark of a great team. It culminates with a slick pass from substitute Drogba to Gudjohnsen, who turns the final pass into the corner.

The strike, which confirms Chelsea's lead at the top will stretch to 13 points after Manchester United's home draw with Blackburn earlier in the afternoon, is his 14th of the season, taking him past Drogba as the club's leading scorer. 'The manager put me on in midfield in the Carling Cup final and said it gave him another option,' says Gudjohnsen. I played there against Barcelona, and in the last three league games it's worked well. It's slightly different for me because I have defensive responsibilities, but I am happy with that.'

As for Mourinho's mood, Gudjohnsen observes, 'It's three wins to the title now and this was a big step forward. It was a difficult one because we were up against a team who have been playing well recently. We were focused, especially when we heard that Manchester United had slipped up. I'm sure the manager has a smile on his face.'

Saints manager Harry Redknapp reserves praise for his nephew Frank Lampard. 'I knew Frank was always going to be a top player because of his attitude and the way he worked at his game,' he says, 'but I didn't know how good he'd become. I've never seen anybody work so hard on the training ground as Frank – except for his dad. But he's different class now and has taken his game on. He's become the complete all-round midfield player. I get real pleasure out of seeing him play because I've seen him grow up since he was a baby. He's fantastic and I'd like to see him become player of the year this year. There are only two candidates: him and John Terry.'

Team

Cech, Johnson, Huth, Terry, Gallas, Makelele, Lampard, Cole (Tiago) Gudjohnsen, Duff, Kezman (Drogba).

Mourinho once again declines to attend the pre-match press conference ahead of the home game with Birmingham, but *The Times* prints an interview given to a Portuguese paper in which he describes Lampard as the most complete midfield player in the game, and launches an outspoken attack on managers-turned-pundits who have dared to describe him as 'arrogant'.

He writes, 'The best job in the world is to be a sacked coach. You get up at 10.30, take breakfast, go for a jog followed by a sauna and a calm surf of sporting sites on the net. Lunch with friends, a siesta, a walk, a meeting with your adviser to see how the markets are doing, a visit to the bank to weigh up the interest rates, or to see if the salary the club is still paying you has cleared the account. Return home, have a great meal with the family. That still leaves time to criticise people you don't know. There are so many coaches in this world who want to work but can't and there are those dashing blades who, through their quality and prestige, could work but don't want to, because life as a parasite fulfils them professionally and economically. Get to work you idle scoundrel! And if you don't want to, let others work in peace!'

Mourinho has no doubts about his best performer of the season: Frank Lampard. 'From August to June, always consistent – the quality of passes, whether passing for possession or depth, short or long, with right or left foot, strength of kick on a static ball or while on the move, fast and constant pace, impressive in defence, in recovery, under high pressure, in one-on-ones or in free space. For me, and I don't say this just because he's mine, he is the most complete player of today.'

SATURDAY, 9 APRIL 2005
CHELSEA 1, BIRMINGHAM CITY 1

Chelsea find it difficult to get to grips with a tenacious City side that deny their midfield time and space to weave its usual brand of free-flowing magic. In the end Chelsea need a late strike from Drogba just to rescue a point, and Arsenal's victory at Middlesbrough cuts the lead to 11 points.

Mourinho leaves Gudjohnsen and Drogba in the dugout with him at the start but it is a strategy that does not work. Kezman returns, while Tiago and Smertin are added to the midfield mix with Makelele rested. Smertin, taking the Frenchman's holding role, ends up being substituted at half-time along with Kezman.

Gudjohnsen and Drogba are the replacements, but it is Birmingham who break the deadlock in the second half when Cole gives away a free-kick with a foul on Emile Heskey. The free-kick is moved forward ten yards after Cole kicks the ball away, and Jermaine Pennant's ball in is for once misjudged by Cech, allowing Matthew Upson to head across goal for Walter Pandiani to slam in a shot from ten yards.

Mourinho puts on Jarosik for Johnson, going with three men at the back, but has to wait for the equaliser. Cole feeds a ball in from the left and Lampard turns to set up Drogba for an easy finish.

Mourinho says he is content with a 'positive point', but admits, 'It was a bad performance in the first half. It looked like a friendly in August. Not enough ambition to win the game.'

It is Mourinho's first words in public for two weeks, which, for a man who can pack a lifetime's worth of controversy into a single press conference, is a stupendously long time.

Mourinho adds that the rumours suggesting he is unhappy at the club are wide of the mark. 'We are fantastic,' he says, 'we could not be better. We have a trophy, we are top of the league by 11 points and we are in the quarter-finals of the Champions League and won the first game. We could not be better. I am happy. The only reason I am not happy is that we did not get the three points against Birmingham.

'In the second half it was a game and we did everything OK except concede a silly goal. But we showed a good reaction with a goal. We put a lot of pressure on them and played to win. We were strong but they fought a lot and defended well. It was a silly goal for us to give away and after that they believed they could get a result. They deserved to go home with a point. It would have been very hard on them if we had scored again near the end.

'Maybe this season has been better than everybody could dream, including me. I always thought we could win the league but to have an 11-point lead with a month to go is better than I thought we could do. It was always likely that there would be a bit of a reaction to the games we're playing now. It's three games in six days and Saturday was the first of two in four days. That's very difficult. We are 11 points in front of Arsenal and it is a comfortable distance. We just have to control it and get the points we need to be champions. For me, being champions today, next week or two weeks' time, away or at home, doesn't matter. I just want to be champions.'

Steve Bruce spends five minutes eulogising on the merits of Mourinho, conceding he can hardly find a fault. 'I think I speak for all managers when I say we've got huge respect for Mourinho,' he says. 'He has been a breath of fresh air for us all. We were getting a bit sick of Wenger v Fergie all the time. There's another one on the block now. Apart from Blackburn once, the Premier League has been contested by Manchester United and Arsenal, and we've got one more in there now. It's taken a hell of a lot of money for Chelsea to get there, but, let's be fair, Mourinho's made some big decisions very quickly. You look how he sent out Hernan Crespo and Juan Sebastian Veron on loan. We are all trying desperately to beat him and we can't – it's as simple as that.'

> **Team**
>
> Cech, Johnson (Jarosik), Huth, Terry, Gallas, Smertin (Gudjohnsen), Lampard, Cole, Duff, Tiago, Kezman (Drogba).

A rare moment of dissatisfaction in the Chelsea camp occurs when William Gallas reveals he is fed up playing out of position at left-back. 'I will continue in this position until the end of the season, but after that things will have to be very clear,' he says. 'I do not like playing left-back. I am not comfortable in that position and it is going to have to change at one time or another. I am sacrificing myself for the team but I am suffering. I know that with the injury to Wayne Bridge and also that of Paulo Ferreira the manager has no other solution than to play me on the left for now. I accept that for the moment but, I repeat, it is becoming increasingly difficult for me.'

Ken Bates drops his £2m legal feud with the club. A Chelsea statement says, 'This settlement has been agreed by Chelsea to avoid wasting more management time and to avoid incurring ever increasing legal fees as a result of the forthcoming trial. In reaching this settlement, Chelsea have not admitted any liability. We are pleased of course that this litigation is now concluded and we wish Mr Bates well in the future.' Chelsea are happy to avoid Abramovich and the club facing scrutiny in the High Court.

Chelsea dominate the nominations for the PFA Players' Player of the Year award with Terry, Lampard and Cech all on the shortlist, along with Thierry Henry – winner in 2004 – Crystal Palace's Andy Johnson and Steven Gerrard.

Chelsea are also represented in the shortlist for the Young Player of the Year award, with Arjen Robben nominated with Wayne Rooney, Cristiano Ronaldo, Jermain Defoe, Stewart Downing and Shaun Wright-Phillips. PFA chief executive Gordon Taylor says he thinks it is 'neck and neck' between Lampard and Terry for the main prize.

Lampard comments, 'I've had a remarkable season with Chelsea. It's difficult to take in the transformation here over the last two seasons. I don't know that I have surpassed the likes of Patrick Vieira and Roy Keane because they are the best and they have been the best in the business for a long time. Vieira is a fantastic player. Every time you play against him you can see what a complete player he is, and Roy Keane has been fantastic over the years. I'm a big, big fan. For me he has been the best in the world – the most complete midfielder I have seen for many, many years. To a certain extent you have to say Steven Gerrard falls into that bracket as well. I know what Jose said but he's my manager and people will rightfully say he's slightly biased.'

After completing their Champions League quarter-final victory over Bayern Munich, Terry has an ultrasound scan on the right thigh he damaged in a clash with Bastian Schweinsteiger. The injury is not as bad as first feared. The scan reveals severe bruising and Terry returns to Cobham for treatment, while other players are given two days off, with Mourinho returning to Portugal for a family holiday.

Terry says the powers of concentration that helped him attain the PFA nomination are down to coaching sessions from Gianfranco Zola. 'Franco used to spend a couple of hours a week working with me when I was in the youth team,' he says. 'He'd say, "Watch the ball. It doesn't matter where my feet go as long as the ball doesn't move." He'd have ten one-on-ones with me and score ten. Then I got better – and he would score nine! But whether it's a winger or a striker, it's crucial to let him know early that you're there. There are always little bits of off-the-ball stuff going on. When I first got into the Chelsea team, opponents would try to pinch your nipples when the ball was up the other end of the pitch. They would also grab your nuts at a set-play or stand on your toes when it was freezing.'

Next up for Chelsea is the showdown with Arsenal, and the good news is that Thierry Henry is out injured. But Terry feels he knows how to handle the Frenchman. 'You've got to get his back to goal and keep moving him away from goal,' Terry says. 'As soon as he gets the ball played into him, get tight to him – but not so tight that he can roll off down the side of you. Keep an arm's distance away, so that if he turns you can get an arm across and give him a nudge. But if you're caught on the counter-attack and it's three against three, you drop off until other players get back.'

Terry adds that he has more trouble with Dennis Bergkamp, and is thankful for Claude Makelele's defensive qualities. 'Bergkamp is so clever at pulling out,' says Terry. 'And if you go with him, the other centre-half is left one against one with Henry. At Chelsea we are lucky to have a defensive midfielder like Claude, who can pick up deep strikers. If Bergkamp drops off to the right, I yell "left shoulder", and if he drops to the left, it's "right shoulder". I think that's all the English Maka knows!'

Arsenal were the last team to beat the Blues at Stamford Bridge – 35 games and 14 months ago. Gudjohnsen says, 'I scored and got sent off in that match, which we lost 2–1. We have moved on since then and are closing in on the title. We are hard to beat and we will keep our form going. We want Stamford Bridge to be a fortress and for us to stay unbeaten for the season.'

Ashley Cole warns that Arsenal have no intention of allowing Chelsea to use them as a stepping-stone to the title. 'If they are going to win it then, fair enough, and good luck to them. But they haven't won it yet, and we don't want them winning it by beating us on the way. We still want to win the league ourselves. Chelsea have to win their games and we are not going to give up. We are on a good run at the moment. We had a tough game at Highbury against them, which we thought we should have won, and we are going to Stamford Bridge without any fear. We are going to go there to try to win the game.'

After the Cole tapping-up affair, Sir Alex Ferguson's reaction to the news that Rio Ferdinand met his agent Pini Zahavi and Peter

Kenyon in a London restaurant is expected. Kenyon insists the meeting was a coincidence but Fergie snaps, 'It may be somebody else's view that the meeting was unfortunate, but it is not my view. My concern is our supporters and I just want to let them know that we are not happy with this. When the chief executive of a Premier League club – with the history they have got in recent times – still sits in a restaurant ... whether it is contempt or just thumbing his nose at us, it is ill advised at the very least.' Ferdinand stresses that he wants to remain at Old Trafford.

Arséne Wenger admits Chelsea have had an exceptional season. 'After 32 games there is no coincidence. You have to respect what Chelsea have done on the pitch. They are 11 points better so that means there was a gap this year. But it is not over yet, we have a chance to close the gap and then there are five games to go.'

There is no comment from Mourinho, but in his place Steve Clarke says, 'We are the top team in London. We beat Bayern Munich, who Arsenal couldn't beat. The league table doesn't lie and the club which has been most consistent is the one which wins the title. Arsenal and Man United have dominated over the past ten years and it is good for football that we are challenging that. The fact people talk about us most weeks tells you we've made it. It's because we are top. When you consider we finished 11 points behind Arsenal last season it's been a good turnaround, and it shows how focused we've been all season.'

WEDNESDAY, 20 APRIL 2005
CHELSEA 0, ARSENAL 0

Wenger shakes hands with Mourinho at the end and finally says, 'Of course Chelsea will win the title now. I always felt that if they didn't lose this game they would be champions – unless someone puts a bomb here! But they are worthy champions because they have been remarkably consistent and that is most difficult in top sport. I can only say congratulations for what they have achieved.'

Clarke claims, 'I thought it was a good game between two top sides. The fans have to be patient and look forward to us being champions. Jose is happy – it was a good result for us and keeps the gap at 11 points. It is going to be difficult for anybody to catch us now. The manager is happy and so are the players. We will set out to get another three points against Fulham on Saturday and then concentrate on the Champions League. We didn't expect Arsenal to roll over but I thought we created the better chances on the night. They started well but we settled down and matched their possession.'

Cheeky Blues fans make Ashley Cole feel at home by holding a placard saying 'Welcome Home'. But Cole doesn't have much to say to Mourinho, who even more cheekily gives him a high-five as the Arsenal defender leaves the field – just as he shook Steven Gerrard's hand after the Carling Cup final!

Without Freddie Ljungberg and Sol Campbell as well as Henry, Arsenal start well. With just two minutes gone Jose Antonio Reyes wins a header against Glen Johnson and Robert Pires thunders a volley against the underside of the bar. Pires wastes an even better chance when he drags his shot wide of the far post after John Terry's attempted clearance is blocked and falls kindly for the winger.

Then Chelsea break and Duff slips the ball to Drogba, but Jens Lehmann saves with his legs. Soon afterwards Drogba slightly overhits a cross that would have set up Joe Cole for a certain goal.

Lampard tackles Pires inside his own box, then at the other end fires just inches wide after Drogba's clever dummy, while the striker produces a clever turn from Duff's cutback but shoots inches wide.

Both sides make changes, with the arrival of Robin van Persie and Jeremie Aliadiere proving Arsenal's need for victory, while the combative Tiago demonstrates Chelsea's resolve as he comes on for Cole. Kezman also comes on for Duff. But neither side can make the breakthrough as the game ends goalless.

Wenger says, 'We knew we'd have to come here and take the initiative because Chelsea like to play deep and hit you on the break. It was important for us to score an early goal and my big regret is that we couldn't take our chances because that would have changed Chelsea's plan and made them come out and play. In the second half Chelsea dropped even deeper, became more cautious and more worried. But we lacked the penetration to finish them off. I will leave it to others to compare the two teams but I can take great satisfaction from the quality of this display and the quality of my team.'

With the title now in touching distance, Lampard already has his sights on sustained success. 'The title is almost there but the hard thing now is to back it up,' he says. 'It's well documented that the second title is harder to win than the first and next season we'll start all over again. Arsenal haven't backed it up but have been a dominant force for the past few years. This year we're the best team. We have to make sure that we're not just the best team this year but the best for future seasons. We're all hungry and are not going to settle for one title. We want to win everything we're involved in and we will play with the same attitude next year.'

Team

Cech, Johnson, Carvalho, Terry, Gallas, Makelele, Gudjohnsen (Jarosik), Lampard, Cole (Tiago), Duff (Kezman), Drogba.

With the Champions League semi-final first leg against Liverpool looming, Chelsea want to rest players without jeopardising their Premiership assault. Clarke insists, 'We're going to put out a team against Fulham that can win the game as we need three points. That would put us very close to the title and then we'd see what happens.' Robben is back in the squad, giving Mourinho the option to rest Cole or Duff.

Mourinho admits he has made errors during the season but says what matters is the final outcome. 'My life in football is about being popular and loved by my team's supporters – and being hated by the opponents' supporters. That's the way I want to carry on because it means we're winning things. Of course I've made mistakes. I can analyse a situation and have the wrong point of view. Of course there will be fights. I can't say I don't like a fight because that's my nature. But sometimes maybe I must be in control of a situation and not react. I always try to do the best for my team. What matters is my club and my players. When we have the cups in our hands we will forget everything.

'I think it is great for English football that a club who has not been champions for 50 years becomes the champion. It is good to run away with this. I can tell you that in Portugal we have been looking for something like this for a long time.'

Mourinho eulogises about his 'Magnificent Seven' – the band of players whose consistent excellence has driven Chelsea to within touching distance of the title. 'Over the season we have had seven players without injuries or suspensions, without bad moments in performances. They have been the big spine of the team: Petr Cech, William Gallas, John Terry, Claude Makelele, Frank Lampard, Eidur Gudjohnsen and Damien Duff play almost every game. The best compliment I can pay Claude is that he has nothing to learn from me. Claude knows everything. He is 32 but because he is out of the French national team, he still has two or three perfect years to give to Chelsea.'

In an especially frank frame of mind, Mourinho then shows his compassionate side by saying, 'Cudicini's situation hurts me. He is fantastic every day in training. He is responsible for Cech performing so well.'

SATURDAY, 23 APRIL 2005
CHELSEA 3, FULHAM 1

It is 50 years to the day since Chelsea last lifted the title and the captain of that side Roy Bentley, now 81, returns to mark the occasion. Robben destroyed Fulham in the game at Craven Cottage and Chelsea are labouring until he replaces Cole. Robben's match-winning display moves Chelsea within two points of just the second title in their history.

Cole gives Chelsea the ideal platform when he swivels onto Drogba's pass and sends a scorching shot past Edwin van der Sar with 17 minutes gone. Drogba squanders two other half-chances, while Cole misses his kick inside the penalty area, and Fulham gradually haul themselves back into the game. Just before half-time Carvalho is guilty of an uncharacteristic error in allowing Collins John to latch onto Luis Boa Morte's pass before finishing. The equaliser comes just seconds after van der Sar races out to deny Duff after the Irishman is sent hurtling through by Drogba.

Robben comes on at the interval and changes the game instantly. Jarosik also comes on for Huth, leaving Duff to drop in behind him at left-back. It is something not even Ranieri managed to come up with, but it gives Chelsea a tremendous threat down the left.

First Robben finds Gudjohnsen but the 'goal' is ruled out for offside, then the Dutchman fires in another shot that flashes wide. Finally he speeds past Moritz Volz and expertly picks out Lampard to score.

Cech tips a fierce drive by Tomasz Radzinski over the bar and foils John's deflected free-kick. But Gudjohnsen makes certain of victory with just four minutes left as he is put clear by substitute Tiago and notches his 100th goal in English football.

Mourinho moans about the Blues' 'ridiculous' midday kick-off. 'A team that plays at 8pm on Wednesday night and then has to play at 12.45pm on Saturday... it is too much. Over the 90 minutes Fulham didn't deserve to lose. They had the fresher legs. I think the result we got is incredible and magnificent and down to the players' character, because at half-time they were dead. I said to them that the only chance was for them to play to their full potential. You have to be super-human to play a huge game on Wednesday night and then again on Saturday morning, and our players are not super-human. It was down to sheer character that we got a fantastic and magnificent victory.'

Mourinho assesses the season so far and says, 'It's not about the treble. The Carling Cup is not such a big thing, but at that time for Chelsea to win a trophy was very important, be it a small or a big competition. But to win the championship after 50 years is very big. Fifty years ago and the fans have not forgotten – this year they will not forget either. Whether it is the players, the staff, the managers ... whoever. Roy Bentley is rightly remembered as the captain of that team and so too will John Terry be of this one. Nobody forgets their names.'

> **Team**
>
> Cech, Johnson, Carvalho, Terry, Huth (Jarosik), Cole (Robben), Makelele, Lampard, Duff, Drogba (Tiago), Gudjohnsen.

Chelsea chairman Bruce Buck says Roman Abramovich is committed to the club for the long haul. 'If you had seen the tears in his eyes in the dressing room in Monaco, you would know this is a committed supporter. You would know how much he cares about the club. His Russian personality is generally to be reserved, but he is hugely excited. I don't see it stopping. I don't see why Roman would sell. If it was the case that he was going to win the European Cup and disappear, why spend £25m on a training ground that wouldn't be built for two years?

Buck also says the spending will slow down. 'We appreciate that the £250m-plus is a lot of money, but we are just playing catch-up. If you look at what United, Arsenal, Newcastle and Liverpool have spent in the last ten years, and then us more recently, by and large we are all similar. If the tag that we have bought success exists, so be it, but I don't believe it is true. I think that money does help and it gets you a long way there, but it doesn't get you over the goalline by a long shot. The answer is to build our academy and bring up more of these younger players, and that is our intention. To bring more John Terrys up the ranks.

Mr Abramovich has invested a lot of money, but I emphasise the word investment. And, on top of that, we have changed our business model, brought in the right sponsors, changed the kit company, the management team, the structure. We have done a lot more than Mr Abramovich throwing money at players and I am not sure we get the credit for that. Although it is difficult to convince people, we are very careful about what we spend, whether it is

£24m on Mr Drogba or £1,000 on pencils. We are careful about every 10p. You have seen the transfer spend go down just in one year and you will see it keep going down. You will see several players come in this summer but also several go out.'

The announcement of a new club sponsor to replace Emirates is part of the realignment. Chelsea are negotiating with Samsung, Siemens and Nokia and the deal will be a Premiership record, eclipsing the £9m a year that Manchester United are paid by Vodafone. The intention is for Chelsea to stand alone from their wealthy benefactor by 2010 and, by 2015 to be eclipsing all their rivals on and off the pitch.

John Terry's remarkable season is recognised as he receives the PFA Player of the Year award from Alan Shearer. Terry says, 'It is unbelievable and the ultimate accolade to be voted for by your fellow professionals whom you play against week in and week out. We have got the Champions League semi-final coming up against Liverpool and are just one win away from the Premiership, so hopefully I am going to be lifting a few more trophies. For Petr, Lamps and myself to be voted in, it was important that one of us won it. It has been a real special season with Chelsea and this just adds to it. I want to thank all of my team-mates. It is my first year as captain and they have helped me a lot, on and off the pitch.'

Terry clutches his precious silverware and refuses to put it down as he discusses Mourinho. 'Jose has been fantastic; I can't speak highly enough of him for what he's done for me personally. He has given me a lot of confidence, gave me the armband at the start of the season and made me believe I'm up there with the best players in the Premiership.'

Chelsea sign a £50m five-year sponsorship deal with South Korean electronics firm Samsung. The deal makes Samsung the club's official sponsor, and the players' shirts will carry the logo 'Samsung Mobile' from next season. It is Samsung's second biggest partnership deal after its sponsorship of the Olympic Games.

Arsenal have a complex eight-year deal with Emirates, worth a potential £100m including the naming of Arsenal's ground and a shirt deal. Manchester United's four-year deal with Vodafone, signed in 2004, is worth a total of £36m.

Peter Kenyon says, 'Over the next five years the plan is quite simple: to turn the world blue. We needed a company that was recognised globally, especially in the UK, China, Russia and America – countries Chelsea are targeting in the next few years. The marketing opportunities are far more critical than the financial sponsorship. I can see a day when we catch Manchester United – on and off the pitch.'

Paul Smith is Chelsea's business affairs director and he believes the gap is already closing on United. 'United have increased revenues as well, but what has affected them is their early exit in the Champions League. That has a big impact on the numbers and within three years we feel we can get close to them.'

An obvious gap between United and the rest is their Old Trafford stadium capacity just shy of 70,000. Arsenal's new ground will be ready for 60,000 in a year's time, but Chelsea are stuck with their 42,449 capacity unless they do something drastic. Smith adds, 'We can't be closer to their [United's] capacity because of the restrictions and regulations. We won't be considering moving right now. Our natural level is probably 60,000, but it can't be done here. We would have to buy all the houses around the ground and knock down the hotels and that won't happen. We want to be big in London and grow the appeal of the club across the city.'

Chelsea are planning to increase the capacity of Stamford Bridge by squeezing 500 extra seats into the Matthew Harding Stand. They have discussed trying to acquire new sites in the area – one idea was the area around Battersea Power Station – but that has also been ruled out. A less likely scheme is that Chelsea will move, on a temporary basis, to the new Wembley Stadium. This has been dismissed as 'pure speculation' and even if Chelsea were interested it would be very difficult for them to gain permission to do so as Tottenham Hotspur have already found out.

Arsenal make Chelsea wait to clinch the title by beating local rivals Spurs at Highbury. Before the match kicks off, among the pubs that line the Fulham Road and Fulham Broadway near the ground, many huddle in the entrances, glued to televisions that hang from the walls, holding banners proclaiming their support for Chelsea. They applaud when Mourinho wanders out of the Chelsea Village Hotel dressed casually in a black and grey tracksuit to whisk his team away in a bus for dinner at a nearby Italian restaurant. It is a nonchalance that suggests they do not care what Arsenal do against Tottenham. In their own minds they have already won the title.

The players' coach arrives back five minutes after the game ends to loud cheers. Joe Cole says, 'We watched the Arsenal game and it would have been nice to have the title in the bag before facing Liverpool. It's still in our hands. We know exactly what we have to do at Bolton.'

The salesman at Fulham Broadway has an impressive supply of T-shirts and flags proclaiming 'Chelsea Champions 2004/05' packed up for the night at the final whistle. But he will soon be doing a roaring trade.

Mourinho wants to keep his men fresh for the semi-final decider at Liverpool, but also wants to finish off the job of winning the title at Bolton. Gallas, nursing a back strain, confirms, 'We want to win the league at Bolton, but it all comes down to how many players are rested – and it could be quite a few.'

Lampard is worried about Bolton's physical approach. He says, 'They scrapped out a 2–2 draw at Stamford Bridge and are too scared of us to try and play football. Their main threat comes from high balls and getting on the end of knockdowns. Teams are realising that to beat us at football is hard because we have good players.'

Bolton are still chasing a Champions League qualifying spot, four points behind Everton in fourth. Sam Allardyce says, 'It's going to be a massive task to get anything out of the game the way Chelsea are going. It's not beyond us but it will be a hell of a result if we can beat them.'

Allardyce taunts Mourinho by claiming Wenger should be known as the 'Special One'. He says, 'Wenger has been the best foreign manager in this country. He is one of the most successful managers there have been here and he showed the way forward in this country with the players he has brought in. Some of the foreign coaches who have come over here have been a disaster. Jacques Santini at Tottenham this season, for instance, lasted no more than two minutes.' But Allardyce adds, 'Mourinho has done brilliantly because he has grasped it in one year. He has swanned into London and Chelsea and said from the start he was going to be successful. He hung his neck on the line and it looks like he is going to achieve. Chelsea should not only win the championship but there is a big possibility they could win the European Cup. They have one of the best-structured defences in the world. In a straightforward contest, we are out of their league. We can only hope we can take advantage of what they have had to go through this week, and what they will have to go through next week at Liverpool. I thought they looked tired and nervy in the first leg against Liverpool. Hopefully, we can catch them out.'

The morning papers are full of headlines of cracks in the camp, based on Robben's reluctance to start the tie with Liverpool and Kezman's frustrations as a squad player. Terry has delayed an operation on a toe injury so could be rested, while Gallas is plagued by a back problem and Duff is out with a hamstring strain. Suggestions that Robben refused to play when Duff failed a fitness test are wide of the mark, and the winger came off the bench for the last 30 minutes.

Chelsea issue a statement insisting the relationship between Robben and Mourinho is 'excellent' and maintain he is 'working hard to get back to full fitness'. Robben's attitude has not gone down well with team-mates.

Despite Kezman playing the last 12 minutes against Liverpool, he is unlikely to be around for much longer. After starting his Chelsea career with four goals in his first three games, admittedly in pre-season friendlies, his confidence was destroyed to such an extent that he was scared to shoot when one-on-one with the goalkeeper. Abramovich took him out to dinner in an attempt to lift him from his depression. Kezman says, 'Abramovich is very close to the group and

I have a good relationship with him. He's a funny guy who, if you didn't know his background, you wouldn't look twice at him. He wears just cheap jeans and a cheap jacket and a normal, casual watch. He understands my problems. Then he calls me and we go out to eat. In everything you can see he is obsessed with football.'

Kezman feels he never received Mourinho's full support and has not been given an explanation for starting just six Premiership games since his £5m move from PSV Eindhoven. He is particularly angry that he was dropped after contributing significantly to the thrilling win over Barcelona. Kezman says, 'It's a pity that Jose Mourinho never stood behind me, never gave me full confidence. I can't score a lot of goals if I am only playing for five or ten minutes. I am number two. Everything I do is not good enough. That's the feeling I have and that's very hard to accept. I respect him because he has fantastic results. From his side he understands my situation but he cannot change anything. He would be crazy to change it. This is the way he works and this is the way he had success the last couple of years. He feels he is the best and he is the most prettiest. You have the world of Mourinho and you have the other world.'

Chelsea fans will toast former vice-chairman Matthew Harding if the team clinches the Premiership title at Bolton. The millionaire businessman was killed in a helicopter crash returning from a League Cup tie at Bolton in October 1996. Rick Glanville, commissioned to write the official history of the club, says, 'More and more fans have said that it would be fitting to win the title at Bolton and then raise a glass to Matthew Harding. I wouldn't be surprised if there wasn't a banner or two among the Chelsea fans tomorrow.'

Harding had big ambitions for the club he had supported all his life and had invested in Chelsea. His widow Ruth says, 'It's a fantastic idea and lovely that the fans still remember him. I don't know what the fans are planning for Bolton but it is a lovely gesture and one which is greatly appreciated by all the family.'

Mourinho illustrates his long-term planning by lining up a deal for Javier Mascherano, the outstanding young Argentina midfield player, who will join them after next year's World Cup finals. An agreement has been reached with Corinthians over the signing of Mascherano, even though the 21-year-old is not scheduled to join the Brazilian club from River Plate until this summer. Suggestions Chelsea have dropped their interest in Gerrard are way off the mark. Mourinho tells his board that Mascherano is potentially a better player than Gerrard and he is also looking at Barcelona's Xavi. But the England player remains high on Chelsea's shopping list along with Joao Alves, a relatively obscure midfield player from Sporting Braga of Portugal. Chelsea are showing exceptionally keen interest in AC Milan left-back Kakha Kaladze. The Georgian has won 35 caps and has been starring in AC Milan's determination to regain their European crown.

Mourinho's determination to dominate for years to come will be illustrated by the next wave of signings. Samuel Eto'o has proved himself at Barca and is again on the wanted list.

When Chelsea last won the title the rest of the country was debating how Britain would cope with the arrival of more immigrants from the Caribbean; the Government promised women working in the Civil Service would have equal pay with men by 1961; Sir Winston Churchill resigned as Prime Minister and Anthony Eden, his successor, quickly called a general election that increased the Tory majority; Princess Margaret announced that she was calling off her wedding to Group Captain Peter Townsend; James Dean was killed when his Porsche plunged off the road in California; in Britain, motorists were being a little more careful, especially when the price of a gallon of petrol rose to 4s 6d.

SATURDAY, 30 APRIL 2005
BOLTON WANDERERS 0, CHELSEA 2

Mourinho takes his place in history as the first foreign coach to win the championship in his first season in English football, and it vindicates the confidence he has had since the day he arrived. Lampard has been immense with goals and performances, and his match-winning brace seals his own contribution to the title as the team's top scorer from midfield. Quite an achievement.

Mourinho's managerial genius combined with hunger, desire and ferocity of spirit are the cornerstones of the title triumph. He immediately expresses his affinity to the club. 'Am I the "Special One"?' he asks. 'No, the whole group at Chelsea is special and no one can say we didn't deserve this title. The players have been fantastic. I am proud of every single one of them and they are worthy champions. But Roman Abramovich, the big boss, also deserves it, and so does Peter Kenyon and his group. This group is really special – that's why I want to stay with them for the maximum time, maybe for longer than the contract I have.'

As his players celebrate in front of the travelling supporters, Mourinho sits in the dugout with his mobile phone. 'I was speaking to my wife and children,' he says. 'They went to Portugal for the weekend but they saw it live and they are happy of course – like me. Football is crazy sometimes. We knew a few months ago we had a lead of some distance but anything is possible – so only now is the moment we really feel we are champions. It's not easy the way we are champions and it was the same story this weekend. This game was the perfect game to be champions because Bolton have a difficult style of play and we had to adapt – and we did. We fought like lions. This squad is incredible. When we play, we play together. When we fight, we fight together. When we suffer, we suffer together. And no one who has any sense of fairness can deny that we deserve the title.'

Lampard says he will remember the moment for ever. 'This is a great feeling and I am proud to have got the goals that have clinched it for us. This is a moment I will enjoy for the rest of my life. I felt I owed the fans one after that miss in midweek against Liverpool. This was the best way to repay them. We wanted to win the league first, now we want to beat Liverpool in the Champions League on Tuesday. It is a great relief after 50 years for the fans and for everyone. Our schedule this season has been so hectic and we have had so many things to concentrate on that we knew it wouldn't be easy. But we always believed we could do it.'

Lampard reveals that Jose Mourinho, within minutes of the title being sealed, has ordered a booze ban on the players. 'We had a little sip of champagne and then the manager got the hump because he wanted us to calm down. Maybe he'll let us have half a glass back at the hotel, but then we will have to be tucked up in bed.'

Lampard also explains why he ignored Carvalho after being sent clear for his second goal. 'When JT won the toss he asked me if we wanted to stay the way we were facing but I just had a feeling that if we are going to score goals and win the title then we might as well do it towards the fans. The first one was great but when I went through for the second I was just thinking to myself, "Don't f*** it up." I think Ricardo Carvalho was with me but there was no way I was going to give the ball to him – he would've put it in the stands! I had tunnel vision at that stage. The first goal was massive for us because we were below par. But it was the second one that really killed Bolton off.'

Lampard also has some words for Arsenal and Manchester United. 'We've proved that the best team wins the league. There have been some harsh words spoken about us not being entertaining and that the best two teams in the Premier League are in the final of the FA Cup. But the best team wins the league and we have done that. You look at Arsenal, who lost at Bolton, and Manchester United, who drew, but we went up there and won. It's time for the others to take a look and know that we are definitely the best.'

Terry reveals how Mourinho – who dashed away from the celebrations to allow his players to take the glory – lost his temper after a goalless first half. 'Bolton probably out-battled us in the first half which didn't please the manager. At half-time he gave us a bit of a bollocking, but we came out and responded well in the second half. The gaffer was fuming. He had a go at everybody, telling us we were 45 minutes from the Premiership and that we had to liven up, that we'd have been better putting him out there than us. And he was right, too. Everybody was under-performing. You're not going to play well every game, so it's about giving 110 per cent. But we didn't do that in the first half. They were first to all the headers and tackles.'

Cole, on as a late substitute, can scarcely believe Chelsea are finally champions. 'I'm a bit dazed to be honest and it will take a few days to sink in,' he says. 'It is the pinnacle of any English player's career to win the league title and we have realised this season just how hard it is. We've got two trophies now and we all want to make it a treble. It's a fantastic feeling. We thought we'd won it after the Arsenal game, but now it's actually happened it's a dream come true for me and all of us. It's hard to believe it's actually happened. There was a stage in the season when I did wonder if I was going to be part of things here. But now, after all that's happened for me in the last few months, it's all worthwhile. I can't see why we can't go on from this to win the Champions League. Why not? We'll be going to Liverpool and we'll be flying now. We just want to get out there.'

Chelsea are set on their way by an inspirational pre-game team-talk from former Bolton star Gudjohnsen, who explains, 'I was very calm for most of it but I did get a bit carried away towards the end of the talk. Nothing crazy – just a bit of shouting. I just said to the lads, "We can make each other champions today." We were all heroes out there, particularly Frank who did brilliantly to get us two goals. He's been such an integral part of the team this year and deserved to get the glory, but it has been a joy to play with all of these lads. Bolton made it really tough for us and we didn't play very well in the first half, so the manager made us fully aware that we were playing for the championship. All of this hasn't really sunk in yet, but together with John Terry and Frank this probably means most to us because we have taken a leadership role in the dressing room as players who have been at the club a few years. All three of us have grown up together and, after the birth of my children, this is my proudest moment.'

Mourinho has to start the match without his two wingers, Duff and Robben, while Joe Cole is left on the bench. There is also a scare in the first minute when Lampard shoots from distance and pulls up, temporarily lame. To the considerable relief of Mourinho and his men, the England midfielder is able to run off the problem. Alongside

Lampard in midfield are the peripheral figures Geremi and Jarosik, who are brought in to add steel to Chelsea's defence of set-pieces. Mourinho learned the hard way from Bolton's fightback to draw 2–2 at Stamford Bridge, and the aerial bombardment immediately resumes. When a long throw-in is not properly cleared, Stelios's snap-shot is held by Cech, while Makelele is booked for his attempts to stop Jay-Jay Okocha's next delivery.

Cech also saves a header from Gary Speed and a shot by Fernando Hierro. The visitors manage only a long-range effort by Lampard in the opening 20 minutes, with the England midfielder shaking off a worrying knock sustained in the process. Then Kevin Davies is left unmarked to meet a lofted free-kick, only to direct his header straight at Cech.

Terry plays on despite having a black eye that restricts his vision in one eye following a clash with Davies just before half-time. Tempers start to fray, especially when Geremi goes down easily under a tackle from El-Hadji Diouf, which earns the Senegal international a booking. Bolton are livid when, from the ensuing free-kick, Chelsea seize the lead against the run of play. Lampard shows great composure in cutting back inside Vincent Candela as he seizes on Drogba's headed knockdown, before picking his spot past Jussi Jaaskelainen. The Bolton keeper is booked for his protests.

Mourinho is concerned with protecting his side's advantage, with the towering figure of Huth soon replacing Drogba. That leaves Gudjohnsen up front on his own, while Chelsea form a five-man defence. But Cech still needs to claw the ball around the post, hurting himself in the process, when Geremi deflects a cross with his head that seems destined for the corner.

Bolton rally once again, but they are caught on the break with 14 minutes left as Lampard races clear. The midfielder has Carvalho bursting his lungs to provide an option to his right, but instead he uses the defender as a decoy before dipping his shoulder and skipping past Jaaskelainen. His finish is assured and sparks delirium on the touchline, with Mourinho dancing for joy and Drogba even seizing an inflatable Premiership trophy from the crowd in expected triumph. He has to wait just 15 minutes longer to repeat the feat, this time for real, as Chelsea's path to the title is complete.

Sam Allardyce is said to have accused referee Steve Dunn of effectively handing the title to Chelsea by failing to spot a perceived foul on Hierro in the build-up to Lampard's first goal. 'The referee has won them this game,' says Allardyce. 'He failed on a major decision, with Jiri Jarosik's foul on Hierro. There was nothing more blatant than that you can see in the game. Hierro was going to win the header but Jarosik just barged into him. The referee waved play on and Frank Lampard got in to score. It's just not on. That's cost us the game, as well as ourselves not punishing them in the first half, when we were hugely on top.'

But Allardyce pays tribute to Lampard, saying, 'I don't want this to overshadow what Chelsea have done over the whole season as they truly deserve to win it. They've been absolutely magnificent and the best player in the world at the moment has to be Frank Lampard. There's no question about that. To play as many games as he does, with the distances he runs and the finishing power he has, it's wonderful. He has been absolutely magnificent all season. You can't take anything out of Frank Lampard. He could play 100 games in a season, that lad. The energy he put in, certainly on the second goal, was amazing. He started in their box when we had the corner and he finished in our box scoring the goal, that's how good he was as well as his quality of finishing. He has to be one of the best players in the world.'

Roman Abramovich parades arm-in-arm with Terry and Lampard on the pitch as the Chelsea pair join the fans singing the owner's name. Abramovich also takes a call from Gianfranco Zola in Italy confirming his job as academy chief next year. Outside the Reebok Stadium, Drogba and Cole hoist themselves out of the skylight in the team coach to dance on the roof in front of fans beside themselves with joy.

Terry is still inside the ground performing his media rounds, gripping a little transparent plastic bag tightly to his side: inside is his shirt from the game, a memento he will treasure for ever. Some of his team-mates threw theirs into the crowd after the final whistle. Others changed into T-shirts with 'Champions' written on them. Terry kept his on his back until he disappeared into the dressing room. 'I've kept my shirt from every game this season and thankfully we've gone and won it. I've kept every shirt and every captain's armband. I'll put them in one big frame. I dreamed of being able to do that when I first started collecting them in the opening four or five games.' It is going to have to be an awfully large frame!

Like Lampard, Terry played in every game of Chelsea's march to the title. He was felled towards the end of the first half by a finger in the eye, and had double vision at half-time because the eye had swelled so badly. Still Terry came out for the second half. 'It feels very emotional,' he says. 'I just want to break down and cry really. I probably will when I get back to my hotel room on my own, when I sit back and watch it on TV.'

Terry finally leaves and takes his place on the team bus. The biggest cheer of all comes when he and Lampard thrust their heads out of the skylight and take the plaudits of the crowd. An hour earlier, the same two players had remained out on the pitch, unable to tear themselves away from the fans.

Team

Cech, Geremi, Terry, Carvalho, Gallas, Tiago, Makelele (Smertin), Lampard, Jarosik, Gudjohnsen (Cole), Drogba (Huth).

Mourinho only gives one interview, to Sky TV, sending a message to journalists that he has no problem with the press but wants the players to bask in the glory.

However, Mourinho tells *Visao*, a magazine in Portugal, 'I made everyone understand you can break with ties to the past where behaviour, preparation of a team and even image go. I helped break several taboos, things that were traditionalist that the English are still hanging on to. They tried to wear down my image, make it more difficult for me to impose myself.' He points the finger at Manchester United and Arsenal, who, he claims, fear and begrudge Chelsea's success. 'It has everything to do with Chelsea: what the club means. First, because the owner is a foreigner and he symbolises external economic power. In addition, the club had not won anything for a long time and now they want to end the successful routine of Arsenal and Manchester United. In other words, everything came together: the Russian millionaire, the arrogant Portuguese, Chelsea as a symbol of the nouveau riche, the institutional power of the two big clubs that are used to winning everything, and who are now scared. They tried to make our success as hard as possible. But our victory in the Premiership could promote a change in attitudes and responsibilities.'

Mourinho's first season has never been dull. Chelsea faced 12 separate disciplinary charges. Two months into the season the club was charged by the FA, along with West Ham, with failing to ensure the proper behaviour of fans during their Carling Cup tie. After the first leg of the Carling Cup semi-final against Manchester United, he described the second half as 'whistle after whistle, fault after fault, cheat after cheat'. Guilty of improper conduct, he was fined £5,000 and warned about his conduct. February was a bad month. Chelsea were fined £15,000 after a brawl in their Premiership match against Blackburn. After the match against Barcelona in the Nou Camp, UEFA charged Chelsea, Mourinho, Clarke and Miles, the club's security officer, with making false declarations about an alleged half-time chat between Anders Frisk, the Swedish referee, and Frank Rijkaard, the Barcelona coach. A £33,000 fine for Chelsea and £9,000 for Mourinho resulted. Mourinho collected another warning for his 'silence' gesture to Liverpool fans during the Carling Cup final, and the affair of an alleged illegal approach to Ashley Cole, rumbles on.

Kenyon hails Mourinho as 'undoubtedly' the best manager in the Premiership and predicts that the 42-year-old will remain in charge at Stamford Bridge for at least another nine years. Chelsea expect to secure his long-term future by finalising the terms of a five-year deal within days. Kenyon believes the coach dreams of building a dynasty that will keep Chelsea at the vanguard of European football for the next decade. 'There's an enormous desire to put Chelsea right up at the top,' he says. 'In order to be a top team, you have to win things more than once and do it over a sustained period of time. That's what attracted Jose to Chelsea. He is a manager that can get us there and I know that is what he wants to do. He wants not to tell everyone that he's the best manager in the world, but to prove that he is.'

Kenyon concedes there will come a time when the club will have to be self-financing. 'We did a lot of activity in terms of getting our squad size right last year, moving 14 players out and bringing seven in. This year it will be a lot less than that. We've a young squad, with an average age of 25, and there's a few selected positions and that's it, so it will probably be about three in to maintain a squad size of 24. We're in a good position and confident we've a squad of players that have not reached their potential, so we will be adding to it in a selective manner, and we've enough in our budget to get the players we want. But it's wrong to say we are going to keep throwing money at the club. We've made a commitment that within five years the club will be profitable and as a consequence of that there are financial parameters. We have invested a huge amount of money – £28om in the last two years on players – and there is a long-term plan in the next five years of recouping on that investment. The team will not suffer in terms of the investment we are planning for it, but we have to move away from the fact we are going to buy anybody and everybody.'

Gallas has expressed interest in joining Barcelona, who contacted his representatives to inquire about his availability, but with two years remaining on his contract he is expected to be rewarded for his loyalty by signing a new deal in the summer. Gallas says, 'Chelsea have the best team spirit I've known in my whole career. Everyone who sees us play must realise how hard we fight for each other. We have absolutely everything. We have great spirit, good players and a manager who gives us the belief that we'll always win. The club have grown up every season and this is good for the future. I want to be with Chelsea and don't want to leave.'

Gary Lineker gives his verdict on Chelsea's season by saying, 'The key moment for me was when Arjen Robben first came into the side as a substitute against Blackburn at the end of October and galvanised Chelsea to a 4–0 win. There is no doubt that they have had their breaks along the way, but when you have as many shots on goal as them you are bound to get deflections and, when you look at the size of their lead, you have to say that those efforts have had little effect on the league outcome.

'People will accuse them of buying the title. But although Mourinho has had a massive budget, you still have to get the right players in and put a team together. If you want proof that money does not give you the right to dominate everything, just look at Real Madrid, who have spent more than anyone and now look certain to finish a second successive season without a trophy. Chelsea have spent big, but they haven't gone out and bought Madrid-style *galacticos*.

'For all his buys, Mourinho has achieved something that untold millions cannot bring into a club: a sense of camaraderie and fierce collective spirit. And although there has been something of a siege mentality inside the club, after all the shenanigans surrounding the Barcelona game and referee Anders Frisk, that consistency and team spirit has been obvious from the early weeks of the season. Of course, when you start well and build up a winning habit, everything is rosy in the garden. But Mourinho had to construct that positive mentality in a dressing room full of new signings and huge egos. That he managed to do so in such a short space of time is remarkable, especially when he was new to the club himself. In fact, managing to adjust so swiftly to the Premiership and all the differing demands compared to other European leagues is perhaps his greatest achievement. Maybe he really is the "Special One".'

Despite his 'special' talents, even Mourinho cannot prevent Chelsea crashing out of the Champions League at Anfield. His immediate reaction is to give the players two days off while he returns to the Bridge to agree a new five-year contract and plan for next season with the vow that his side will come back even better. Mourinho says, 'I am delighted to be signing this new contract. My heart is with Chelsea and the fantastic group of players I have. They have done a great job this season. But the vision of the owner and the board for the future of Chelsea is also one I want to be part of. I'm totally behind this project and their support in achieving it means Chelsea is the place where I will be happiest in my work. I cannot imagine another club or situation where I would be happier.' Kenyon says, 'This is great news for everybody concerned. This deal demonstrates Jose's commitment to Chelsea and also our certainty that he is the best manager to take the club into a new, exciting and successful era.'

Mourinho waited until he knew Chelsea's European fate before agreeing the deal. He adds, 'The new deal is very important for me and I'm very happy with it. I promise we will be even stronger next year. This season we won two out of four trophies and next season we will compete for five because we are also in the Community Shield. We'll be out to win two or three of those. I know what the club want for the future and we want the same. We all know that this season was a good start – not the end, but the start. We want to win more titles and my players are the same. We were very happy with this season but we want more for our lives and our careers. The club and the owner are the same. And to have a five-year contract is very good in family terms. There is now no doubt that our lives are in London and that is important for my children. When my family situation is stable, that is better for my professional situation so I can be completely focused towards Chelsea. I think my players will be happy with the news, as they will be with me for the next five years. It is also good for the fans as I feel we have established a good relationship and they are happy with what I have brought here.'

Chelsea insert a hands-off clause worth more than £5m into his new contract. His new deal is worth £5.2m a year, but the real value could be as much as double that with more success. Mourinho's contract contains a clause stipulating that his next employers must pay Chelsea the value of his contract for a year should he leave within the next five years.

championship,' he says. 'What I can also say is that there are not many times when the best team wins the Champions League. In the Premiership things can happen, you can make a mistake one day, you will have players missing another day, you will have bad luck or good luck in other days but at the end, when the battle is over, the best team always wins the title. That is why the Premiership was our top target. We wanted to prove we are the best. In the Champions League it is different; it is cup football and an example is Porto when we scored a goal in the last minute to give us the game against Manchester United. This season Chelsea are out of the competition because of a ghost goal. If, in the Premiership, we lose a match to Liverpool through a ghost goal, it is not a problem because you have more matches to recover from that defeat. In our case, though, we are out of the Champions League despite the fact that, as everyone knows, we did not concede a single goal in the semi. That is cup football for you. Last season Porto scored in the last minute and went through. This season, Gudjohnsen could have scored in the last minute to put us through or the linesman could see the same as everybody else and not give a goal. So to win the Premiership and prove we are the best makes me very happy because we are a young group who has worked together just this season. To win two out of four trophies was very good and just what we want at the beginning of a wonderful Chelsea period.

'The priority is to keep the champions – make sure you don't lose the important players. This club has conditions for that. We will keep our group of champions and we will improve it. If we look at the left-back position for example, we have only Wayne Bridge. We can improve on that place before next season. When you look at the attacking players we can say we need another one and in midfield we can keep them all and maybe add another one. We also have a lot of players in the group who have been in England for just one season. It is not easy, in my opinion, to adapt to football here so these players will be better next season.

'My contract is for five years from now. It means the club very much wants me to stay and I also want very much to stay. We are committed. We want to work together for the future of this club. This season was not the end, just the start. To win the championship after 50 years was a fantastic achievement. We must look forward now to win more silverware, not after another half a century but year after year.

'Now I am emotional with my players, but that won't last for ever. I can be in love with my players for what they have achieved this season but if they don't do it again next year I won't be in love any more. I cannot say to John Terry, "You are my captain and the Footballer of the Year and you have been fantastic so I promise you will always play next year." He has got to continue performing. Petr Cech has been absolutely fantastic. But next year he must want to prove again that he is the best keeper in the world. Claude Makelele must look to finish his career at Chelsea with even more trophies. Everyone must be hungry to improve. I will not have anyone thinking their place in the team is already waiting for them just because they have been fantastic this season.'

With the dust still settling on this year's achievements and three Premiership games still to go, Mourinho is already putting in the groundwork for next season. 'There was a scream of victory at Bolton, but this game against Charlton will be the last day for enjoyment,' he says. 'The day after we went out of the Champions League at Liverpool I had a meeting with Roman Abramovich, Peter Kenyon and director Eugene Tenenbaum to prepare for next season. I spoke to my players and told them a lot of people would be jumping for joy because we did something great. But we are not happy. We want much more. Some players in football win one simple, small cup and they are up on the moon. And they can sleep happily with one trophy. But I cannot work with players like that. Winning the Premiership is just the start of the process at Chelsea – not the end of it. I am always looking forward, never backwards.

'We will be back for pre-season training on 6 July and I expect to have all the new signings in place by then. Last year I did not arrive at Chelsea until the end of May and I had just one month to make a lot of changes to the playing and coaching staff. This time I only need to make a couple of changes and I have two months to do it. So it will be much easier. It will be difficult for me to sign any English players because to improve the squad I need the very top players. But the best Englishmen are already with the top Premiership clubs. In Italy it's easy because AC Milan are not afraid to sell to Inter or Juventus. But here Chelsea and Manchester United will not swap players because we're scared they will perform well for our rivals.'

Abramovich pledges his commitment to the club, vowing to make them the biggest in the world in a special address to the fans in the match-day programme for the Charlton game. 'I view this championship as just the beginning of a new era for Chelsea and would like to reiterate my long-term commitment to the club. Much has been said about the financial outlay over the past two years. However, this must be seen in the context of placing Chelsea on a level playing field with the other top clubs in England and Europe for a sustained period. We have made solid investments on the field in players, management, training facilities and an academy that will nurture the next generation of home-grown talent.

'Off the field, a team of executives and senior managers has been put together to grow the business and capitalise on the playing success. All of this is a deliberate, long-term strategy with the aim of building the most successful football club in the world in the next ten years and beyond. Under chairman Bruce Buck, chief executive Peter Kenyon and Jose Mourinho, we have a strong leadership team that shares my vision.'

SATURDAY, 7 MAY 2005

CHELSEA 1, CHARLTON ATHLETIC 0

It's a day of celebration as John Terry lifts the Premiership trophy, 50 years after Chelsea's last league triumph. The players are still on the pitch nearly two hours after the final whistle as Mourinho quietly leaves the stadium with wife Tami and kids Matilde and Jose.

'I am happy, I am tired and I need a holiday,' Jose declares. 'But now we look ahead. Enjoy today because tomorrow we start planning for next season. It's not in my nature to be happy with what I have got now ... I want more.'

Chelsea's unbeaten league run stretches to 27 games. Carlo Cudicini, appearing in his first league game of the campaign, has the satisfaction of keeping the clean sheet that takes Chelsea past the Premiership record of 24 in a season. Mourinho reveals his team started celebrating on 15 January when they won at Spurs and Arsenal lost at Bolton. In his programme notes he simply lists the 102 members of his staff – from captain to cook – and declares, 'These are my champions.'

However much Mourinho and his players are still smarting at their Champions League exit, thousands of fans inside Stamford Bridge do not allow that defeat to spoil their day. They chant for Abramovich and for Mourinho, they 'stand up for the champions' and they hail Terry and Lampard. And that is just before kick-off.

Compared to the celebrations, the match is merely a sideshow. Chelsea wait until the final minute before Lampard is brought down on the edge of the box. The foul looks to have been outside the area and contact is, at best, minimal, but the penalty is still given. The ball is handed to Makelele, whose first effort is saved, but he nets the rebound with a mishit to score his first goal for the club in his 94th appearance.

His team-mates joke that he doesn't even come close to scoring in training: in penalty practice on Friday he missed two out of two! But that doesn't stop the players ushering him forward to the spot. When he finally forces the ball over the line, Makelele is promptly buried under an avalanche of team-mates, a testimony to both his talent and popularity. Charlton just have time to kick off again before ref Mike Riley blows the whistle to allow Chelsea's celebrations to begin.

Mourinho insists his players disobeyed his strict orders. 'I said if there's a penalty – Frank Lampard. If there's a penalty in minute 90 with us leading 2–0, then Makelele.'

But the late winner is deserved, even though it is so fortuitous. Chelsea create several first-half chances, but Lampard directs one free header over the bar and Gudjohnsen volleys another effort wide. Charlton are indebted to keeper Stephan Andersen, who produces one acrobatic save to tip a fierce drive by Cole onto the bar, while he is also out quickly to foil the midfielder as he breaks clear. Cole clips another shot wide of the far post, but Charlton also threaten on the break, Jonathan Fortune lifting one half-chance over the bar and directing another effort inches wide. Charlton's goal continues to live a charmed life after the restart, with Terry rising to meet Johnson's deep cross, only to crash his header against the face of the bar.

Cudicini is required to produce an excellent save to tip Matt Holland's drive around the post. Still Chelsea press and still they waste openings. Lampard clips the ball through to Cole, who fires that chance wide before promptly flashing another effort over the top.

Mourinho needs goals, but instead opts for sentiment, bringing on third-choice keeper Lenny Pidgeley for his first-team debut with nine minutes left. Pidgeley is soon called upon to make an important block, but the real drama is reserved until the last minute when Makelele strikes his late penalty winner.

The Premiership trophy awaits and Stamford Bridge's celebrations can finally begin in earnest. There is an elongated presentation ceremony as all the backroom staff are individually introduced and paraded before the fans and make their way to the winners' podium before the players. Mourinho explains, 'On the pitch I got my entire staff together and said to them, "Enjoy the day because tomorrow we must think about the future."'

Before the 2005 team lift the trophy, 13 members of the 1955 side are brought out with the old Football League trophy. Terry and Lampard hand over the trophy to them that was never publicly presented 50 years ago. It is a wonderful addition to the occasion. Then it is on to the main event. 'Are you watching Arsenal!' and 'Chelsea are back!' are sung with gusto as staff and players are brought out of the tunnel one-by-one. Many Charlton fans sportingly stay behind and clap. Roy Bentley and Stan Willemse, legends from 1955, carry out the Premiership trophy and Terry lifts it to the accompaniment of explosions and streamers.

There are tears and much singing as no one wants to go home. An impromptu football match breaks out between the players' kids in front of the Shed, and Cole is booed when he joins in. Finally the team reluctantly troop off down the tunnel, Lampard, Terry, Gudjohnsen and the trophy the last to leave.

One banner reads 'What blip? Chelsea FC Champions 2005', while another simply states 'Jose Mourinho for Prime Minister'.

Team

Cudicini (Pidgeley), Johnson (Jarosik), Terry, Carvalho, Gallas, Makelele, Cole, Lampard, Tiago (Forssell), Geremi, Gudjohnsen.

TUESDAY, 10 MAY 2005

MAN UTD 1, CHELSEA 3

For the first time in 103 league matches, United are beaten after taking the lead. Goals from Tiago, Gudjohnsen and Cole not only inflict United's only home league defeat of the season, but also allow Mourinho's men to rewrite the record books. Victory means Chelsea break United's Premiership records for points and wins in a season. After going behind to Ruud van Nistelrooy's goal, Chelsea take total control. Those United fans who remain to the end clap Chelsea off the pitch. Sir Alex Ferguson now knows just how far his team are behind Chelsea.

While United's in-house television channel hosts a debate on whether Chelsea are worthy champions, Ferguson lauds Mourinho's 'formidable achievement'. Writing in his programme notes, Ferguson promises 'no cheap Portuguese plonk in the manager's office tonight, but fine wine deserving of a champion.

'For a manager new to the country and the English game, breaking entirely new ground, it is a formidable achievement. We know Chelsea have raised the financial stakes but money isn't the total reason for success. There's still a team to be built, balance to be created, tactics to be applied and spirit generated. All this Jose has done. To come into the Premiership and leave us all standing is brilliant and everyone at Manchester United offers sincere congratulations.'

Ferguson makes his players form a guard of honour for Mourinho's title-winners – a sporting gesture, although possibly done to remind his charges that their standards have slipped. Roy Keane does not look comfortable with the whole plan. The Chelsea team emerge to a chorus of boos from the crowd. Wayne Rooney and Gary Neville scowl. It is one of the more surreal moments of the season. 'Have you ever won the Treble?' comes the query from the Stretford End. Chelsea fans react by chanting 'One Malcolm Glazer'.

Keane is soon cautioned for catching Cole, and is lucky not to walk for upending Lampard. By then United are ahead, with Keane and particularly Wayne Rooney playing their parts in Van Nistelrooy's eighth-minute poacher's goal. From the wreckage of a United corner, Keane lays the ball back to Paul Scholes, whose firm shot is diverted by Robert Huth to Rooney. The England international drills the ball into the box for Van Nistelrooy to pounce from close range with a confident flick. Johnson is guilty of playing the Dutchman onside and failing to react. Chelsea's defence is simply not the same without Terry.

Chelsea respond stylishly to the rare indignity of falling behind in a Premiership game. Within ten minutes the new champions are level. Tiago collects possession 35 yards out and spots the United players are dropping off him expecting a pass, so he lets fly. His beautiful arcing shot rises and dips, leaving Roy Carroll completely bemused in the United goal. Carvalho then denies Van Nistelrooy with a wonderful late interception, while the busy Rooney also goes close. Cole also sends a curling shot narrowly wide in a competitive first half.

After the break Darren Fletcher is unlucky not to match Tiago's attempt as his effort cannons off the woodwork. And it is not long before Chelsea are in front as Lampard feeds Tiago, whose driven low pass is controlled by Gudjohnsen. The Icelander waits for Carroll to commit himself and coolly dinks the ball over the on-rushing keeper.

Gaps begin to appear in the United defence and another Chelsea goal seems more likely than an equaliser for the home side. Sure enough, inside the last ten minutes, Wes Brown's clearance is cut out by Lampard, who darts into the area and cuts the ball back for Cole. There are clear suspicions of offside as he turns the ball home, but the travelling Chelsea faithful are not bothered.

In happier times Sir Alex would pick up the microphone after Manchester United's final home game of the season and deliver a victory speech to the masses. Now Chelsea have established a new order to English football, United's manager is silent. Instead, Old Trafford hears the clanking of emptying plastic seats long before the final whistle. Those who stay see Ferguson's players embark on a lap of 'honour' with heavy hearts. Ferguson is in denial afterwards, pontificating about a 'marvellous spectacle' while neatly swerving any possible criticisms of his team. But there is one brief moment of acceptance that they have come up against superior opponents. 'Once Chelsea's second goal went in they were worthy winners,' he says. 'Chelsea played like you expect champions to play – with authority.'

Mourinho describes beating United's record points total as 'perfect'. 'The record was our motivation,' says Mourinho. 'We wanted to beat it and this is a special moment. It is the perfect way to do it – at a great stadium against a team who in Sir Alex Ferguson have a manager who leads by example in success and fair play.'

Team

Cudicini, Geremi, Huth, Carvalho, Gallas, Makelele, Johnson (Jarosik), Lampard, Tiago, Cole (Grant), Gudjohnsen (Morais).

There is only ever going to be one winner of the Barclays Manager of the Year award. Mourinho's landslide victory in the championship race earns him the required majority in the voting panel's ballot. Only once has the champion manager not been given the award. In 2001 when Ferguson led United to the title, George Burley won it after lifting Ipswich Town to an unexpected fifth place. It was also the year Gerard Houllier won three trophies with Liverpool. David Moyes and Rafael Benitez have valid claims this year, but they are still not going to deny Mourinho.

SUNDAY, 15 MAY 2005
NEWCASTLE 1, CHELSEA 1

Mourinho concedes that he will struggle to surpass this record-breaking season as Chelsea move on to an unprecedented Premiership haul of 95 points and set yet another record for the fewest goals conceded in a season – a mere 15. Mourinho observes, 'The record does make you realise this season has been magnificent. It has been fantastic and that is why I want to stay in this country. It is the best football country in the world. Our objective will be to be champions again and improve in certain aspects, but we know next season will be harder because people know the side and what we can do.'

Newcastle are gifted the lead when Geremi inadvertently diverts the ball in after Alan Shearer rises to head on Charles N'Zogbia's 32nd-minute corner. The home side's advantage is short-lived. Celestine Babayaro misjudges Lampard's through-ball and resorts to fouling Gudjohnsen inside the penalty box. Lampard steps up to beat Given, driving the ball straight down the middle, despite losing his footing as he strikes the ball, for his 19th goal of a memorable campaign.

After the break, Jermaine Jenas miscues from close range and Cudicini does well to palm away Patrick Kluivert's header. Shay Given also excels with a save from Gudjohnsen and somehow claws an effort from Jarosik away at the death.

Mourinho generally takes the biscuit, but this time he takes two – as he is walking away from the press room, Mourinho smiles and grabs a couple for the journey back to London. His Chelsea team, missing eight of their significant contributors this season, have just extended their Premiership points record by one and but for a brilliant reaction save by Given from Jarosik near the end, it would have been three.

Chelsea's record on the road is 15 wins, three draws and one defeat. Their total of 95 points – meaning they finish 12 points ahead of Arsenal – will take some matching. So will the record 25 clean sheets.

'It is an unbelievable record,' says Mourinho with all the modesty he can muster. 'Ninety-five points is a lot of points. The clean sheets gave us a big push to be champions. At the beginning of the season, when we were not so fluent, clean sheets gave us a lot of points. People said Chelsea were boring, but Chelsea were building.'

And Mourinho has not finished building just yet. 'We started thinking about the next campaign a few months ago,' he says. 'It's easy to prepare for next season as we have a group of champions and want to keep them. We want to make two or three adjustments but we have the base.'

Team

Cudicini, Geremi, Huth, Carvalho, Johnson, Cole (Morais), Makelele, Lampard, Tiago, Jarosik (Watt), Gudjohnsen (Oliveira).

The Champions League

'I HAVE TO DEFEND WHAT IS MINE. THE CHAMPIONS LEAGUE IS MINE AT THE MOMENT. I AM THE LAST WINNER AS MANAGER OF THE CHAMPIONS LEAGUE – SO IT IS MY COMPETITION.'

Jose Mourinho

Chelsea's Champions League campaign couldn't start with a more controversial and intriguing draw in Monte Carlo. Jose Mourinho will begin the defence of the Champions League he won with Porto in a group that includes CSKA Moscow, a team sponsored by Roman Abramovich. The other teams in Group H are Paris Saint-Germain and Porto.

Chelsea's Russian owner has ploughed £40m into a sponsorship deal with CSKA – and the multi-billionaire's links to both clubs spark an investigation by UEFA. Ironically, Abramovich was in Scotland to cheer on CSKA as they reached the group stage by beating Rangers in the qualifiers and he was invited into the dressing room afterwards to congratulate the team.

His oil company, Sibneft, is the club's main sponsor and UEFA spokesman William Gaillard says, 'This has to be looked at thoroughly to see whether there is a controlling interest by Abramovich in CSKA because the teams are in the same group.'

After carrying out a week-long investigation, UEFA declare themselves satisfied that Abramovich does not have a controlling interest in CSKA Moscow. A UEFA spokesperson says, 'The investigation is over.'

Anyone who thinks Mourinho cares only for big-money signings should see him on the morning before the Champions League draw. He is watching Chelsea Under-13s from behind one of the goals. 'That's the second time he's been down here in two weeks,' says Chelsea's academy director Neil Bath.

'Jose's produced a document for the [academy] coaching staff and scouting staff which sets out the philosophy he'd like to see,' says Bath. 'He's very clear about the type of player he'd like coming through. He wants players who are physically, technically and tactically capable of playing in the first team and have experienced the systems of play and the typical training methods that he implements. So we have spent time watching his training sessions and reading up on his philosophy.'

As they approach their opening Champions League tie in Paris, Chelsea have kept four consecutive clean sheets in the Premiership. Mourinho says, 'It's important to be strong defensively. It's about being compact and that can be beautiful.'

Striker Didier Drogba expects a hostile reception from the Paris crowd because of his Marseille associations. So far this season PSG have failed to win a single league game and are 14th in the table. Mourinho is even tempted to alter his usual safety-first approach. 'If you start the group stage at home, you have to win. Away, you have to get a point. If we leave Paris with a point, normally it is good for the next stage. But that is not the way we are thinking. We come here to play with a victory in mind. We are not going to play a defensive game.'

TUESDAY, 14 SEPTEMBER 2004

PARIS SAINT-GERMAIN 0, CHELSEA 3

Jeered by PSG fans from the moment his name is announced, striker Didier Drogba has cause to laugh after his two goals secure an away victory that already makes Chelsea's progression to the second round look a safe bet.

In fact, the only real surprise is that it takes Chelsea 29 minutes to take the lead. Joe Cole's clever turn brings the corner that results in the opener. Frank Lampard floats in a cross from the left, goalkeeper Lionel Letizi flaps at the ball and John Terry can hardly believe his good fortune as he nods in. Mateja Kezman is brought down for a free-kick 15 minutes from time and Drogba picks his spot over the wall, leaving the keeper without a prayer.

The game is settled in added time when Tiago wins the ball and Cole instantly releases Kezman through on the left. The Serb, on for Gudjohnsen, shoots straight at Letizi, but Drogba is perfectly placed to stroke home the rebound. Each time he scores the man from the Ivory Coast cups his hands to his ears in mockery of the home fans, mimicking the goal celebrations of their Portuguese striker Pauleta, and blows kisses at them for good measure.

Jeered mercilessly by PSG supporters throughout the game, Drogba walks off bare-chested when the final whistle blows. Drogba admits, 'I did wind them up but they wound me up a bit as well, didn't they? I lost against them three times for Marseille last season so it was important for me to score and for the team to win. We're very pleased. The manager said we could win and we wanted the three points so we could be top of the group because we know we are the sort of team that should be top.'

Mourinho adds, 'People always want to talk about the dark side of football but Didier showed tonight why I pressed my board to bring him to this club. He was the man of the match, scored two goals and respected everybody. He only wanted to show how much he loves both countries. If you love football, even if you're a PSG supporter, you should only be pleased with the performance you saw Didier give.

'We played top-class football and controlled the game from the first minute to the last. Our use of the ball was superb and we were in charge of the tempo and pace of the game while defensively we were incredible again. We could have scored more goals but we made it look easy. That was a measure of how well we played because Paris were not an easy team to beat.'

Lampard too hails Drogba. 'Didier's got pace, power and great finishing ability and can get us 20 or 30 goals this season, like Thierry Henry does for Arsenal. We've been lacking a player with real pace and power and now Didier's doing it. He's very strong, has good feet and is very willing to run for the team. It's nice to have a big figure up front that you can pick out straight away.'

Team

Cech, Gallas, Ferreira, Terry, Bridge, Lampard, Cole, Tiago, Makelele, Drogba, Gudjohnsen (Kezman).

Mischief in the fixture calendar brings FC Porto to Stamford Bridge four months after Mourinho led Porto to victory in the European Cup. Chelsea are like Mourinho's Porto in that they play a midfield diamond and largely leave the job of winger to their full-backs. Chelsea also guard the ball jealously. 'You can see some of last season's Porto in the way Chelsea now play,' says Tiago. 'Maybe it's in the possession of the ball, maybe in the organisation of the game, especially in midfield, which is tight and quite close together. They had Deco, but apart from that I think we have more attacking options. I don't think you can call us a defensive team.'

Abramovich paid £33m to Porto for defenders Paulo Ferreira and Ricardo Carvalho. Porto also sold Deco to Barcelona and Pedro Mendes to Tottenham. Despite their newfound wealth, Porto are struggling. Going into the weekend, they have drawn all three of their domestic Superliga matches and, in their opening Champions League contest, they could do no better than manage a goalless draw at home to CSKA Moscow.

With six wins and two draws in his first eight matches, the only thing upsetting Mourinho is what he perceives to be persistent and unfair criticism of his tactics. Chelsea are not exactly playing with the panache of Arsenal, but in their ability to retain possession and control the tempo of a game, Chelsea are showing a tactical intelligence that Arséne Wenger and Sir Alex Ferguson have seldom coaxed from their sides.

WEDNESDAY, 29 SEPTEMBER 2004

CHELSEA 3, PORTO 1

The match begins with an unsavoury incident as Jose Mourinho goes over to shake the hands of Porto fans before kick-off and a yob pushes forward and spits on his shirt. Disgusted at what has happened, Mourinho takes a step back and security guards manhandle the idiot out of the ground.

Revenge is not long in coming. After seven minutes, Chelsea score their first goal when Damien Duff flicks the ball over the head of a defender for Eidur Gudjohnsen to hook a first-time cross into the middle where the unmarked Alexei Smertin drives a shot deep into the far corner for his first goal for the club. It brings the former Porto boss to his feet in celebration – not far from the Portuguese fans – which, in turn, produces a warning from the fourth official for Mourinho to cool it.

Didier Drogba, the second most expensive striker in the Premiership behind Wayne Rooney, does his best to give Chelsea fans something to celebrate following the Old Trafford wonder kid's amazing hat-trick against Fenerbahce. With Chelsea coasting on the back of Smertin's opener, he strikes with a header from a Duff free-kick in the 50th minute to reignite the game.

Benni McCarthy then gives Porto a lifeline by netting a 68th-minute rebound after Petr Cech fails to hold a stinging shot from Carlos Alberto that skims John Terry's head. The Chelsea skipper, though, takes just two minutes to respond, diving full length to head home Frank Lampard's free-kick.

After the game, a jubilant Mourinho lavishes praise on a group of players he clearly believes is good enough to bring the Champions

League trophy to Stamford Bridge. 'It's great. We've beaten the European champions, have six points and are in a fantastic position to go through to the next stage.

'I have a fantastic group of players at Chelsea. We have the right personalities, the right characters and for me it's amazing to see the way they fight in every match. At some of the top clubs the big names think more about themselves than the team. But my big players play for the team. That is why no one has beaten us in nine matches.'

Porto manager Victor Fernandez acknowledges the value of Lampard's deliveries from set-pieces. 'One of our problems was Lampard at free-kicks because we were playing against some of the best headers of the ball in Europe.'

Chelsea have now ended a run of four successive Champions League draws at Stamford Bridge. Considering they reached last season's semi-final, it comes as a surprise that this is only their second home win in seven European matches.

It also marks the end of a record-breaking run of 12 Champions League games without defeat for Porto and continues a sorry run in which they have been beaten seven times in eight trips to England. The 1–1 draw, when they knocked out Manchester United last season, was the only point they gained.

> **Team**
> Cech, Ferreira, Carvalho, Terry, Gallas, Smertin, Makelele, Lampard, Duff (Tiago), Gudjohnsen (Kezman), Drogba.

Jose Mourinho pens a personal letter to UEFA chiefs begging them not to punish his old club after UEFA announce they will be taking action against Porto following the spitting incident at Stamford Bridge.

Helder Mota, the fan who spat at Mourinho, is a member of FC Porto's fanatical Super Dragons supporters club. He describes Mourinho as an old pal and makes wild claims, fiercely denied by

Mourinho, that the Chelsea manager has been sending his wife saucy text messages. 'When I saw Mourinho, the blood came rushing to my head and I couldn't stop myself. It was everything: the fact that he was texting Luciana behind my back, the fact that he abandoned Porto and the fact that we used to be friends. On Wednesday he didn't even acknowledge me when he came to within feet of where the Super Dragons were to sign autographs. I ran up to him and spat in his face twice. Four stewards threw me out of the ground and I had to watch the match on TV.'

Mota has also admitted making a death threat against Mourinho the night before the Champions League final. 'Spitting at Mourinho is only half of what I want to do to him. I am prepared to go to prison over this.' Mourinho is taking Mota's threats seriously and has informed police. Chelsea will also increase security for Mourinho during the return match in Porto.

Chelsea face CSKA Moscow in a week when plans to make a musical of Roman Abramovich's life are announced at the same time as the Russian government continues to investigate his finances. Mourinho says, 'CSKA are a very good side. They went to Porto and did not concede a goal. That shows how strong they are. If they get points against us at Stamford Bridge or in Moscow, they'll be in a very strong position.'

Mourinho's main worry is the form of Vagner Love, the Brazilian whose goals have taken CSKA to the top of the Russian league, which they lead by one point with four games to play. CSKA bought Love in the summer for £6m, with money provided by Sibneft. With Drogba injured, Mourinho has no choice but to pair Kezman with Gudjohnsen up front. The Serb has yet to score in ten appearances for Chelsea.

Drawing a blank at Manchester City resulted in Chelsea's first defeat under Mourinho at the weekend. Now he expects a response. 'We do not lose much and we did not enjoy the taste. I have no doubts my players will give me a good answer.'

WEDNESDAY, 20 OCTOBER 2004
CHELSEA 2, CSKA MOSCOW 0

Before the match, Jose Mourinho is presented with the European Club Manager of the Year award by Sir Bobby Robson. In the crowd, the contingent of Moscow fans holds up a giant banner with a message to Abramovich written in Cyrillic script: 'Abramovich, give us three points'. But their team begins as though it does not need any help from the man who pays £10m a season to have the name of his oil company, Sibneft, on their shirts. Chelsea are soon on the back foot as CSKA come out fighting.

However, in the ninth minute, Chelsea make the Russians pay when they expose their defensive frailties with a Frank Lampard corner to the back post. Eidur Gudjohnsen rises high above the defenders to nod the ball back across goal and John Terry stoops to head it across the line from close range. It is his third goal of the season and maintains his record of scoring in every Champions League game this campaign. Then there is a scare for the home side. Early substitute Laizans takes a corner that skids across the area, bounces off Gudjohnsen's back and is heading for the top corner until Petr Cech arches his back to produce a fine reaction save and tip the ball over.

CSKA's aerial weakness at the back undoes them again in first-half injury-time from another Chelsea dead ball. Duff swings over a free-kick from the right-hand side of the area and Gudjohnsen runs unchallenged between two defenders and leaps to power his header past Igor Akinfeev. It is only the Iceland striker's second goal of the season but it gives Chelsea a commanding lead at the top of Group H.

Later Mourinho hails goalkeeper Cech. 'The boy is doing fantastic for us. The first half was very difficult for us. They started the game better and had one or two good chances. Our goalkeeper made one or two great saves and the second goal came at the right time for us mentally.'

Chelsea could not have done better than win their first three group matches, but efficiency rather than excitement has been the keyword tonight. The lowest crowd of the season – 33,945 – is a big surprise. These big European nights used to be special, highly charged occasions. Mourinho says, 'I like a full stadium. Maybe it wasn't full because of Chelsea's past record at home in the Champions League. But now that we've beaten Porto and CSKA, maybe they'll all come to see us play PSG.'

However, a win in Moscow will guarantee Chelsea top spot and that would render the visit of PSG largely academic.

Team

Cech, Bridge, Terry, Gallas, Ferreira, Lampard, Duff (Cole), Smertin (Parker), Makelele, Kezman (Tiago), Gudjohnsen.

Former Chelsea manager Claudio Ranieri's honeymoon at Valencia is over after they are thrashed 5–1 at home by Inter Milan in the Champions League. Valencia face an uphill struggle to qualify for the second stage after losing two of their first three games.

Alexei Smertin claims Chelsea are now the biggest team in Russia. Smertin is a hero in his home country, where his popularity is similar in stature to that of David Beckham, Steven Gerrard or Michael Owen in England. 'Chelsea is the most popular team in Russia now. English football is now so big in Russia that they can watch every Chelsea game. Every time I come home they want to know what is happening here.'

Mourinho's side need just a point in Moscow to claim their place in the last 16 of the European Cup and they trail Premiership leaders Arsenal only on goal difference. But he plays down growing expectations of a double by claiming clubs from Europe's biggest leagues cannot conquer the continent as well as their own country. Since United did it in 1999, Porto are the first team to have won their domestic title and the Champions League in the same year. 'I know Manchester United won the title and the Champions League in 1999 but it's really difficult. It happens once in a lifetime. For me it's happened twice in the last two years [with Porto]. I don't think this will be the third consecutive year.'

Mourinho and his players arrive in the Lokomotiv Stadium on the same coach as Roman Abramovich. Conspiracy theorists have been claiming any result other than a Chelsea victory will be 'a fix' to help CSKA qualify. When Abramovich steps off Chelsea's team bus before training, he is clearly relishing the build-up. On Sunday he is also seen mingling in a hotel with visitors who include Sir Bobby Robson. But it comes as no surprise that he does not join Chelsea players and coaches on a visit to Red Square where hard man John Terry braves the cold in shorts and flip-flops.

Mourinho insists this is just another game for Abramovich, which is hard to believe. The Russian is on home soil and, as well as his sponsorship of CSKA, he is also a close friend of the club's president, Evgeny Giner, and has been to at least one of their home games this season.

Mourinho offers an insight into Abramovich's involvement with the squad. 'He's very committed with us. He's not just the owner, he also wants to win like the pros. Every single match since the beginning [of the season] he's been involved … he feels part of the group and also the group feels he's part of us. We are always very comfortable when he is with us and I think he feels the same among the pros.'

Much interest in Moscow centres on whether Smertin will play. Mourinho says, 'I have to choose not with emotion, with heart, with relations with countries but with what is best for the team.'

Victory will allow Chelsea to turn their attentions to the Premiership. Indeed they face Arsenal just five days after their final Champions League group game, away to Porto, which may be meaningless by then. A result here could make the twin challenge less of an impossible task.

TUESDAY, 2 NOVEMBER 2004
CSKA MOSCOW 0, CHELSEA 1

Mourinho hails Arjen Robben as his 'extra dimension' after the Dutchman's first goal enables Chelsea to become the first team to qualify for the last 16, with two games to spare. Robben's sweetly stroked first-half finish is enough to complete Chelsea's perfect passage through Group H.

The build-up to the 23rd-minute goal is elegant as Robben slips through to find Damien Duff's diagonal run before racing into the box to receive the Irishman's back-heel. The finish is sublime, as Robben allows the ball to run beyond the lunge of Sergei Semak before looking up and passing it left-footed into the bottom corner.

Roman Abramovich grants himself a small grin as the ball rolls into the net. Nearby, former Russian President Boris Yeltsin suggests his vodka supply has not yet been entirely cut off as he throws a minor tantrum in the directors' box. The Russian elite are out in force.

By half-time Chelsea have conceded ten corners – the most they have given away in any game this season has been 11, also against CSKA. But the key to their success here is the rapid transition from rock-solid defence to rampaging counter-attacks – the hallmark of Mourinho's Porto. Robben is a particularly useful asset when you play this way.

Chelsea have a close call when Brazilian Vagner Love blasts a second-half penalty high over the bar after Glen Johnson's wild foul on Yuri Zhirkov. Mourinho says, 'Glen has to play these matches to learn from his mistakes. He has to control his position and avoid sliding tackles.' Johnson, making just his second start for Mourinho, travels back to London wondering if he will get another chance.

Chelsea have conceded only four times in 16 matches this season and their performances will have been noted in Madrid, Barcelona, Milan and Turin as well as Highbury and Old Trafford. Today John Terry and Ricardo Carvalho have been all but impenetrable in front of

Petr Cech, while midfielder Scott Parker has shown how determined he is to be considered for a first-team place.

Robben, who linked so brilliantly with Duff before firing home, says, 'It was a great goal to score and I finished it quite well. I knew what I was doing and last year in the Champions League I did exactly the same, going one way and shooting in the other corner. It was a great combination with Damien and a good finish. I'm sure we can play in the same team – I've always said that.'

John Terry believes Chelsea's magnificent Champions League performances have sent shockwaves around Europe. 'Real Madrid and AC Milan may be the best teams in Europe, but the way we're playing at the moment I'm sure we can match them, if not better them. We've looked very solid in the Champions League so far and are sending out a message to the rest of Europe. It was a great performance and four wins out of four is a fantastic start. We've been scoring a lot more goals and have only conceded one in four games, which shows how well we're playing.'

Having now won the group, Chelsea are free to focus on the Premiership until the knockout stages begin at the end of February, though there will be no let-up from Mourinho. He says, 'We will face the next stage against the second-placed team but I promise CSKA that we will play exactly the same way against PSG and Porto. Anyone who thinks we will take it easy is making a big mistake.'

Team

Cech, Johnson, Terry, Carvalho, Gallas (Ferreira), Duff, Parker (Tiago), Lampard, Makelele, Robben, Gudjohnsen (Kezman).

Chelsea lodge an official complaint with UEFA because around 50 of their fans with tickets were stopped from entering CSKA's ground and missed most of the first half. UEFA will also investigate a flare thrown from the crowd at Petr Cech.

After being out for five weeks following a groin operation, Didier Drogba returns to the squad for the encounter with Paris Saint-

Germain. 'The team is improving because of time together,' Drogba says, 'and it is easier to come back into a winning team. I will have to give my best.'

The French club are third in the Group H table with four points and desperately need good results to progress. 'We want to win these last two matches,' says Mourinho. 'I will make some changes and rest some players, but the team I put out will still be a good one. The truth is, though, that my team have done the job in the Champions League while Paris Saint-Germain and Porto have not.'

When Mourinho left the pitch in the Lokomotiv Stadium after victory over CSKA Moscow, he made a promise to Valeri Gazzayev, the CSKA coach. He assured Gazzayev that, even though they were through to the last 16, his team would not be relaxing in their final fixtures against Paris Saint-Germain and FC Porto. 'In the players' tunnel,' Mourinho says, 'I told the Russian coach that he could be sure that my team would be fighting for results against PSG and Porto. If CSKA want to be the second-best team in the group, it is up to them.'

'This is not a dead match,' he insists. 'I told the players that we are better than PSG, but motivation will make the difference. The players have to fight for a position in the team and I look not at their faces, who they are or how much they might have cost. I look for what they can give me in the performance.'

WEDNESDAY, 24 NOVEMBER 2004

CHELSEA 0, PARIS SAINT-GERMAIN 0

Ominously, PSG have failed to win an away game in Europe for seven years. Despite the sell-out crowd at Stamford Bridge, this game proves that dead group matches are a turn-off. The French club have plenty more to play for with qualification between them, Porto and CSKA Moscow still in the balance but the match never catches fire.

Jose Mourinho rests nearly £80m worth of talent in Petr Cech, John Terry, Eidur Gudjohnsen, Damien Duff, Claude Makelele and Tiago. In come Carlo Cudicini, Glen Johnson, Joe Cole, Scott Parker and Mateja Kezman. Didier Drogba returns from injury to sit on the bench but Chelsea still lose their 100 per cent record in Group H. Having already reached the second phase before the game starts, Chelsea do not create a real chance until the 81st minute when Drogba fires straight at keeper Lionel Letizi.

Still the game presents a rare chance for some of Mourinho's squad to press a claim to the first-team in the build-up to their crunch match with Arsenal at Highbury. Chelsea certainly start brightly enough as the lively Arjen Robben probes and presses for an opening, while Kezman looks a constant threat.

Joe Cole, one of the players with most to prove, sets up Kezman but the Serb has rarely shown the sort of goalscoring form which made him such a threat for PSV Eindhoven and once again he wastes a good opening from 20 yards. Ironically the best entertainment comes from the rollicking Mourinho gives Cole from the touchline for being badly positioned at a free-kick just before the break.

At half-time Mourinho proves that not even the in-form Robben is irreplaceable as he takes off the Dutchman and sticks on Duff to try to give his team fresh impetus. But Mourinho's second-choice team do not manage a single shot on target until the 60th minute when skipper for the night Frank Lampard produces an effort on the turn that is easily saved.

The PSG fans are busy barracking Drogba, who comes on in place of Kezman, for his Marseille connections, while Mourinho then throws on Gudjohnsen for Lampard. Drogba's comeback after seven weeks on the sidelines turns out to be the only highlight. He has a chance to gain revenge for the taunts of the visiting French fans just minutes after coming on but his well-taken 'goal' is disallowed for offside.

Mourinho makes no excuses for sending out a much-changed side. 'The fact that I rested a lot of players was good. My attitude will be the same against Porto in the sense that we will try to win. We did not give the match to PSG – they had to fight.

'All my players are playing regularly and for their national teams, so if I cannot give them a rest – we don't really need the points to get through – then I am stupid. We tried to win and had some chances, the last of which was a great one and could have killed the game.'

For PSG coach Vahid Halilhodzic it is very much a case of mission accomplished as his team keep alive their hopes of making the last 16. 'This result puts us in good stead to hold on to second place in the group,' he declares.

Reflecting on the end of Chelsea's perfect record in the Champions League, Mourinho says, 'It's nice to have a 100 per cent record. But the first objective in this competition is to go through.'

Team

Cudicini, Johnson, Carvalho, Gallas, Bridge, Smertin, Parker, Lampard (Gudjohnsen), Cole, Kezman (Drogba), Robben (Duff).

Chief executive Peter Kenyon's appraisal of the manager he's worked alongside for four months hasn't changed. 'Jose has all the traits of someone who's supremely confident in his own ability, has a firm belief in what he's trying to do and, above all, has a minutely detailed approach to the game. He's created a complete team ethic, a squad that's totally together. His methods of coaching are challenging and interesting and he's a natural leader: someone who commands total respect.'

Meanwhile, Jose Mourinho's lawyer asks judicial officials to provide extra security when he returns to his old club Porto. Under Portuguese law, the Porto supporter who spat on Mourinho is barred from the return game. When asked if he needs bodyguards, Mourinho says, 'Yes. If you visit Palermo [Sicily] you probably also need [them].' This remark arouses much indignation on the Italian island. Banners at Palermo's home match against Atalanta read, 'Mourinho – Champion of Ignorance'.

Mourinho relates how his greatest triumph – managing the European champions in 2004 – nearly turned into a nightmare. The evening before Porto beat Monaco 3–0 in Gelsenkirchen, Mourinho took a call. It was from a well-known figure in Porto's underworld. 'The person on the other end told me, "You think you're the best, you bastard. We won't do anything now because you have a final tomorrow. But as soon as it's over, consider yourself a dead man because we'll get you. As soon as you get back to Porto, your fate is sealed. You don't have a chance." I replied, "You must be mad, I don't know what you're talking about."'

Porto president Pinta da Costa adds to the controversy by claiming that Mourinho deserves the threats because of his 'bizarre' behaviour and insists he left the club in a mess by quitting with two years left on his contract.

In these circumstances, Chelsea change their travel plans, bring in private security guards and take police advice on whether Mourinho will be breaking UEFA rules by ducking public appearances. The team will not train on the Porto pitch before the game and Mourinho will skip UEFA's compulsory pre-match press conference.

Chelsea receive a police escort from the airport to their hotel and Steve Clarke admits, 'We are expecting a hostile atmosphere but that is the case in all European away matches. I don't know how Porto's fans will react to Jose. All I know is that, if he won the European Cup for Chelsea and then came back to Stamford Bridge with another club, Jose would get a fantastic reception.'

If Porto fail, the beneficiaries will be CSKA Moscow – the club Abramovich sponsors. Da Costa makes it clear he will not be shaking the hand of Mourinho but the Chelsea coach will find at least one friendly face in the Porto ranks. Defender Pedro Emanuel insists, 'Meeting Mourinho again is going to be very special. He was the person who brought me to Porto and who took a chance on me. I had an excellent relationship with him because of all the good work he did during his time at this club.'

Ricardo Carvalho who, along with Paulo Ferreira, followed Mourinho from Porto, says, 'Porto may have won the Champions

League last season but Chelsea have a better side. I believe Jose, myself and Paulo will get a good reception. Ninety per cent of Porto's supporters will cheer us, I think, because we had such happy times together. But if I foul a former team-mate on the edge of the penalty area as he is about to shoot, they might not cheer me any more.'

TUESDAY, 7 DECEMBER 2004
FC PORTO 2, CHELSEA 1

Ruthless Mourinho shatters any hopes that he will make things easy for his old side when he fields a powerful-looking team. However, Porto are desperate to avoid becoming the first defending champions to crash out of the competition at the group stages and they are also motivated to prevent their ex-coach Mourinho from being the man who knocks them out. They also cling to the fact that, in seven matches on their home turf, they have never been beaten by English opposition.

This, however, is no ordinary English opposition. Chelsea soak up their early pressure, then have the best of the first-half chances. Wayne Bridge sends a right-foot shot narrowly wide of the far post after just three minutes. Didier Drogba then connects with a Frank Lampard cross, forcing keeper Nuno E Santo to push his header against the bar.

Damien Duff strikes on 33 minutes. A solo run is capped by a powerful strike which Nuno lets slip through his fingers to prove exactly why he is normally on the bench when Victor Baia is fit. The Porto game provides compelling evidence that Chelsea function best when playing 4-3-3. As the game progresses the lack of width in Mourinho's midfield diamond, part of tonight's 4-4-2 system, becomes all too apparent.

Diego responds with a stunning goal on the hour. Petr Cech is left rooted to the spot as the Brazilian playmaker sends a 25-yard volley scorching past him with such ferocity that it nearly leaves a hole in the net. Benni McCarthy then strikes with a header to inflict the first defeat on Chelsea in the Champions League and only the second reverse of the season.

In reality, this defeat is more damaging to Mourinho's pride than to his side's long-term prospects. Scott Parker is singled out for particularly harsh treatment, when he is berated at Oporto airport for failing to block Diego's second-half equalizer. Mourinho even goes as far as to question his players' motivation. 'My players were happy with the draw and looked comfortable but Porto had extra motivation.

'The night was a big sensation for me. I worked very hard to detach myself and did my best to win the game. It's a special stadium for me because for two years it was mine. I tried to come here to win and I am frustrated we lost.'

The Blues boss is seething at the defeat but insists it will not affect his build-up for Highbury. 'You can't make any relation between this match and Arsenal. If you could then I'd have played the team that will start against Arsenal – including Claude Makelele and Arjen Robben.'

Before this setback, Mourinho has lost just once in his 24 games in charge. The home supporters further ruined his night by taking out their early frustrations on Drogba and Gallas, who suffered abuse from every corner of the ground, with monkey chants drowned out only by the support of the travelling Chelsea faithful.

The worst came in the 18th minute when Drogba was clattered by Derlei. Mourinho and the rest of the Chelsea bench leapt on to the pitch to register their anger but the home fans responded with the re-emergence of the vile monkey chanting to mar what had previously been a good-natured contest. All in all, a fairly depressing evening.

> **Team**
>
> Cech, Gallas, Terry, Carvalho, Ferreira, Smertin (Tiago), Lampard, Parker, Bridge, Duff (Robben), Drogba (Kezman).

The possible opponents for Chelsea in the Champions League draw in Nyon are Real Madrid, Barcelona, Bayern Munich, PSV Eindhoven and Werder Bremen. David Beckham claims Europe's elite will be trembling at the prospect of drawing Real Madrid in the knockout phase. The England skipper was instrumental in Real's crucial win behind closed doors in Rome, as Ronaldo's early strike and a Figo double sealed victory over Roma.

For his part, Michael Owen says he would love to face an English club. 'We are very happy to have qualified after winning a very difficult game in Rome,' says Owen, who only played the last five minutes of the encounter. 'I would like to play Chelsea or Arsenal because I think it would be a very attractive fixture.'

Joe Cole meanwhile is hoping Chelsea will be paired with one of the big Spanish sides. He says, 'I'd love to play against either Barcelona or Real Madrid and I'm sure, whoever we play, the games are going to be very tight. Whoever we get, I'd like to think we'd have a very good chance of winning and making it through to the next stage.'

Mourinho is more specific: he wants to be paired with the Catalan giants. After all, he learned his trade at the Nou Camp under Bobby Robson. 'For emotional reasons, I'd like to play Barca. First of all I love the club and the city; I spent four incredible years there. And the second reason is because everyone says they're Europe's best, who play beautiful football. I'd like to play them.

'Everyone is tipping them to win the competition. They play great football and it would be two incredible matches. The Spanish leaders against the English leaders would be a fantastic game – the most powerful tie of the draw. But there are a group of fantastic teams we could play – Barca, Real Madrid, Bayern Munich, Werder Bremen and PSV – and they would all be tough. You always want to play the big teams, the big managers and the big players. But I don't like to play against Italians, so I'm glad we can't face AC Milan, Inter and Juventus.'

As group-winners, Arsenal and Chelsea get to play their first-leg games away. When the draw is made, Chelsea are matched against the 16-time Spanish title-winners Barcelona just as Mourinho predicted.

Barcelona have met Chelsea once before in the Champions League, at the quarter-final stage in April 2000. The Catalans overturned a 3–1 first-leg defeat at Stamford Bridge to go through 6–4 on aggregate after a 5–1 extra-time victory at the Nou Camp.

Mourinho shrugs off the dangers of facing the runaway La Liga leaders by claiming his number one priority is to see Chelsea crowned as English champions for the first time in 50 years. 'Chelsea are a strong team now – but we are in a fight with Arsenal, Manchester United and Everton. We are in a good position. I don't like the word fear in football because I don't believe in fear.

'In their league Barcelona are in an even better position because they have no opponents. Barcelona are alone. Real Madrid and Valencia are too far behind; Deportivo La Coruna have been very poor this season. Barcelona are in a comfortable position so maybe they can prepare for the Champions League in a different way to us.

'At Porto, I could rest eight or nine players before a Champions League game because I had the championship in my pocket by December. In the Premiership we have to fight until the last kick, so maybe they have an advantage. Week after week, match after match, it is harder in England than in Spain.

'I've never won the Premiership and I like to win new things. The Premiership is the ultimate test. It takes a great team to win the Champions League – but the great teams still need luck. There are almost 40 games in England and only the best team wins.'

Mourinho reckons he learned the skills that have made him Europe's hottest boss working under Bobby Robson and Dutchman Louis van Gaal at Barcelona. He left four years ago after helping break Chelsea hearts in that epic 6–4 Champions League quarter-final double bill. He says, 'I go back to Barcelona as European Champion and Chelsea manager. I have a friend in every corner, so it will be a very emotional time for me. But I am keen to play against them because they want to win and play football the pure way. Barcelona is more than a football club; it represents a country. Catalonia is for them a country and Barcelona is its face around the world.

'My son, Jose, was born in Barcelona and has a Spanish passport;

he is a little Catalan, so my blood is speaking here. But he will be supporting Chelsea.

'Chelsea are one of the best clubs in England; we hope they can be the biggest in a few years. Barcelona are a massive club but, as a football team, they are not better than us. When I was assistant manager there, we played Chelsea and they were two great games. Chelsea were a good team then, a young Gianfranco Zola with good players around him. It was Luca Vialli's time and they won a few trophies. We won almost everything at Barcelona.'

Meanwhile, Barcelona star Ronaldinho hints he might be interested in joining Chelsea at some stage in the future. Striker Samuel Eto'o, who has 12 goals for Barca, sets great store by his team-mate and says, 'Ronaldinho is worth half of Chelsea's players. That's our great advantage on the field.'

But Eto'o, who is African Footballer of the Year, insists Chelsea do not always get their man – he knows because Chelsea have missed out on him! The £18m ex-Real Mallorca star says, 'Several times I've been close to signing for Chelsea but the deal was never closed. Now they'll have me on the other side in the Champions League and they'll come out as losers. This is a very special game for everybody involved. The whole world seems to think Chelsea are invincible and the best team in Europe, but I want to help Barca prove that is not true.

'The attack of Chelsea? It does not worry me. For a start, Robben is injured and Drogba is not better than me. Ivory Coast have never beaten Cameroon. I am the best African player, not Drogba. All the world knows that. What has Drogba won? It is fair to say that Chelsea's defence is a very good one but they have not played Barcelona. John Terry, Carvalho and Paulo Ferreira are all good players but they will not be able to cope with my speed or the football of Ronaldinho and Deco. We all know that Petr Cech has not conceded a goal for a long time but then again he has not played against me.

'Playing Barcelona will be a nightmare for Chelsea at the Nou Camp and in London. We must be favourites for the tie because Barcelona are a better team than Chelsea. This game will be the best clash in Europe – the fans just can't wait for the games to start. Let me assure you I am not an arrogant person, but I have been preparing for this round with the maximum concentration. I want to play to 200 per cent because it is a final of champions for me. I dream that we beat Chelsea and then go on and win the Spanish title and Champions League final.'

Mourinho says, 'My dream final would be Chelsea v Arsenal. English football hasn't won enough in Europe; that's not right. It's time to put an end to that injustice.'

Chelsea continue to excel in their quest for the title until 'the blip' finally arrives, but from an unexpected quarter with the loss of one of their key players, Arjen Robben, who was kicked soon after scoring the early winner at Blackburn. Once the swelling subsides, the diagnosis is two cracks in the foot and an absence of at least six weeks. Barcelona boss Frank Rijkaard is delighted that Robben will miss their Champions League clash. 'The injury to Robben is bad news for Holland and Chelsea but excellent for Barcelona. We will not have to face one of the best European players of this moment and it will make playing them less complicated for us. Robben is the best forward Chelsea have – and Mourinho knows it.'

Rijkaard is a meticulous manager and has spent time analysing the way Chelsea play. 'I've seen some matches on the telly, they are a great team. Very functional ...'

That subtle put-down highlights Barcelona's contrasting reputation for playing football rich in finesse and skill. The personal battle of the coaches will be as fascinating as the on-field struggle. Though there are obvious similarities, both being sophisticated, 42-year-old multi-linguists oozing self-worth, there is a plain distinction. If Mourinho's searing ambition is motivated by his failures as a player who never came close to the first rank, Rijkaard will always form one point of a sublime triangle of Dutch talent alongside Ruud Gullit and Marco van Basten. Rijkaard has won the European Cup three times – twice with Milan and once with Ajax – and could become one of the few men to lift the trophy as both a player and manager.

Acknowledging Rijkaard's 'fantastic' playing legacy, Mourinho remarks that, as a manager, his counterpart 'has zero trophies and I have a lot of them'.

'I haven't met him yet,' Rijkaard replies. 'All I know is what we see on TV or read in the papers. Our papers are very interested in him because he worked here once.' Rijkaard is surprised by the possibility of verbal sparring. 'You call them mind games? How do they work?' After hearing a few examples of Mourinho's more cunning jibes, Rijkaard laughs loudly, 'Thank you! Thank you! I look forward to this kind of game. What has he said so far?'

The Dutch manager prefers to remain aloof. 'I didn't have a big reaction when our name came out with Chelsea. Even before the draw I said it doesn't matter who we play. When you're down to the last 16, there's not much difference between Team A and Team B. Maybe it's better we play Chelsea. In a clash between big teams, you know your players will concentrate. They have to play very well against Chelsea to go through.'

He recognises the danger. 'Chelsea have good team spirit and their defence is very strong. They are disciplined but they also have some wonderful players – especially in midfield. Robben is important to them because, when he is fit, he gives them something extra. They are also dangerous because they're being challenged to do great things. You can see they're hungry. So all this makes them one of the best teams in Europe.'

Rijkaard will find it hard to avoid talking about Mourinho. 'I can't say yet if I will like him. How can you really judge a man until you come face to face? Maybe I'll find out what he's really like over these next few weeks. I know he's very successful but we'll learn a little more about both him and his team. He can say the same for me. So, sure, when we finally meet, it could be quite a moment.'

Ronaldinho picks out Lampard as the biggest danger to his dreams. 'Lampard has been outstanding for Chelsea all season. Chelsea remind me very much of Barcelona. They have very good individual players all over the pitch, but it is their spirit that stands out above all else. Chelsea's strength is their defence, but also the fact that they play as a team. They all play for each other at all times. They have many great footballers. We must be aware of every single one of them for this tie.'

Deco takes a swipe at Mourinho's Chelsea for conquering a poor quality league. 'It tells you everything about the Premiership and how much easier it is than the Spanish league that Chelsea have won eight in a row during this season. The Premiership is full of mediocre and, frankly, very poor teams.'

Mourinho prepares Chelsea for his biggest game since arriving in English football. 'I have to defend what is mine. The Champions League is mine at the moment. I am the last winner as manager of the Champions League – so it is my competition. I have to try and fight for Chelsea and I have to try and fight for myself by defending my cup until the last moment. Maybe winning the Champions League enabled me to come to a big football country like this. The competition means a lot to me. At 42, I am very young as a manager. I have 15 more years to work in football. I hope to get that taste of winning the Champions League again. But it is so difficult to win. You can perform well, have a good team and have big ambition. But make one mistake and you are out of the competition – even if you don't deserve to be.'

In another swipe at Barca, Mourinho adds, 'Barcelona have a great club. But in 200 years of history, they have won the European Cup only once. I have been managing for a few years and I have already won the same amount.'

Mourinho feels Chelsea are not as good as his Porto side yet but he is working with better players. His squad are still two years from reaching the kind of technical standards that helped Porto to Champions League glory. Mourinho says, 'We have better players than the Porto squad of last year, but in my third year at Porto we had a better technical team. They knew everything I know. They knew how to adapt, change from system to system, when to press high or to block low.

'Porto won the Champions League in their third year – here at Chelsea it has been seven months. The contract I have with Chelsea is for four years. By the time we get to the third or fourth year then I think you will see my best Chelsea team. We still have a way to go. The beginning of the next season will be very important for us to make steps ahead. There are things I do not want to work on now. I really don't want to mix things before the players are ready on the tactical side. You can't jump phases, there has to be a steady progress, achieving things step by step. So Chelsea have the better players but maybe Porto had the better team.'

Chelsea's fate against Barca depends on how they cope with the absence of Robben. Mourinho's method of dealing with the problem is to ignore the Dutch winger completely. 'I don't want to think about Robben. The best way to face an injury to a very important player is to forget the player. I don't speak with him. When my fitness coach says he is ready to play, I will jump, but at this moment I don't want to think about him. He cannot play so I have to work and support the other players.

'I will never give missing Arjen Robben as an excuse for anything – we have players to work with without him. It's unfair to put more pressure on Damien Duff in Robben's absence. I didn't see Damien play for Blackburn in the flesh but I know the reason Chelsea bought him was because he was playing outstanding football there. But I doubt if he has had a better season than the one he is having. He has been fantastic.'

Mourinho has already formulated a plan he believes will neutralise Eto'o and Ronaldinho and his self-belief is illustrated by his suggestion that his first six months at Chelsea have already begun to transform the face of English football.

Chelsea's preferred 4-3-3 formation has been adopted by Manchester United, other Premiership sides and was tried – unsuccessfully – by Sven Goran Eriksson in the draw with Holland. 'The long-ball tactics still exist, but the traditional 4-4-2 is changing,' he says. 'In two years it will all be very different.'

Meanwhile, John Terry stars between the sticks in a training session at Stamford Bridge but twists his ankle. Terry and his team-mates thrill hundreds of children who have arrived for guided tours of the Stamford Bridge set-up. Despite hobbling, Terry does not disappoint the watching youngsters and signs all their autographs – as do the rest of Mourinho's men. He says, 'Ronaldinho is the one player in the world who stands out at the moment. His all-round game is great, with his skills and his quick feet so it will be good to play against him. But they've got quality all over the pitch: Eto'o looks fantastic and he's full of goals. However, we've got quality in our side too, and we'll be going to the Nou Camp full of confidence.'

Roman Abramovich is pictured next to European Footballer of the Year and possible transfer target Andriy Shevchenko at an Italian awards ceremony, as AC Milan prepare for their big Champions League tie with Manchester United.

After being dumped out of the FA Cup 1–0 at Newcastle, Chelsea fly direct from Newcastle to Barcelona on Sunday night and hold light training the next day at the city's Olympic stadium. Mourinho insists three injured players travel to Spain in a last-minute attempt to get them fit. The problem with Duff's knee and Gallas's groin does not deter Mourinho from bringing them to Barcelona in the belief they can recover in time.

There is also private optimism about Drogba's chances of recovering from a thigh strain in time. He has not played for Chelsea since their Carling Cup defeat of Manchester United and the player is told that he should be prepared to face Barcelona. Kezman is a shock potential starter at the Nou Camp alongside Gudjohnsen after Duff picked up a knee injury against the Magpies. The Blues are also missing Wayne Bridge, who left St James' Park with a broken ankle and lower leg, while Gallas is also struggling.

Mourinho recalls what he sees as the most significant moment from the last 12 months. 'My players are crazy to win something important. When we were in the USA last summer we were together 24 hours a day and talked a lot and exchanged feelings. The message that came over clear from that is that, while it is a club full of stars and rich players who have earned a lot of money, only Claude

Makelele and the ones I brought from Porto have won titles. The others: zero. When I said that to them, they said, "You are right, it's true." So I said, "If I'm right, why didn't YOU win anything? And if I'm right, why don't you try to follow my concepts and projects?" That is what we have done. I now have a very ambitious squad.'

So when Ronaldinho, Deco and co come calling, Mourinho will expect his 'three team leaders' to stand firm. 'Psychologically, the leaders are Terry and Lampard,' Mourinho explains. 'Tactically the leader for the organisation is Makelele.'

Meanwhile, Barca's quest for a first La Liga title since Mourinho was assistant to Louis van Gaal in 1999 comes closer as they open up a seven-point gap over Real Madrid. Deco scores both goals in Barcelona's 2–0 win over Real Mallorca, while Real lose 2–0 at home to Athletic Bilbao. The mood in the Catalan capital could hardly be better ahead of the visit of Chelsea.

Mourinho tells his players there is no room for doubt. 'You must be confident and act like this before this sort of match. I keep saying to the players that when you have a bad result or injuries you mustn't look back and forget what you have to do in the future. I can't say, "I don't have him or him, so we can't expect to get a good result." We must find another way. We still have many good players and have to adapt the way we're playing. We are without Robben and Duff so we have to change. When we go out there, we still have to fight for a good result. You have to think positively and realise there are 180 minutes, maybe more – and that it will not be easy for them in London.'

Mourinho proudly boasts he has *never* lost two games in a row as a manager. 'We are confident,' Mourinho says, before illustrating the point in a barbed answer to a journalist's question. 'In the eight or nine years since I was here I have progressed in life, I've evolved. You haven't.'

He then dispenses with the usual tactic of keeping his line-up plans close to his chest by naming what he believes will be the Barcelona team, followed by his own.

'We have one more session but I think Drogba plays, Gallas plays;

Duff I don't think so,' says Mourinho, before predicting the team Barcelona will field. Then he adds, 'You want to know my team? All right: Cech, Paulo, Ricardo, Terry, Gallas, Tiago, Makelele, Lampard, Cole, Drogba and Gudjohnsen.'

In typically mischievous style, Mourinho attempts to plant an element of uncertainty in Rijkaard's mind by naming his team early. Duff, he says, will not be fit. Yet Duff trains and has not given up hope of making a surprise appearance.

Rijkaard is reluctant to bite back and says, 'There is no need to respond.' But, when the former Dutch star is asked why he has given his players a couple of days off and not sent anyone on a spying mission to Stamford Bridge, while Chelsea are in Spain working hard, Rijkaard cuts loose. He says, 'Chelsea show up three days early, train behind closed doors and then announce their line-up. What was the point of training in secret then? But you can say what you like before the game – the match tells you the truth. Most coaches think that the players deserve to know the team rather than the press. But Chelsea are in an unusual situation now. They've just been knocked out of the FA Cup and Manchester United are closing in on them in the Premiership. Let's see how all that will affect them. A lot of times when people talk before games it's a sign that they aren't at ease with the match to come – not very calm. I'm not worried.'

Mourinho's bullishness during the build-up could backfire. As Ronaldinho observes, 'Chelsea may think they are motivated for the match. But Mourinho says he has never lost two games in a row as manager – and that has motivated us even more. Hopefully, we can make him suffer two defeats.'

WEDNESDAY, 23 FEBRUARY 2005

BARCELONA 2, CHELSEA 1

When the same two teams met in the Nou Camp four years ago, referee Anders Frisk dismissed full-back Celestine Babayaro and awarded Barcelona two penalties as the Spanish side romped to a

5–1 victory in extra-time. Blond-streaked Frisk is widely regarded as one of the top officials in world football, but games he is involved in rarely pass without the 42-year-old Swede leaving a lasting impression. So it proves this time.

Chelsea start off solidly in defence as Barcelona make good use of the flanks. Mourinho springs a major surprise by including Damien Duff – a day after insisting it was 'almost impossible' for the winger to recover from a knee injury. And it is Duff who speeds on to Lampard's pinpoint 40-yard pass to collect with precision control and then flick a cross towards the unmarked Joe Cole, which right-back Juliano Belletti slides in at the near post in the 33rd minute. Then after Belletti's own-goal rocks Barcelona, Didier Drogba misses a golden chance to put the tie beyond doubt a couple of minutes later, shooting wide with only keeper Victor Valdes to beat.

The game erupts in the 55th minute when Swedish referee Frisk dismisses Drogba after a legitimate attempt to reach a back-header in a challenge with Valdes. A series of rash challenges by Drogba leads up to his second-half dismissal – and his reluctance to leave the pitch may prompt a UEFA punishment. Both players go down, but Drogba picks up his second booking, having earned a first-half yellow card for a foul on Rafael Marquez. It leaves the Blues with ten men for the second game in a row. Their sense of injustice is heightened by Barca fans chanting racist abuse at Drogba – monkey chants fill the air as he trudges towards the visiting dugout.

Not long afterwards, Maxi Lopez squirms clear of William Gallas in a crowded area – after a move involving Ronaldinho and Samuel Eto'o – before finding a glimmer of space to angle a right-footer into the far corner. Worse follows in the 73rd minute when Lopez's mishit cross-shot from the right is left by Carvalho as Eto'o emerges from between two Blues defenders to slam home an eight-yard winner.

Mourinho has now suffered two losses in a row for the first time as a manager, but it is the manner of the defeat, the harsh dismissal of

Drogba, and a fracas at the interval and that push the manager into hyper drive.

The London club plans an official complaint about Rijkaard's conversation with the referee at half-time. Mourinho is upset at what he sees as fraternisation between the Swedish referee and Barcelona's manager, plus the fact that Chelsea went down to ten men so soon after the interval. It is a carbon copy of Mourinho's rant accusing Sir Alex Ferguson of attempting to influence referee Neale Barry during the first leg of last month's Carling Cup semi-final. Mourinho is so angry that he refuses to take part in any post-match interview, a violation of UEFA regulations that is likely to result in a fine.

There are also suggestions of a scuffle involving Rijkaard's assistant and Mourinho, in which it is reported that Henk Ten Cate assaulted the Chelsea manager with a kick to the backside. Though Chelsea take no steps to indicate the thrust of their submission to UEFA, they do move to douse these particular wildfire rumours.

There has, however, definitely been a dispute between Ten Cate and Chelsea's goalkeeping coach Silvino Louro as well as their head first-team coach Baltemar Brito. The Chelsea coaches walked on the wrong side of the players' tunnel – where a barrier separates home and away players and staff – precipitating heated words and a minor scuffle. Mourinho also booted Barca midfielder Xavi Hernandez out of the Chelsea dressing room. He refused to shake Xavi's hand.

Later Frank Rijkaard confirms that he did chat to Anders Frisk but insists, 'I was not the cause of the incident. I said, "Hello, pleased to meet you," to the referee. I said something about the game in a very polite and informal way. So the reaction of the Chelsea side was a little bit exaggerated. It is not true that the referee went into our dressing room and I am glad this rumour has come out because now it all seems even more ridiculous to me. Maybe they want to start something and make it worse than it is.'

Defender Rafael Marquez accuses the Londoners of making

excuses. 'Everybody could see who was the better team out on the pitch. Chelsea are just angry because of the defeat. Everyone had talked about Super Chelsea before the game, but I didn't see anything super out there. The only team that played football was us. When a team just waits for their opponents or the referee to make a mistake then it makes you angry. Even when Chelsea scored, we weren't desperate because they had done nothing.'

Ten Cate also weighs in, 'Football is supposed to be for fun. The paying public don't go and buy tickets to go and see the boring football that Chelsea played. They had very few shots on goal while we had many. We could have won by even more goals. The only team playing proper football was us.'

Jose Mourinho's philosophy, which he restates, is that 'when the game is finished, the next one has already started'. The return at Stamford Bridge will be a true test of his managerial mettle.

Team

Cech, Terry, Ferreira, Gallas, Carvalho, Makelele, Lampard, Cole (Johnson), Duff (Gudjohnsen), Tiago (Smertin), Drogba.

The Dutch contingent are ganging up on Mourinho. Johan Cruyff backs up the 'boring' attack by Barca, while Tottenham head coach Martin Jol maintains there is nothing wrong with speaking to officials – it is a common occurrence in European football. Cruyff says, 'I'm sure Mourinho is going to be the best coach in the world but I don't support his type of football. It bores me to sleep. I recognise that Chelsea defend very well but it's not what I want to see. Chelsea are a copy of Porto, a max-mix of English and Portuguese football but playing only on defence.'

Mourinho finally gives part of his version of the row with Rijkaard and Frisk in his media press conference ahead of the Carling Cup final. Mourinho maintains that his Barcelona counterpart and the referee talked 'in a private place' rather than the tunnel. 'Sometimes you can talk to the referee, but usually in a common space. It is different in a tunnel with 20 people around. You can't say you can't communicate or there should be a wall. But it is another thing to talk to a referee in a private place.'

In his weekly column for Portuguese sports supplement *Record Dez*, Mourinho calls for Italian Pierluigi Collina to take charge of the second leg. 'Something was said to me in London, that the referee will be Collina, the best in the world, independent, above all pressures. The perfect referee.

'In Barcelona, the referee was inefficient. It was an adulterated result. When Deco produced a ridiculous dive in the area, the referee didn't show him a yellow card. When I saw Rijkaard enter the referee's changing room at half-time, I couldn't believe it. When Drogba was sent off, I wasn't surprised. When the game finished I breathed a sigh of relief. Drogba wasn't unlucky. Unlucky is when you waste a shot in front of Valdes. The red card was not unlucky. It is a fact. It is wrong.

'In Barcelona the team that played best won. However, they only did that against ten; I think the game would never have been lost if it had been 11 against 11.'

UEFA spokesman William Gaillard says, 'We have made no decision at all on this [who will referee the second leg]. The normal procedure would be for it to be decided at the end of this week. If Mourinho thinks it is Collina, you will have to ask why he thinks this. We have eight excellent referees and eight ties, the only thing we do know is that it will not be Anders Frisk because we never have the same referee for both legs.'

Claudio Ranieri is sacked as Valencia coach just eight months into his second spell in charge of the Spanish champions. The decision is taken at a board meeting brought forward following the club's shock elimination from the UEFA Cup by Steaua Bucharest.

Hours before the Carling Cup final, chief executive Peter Kenyon confirms the club will be forwarding a report to UEFA about Rijkaard's dialogue with Frisk, but the complaint will not be heard until the tie is over.

Medical experts predicted Arjen Robben would be out for six weeks, but Jean-Pierre Meersseman, the Belgian chiropractor who is treating Robben, believes the Dutchman has a chance of facing Barcelona.

Robben has been receiving treatment from the AC Milan club doctor following the personal intervention of Roman Abramovich who phoned vice-chairman Adriano Galliani to request the club's medical coordinator fly to London to see the player. Meersseman says, 'Abramovich asked Galliani if I could treat Robben and I suppose he said yes because I came to London. They are very good friends and Galliani was happy to help. There has been a great relationship between Chelsea and AC Milan for the last couple of years. Abramovich knows Galliani well and the Russians are on good terms with our Prime Minister, Silvio Berlusconi.'

It is highly unusual for one club to provide such assistance to a direct rival and it is a measure of the extent of Abramovich's influence. 'I hope he can be back in time to play against Barcelona and I will try to help him make that happen,' says Meersseman. 'I put everything right with Arjen's foot the last time I saw him 12 days ago. He had a fracture on the cuboid bone and his third metatarsal. I corrected one fracture and we adjusted the bones around it. I also needed to balance the muscles and we worked on his posture too. I know he was pleased with what I did and now he is running again.'

Barca's French star Ludovic Giuly is given the all-clear to play at Stamford Bridge but Rafael Marquez is out. It is a boost for Barca who had said earlier in the week that they did not think Giuly would play.

The pain of the Champions League calamity against Monaco last season still gives Eidur Gudjohnsen sleepless nights. 'Whenever I am reminded of what happened in the competition last year it is something that keeps me awake. First of all we came so close and secondly it would have been a fantastic achievement for me to go into the Champions League final. There was a real feeling among the players that we had a great chance because we were so close.

'We were 1–1 in Monaco with a man advantage on the pitch and when you think back to that night it just looks like a cock-up really.

Then we got off to a flier at home and were 2–0 ahead and we were thinking, "This is it, we just need to see this game out." But they hit us on the break just before half-time and got back into it. It deflated the team a little bit. We had the tie won twice, but maybe it was due to a lack of experience. We should have settled for the draw in Monaco.'

Fulfilling the prediction made by Mourinho, Pierluigi Collina is named as the man in the middle for the Barcelona game. Collina, who handled the World Cup final between Brazil and Germany in 2002 and the 1999 Champions League final between Manchester United and Bayern Munich, will quit in the summer for a desk job as *designatore*, the man who appoints referees for Serie A fixtures.

Frank Lampard calls on Chelsea fans to generate a special atmosphere. 'We have to use our crowd to help get a result in the second leg. What happened with Didier in Barcelona was difficult. We were in a really good position with 11 men but the sending-off changed that. It was a harsh sending-off but at a place like that, with the noise of the crowd, decisions were going to go their way. Now it's our turn. We have to stop them scoring which will be tough with the players they've got, but it's achievable.'

The all-for-one mentality fostered by Mourinho should give Chelsea the edge as Lampard says, 'The pre-game talks we do are really good. We do them in a huddle, with our arms round each other's shoulders and everybody – the physio, everyone – is involved. John Terry's really into it from the start when he does his but I build mine up a bit more. I gave the one before the Barcelona game – there were three or four F-words but not as many as you might get in John's. There were a couple of stutterers at first and some of the lads like William Gallas were a bit shy. But it's a good thing for us – it helps every member of the squad feel important and that they've got a role.'

According to 'Lamps', revenge is in the air. 'There's been a lot of talking from them since the game; they've been giving out stick to our manager, our team and to certain individuals. You can ignore it or say it doesn't bother you, but when I see opponents talking about us, I want to do something about it. That's why I can't wait for them to come over here. I'm certainly surprised that experienced pros like theirs have spoken out halfway through a game like this. They've been a bit premature because they've now got to face us on our own pitch and in front of our own fans and it will be very different to how it was at the Nou Camp. It's all got a bit personal, and that's given the match even more of an edge.'

Raising the stakes further, Ronaldinho suggests Chelsea are a dirty team. 'I was bruised all over after the game and I can count on half of one hand the number of Chelsea players who played the game in a clean fashion.'

As the verbal war intensifies, Mourinho changes the time of his pre-match press conference so he can have the last word. Originally, Mourinho was going to speak at 4.30pm. Now he plans to give his sermon at 7pm, half an hour after Frank Rijkaard's.

In Barcelona it was Mourinho who spoke first before the match and took the unusual step of naming his own side, as well as predicting Barcelona's team. This time Mourinho wants the benefit of hearing Rijkaard's address to the media before he offers his own thoughts. He believes the psychological warfare can have a significant impact on the result.

The Dutch coach is bemused by the change of times for the press conferences but feels to complain would be to play into Mourinho's hands. Rijkaard can't resist a dig when he jokes Robben could line up for Chelsea. When asked to guess tonight's Chelsea team, Barca boss Rijkaard says, 'One, Robben. Two, Robben. Three, Robben.'

Rijkaard attempts to broker a fragile peace, even if Mourinho cannot resist restoking the fire. Rijkaard is in conciliatory mood after a fortnight of squabbling, the likes of which the competition has rarely seen. 'Jose is doing a great job at Chelsea,' he says.

Mourinho provocatively suggests he would prefer Frisk to be in charge. 'If you ask me which referee I would want for the game, I would say Frisk, because maybe he would help us in the same way that he helped Barcelona. Instead we have a referee who will not have a direct influence on the result.'

Mourinho does pay the Spanish club a compliment. Again, though, it contains a sting in the tail. 'Barcelona have great qualities and play such beautiful football, that they should not have to dive so much.'

Chelsea can go through with a 1–0 win. But Robben has lost his race against time to make the bench. Instead Parker is set for a surprise comeback as substitute. After all the mind games and criticisms, Joe Cole expresses Chelsea's hunger for success. 'Victory would be very sweet, with all the controversy and drama that has gone on,' says Cole. 'That's what inspires us.'

Around 42,500 will pack into the Bridge, but the club with ambitions to be the biggest in Europe could have sold another 10,000 seats with ease.

TUESDAY, 8 MARCH 2005

CHELSEA 4, BARCELONA 2
(CHELSEA WIN 5–4 ON AGGREGATE)

Chelsea earn a place in the folklore of the European game with this magnificent victory in a spectacle of explosive drama and swaying fortunes. Having been accused of negative tactics in the Nou Camp, Mourinho bravely fields Mateja Kezman just ahead of Eidur Gudjohnsen. Kezman makes an immediate impact, surging down the right flank after Frank Lampard wins possession before producing an inviting cross for his strike partner. Gudjohnsen's first touch takes him past Gerard, before he lunges forward to power his shot past Victor Valdes with just eight minutes gone. That is, in itself, enough to take Chelsea through, but their tails are up and Lampard volleys over the bar on the turn from just eight yards out.

When Joe Cole's shot is deflected, Valdes can only parry the ball and Lampard is on to it in a flash to finish. 'Boring, boring Chelsea' rings out ironically around Stamford Bridge. Then Cole produces more midfield inspiration, driving a through-ball for Duff to scamper onto and roll underneath the body of the stranded Valdes.

That should be game over. Instead, Barca surge back. Petr Cech denies Samuel Eto'o at full stretch and Ronaldinho rises to direct a bullet header just inches wide from a Barca corner. Then Paulo Ferreira, with his back to the ball, handles unnecessarily, Ronaldinho converts the ensuing penalty even though Cech guesses right and gets a hand to the ball. The tie is transformed. Barcelona only need one goal to go through and, even though Cech again performs acrobatics to deny Deco, Ronaldinho conjures one of the greatest goals ever in this tournament – an all-time classic!

Swivelling his foot and his hips with Ricardo Carvalho in front of him, and with minimal back-lift, he crafts a shot that curls into the far corner, leaving Cech motionless. Eto'o also skims a shot over the bar from Ronaldinho's inspired through-ball, but Chelsea rally and Cole strikes the post, with Duff just failing to convert the rebound as he stretches. And that is all in the first half.

It is so action-packed that Ferreira can be forgiven for believing the full 90 minutes are up when he swaps shirts at half-time with Ronaldinho! Ferreira is withdrawn soon after the restart after suffering a torrid time at Ronaldinho's hands, with Glen Johnson the next to be run ragged by the Brazilian.

However, John Terry and Lampard lead the revival as the match continues to fizz with excitement. Lampard twice comes close, but Cech scrambles Juliano Belletti's long-range effort around the post and then produces an incredible save from Carles Puyol. Valdes is also equal to a thunderbolt from Cole, while Lampard and Gudjohnsen both threaten. Pushing forward, Chelsea leave themselves open to the counter-attack and, when Cech tips Andres Iniesta's shot onto the post, Eto'o fails to punish Johnson's hesitation and blazes over. That is the let-off Chelsea need. When Terry heads home Duff's corner, Barcelona's pleas for a foul on Valdes are ignored.

Mourinho immediately introduces Tiago for Gudjohnsen and

then Huth soon follows amid a frantic final spell as Deco flashes an injury-time free-kick just wide.

When the final whistle blows and Terry's 76th-minute header has sent the Blues roaring into the last eight after a nail-biting tussle, Mourinho dances along the touchline and flings himself into an ecstatic sea of players – later he insists Chelsea's amazing win is sweeter than his Champions League triumph at Porto.

Mourinho says, 'I'm so happy to beat the side supposed to be the best in the world. Even after I won the Champions League final with Porto, I did not celebrate like I did tonight. Tonight the game was changing every five minutes and the result was in doubt right up to the whistle.

'I was just about to put Robert Huth on at centre-forward when we scored, so I put him on at centre-half! Had they scored in the last seconds, we'd have gone out. That's why it felt so good to win. There was absolutely no time to breathe and enjoy the moment but this has been an unbelievable night and a magnificent game. We scored four, hit the post and should have scored six or seven. Barcelona scored two and could have had four or five. But the reality is over two legs we've scored five and they have four.

'That shows the difference between the teams. Over 180 minutes the best team goes through. But the point of the night is not beating Barcelona. The point is getting to the quarter-finals.'

Now it is Rijkaard's turn to feel aggrieved. He accuses Chelsea of lies and insults after being involved in a tunnel brawl following taunts from Chelsea's Portuguese scout Andre Villas. Villas sparked a brawl by blowing kisses at Rijkaard after the final whistle. Rijkaard had to be pulled away by heavy-handed stewards before Eto'o, Ronaldinho and Puyol all waded into the fray.

Rijkaard rages, 'I am always bitter when I lose and tonight I am even more bitter because of all the lies they told before this game and the things they created. Some guy came forward and insulted our bench and I don't want to say what I think of him. I wanted to win this game even more than usual because of all the stuff surrounding the build-up. So it hurts me even more to be leaving after this defeat.'

The club's astonishing victory is marred by ugly scenes and Eto'o claims he was called a monkey by a steward. 'Chelsea going through is a disaster for football,' he tells the Barcelona-based newspaper *El Mundo Deportivo*. 'And if this team wins the Champions League, it would make you want to retire. With so much money and so many players, what they do is not football.'

Steve Clarke has a different viewpoint. 'We think we are one of the best teams in Europe and having a deficit from the first leg made it difficult for us to go through. The boys went out with great belief and got there in the end. We felt a little aggrieved that we lost the first game and set out to put that right. It was a very good start and I think we proved we can be an attacking force if we have to be. We've proved that all season. We are formidable at home and set out to put them under pressure.'

Chelsea captain Terry has the knack of scoring vital goals – but there's been nothing to match his late winner. Terry says, 'What a great feeling. It's right up there with the best. Our pitch is a lot tighter than the one at the Nou Camp and we knew that if we could put them under pressure, they wouldn't like it. I don't care about the things their players said before the game. Today is about Chelsea. That sent out a message to the whole of Europe. There's still a long way to go and a lot of quality teams left, but I'm sure there will have been a lot of people watching who are afraid of us now.'

Abramovich appears in the dressing room as usual at the end. Gudjohnsen observes, 'Mr Abramovich likes to soak up the atmosphere, see how the lads react. Every win gives you pleasure but this was extra special with the magnitude of a match with Barcelona and all that had been said. You can say what you want in the press, but the real answers are delivered on the football pitch. That's where you answer every critic. Chelsea have gone from a big club to a massive club. The manager has given us a winning mentality. We work together; there are no individuals. There is such a good team spirit that starts with John and Frank. It's important the Englishmen let the foreign players know the culture of English football. I'm also considered English!'

Team

Cech, Ferreira (Johnson), Terry, Carvalho, Gallas, Makelele, Cole, Lampard, Duff (Huth), Kezman, Gudjohnsen (Tiago).

According to Frank Lampard, Chelsea's amazing triumph was inspired by criticism from the Spanish giants. 'A lot was said from the Spanish side before this game but I think we showed a lot of people in Europe that we have the character and ability. The idea that we're boring was shown to be wrong. I thought that all the talk from Barcelona between matches was a bit strong because it was only half-time. I think that's part of the reason why we started so strongly. It gave us an extra edge. Some of Barcelona's possession play was fantastic but the game's not all about possession.

'I was still confident at half-time that we would win the game. We just had to be patient. Barcelona have done a lot of talking but we were clever enough to realise that there were 90 minutes to go. The performance we put in shows we're a top, top team. We're an English team with a lovely mix of English spirit, great foreign players and a foreign manager who is very tactically aware and he got straight into the spirit of the English game. It was one of the most satisfying games I've played in and is up there with the Champions League win over Arsenal last season.'

Of all people, Johan Cruyff is now backing the Blues. 'Chelsea could be European champions thanks to having one fundamental player – Lampard. I looked at the Chelsea team and I thought that Lampard would really fit in well in the Barcelona team. He would make Barcelona stronger in midfield. At the same time he would benefit from playing for Barcelona. He is a very attacking player and Barcelona always play attacking football. He would score far more goals. One other player who would be good for Barcelona is Duff. He is one of the few players who can really play on the wing. Barcelona are a really good footballing team. They are a team who use their wingers, and on the left he would really give them something special. Barca failed in defence because they played too many horizontal balls against a rival that is dangerous in this type of game.

'Mourinho makes his team play defensive all the time. I have no joy in watching Chelsea. It is a shame because I like English football. But Chelsea do not play like the English. They play like the Portuguese: defensive and only looking for counter-attacks.'

With Real Madrid crashing out at Juventus, there are no Spanish teams in the European Cup quarter-finals for the first time in 12 years. But some of the great names of European football still stand between Chelsea and a place in the last four. The quarter-finalists are made up of six former European champions, with the other two places going to Chelsea and Lyon. Clubs from the same countries are no longer kept apart in the draw, so it is possible that Chelsea and Liverpool could meet in the next round in what would be a repeat of the Carling Cup final.

David Beckham is tipping Chelsea. 'Mourinho has been there and done it and will have that experience for his players and his team. Seeing the way Chelsea beat Barcelona and the way they've been performing all season, they have to be major contenders to win the Champions League this season. They're the new *galacticos* because of the way they've been playing. They have the money of Roman Abramovich to keep taking them on as a club. They also have a new young manager and no one has seen anything like him before. Mourinho has got the confidence and the arrogance to keep the pressure off his players and you have to respect him for that. Chelsea have a very good mixture of excellent young English players and talented foreigners who have come in and performed right from the off. People thought it would take quite a while for all their new signings to gel. But they've won trophies straight away.'

Meanwhile, referee Anders Frisk announces that worries over his own and his family's safety have prompted him to quit refereeing. 'The threats toward me have escalated the last few weeks after the Barcelona–Chelsea game,' Frisk says on Sweden's football federation website. Frisk, ironically a big Chelsea fan, says he has received death threats since the match. 'It's not worth carrying on ... My safety and the safety of my family goes before anything else. These last few weeks have been the worst of my life. I still say that what I did in Barcelona was correct.'

Frisk tells the newspaper *Aftonbladet*, 'Chelsea have supporters in many parts of the world, so all of them [the threats] didn't come from England. Soon it will be impossible to referee a Champions League match if the clubs can't accept defeat or a player being sent off.'

Mourinho is blamed by Volker Roth, chairman of UEFA's Referees Committee, for the incidents that led to Frisk's retirement. Roth says, 'People like Mourinho are the enemy of football. It's the coaches who whip up the masses and make them threaten people to death. We can't accept that one of our best referees is forced to quit because of this.' Swiss referee Urs Meier, who suffered a hate campaign by England fans after disallowing a Sol Campbell 'goal' against Portugal at Euro 2004, says, 'It's not OK for a coach to put this much pressure on a referee. He [Mourinho] has to be punished.'

But Mourinho insists he is not to blame. 'Mr Roth, he has only two ways out – he apologises or he will be sued. I regret that Frisk has decided to leave football. If as some people say his decision is associated with the criticism of his exhibition in the match against Barcelona, I find it odd. Every day, everywhere, there are criticisms like these from coaches, directors and players. It is a normal situation. A referee with the experience of Mr Frisk would not take such a drastic decision because of criticism of his performance at Barcelona. If there are other motives I do not know them and I would like them to be known. If it has something to do with the threats – which should obviously be condemned – then it is a police case.'

Sepp Blatter, the FIFA president, calls on football professionals to show greater respect to officials. 'I am appalled by the verbal attacks directed at referees and it is often such extreme behaviour that sparks off trouble among supporters.'

Mourinho faces a ban from the touchline and the dressing room for the quarter-finals if he continues his war of words with UEFA. Gaillard, UEFA's director of communications, confirms that Mourinho's latest outburst has been 'added to the file'.

UEFA distance themselves from claims by Roth that Mourinho is an 'enemy of football'. Spokesman William Gaillard says, 'Roth has our full support and respect but he's not a UEFA employee. He was reacting as a private person, a referee. UEFA have never said Jose Mourinho is an enemy of football. We are looking into respect for referees as a whole. There is nothing in our statement about Chelsea or Mourinho.

'UEFA have never said that Mourinho caused Frisk to resign. This is a big logical jump. All we're saying is that some statements from managers and players are misconstrued by the public at large who are not mentally stable.'

Mourinho's conduct in Barcelona will be considered by UEFA's disciplinary body. 'It was never Mourinho's intention to whip up feeling against Frisk, but we would ask all managers to be careful and refrain from making these statements,' says Gaillard. 'We want to have a good relationship with Chelsea. No one becomes a pariah. When the Chelsea delegation come for the draw tomorrow they will be warmly received by us.'

Behind the scenes, though, friction remains, with UEFA leaking the substance of Chelsea's response as to why they took the field late for the second half – because they were 'too nervous' – and as to why Mourinho failed to attend the mandatory press conference – because he was too upset. A high-ranking source on UEFA's control and disciplinary body lets it be known that 'eyebrows will be raised both about what they did and about their evidence'. Clearly an irate UEFA do not accept Chelsea's version of events: that Rijkaard entered Frisk's room at half-time.

Mourinho maintains he is still anxious to avoid the Italian sides in the draw. 'They are the most difficult teams to play against in Europe, as you can see by their records. Playing an Italian team is not the same as Spanish or French. We must be a team with thinking qualities. You can't play with the heart or by instinct. You need to be clever enough to play with the brain.'

Bayern chairman Karl-Heinz Rummenigge wants to avoid Chelsea, describing them as 'one of the strongest teams in the Champions League. We would prefer to avoid them at this stage. If we are to meet them, then I would prefer it to be one round later.'

In the event, the draw is intriguing, pairing Chelsea with Bayern, AC Milan with Inter Milan and outsiders Olympique Lyon and PSV Eindhoven together. Liverpool play Juventus for the first time since the Heysel Stadium disaster at the 1985 European Cup final in which 39 fans died after a riot by Liverpool supporters.

So it's sod's law for Rummenigge as Bayern get the draw he did not want. It will be the first time the pair have met in European competition. The winners will be matched against the winners of Juventus versus Liverpool in the semi-final.

Bayern Munich boss Felix Magath claims, 'Three months ago we would have had no chance against Chelsea. But the winter break we had in Germany will make a big difference and now is the ideal time to strike against Chelsea.'

The first leg at Stamford Bridge will be Chelsea's 49th game, six more than Bayern, who had a six-week break over the Christmas and New Year period. Chelsea have never lost a tie to a German team. Mourinho says, 'There are no easy adversaries; there are only feelings and facts. Everybody wished for Lyon or PSV, but I wasn't that keen on Lyon because they are an extremely organised team. They are a second Porto. Last season if it hadn't been Porto, it would have been them. They are a true team. Bayern are powerful, they have good players and are a typically German team.'

The Germans are going for a treble of their own and director of football Uli Hoeness is full of bravado. 'Chelsea, with the away game first, was exactly the draw I wanted. Chelsea have a good team but we showed against Arsenal we can raise ourselves to the task. This is a super draw.'

Bayern also take the opportunity to confirm their interest in Chelsea's German centre-back, Robert Huth. Hoeness says, 'We have already spoken with Chelsea and his agent.' Jurgen Klinsmann, Germany's national coach, says Huth must play regularly to be certain of a place at the World Cup. The £5m-rated centre-half comments, 'I've always said I would be interested in playing in Germany. Obviously I have the pressure to play for a club where I will be guaranteed first-team football because I know I need that to stand a chance of playing in the World Cup.'

Huth backtracks within days. 'I'm staying here [at Chelsea], unless the club wants to get rid of me. It's not an issue, even if some people say it is.'

Didier Drogba makes a public apology to referee Anders Frisk. 'I would like to apologise to Mr Frisk if I might have, in any way, prompted him to end his refereeing career,' he tells French television channel TF1. 'I really hope he will change his mind. Soccer needs great referees and Mr Frisk is one of them. Everyone makes mistakes and referees are human, we have to accept that.'

The Swede says he will not go back on his decision despite efforts by UEFA and the game's worldwide body FIFA to persuade him to change his mind. In an interview with the *Sunday Times*, Frisk describes the period after the game in Barcelona as 'the worst 16 days of my life'. Without naming Mourinho directly, Frisk is quoted as saying, 'He violated my integrity. When you attack something that is so important to refereeing and so important to my culture, as well as to this fantastic hobby I have had for the last 26 years, of course you [inflict] hurt.'

Mourinho drops his threat of legal action against Roth and has privately promised not to criticise match officials in public as part of a peace deal between the club and the European game's governing body.

Mourinho is finally charged with bringing the game into disrepute by UEFA. Assistant manager Steve Clarke and security officer Les Miles are also in the dock for 'wrong and unfounded statements' after the tie in Barcelona. A statement is issued by UEFA: 'These charges relate to making false declarations, notably in the complaint sent by Chelsea following the UEFA Champions League match against Barcelona on February 23. By further disseminating these wrong and unfounded statements, Chelsea allowed their technical staff to deliberately create a poisoned and negative ambience amongst the teams and to put pressure on the refereeing officials.'

The trio face fines or touchline bans. In response, Chelsea will only say that they are 'reviewing their position'. Mourinho has blown any chance of covertly getting around any restrictions that may be imposed. UEFA will be wise to certain passages in his authorised biography in which he boasts of using a 'small, sophisticated telecommunications device' to relay tactical messages and order substitutions when he previously faced a touchline ban while manager of Porto.

William Gaillard issues a detailed and highly damaging set of charges, which include 'basically using lies as a pre-match tactic'. He accuses Chelsea of 'trying to qualify for the next round by putting pressure on referees and officials'. He says, 'There is a clear contradiction. They say Clarke and Miles saw the meeting but we know by looking at that, from where they were, they could not have seen anything. Then Mr Mourinho says in a signed article that he was the one who saw it, which again is false. What we do know from the reports from the referee and the venue director is that Mr Mourinho came out of the dressing room and shouted in a quite aggressive way at Anders Frisk, "Can I also come into your dressing room?"' UEFA will even use plans of the stadium at the hearing to prove that Chelsea have concocted their story.

Who saw what in a tunnel is normally a petty issue, but the UEFA hierarchy is furious as Mourinho keeps casting doubt over the integrity of its staff.

After discussions with senior UEFA officials at the draw, Chelsea are prepared for disciplinary action, but the force with which it is delivered comes as a shock to many at Stamford Bridge. After Gaillard's remarks, they can expect no leniency. UEFA are also awaiting reports about the brawling at the end of the second leg at Stamford Bridge.

Chelsea are standing by their original allegations and considering their legal position. Chelsea are also seething at the inflammatory language. Senior figures fear the club have already been found guilty and some are even questioning the independence of the Control and Disciplinary Board.

Chelsea demand that Mourinho gets a personal hearing. Under UEFA rules disciplinary matters are usually dealt with via paper submissions, though in exceptional circumstances they will allow oral evidence. Six of the nine members of the Contol and Disciplinary Body are or have been UEFA match delegates. The chairman of the body is Josep Luis Vilaseca – a Spaniard with links to Barcelona – but UEFA insist members of the panel are neutral.

Whatever judgment is made, Uli Hoeness insists he wants Mourinho in the dugout against Bayern. 'We hope Mourinho is in the dugout for both of the games. We want to meet Chelsea at their best and that means with their coach on the bench. It would be a real shame if he could not guide his team from the dugout.'

To add to a growing sense of the absurd, there are media reports that the visitors' dressing room at the Bridge was trashed by Barcelona's stars and there appears to be photographic evidence that wood panelling was damaged.

And just as UEFA are attempting to curb Mourinho's excesses, the Chelsea coach is to have his own television show! The 50-minute live show will be broadcast monthly in Portugal and, given that Mourinho is said to be 'willing to talk about anything but politics', there is potential for more controversy. The first show is scheduled for 18 April at 9pm – after the watershed.

Meanwhile, chairman Bruce Buck meets with chief executive Peter

Kenyon to plan Chelsea's defence as William Gaillard accuses the club of turning their problems with UEFA into a vendetta. Gaillard is a central character in the feud. A former media director of the International Air Transport Association, he had to reassure the public about worldwide airline safety in the aftermath of 9/11. Gaillard, 53, quit to become UEFA director of communications a year ago.

Chelsea's lawyers are trying to convince the disciplinary panel to dismiss the case and will cite Article 6 of the European Convention on Human Rights, governing the right to a fair trial. Mourinho reportedly says, 'They have taken sides without listening to our side of things and we have already been found guilty before UEFA passes judgment. We simply passed on what we saw – not in my case because I could not see, but those who work with me saw. And when they tell me what they saw I believe them.' The quotes attributed to Mourinho in the newspaper *La Vanguardia* provide an untimely reminder of his ability to court trouble. Chelsea move swiftly to deny that Mourinho uttered the words.

All in all, the situation has reached a farcical stage, with Chelsea saying that Mourinho did not say something about an event that UEFA say did not happen.

On the eve of the hearing, a five-game ban to include the Champions League final is being touted. But Chelsea stick to their line that Steve Clarke and Les Miles saw Frank Rijkaard in an area forbidden to coaching and playing staff and reported their concerns to Jose Mourinho. They are also claiming that there are many inaccuracies and discrepancies in UEFA's report.

In the event, Mourinho is handed a two-match touchline ban and a 20,000 Swiss francs (£8,900) fine, Clarke and Miles are reprimanded and the club receives a 75,000 Swiss francs penalty (£33,000). Significantly UEFA withdraws its key allegation that the club manufactured a conspiracy that 'created a poisoned and negative ambience'; UEFA privately concede Gaillard overstepped his authority.

Mourinho stays away from the hearing. Peter Limacher, head of

UEFA disciplinary services, says, 'As far as the touchline ban is concerned, a team manager who is suspended from carrying out his function may follow the match, for which he is suspended, from the stands only. He is not allowed in the dressing room, tunnel or technical area before and during the match and he is not allowed to get in contact with his team.'

Claude Makelele is not too worried about the ban. 'Jose's absence will not affect us totally although it will be a blow. Mourinho has a massive presence and having him on the bench helps us enormously. Mourinho is a marvellous boss and can change a game with his instructions. That talent makes him the best boss there is. He has the ability to think on his feet regarding his substitutions and the positional or tactical changes to the shape of the team. We just look to Mourinho on the bench and we instantly know what we are doing and what we need to correct.'

Chelsea are unbeaten in their last nine home Champions League games – their last defeat was against Besiktas in 2003 – but Bayern Munich striker Roy Makaay reckons Chelsea are weak at the back and have taken too much for granted. He says, 'I know Mourinho from my time in Spain when he was Bobby Robson's assistant. Now he is the coach and things are going well for him, but the good results are perhaps going to his head. I don't like it that he takes it for granted that they will knock us out. They say that Chelsea have the best defence in Europe, but they still haven't played against Bayern. Playing the return leg in Munich will give us a slight advantage, but we can't afford to drop our levels of concentration. Maybe this fame that they have will end after these two games.'

Germany's national newspaper, *Bild*, does not mince its words either. 'And you thought Bayern were arrogant? Meet Chelsea's manager-lout' is their headline, while underneath are some of Mourinho's more outrageous quotes.

Meanwhile rumours spread that Mourinho is set to quit Chelsea over the club's failure to fully support him against UEFA. The club are not appealing against UEFA's decision, believing that this would almost certainly lead to a longer ban for their outspoken coach. Roman Abramovich flies in to London to talk with Mourinho, something he always does before a game. But this time the headlines shout, 'Crisis!' Mourinho's agent, Jorge Mendes, joins the talks to provide even more 'evidence' that Mourinho's future is on the line.

Mendes is there to help deliver the message – some of Europe's biggest clubs are understood to have been in contact, with tentative enquiries as to whether Mourinho would be keen to move. However, Mendes is not demanding an improved contract or making threats. He wants reassurances for his client.

Mourinho, though, is not genuinely close to resigning, but he and his employers realise that the matter has to be resolved before it escalates further.

Certainly Chelsea do not want to lose the coach who has taken them to the brink of a first title in 50 years. Mourinho, equally, prefers to remain at Stamford Bridge despite numerous other offers. 'He likes Chelsea, the players, the club and the country,' says a friend. 'It is not important that he has offers from anywhere else. But Jose is not someone to keep his mind in his pocket. Remember the way he left Benfica; he wanted to clarify his situation with the president, a public statement that he would be the coach the next season, but it did not happen. Jose just wants to work in clear waters.'

The cracks in the manager's relationship with the club hierarchy are confirmed by his assistant Baltemar Brito, who also reveals Mourinho will watch the Bayern game in a 'private place' on television and there will be no contact with the bench via mobile phone or any other means of communication.

When asked about the manager's future at the pre-match press conference, Brito does nothing to silence the persistent rumours. He says, 'When Jose comes to a club or starts a new job, he gives 100 per cent and expects 100 per cent back. Jose is not too happy because he feels slightly hard done by around the ban situation.' It is the first public acknowledgement of a problem but Mourinho is keeping his thoughts to himself.

For the first leg against Bayern, UEFA appoint hardline referee Rene Hemmink, 6ft 6in and 17st, who abandoned a game in October between Den Haag and PSV Eindhoven with ten minutes to play after racist chants from fans. Hemmink was in charge of Chelsea's goalless draw with Paris Saint-Germain in November.

Bayern boss Felix Magath is careful not to follow Ottmar Hitzfeld in describing Mourinho as arrogant. 'If I don't know the person, I can't make judgments,' he says, 'but I am clearly aware of Jose Mourinho's great achievements.

'The advantage of having the return leg at home is that Chelsea must do something tomorrow,' he continues. 'They can't just rely on counter-attacks but they will have to bring the game to us and that could help us. I believe that tomorrow we will not lose and that we can score one or two goals. Germany have the winter break so our players now are fresh and in top condition, whereas England has played non-stop until today. I think there were signs of that when we played Arsenal.'

Despite the ban, Mourinho will get his chance to do his stuff at half-time after all. UEFA will be unable to stop him addressing any of his players – and the nation – who are watching television when his advertisement for American Express airs for the first time during ITV's coverage of the match. That'll do nicely, then.

WEDNESDAY, 6 APRIL 2005
CHELSEA 4, BAYERN MUNICH 2

Mourinho is supposed to be the man who isn't there but his presence is everywhere on a night of mystery and intrigue, cloaks and daggers.

He is there in the banners, then in the boos that greet the playing of the UEFA anthem before the tie and in the words of support from John Terry in the programme. Chelsea add to the melodrama by refusing to give any clues as to his whereabouts, except to say he is 'in a quiet place'.

Mysteriously, notes are being passed around among his assistants in the dugout. Are they from Jose? Is he in a health club a mere 50 yards away? Someone says he is in the Chelsea Village Hotel, holed up in a room overlooking the pitch. No one knows for sure, although one paper manages to snap him leaving in a baseball cap and tracksuit top.

Mourinho's ban has created a siege mentality at Stamford Bridge, which is immediately evident when Chelsea fans boo the UEFA anthem before the game and chant Mourinho's name to drown it out. 'Jose,' a giant banner says, 'They May All Hate Us But We All Love You'. Another reads, 'Jose Is Simply the Best'.

Soon Frank Lampard shows there are leaders on the pitch as well as off it. And two left-footed goals demonstrate how he is maturing into arguably the best midfielder in Europe. After substitute Bastian Schweinsteiger capitalises on a rare instance of fallibility from Petr Cech to cancel out Cole's deflected early opener, it looks as if the absence of Mourinho could prove costly. At this point it looks as if the remainder of Chelsea's season hangs in the balance. Enter Lampard ...

His first, which puts Chelsea back in front just seven minutes after Schweinsteiger's equaliser, is simple in construction; Glen Johnson's high ball is knocked down by the head of Drogba, for Lampard to take a step back before steadying himself and directing a low accurate shot past goalkeeper Oliver Kahn.

The next is even better as Makelele clips the ball into the box. Lampard controls it on his chest, then spins 100 degrees to produce a thunderous finish on the half-volley – a special strike.

The Germans are unable to deal with the long-ball tactic, with Drogba making life a misery for the centre-backs Robert Kovac and the Brazilian Lucio. Later Owen Hargreaves is rather unflattering about Chelsea's style, describing them as a 'long-ball' team who resorted to direct tactics because they could not pass their way through the Bayern defence. Taking advantage of costly absences in the Bayern ranks, where Roy Makaay has joined Claudio Pizarro on the sidelines denying Felix Magath's side two players with 40 goals between them this term, it is all looking so good, particularly when Drogba forces the ball home from close range with only ten minutes remaining.

Yet deep in stoppage time comes the final twist on a night that is becoming, in its own way, as dramatic as those unforgettable events against Barcelona. This time, Ricardo Carvalho's tug sends Michael Ballack into sufficient histrionics to alert referee Rene Hemmink. Terry later accuses Ballack of diving to win Bayern's late penalty, which the Germany international successfully converts, as Chelsea become embroiled in yet another Champions League refereeing controversy.

Magath says that Ballack's goal has raised his side's chances of overturning the two-goal deficit in Munich. 'It was good to get the goal before the end – it has given us hope,' he says. 'We will also hopefully have some of our other players back for the return game. We had difficulty coping with the high balls and it was disappointing to concede four goals. This was an exception for us tonight. Normally we cope with such tactics.'

Magath hopes to have Makaay and Pizarro back for the return. "But only three teams have ever overturned a two-goal deficit in the Champions League at this stage and, with Lampard so imperious, Mourinho's men will fancy themselves to score in Munich.

A further note of controversy emerges: did Mourinho use coaches Rui Faria and Silvino Louro as contact points to deliver messages to his assistants Clarke and Brito? There was certainly some very suspicious behaviour by the man in the hat, fitness coach Faria. Faria, rarely on the bench, was wearing a 'beanie' hat and seemed to be leaning back and listening to an earpiece on several occasions before scribbling notes and speaking to Clarke and Brito. Goalkeeping coach Louro, at the centre of punch-up claims in the tunnel after the Barcelona game, appeared three times clutching a piece of paper – and three times it led to a Chelsea substitution. During the second half, UEFA press officer Hans Hultman was seen standing by the home bench keeping watch on the trio and, in the 75th minute, he asked fourth official Pieter Vink to question Faria. Later Brito denies having any contact with Mourinho during the match.

Bayern promise an electrifying second-leg performance at the Olympic Stadium. 'We want to attack so hard that the stadium walls are going to shake,' says Bayern's director of football Uli Hoeness. 'We have to take them down, and that's that. We've got to get two goals – it doesn't matter how. I'm very confident.'

Team

Cech, Johnson (Huth), Carvalho, Terry, Gallas, Cole (Tiago), Lampard, Makelele, Duff, Gudjohnsen, Drogba (Forssell).

One mystery is solved soon after the game. It transpires that Mourinho watched the Bayern match on a huge plasma screen television inside the Chelsea Club & Spa, which is part of the Chelsea Village complex.

And just after 11pm, as the crowds drift away, Mourinho's agent Jorge Mendes slips through the entrance to the Chelsea Village Hotel. A few minutes later Kenyon also rounds the corner, passes the old Shed End, but heads in the opposite direction towards the VIP car park. A new contract has been finalised for Mourinho and they can both go home safe in the knowledge of a job well done.

Of course, Roman Abramovich was always going to give Mourinho exactly what he wanted. But talks were brought forward because Mourinho was so exasperated when he read the comments from chairman Bruce Buck after the UEFA ban was announced, when the Chelsea chairman declared the hearing to be 'full and fair'. Mourinho feels the club has not been backing him and Buck's remark added salt to the wounds.

Chelsea can now justifiably claim there has been a cover-up over what really happened in the Nou Camp during the Champions League first leg on 23 February. The club always insisted referee Anders Frisk spoke to Frank Rijkaard outside his room and remain adamant that such a conversation took place – a claim now supported by UEFA. Chelsea's version of events is now backed up by the venue director's own report to the UEFA disciplinary panel.

Above: In 1997, Jose Mourinho had his first taste of success as assistant to Sir Bobby Robson at Barcelona. The pair are pictured here at the UEFA Cup Final against Paris Saint-Germain in 1997. ©*Getty Images*

Below: Nuno Valente of FC Porto hugs his manager, Mourinho, after winning the Champions League Final against AS Monaco. ©*Getty Images*

Above: Jose Mourinho in action as he directs Chelsea's Wayne Bridge during a match against CSKA Moscow in his early years as manager at Stamford Bridge. His holding out four fingers suggests a change of tactics.

©*Jim Watson/AFP/Getty Image*

Below: Mourinho oversees his players' warm-up during a Chelsea training session in 2004.

©*Getty Images*

Top: Mourinho and players Petr Cec (*left*), Frank Lampard and John Terry (*right*) gaze down at the trophy after being crowned Premiership champions in May 2005.

©Adrian Dennis/AFP/Getty Images

Middle left: Carling Cup victory after beating Liverpool at the Millennium Stadium in Cardiff.

©Rebecca Naden/AFP/Getty Images

Middle right: Mourinho proudly lifts the FA Cup trophy, presented by Prince William at Wembley. *©Getty Images*

Left: John Terry and Frank Lampard celebrate the amazing achievement of winning back-to-back Premiership titles – Chelsea are the only club besides Manchester United to do so in the Premiership era. *©Getty Images*

The evident respect and admiration between the Chelsea players and manager: Mourinho celebrates victory against Barcelona with Frank Lampard (*above left*) sharing a joke with striker Didier Drogba (*above right*) and embracing Lampard and John Terry following a Premiership match against Arsenal (*below*).

Above: Family first for Jose Mourinho. Here he is with wife Matilde, known as Tami, at a lunch with the President of the Portuguese Republic. *©Getty Images*

Below: Mourinho poses with son, Zuca (*left*), and daughter, Matilde (*right*), and the Barclays Premiership trophy at Stamford Bridge. *©Getty Images*

Above: New beginnings at Inter: Mourinho holds the trophy aloft after winning the UEFA Champions League final.

©*Getty Images*

Left: Cristiano Ronaldo celebrates with his Real Madrid team mates as Jose Mourinho leads them to victory in a La Liga match against RCD Mallorca.

©*Getty Images*

bove left: Jose Mourinho addresses the press as he returns to Chelsea for a
cond managing stint in June 2013. ©*Getty Images*

bove right: Mourinho's legendary status among Chelsea fans made him a
opular choice to replace Rafael Benitez. ©*Getty Images*

elow: Back in action: Mourinho watches from the sidelines during a Premier
eague match between Chelsea and Norwich City in May 2014. ©*Getty Images*

Back where he
belongs.
©Getty Images

It really is astonishing that UEFA apparently chose to ignore the written testimony of the man at the centre of the dispute. The 25-page report compiled by investigator Edgar Obertuefer for UEFA's Control and Disciplinary Body does not appear to contain a single reference to the referee's version of events.

Chelsea contacted UEFA to ask for Frisk's report and, when it arrived a day later, they discovered that the Swede had bolstered their version. Frisk said that Rijkaard approached him on three separate occasions until he finally lost patience and told him to return to his own dressing room. Although UEFA confirm that Chelsea have 'waived the right to appeal', the club are discussing whether or not they can pursue other avenues to seek redress as they feel Mourinho, who is still furious they did not appeal, has been made the scapegoat.

UEFA are in no mood to wipe the slate clean for Mourinho, but the failure to bring Rijkaard to book is rapidly becoming a farce. Chelsea, though, will be punished following events during the first leg against Bayern. As is mandatory under UEFA law, the club will be fined because they had four players cautioned – Drogba, Carvalho, Gallas and Makelele.

Frank Lampard's last trip to the Olympic Stadium, Munich, was for England's unforgettable 5–1 World Cup triumph in September 2001. He says, 'It can be an imposing ground, especially with their fans and the atmosphere they're going to produce. But we don't believe in giving things up when we have them in our grasp.'

Mourinho admits that his role in the dugout will not be as vital as the preparation of his squad. 'I am not on the bench but the players are on the pitch. And as I have been saying to them, our work – the management team's work – is done during the week. During the 90 minutes my direct actions are not that important. I never say after a first leg, the result is good or bad, because you never know. In the first leg, I never feel the pressure of having to win or not concede. The second game will be more important than the first, like against Manchester United in the Carling Cup semi-final. We played them at home and couldn't beat them, but we didn't panic and we went away and won the second leg. I think the players are well prepared.'

As they arrive in Munich every member of the party is still livid about the long-ball tag. Joe Cole says, 'If anyone really thinks we can't play football they should look at any of our last ten games when we've carved teams open with our passing movement. Of course we can pass the ball. But we played a more direct game against Bayern because we felt they couldn't deal with it. There wasn't a moment when somebody told us to start looking for Didier in the box. It just happened naturally.

'Sometimes you need to fight and sometimes you need to get the ball quickly into the box. What's the point in playing pretty stuff if it's not effective? Why should we play to Bayern's strengths? The way we played last week was very effective because we scored four and should have had more.'

But Magath is plotting an upset. 'We are capable of scoring two goals in 45 minutes and that is what we need against Chelsea,' he says after his side recovers from going a goal down to beat Borussia Moenchengladbach 2–1 in the Bundesliga. 'That will comfort us, even in the Champions League. We can now go into that game with added self-confidence. We go into the game convinced we can knock Chelsea out.'

Chelsea deliver another snub to UEFA by putting fitness coach Rui Faria and fringe striker Mikael Forssell up for the pre-match press conference. The event degenerates into farce as Faria arrogantly fields questions about his infamous woolly hat and launches a personal rant against UEFA's touchline ban on Mourinho. Faria denies he passed on mobile phone messages to Brito and Clarke at Stamford Bridge and adds that he had nothing to hide under his hat!

Faria is dubbed 'Mini Mo' the next day in the press. Unable to keep a smile off his face as he winks at his audience, Faria shows he is a chip off the Mourinho block as he declares himself a 'Special One' in his own way. UEFA representative Wolfgang Eichler, close to tears when he realises what Chelsea are doing (poor chap), says, 'I'll be reporting everything that has gone on to UEFA. Just look at the difference. Bayern put up Magath, Kahn and Hargreaves and Chelsea did this.'

But Bayern are not interested in Mourinho's latest tricks. Hargreaves jokes, 'They were handing notes around like naughty schoolchildren in a class. We saw the TV clips. It's not a big deal and we're not going to be sidetracked by the circus.'

Meanwhile, experienced goalkeeper Oliver Kahn calls on his lightweight team-mates to stand up and be counted. 'It was a big shock to me to concede four goals last week. It was unprecedented in Bayern's Champions League history. That result has come as a real warning to us and we will only have a chance of turning this match around if we don't let Chelsea catch us by surprise again. They are known for their aggressive style and their powerful physical contact. We must respond with aggression and a firm resolve of our own. Otherwise we will lose.'

The incorrigible *Bild Zeitung* chooses the game as the subject for its front-page headline: 'Bay-Bay, Chelsea'. On the football page, there is a cut-out paper aeroplane to be aimed at the Chelsea dugout with messages in English purportedly from Jose Mourinho: 'Substitute Drogba and Lampard!'

TUESDAY, 13 APRIL 2005
BAYERN MUNICH 3, CHELSEA 2

Mourinho arrives on the front seat of the team bus with an air of affected nonchalance: feet up and eyes shut. If his entrance is unusual, his exit is spectacular. As most of the stadium's photographers train their lenses on the VIP seats, Mourinho suddenly appears on the giant screen in the stadium; he's back outside and stepping into a beige Munich municipal taxi for the short ride back to the team hotel. A Chelsea spokesman later announces that Mourinho's 'privacy' had been invaded at the stadium. He fully intended to watch from the VIP area but felt harassed by cameramen and left the ground minutes before kick-off.

Once the whistle goes, Bayern make good their promise to take the role of aggressors and Robert Huth makes an inauspicious start to life as a right-back when he is skinned by Ze Roberto down the wing. The Brazilian cuts the ball back to Michael Ballack in the area and only a flailing leg from Cech keeps the shot out.

Down the opposite wing comes Bastian Schweinsteiger who begins by causing equal trouble for William Gallas, the young German inflicting the old-fashioned 'nutmeg' humiliation on the French full-back on 18 minutes and then going on to beat Lampard before unleashing a cross that curls menacingly across goal.

Yet Bayern have to beware of Chelsea on the counter. In fact, after just a few minutes, Lampard's ball over the top sends Drogba away behind the square backline with the flag staying down, but Oliver Kahn, racing from his goal, just gets his foot there first to clear the danger. Before the half-hour, Chelsea take a daring lead. The goals Lampard keeps scoring, and the games he has dominated, mean that his triumphs are no fluke. But when he strikes his 15th of the season, the ball goes in after a big deflection off a defender, just like Cole's first last week.

Michael Ballack is swiftly up to his first-leg trick of diving but the Spanish referee nips that tactic in the bud. There are two scares for Chelsea before half-time, not least when Ze Roberto offers further evidence that Huth is not a natural full-back by beating him down the flank and cutting back another inviting ball. But Ballack wastes his best chance when Huth misjudges a header and presents the midfielder with a simple chance from close range. The talented midfielder cannot keep his shot under the bar.

Duff is then presented with a glorious chance to kill the tie. Lampard's innocuous free-kick is allowed to trickle through to the Irishman and, holding off Willy Sagnol's challenge, he shoots from close range. Somehow Kahn turns the ball away.

The Bayern goal arrives on 65 minutes and, by then, the home side are in control. Sagnol crosses from the right and Ballack, who has established himself as the match's most influential man, produces a stunning header. Cech is equal to it, but turns the ball against the inside of the post and, as the ball ricochets back along the line, it is turned in by Pizarro. The Chelsea defence is no longer looking invulnerable. Pizarro's tap-in means only one clean sheet in the past 11 games.

Bayern pour forward. Within four minutes Huth deflects a Bixente Lizarazu cross on to Cech's bar. From the corner Ballack once again proves dominant in the air and it requires Eidur Gudjohnsen to volley off the line.

Out of nothing, Chelsea appear to seal the tie with 11 minutes remaining. Cole makes the crucial breakthrough, running unselfishly to keep the ball by the corner flag. As the defence expects him to waste valuable time, instead he crosses from the left for Drogba to power-flick his header past Kahn into the far corner. Drogba, kicked twice by Kovac, who is eventually booked, takes revenge by climbing above the Croat to score.

Bayern manage to rouse themselves from the depths of a display that sees most of their supporters exit before their winning goals go in. The first comes from Jose Paolo Guerrero, who turns in Schweinsteiger's cross from the right at the near post. Then in injury-time Mehmet Scholl scores with the last kick of the game. It is the first time that Mourinho's Chelsea have conceded three goals but they are through. In the semi-finals Mourinho's team will play against either Liverpool or Juventus, who face each other in Turin tomorrow night.

While the game is going on, UEFA officials confront fitness coach Rui Faria during the half-time interval to prove he is not in communication with Mourinho. Faria is ushered into a side room and told to remove his hat after allegations he has been passing on messages from Mourinho to Brito and Steve Clarke during the first leg. Despite protests from Faria, who claims such a request is not in UEFA rules, the Chelsea coach duly removes his hat to prove he has no communication device attached to either ear.

Chelsea have a fitness scare over Terry, who admits that his leg is 'in bits' after the match. Terry has a week to recover before the home game with Arsenal. But the next round of the Champions League is even more important.

Can Mourinho become the first manager in the modern era to win the European Cup with different teams in successive seasons?

Team

Cech, Huth, Carvalho, Terry, Gallas, Makelele, Cole (Morais), Lampard, Gudjohnsen (Geremi), Duff (Tiago), Drogba.

After the match Mourinho goes window-shopping in Maximilianstrasse, Munich's equivalent of Chelsea's Sloane Street, until his team return. When they do, around midnight, he joins his players and staff for a celebration party thrown by Abramovich at Munich's trendy Cafe Roma restaurant, a regular haunt of the rich and famous just 400 yards from their hotel, the five-star deluxe Hotel Kempinski. As he makes his way out through the hotel lobby after the game, Mourinho is applauded on his side's victory.

Later John Terry follows his team-mates through Gatwick airport 20 paces behind them. He returns from Munich with only one leg in complete working order. But he has managed what so few traditional English hard men have achieved in European football before: aggression and dominance without loss of temper.

The tone for the night was quickly set. The clattering of Kahn by Terry and the long balls to Drogba in the first leg had been part of a successful tactical ambush by Mourinho; then Terry and his team-mates did a remarkable job of subduing a Bayern side intent on revenge.

Liverpool Manager Rafa Benitez announces he is 'proud and delighted but not surprised' after his side secure an unexpected aggregate victory over Juventus in Turin. Liverpool have sealed a first-ever all-Premiership semi-final against Chelsea, which also guarantees an English side will be in the final. Benitez says, 'Chelsea have won three times against us already this season. But over the last two games we have got closer and maybe next time we will manage it. We certainly have a lot of confidence when it comes to the Champions League, though it will be difficult. Chelsea are top of the table and, for me, are the favourites. But we have nothing to lose, only something to win.'

Defender Jamie Carragher believes Gerrard will snub a £35m move to Chelsea if Liverpool can knock them out of the Champions League. Carragher says, 'Why would anyone want to walk away from a club who had reached a European Cup final? These are good times at Liverpool at the moment and this result shows the club are going places. We're desperate for him to stay but it's his decision. If we get to the Champions League final, it must have an influence.

'For me, Stevie G is the best in England and he'll be out to prove that against Chelsea. I want to be in the final – we all do – because we all want success. If Stevie has a decision to make at the end of the season, that's up to him. But the club will move on whatever happens, although we're all hoping he'll stay.'

Benitez knows Chelsea are overwhelming favourites to make it through to Istanbul. But his side's own European pedigree must disturb even the single-minded confidence of Mourinho. 'All the pressure is on Chelsea. If you spend £10,000 on a suit, you'll get a better suit than if you spend £1,000. You might think it's the same with football – that, generally, if you spend a lot of money you will win. But this is different. You only need one goal to win and that can come from a corner or a free-kick, or something you haven't even thought about. In Spain, Real Madrid and Barcelona spend all the money, but Valencia still won the title, so you can see football is so different to anything else. Chelsea are one of the best teams in the world and are favourites ... but we can beat anybody on our day. We will go without any fear of Chelsea or the game.

'We're the underdogs because they're one of the best teams in the world. But the way we beat Juventus in the quarter-final was important because it made the players believe we can win games we're not expected to. It is just a case of mixing what is in the heart with what is in the brain. The important thing is that we are not afraid of Chelsea.

'Against Chelsea, I've identified what I believe are weaknesses and we've been working hard on ways to give them problems. But

Mourinho will be doing the same. Away from home in the Premiership we sometimes have three or four weaknesses. At home, I hope one or nil. When you lose by only one goal, you know you're very close. They'll play like they play in the Premier League, I'm sure, but we'll be treating this as a European game. I don't know why exactly it's been that different between Champions League matches and the Premiership. Maybe the players feel it's more special in the Champions League. If you'd said to me six months ago that we'd be playing at Anfield against Chelsea for a place in the Champions League final, I'd have taken it.'

Luis Garcia is out for revenge after the Carling Cup final. 'The final left a bad taste because we should never have lost. Now it is the moment for revenge. It is the best time of the season to play this semi-final because we have key players coming back from injury and we are playing a better game. To play the final of the Champions League is a dream for any player and we are only 180 minutes away from it. I've fixed our defeats against Chelsea in my heart and to beat them now would be magnificent.'

It has taken foreign leadership to make English football a Euro force again. Mourinho claims, 'English football needs to adapt to Europe in certain aspects. English managers are very good. But maybe the mentality of me and Rafa Benitez to play in a more tactical way gives us a little bit of an advantage.'

Mourinho is ready for an ear-bashing from the Scousers who will be within touching distance behind his dugout. After Gerrard's own-goal equaliser in Cardiff, Mourinho was sent down the tunnel for putting his finger to his lips and telling their fans to be quiet. He also had a running verbal battle with Jamie Carragher, who did not like Mourinho shaking hands with the Liverpool players. 'I told him where to go and he said the same, so it's 1–1.'

Mourinho adds, 'My reception is always bad from rival fans and always negative. I think that is normal; it's not just Liverpool fans but every fan. They sit behind me and can almost touch me. I think we are a special club because we give opposition fans the best seats in the stadium. When we go to Liverpool, Newcastle and Manchester

United our fans are stuck up on the moon at the top. But they come here and get the best. That shows we are special. They always try to disturb me a bit but I try to calm them down and be nice to them.'

There are stirrings of unrest when defender William Gallas says that Barcelona are keen to sign him and Mateja Kezman announces he wants to leave because Mourinho will not give him a regular place. Gallas's revelation comes a fortnight after he spoke about wanting to clarify his situation at Stamford Bridge at the end of the season when he made it plain that he was uncomfortable at left-back. Frank Rijkaard regards him as a central defender. 'Yes, Barcelona want to sign me,' Gallas tells the city's newspaper *El Mundo Deportivo*, without stating whether a move there would interest him. Mourinho is expected to try to persuade him to stay to compete for a place in central defence once he signs a new full-back.

Meanwhile Damien Duff has an injured left hamstring and needs a late fitness test. He trains on his own the evening before the game against Liverpool but is seen to grimace repeatedly while doing shuttle runs. Arjen Robben, though, could be fit but he is still being treated for a sore ankle after playing 45 minutes against Fulham.

WEDNESDAY, 27 APRIL 2005

CHELSEA 0, LIVERPOOL 0

At 5pm Damien Duff fails a fitness test on his hamstring. Arjen Robben is in a slightly better condition but his ankle problem means he can only come on for the last half-hour and, lacking these two creative forces, the game heads towards a goalless draw as Liverpool dig in. Chelsea are unaccustomed to being without both Duff and Robben. Excluding two FA Cup ties for which Mourinho rested players, this is the first time they have started without either player since mid-September.

The game is tactical rather than end-to-end. Throughout its 90 minutes, goalkeeper Jerzy Dudek makes no noteworthy saves but Petr Cech has to pull off two to avoid a perilous away goal before the trip to Liverpool. It falls to Joe Cole to provide the bulk of the team's runs from his flank because Eidur Gudjohnsen, on the left, always moves inside to link with the midfield.

Gudjohnsen does, however, release Cole with a pass that springs the offside trap after 14 minutes but, although Didier Drogba's power sees him get the break of the ball from the ensuing cross, he badly screws his finish wide with only the keeper to beat. Within five minutes a better opportunity is manufactured on the left. When Drogba lays play out to William Gallas, he works the ball on to his right foot and flights in a deep delivery. The diminutive Cole outjumps Djimi Traore and heads down but Frank Lampard inexplicably fires over from point-blank range.

Gathering a pass from Xabi Alonso in the 19th minute, John Arne Riise, having put the ball on to his unfavoured right foot, comes across Ricardo Carvalho but can do no more than steer the ball straight at a relieved Petr Cech. Six minutes before half-time the goalkeeper makes one of the best saves of this tournament when, after going one way, he somehow manages to recover and tip away a goal-bound Baros header.

'Welcome Home Stevie G – Another OG Please,' reads a cheeky banner in the Shed, a double-edged reference to the glancing header past his own goalkeeper that gave Chelsea a late equaliser in the Carling Cup final. Gerrard's battle with Lampard for supremacy in the central areas sets England's two strongest midfield men in direct opposition, with the added piquancy of a possible link-up next season.

'There's only one Steven Gerrard,' sing the blue-clad fans in the North Stand as he collects Alonso's short free-kick in the last minute and slices a 30-yard pile driver into Row Z of the Shed – interestingly, his ritual post-match handshake with Mourinho is not accompanied by eye contact. Meanwhile, Alonso is cautioned for a disputed foul on Gudjohnsen and leaves the arena pointing angrily at the Icelandic striker, implying he coaxed the booking from the referee. The booking will keep him out of the second leg.

There is no sign of panic from Mourinho at the end, though. He slaps hands contentedly with Steve Clarke at the final whistle. It turns out Mourinho is one of the few people who can be inspired to a bout of nostalgia by a goalless draw at home. Mourinho's conviction that Chelsea will secure passage to the final is unswerving. 'We need to be strong mentally but I think the pressure is on them. At this moment 99.9 per cent of Liverpool people think they are in the final but they are not. It's an easy thing to come and play for a draw, and they defended well, but it will be different in the second leg. I like this situation very much because it is now like an FA Cup tie with the result being decided over 90 minutes.

'Don't forget that Manchester United drew 0–0 here in the first leg of the Carling Cup semi but we went up to Old Trafford and won the second leg. And in last season's semi-final with Porto, we were held 0–0 at home by Deportivo La Coruna but they lost Mauro Silva through a booking late in the game and we beat them at their ground. Tonight Liverpool have lost Xabi Alonso for next Tuesday's game so there are a lot of similarities.'

Rafa Benitez refuses to abandon the belief that his team will snatch a place in the final. 'They did not have a shot on goal and that was because we controlled the game. If someone had said at the start of the season, we'd play at Anfield for a place in the Champions League final, I'd have thanked them. But tonight I am a little disappointed we have not won.'

On the final whistle Liverpool celebrated as if they had won a trophy, but Eidur Gudjohnsen believes that they will feel the pressure in front of their expectant public. 'We're not going to panic and will go to Anfield full of confidence. It'll be a difficult game but they have to come at us as they're playing at home. That could work in our favour as they're under pressure but we'll go out to win the game as we normally do.'

Team

Cech, Johnson, Carvalho, Terry, Gallas, Tiago (Robben), Makelele, Lampard, Gudjohnsen, Drogba, Cole (Kezman).

It transpires that before the first leg with Liverpool Mourinho asked Arjen Robben to begin the match after Duff failed a late fitness test, but the Dutch international declared himself not fully fit despite being cleared by the club's medical staff. The media interpret this as a conflict between the star and coach, which is strenuously denied. Although frustrated by the player's stance, Mourinho understands Robben's predicament and has resolved to ration his playing time strictly until the end of the season.

Steven Gerrard warns that, when Chelsea visit for the return leg, Anfield will be no place for faint hearts. 'We need 11 gladiators and the subs and the fans have all got to be ready as well. Anfield is the best place for a big European night by a mile and Tuesday night is going to be a great spectacle for everyone. The confidence running through all the players on these occasions is incredible.

'The Carling Cup was a huge disappointment. It was not my day then but hopefully it will be my day next month when I get the chance to lead the boys out in another final. The important thing before the game at Chelsea was to stay in touch and give ourselves a fighting chance in the second leg. It was a good performance; it's a massive achievement to get a clean sheet at Stamford Bridge. But we know we are not home and dry. Chelsea are a brilliant side capable of coming to Anfield and beating us. We will show them a lot of respect – but it's going to be some night.'

The Chelsea players are oozing with confidence after encouraging words from their coach. Ricardo Carvalho insists, 'Chelsea will get into the final – and that is for certain. I am very confident. We will run out at Anfield with our heads held high. We know we're capable of winning. We have what it takes to score goals and win up there. It was important for us not to concede in the first leg. Now we know we have to score in order to win the tie – and we will do all we can to achieve this. The main priority for us now is to reach the final of the Champions League.'

As the war of words grows, Rafa Benitez tries to turn the tables on his Chelsea counterpart by insisting all the expectation lies with Mourinho. 'Chelsea are saying that we are too confident, but I think that only goes to show that they are worried. What they are trying to do is put the pressure on us because they know that in reality it is them who are under all the real pressure.

'When you have the most expensive team in the world then you need to win titles to justify that. Chelsea have spent £200m. They should be expected to win the Champions League after spending that kind of money and that's why they now feel under so much pressure. I know people think that if Chelsea score, we cannot win because of the away goal, but that is something that does not concern me. The only issue is that we win the match. If Chelsea score once, then we have to score twice. If they score twice, then we have to score three times. I don't think about the away-goals rule, I only concentrate on winning the game.'

Before the second leg, Robben is still not fully fit but says he is willing to risk it. Robben, left out at Bolton as the Blues clinched the Premiership title, says he will put his hand up for selection at Anfield even though he does not think his body is up to it yet.

Mourinho is not giving too much away about his plans – apart from admitting his continued doubts over Robben and Duff. Asked whether Liverpool will miss the suspended Alonso, he replies, 'They'll miss him no more than we miss Robben or Duff in other matches and maybe tomorrow again. Alonso is a very good player, of course, but they have Igor Biscan, Steven Gerrard, Dietmar Hamann and Harry Kewell. They have a lot of solutions. For us, it's more difficult as we only have two wingers. If we lose one, we are in trouble. If we lose two, then it's a problem that you cannot solve.'

Mourinho invites the Kop to make as much noise as they can. The new Premiership champions, their manager says, are unafraid to claim their European Cup final place in one of the most imposing football stadiums in the competition's history.

Both Mourinho and Benitez insist that the pressure to triumph in the Premiership's private European battle is weighing more heavily on their opponents and yet neither can deny that defeat will irredeemably scar their season.

Mourinho bemoans the relentless tide of crucial fixtures that pile up week after week in England. Chelsea beat Bolton to clinch the Premiership on Saturday which allowed his team just one hour's celebration – 'no families, no wives, no kids, no dinner, no champagne, nothing to enjoy' – before they had to begin preparations afresh for the Liverpool game. He dismisses the magnitude of the achievement that awaits him – winning two successive European Cups with different teams – but says his team have not been affected by the exhausting pursuit of the Premiership.

'They [Liverpool] have more power in their legs but we have more power in our minds from winning the championship,' Mourinho says. 'It is more difficult to win the Premiership than the Champions League. You have to go all over the country in all conditions, in wind and rain, sleet and hail, on good pitches and bad ones and in the north and the south, and all the time under pressure from United and Arsenal.'

Duff and Robben are both consigned to the bench after failing to fully recover from injuries, while several other players are shattered following their efforts in winning the Championship at Bolton on Saturday. But Mourinho says, 'Motivation can make miracles. Chelsea are tired but ready to go to the final. Liverpool rested six or seven players this Saturday, but with a little more effort we can get to the final. We played our best team at Bolton because winning the title would help us forget our fatigue. We're confident that we can win.

'I said last week that details could make the difference. At Stamford Bridge the game was very balanced but we deserved to win 1–0. Now I think the game will be very balanced and only a detail will determine who goes to the final.'

TUESDAY, 3 MAY 2005

LIVERPOOL 1, CHELSEA 0
(LIVERPOOL WIN 1–0 ON AGGREGATE)

After the stalemate at Stamford Bridge, the last thing anybody expects is an early goal, but Liverpool seize the initiative after four minutes. Steven Gerrard plays a delightful first-time ball over the top to Milan Baros. Petr Cech collides with the striker as he rushes out, but referee Lubos Michel allows play to continue. Luis Garcia hooks the ball towards goal and the linesman rules his effort has crossed the line despite Gallas's desperate last-ditch clearance.

Having given his side the lead, Garcia almost gifts Chelsea an equaliser midway through the first half. He is caught in possession on the edge of his own box by Frank Lampard who feeds a ball through to Joe Cole, but the angle is acute and he lifts his shot over Jerzy Dudek but wide.

It is the same at the start of the second half as it becomes blue attack against red defence. Jamie Carragher is awesome at the back as Liverpool see off wave after wave of Chelsea attacks. A tiring Baros is replaced by Djibril Cisse on the hour.

Two minutes later, Didier Drogba curls a free-kick just over the bar as Dudek waits to make his first save. Liverpool concede a free-kick in a dangerous position on 68 minutes and this time Dudek is called into action. Lampard's free-kick is sweetly struck and heading for the bottom left-hand corner, but the Pole makes a superb save at full stretch to turn the shot round the post.

Ricardo Carvalho escapes a booking for a foul on substitute Harry Kewell which would have forced him to miss the final had Chelsea made it to Istanbul. Mourinho introduces Arjen Robben for the disappointing Joe Cole and Mateja Kezman for Tiago. Robben is instantly in the thick of the action, seeing one effort superbly blocked by Carragher and then firing over.

In a last act of desperation, giant centre-back Robert Huth is sent on up front in place of full-back Geremi. But the next chance falls at the other end as Djimi Traore's cross drops perfectly for Cisse. The Frenchman's header is weak and straight at Cech.

Chelsea then waste a glorious opening of their own. Drogba looks odds-on to bury Robben's centre from the left, but he misses the ball completely and it rebounds off Traore for a corner. Carvalho is then almost caught out at the back on a rare Liverpool raid. He gifts the ball to Cisse but his shot is deflected just wide of the post with Cech scrambling across his goal.

Chelsea have a glorious chance to level deep in injury-time. Terry launches himself to win a header in the box and Dudek flaps at the ball, gifting Gudjohnsen an incredible opening at the far post. But staring at goal, he snatches at his shot and it goes inches wide. The final whistle sounds soon afterwards.

Rafa Benitez claims that he always believed he could outwit Mourinho, 'I said that, with our fans behind us and the players playing so well, we had a great chance of winning – and we have. Yes, they put us under pressure but we controlled it more in the second half. The boys are jumping around; it's very joyous in the dressing room. The whole team was superb.'

Mourinho, who congratulated all the players and Liverpool staff individually on the pitch, backs Liverpool to lift the European Cup. 'They were lucky and the best chance came in the last minute, when, if we had scored, we would have killed Anfield. So maybe it was good not to happen.'

Despite this Champions League semi-final defeat, Mourinho insists that Chelsea will rightfully still be hailed by their fans for their title success. He is frustrated, claiming the 'best team lost' as Benitez's side benefited from a controversial refereeing decision when Luis Garcia's fourth-minute goal was allowed to stand, even though Gallas appeared to clear the ball before it crossed the line.

'My players are still heroes, for sure. They have done what nobody at this club has done in 50 years. They won the Premiership. So for me, they are heroes. They can lose and lose, but if our group is so solid and so strong, for me they will always be my heroes. I think the fans have the same feeling as I do for my players.'

Even in defeat, Mourinho has lost none of his innate self-belief, claiming he still regards himself as the 'Special One'. 'For sure I am. You want to try and succeed in your job like I have done in mine inside three years? You have no chance,' he tells one reporter. 'Of course, the players are upset. Everyone reacts differently but they are all sad. William Gallas is crying but he is not more unhappy than me.'

Mourinho adds, 'What can I say? Just that the best team lost. No doubt, that is for sure. The best team didn't deserve to lose. But football is sometimes cruel and you have to accept the reality. Sometimes it goes for you and sometimes it goes against you. Now I hope Liverpool can win – with all my heart I hope that.'

Meanwhile as tears roll down the battered and cut face of Gudjohnsen. A slashed shot across the face of goal in the sixth minute of injury time was the difference between Chelsea booking their trip to Istanbul and returning to London as unfulfilled champions. Gudjohnsen says, 'It was a tight angle and actually Jamie Carragher cleared it off the line. I controlled the ball, hit it quite well and thought it was going in, but it came off Carragher's thigh. I would have loved to see the net move at that moment, but it seemed that Carragher cloned himself last night. He was just about everywhere.'

Gudjohnsen is more composed than after last year's semi-final defeat, but insists that the pain inside hurts more this time. 'It was even more disappointing than last year because we're a better team and more mature. It's a bitter disappointment, but we've taken a big step forward this season. We've won two trophies. After getting over this result, we'll bounce back with a smile on our faces.'

Mourinho sees grounds for optimism. 'This is an historical group of players for the club and I hope the fans give them the credit they deserve. The group are together and next season we will be together again. We don't change the group; we can have two or three new players and no more than that. Now though, at the end of the season, I want the Chelsea fans to show these players the love they deserve.'

Mourinho gives his players two days off before Saturday's league game against Charlton but confirms that he, for one, is not resting on his laurels. 'I want the players to rest. But I will be at Stamford Bridge tomorrow starting to prepare for next season. It will be coming soon and it will be another chance to get some trophies.'

> **Team**
>
> Cech, Geremi (Huth), Carvalho, Terry, Gallas, Tiago, Makelele, Lampard, Cole (Robben), Drogba (Kezman), Gudjohnsen.

Computer technology later shows Luis Garcia's strike did not cross the line. Sky's hi-tech image reveals Gallas cleared the ball in time and the goal should not have stood. Sky commentator Andy Gray insists the computer programme, developed from Israeli missile technology, proves Slovakian linesman Roman Slysko got it wrong.

But Slysko says, 'I believe my decision was correct. My first feeling, which I remain convinced of, is that it was a goal. I am 100 per cent convinced. I saw it clearly. I was adequately positioned for that situation. It was a very hard situation and under those circumstances you only have a few hundredths of a second to react. There will always be those kind of situations in football matches. There was also an incident just before involving Petr Cech and Milan Baros which could have resulted in a penalty and a red card.' Cech insists his challenge on Baros in the lead-up to the crucial goal did not warrant a spot-kick or sending-off. 'I just occupied the space,' he says. 'Milan hit the ball and then he jumped into me. In my opinion it could not be a penalty.' But Baros, Cech's international team-mate, raps, 'It should have been a penalty. He flew at me. I think he even did not hit the ball. But it is not important now.'

Referee Lobos Michel observes, 'I believe Chelsea would have preferred the goal to count rather than face a penalty with just ten men for the rest of the game. If my assistant referee had not signalled a goal, I would have given a penalty and sent off goalkeeper Petr Cech. Jose Mourinho shook my hand after the game and did not complain about the goal. I appreciated his gesture. I was quite ready to explain everything, but no one asked me about the situation.'

Mourinho is again under attack by UEFA. Lars-Ake Bjorck, the Swedish vice-chairman of UEFA's referees committee, responds to Mourinho's criticisms of the referee in the *Telegraph*, saying, 'It is unbelievable he does not have the decency to learn anything, especially considering that he was recently punished with both a suspension and a fine. This damages football a lot. We can only hope Mourinho's initiatives do not have the same consequences this time.'

But it is a far more hostile comment attributed to the same official in the *Sun*. 'It's unbelievable he hasn't got the brain to learn from his mistake last time. It's incredible, especially when you put in mind he recently was punished hard with both suspension and payment charges. If UEFA get a report we will treat it rapidly. This kind of statement damages football and everything around football.'

Swedish head of referees Bo Karlsson says he hopes Slysko does not suffer the same fate as Anders Frisk. 'I hope with all my heart this linesman will not get the same terrible threats Anders got,' says Karlsson. 'We can only hope Mourinho's words will not bring the same, bad, sad consequences as last time.'

The defeat is still sinking in for John Terry. 'We are absolutely devastated at going out in the semis again – especially as we reckon we were the better side and their goal should never have been given,' he says. 'We feel it should have been us in the final but it wasn't to be. Hopefully, next season we can win the Premiership again and reach the final. We believe it will be our turn next. It's something all the lads wanted desperately – and over the two games we felt we deserved to go through. We've stepped up the ladder this season by winning the Carling Cup and the Premiership, which was a massive achievement. It's still been a great season for us but this defeat will put a bit of a downer on things. It was especially disappointing to go out at this stage for the second year running. Having come this far and beaten teams like Barcelona and Bayern Munich we felt we could go all the way and win it. We've played Liverpool five times this season and they've beaten us only once, so I think overall we are entitled to feel we are the better side.'

William Gallas, who wept on the pitch at full-time, says Chelsea's stars went missing at Anfield. 'We were one match from the final. Why couldn't we get there? You shouldn't be tired with just one match remaining to be played. We should have played with our hearts and minds. That had been our strong point all season. Not this time.'

Eidur Gudjohnsen says he and his team-mates will be back in a positive mood by the time the Premiership trophy is presented. 'We should try to enjoy the moment and still remember that is has been a very successful year and we'll be even more together next time.'

The FA Cup

'I CAN SEE WHAT THE FA CUP MEANS NOW AND I THINK IT'S FANTASTIC.'

Jose Mourinho after Chelsea's FA Cup tie against
the League two team, Scunthorpe United.

The late Brian Clough was Brian Laws' manager at Nottingham Forest. Laws, now boss of Chelsea's third-round FA Cup opponents Scunthorpe, considers it a privilege to have served under Cloughie at the City Ground for five years. Laws can see many similarities between his old boss and Jose Mourinho. 'They used to call Cloughie "Old Big 'Ead", but Mourinho should be known as "Young Big 'Ead" because he is only 41!' says Laws. 'And having heard Jose in interviews, he does remind me very much of how Cloughie used to act. But that is not just about being big-headed. It is more of an arrogance or confidence – not only in himself, but also in his players. Cloughie had a great belief in us and he was prepared to upset people with it. He just didn't care. And I think that is where Mourinho has shown his colours. He marched into Stamford Bridge and said straight from the start that he knew his team were going to win things this year – and I find that really refreshing.'

Laws adds that he felt like he had 'won the lottery' after drawing Chelsea. He was doing his Christmas shopping in Sheffield with his wife when the draw was made but managed to watch it in an electrical goods store. 'I was in a television shop at the time, and saw it 40 times on 40 different screens. They must have thought I was an absolute lunatic, because I was screaming and jumping up and down. That's just how much it means to me and this club. We're not going to Chelsea just to lap it up and say, "Thanks very much." We're going to try and cause an upset.'

Chelsea's chief opposition scout Andri Villas warns they must not take Scunthorpe lightly. 'For a Division Two team they have good organisation. The principles are direct football, but direct football with some basics and quality. The guy who impressed was Peter Beagrie, with his experience. In one-to-ones he can still beat defenders.'

Beagrie was watching from the comfort of his settee when he heard the draw, but could have done without the reaction of his nine-year-old son. 'Dad, you're going to get hammered,' said Sam. The last time he played at the Bridge he was marked by Mario Melchiot, and before that Albert Ferrer. 'Maybe they will go easy on us this time, and only play Glen Johnson! If we had been playing Arsenal or Manchester United, they might have put out a team of fringe players, but even Chelsea's youngsters are worth £6m–£7m. The likelihood is that, whatever the line-up, it will be worth about £150m. In those circumstances, all we can ask is that we don't embarrass ourselves. If we can keep the score-line below five, we'll have nothing to be ashamed of.'

Jiri Jarosik experiences English football for the first time after signing three days earlier. He says, 'I hope I will become an important part of the squad and help Chelsea to achieve their goals for the season. There is a great chance for me here, and I will do everything to take it. Jose Mourinho explained the situation in Chelsea to me and said that I will certainly be given my chance.'

Keeper Paul Musselwhite is sure Steve Clarke, Mourinho's assistant coach, will warn his superstars about the perils of facing the League Two side. Former Scotland international Clarke was Chelsea's right-back when they were hammered 4–1 in a League Cup clash at Glanford Park in 1988. Musselwhite played in goal for the Humbersiders that day as a teenager. Seventeen years on he cannot wait to get to grips with Clarke's Chelsea. He says, 'Obviously it's a bit different from 17 years ago because Chelsea are now a team full of superstars. But they still had a very good side back then with Kerry Dixon up front. And they won the old Division Two title that season. I was a kid of 19 playing just my ninth game for Scunny – but we were brilliant that night and battered them. We did the same in the second leg at Stamford Bridge when people down at Chelsea thought it would be easy for them to get a result. Their fans were so sure they would do it that only 5,000 turned up at the Bridge. But in the end we drew 2–2. I don't suppose many of their top players now have even heard of Scunthorpe. But Stevie Clarke will remember that game. So I'm pretty sure he will have revved up his squad and told them not to take us too lightly.'

Clarke admits, 'I've tried not to tell the players about it. I'm too embarrassed. It was a humiliating night for all of us. We'd just been relegated from the old First Division. But it was still considered a big upset. It was 1–1 up there for a long time and then the roof fell in on us, as it often did for Chelsea in those days. I think they scored three goals in five or six minutes. I remember walking off feeling so ashamed. We thought we could turn it around at Stamford Bridge but could manage only a draw. It is a reminder of what can happen in cup competitions. We've done the same preparation for Scunthorpe as we would for Arsenal, Manchester United or Barcelona. We don't treat them any differently.'

SATURDAY, 8 JANUARY 2005
CHELSEA 3, SCUNTHORPE UNITED 1

Jose Mourinho presents Brian Laws with the five-page dossier he has had compiled in preparation for the tie to show that Chelsea are taking nothing for granted. Yet the match proves even tougher than the score-line suggests.

Striker Paul Hayes' smart eighth-minute turn and shot through Cudicini's legs puts the 6,000 travelling fans into ecstasy. Then, after Kezman's volley and a cruel own-goal by Crosby have restored the natural order, substitute Cleveland Taylor is the width of the post away from putting Laws' men back on level terms.

Only a late close-range strike by stand-in skipper Gudjohnsen kills the game off and Laws says it is a day his side can be proud of. 'Chelsea treated us like kings – but we nearly took a ransom. We showed that they're only human beings and not from another planet – even if they can play like they are. Jose came in and gave me the scouting report he'd compiled on us. I was ready to swap him mine, although I'm not sure he needs it too often. The only weakness I'd spotted was that the pies were cold. But after the game he said to me, "If we keep on being that lucky, we'll win the Premiership." That was a nice touch and he made my players feel very special. It's easy for the big clubs to ignore the smaller teams but he couldn't have done more.'

Goalscorer Hayes is also full of praise for Mourinho. 'Scoring that goal was a dream come true – I just assumed I was going to wake up. But the whole day was fantastic, thanks to Jose Mourinho. He was brilliant towards us. He showed us around, let us go into both dressing rooms, and after the game he said "well done" to each of us on the pitch and came into the changing room as well.

'Jose told us that we could go into the home dressing room and talk to anybody we wanted to and get any autographs and shirts. I got Joe Cole's, which is the one I really wanted. He didn't have to do any of that, but he did. I've seen him called arrogant and rude but he couldn't have done more to make our day great.'

Mourinho rests Terry and Gallas, with Smertin given a run-out at centre-half alongside promising young defender Steven Watt. Cech has not conceded a goal in over 500 minutes; it takes his replacement Cudicini just eight. Sparrow picks up some scraps carelessly left by another Chelsea reserve, Nuno Morais, and clips in a cross to Hayes' feet. His turn is sharp enough to leave the hopeless

Smertin on the seat of his pants and the Scunthorpe striker drills a low shot between Cudicini's legs.

Drogba passes up the chance to tackle Sparrow in the build-up – a snapshot that gives you the picture of Chelsea's early approach to the tie. Chelsea don't underestimate Scunthorpe – they just don't estimate them at all.

A slice of normality is brought to proceedings when Gudjohnsen swings over a cross and, after Drogba's token effort to challenge, the ball falls to Kezman, whose precise volley produces the equaliser.

Then Drogba isolates himself against Byrne and races past him in three strides. The Chelsea striker's intended low cross is a touch sloppy but the hapless Crosby cannot break his lumbering stride and merely wrong-foots Musselwhite with his unwitting diversion.

Chelsea preserve their lead by Cudicini's full-stretch save from Taylor's ten-yard header that shakes the post. But Gudjohnsen wraps up the victory with a six-yard finish five minutes from time after shots from Robben and Cole are saved and the rebound falls to him unmarked close to goal. He smashes the ball into the roof of the net and turns to signify the cup fighters have finally been finished off.

Laws observes, 'We were very much on top in the first 20 minutes – there was only one team in it and we were looking the more likely to score. But as the game went on the Chelsea players stepped up a gear. They knew they had to get a result. But overall, the players did the town, the fans and the club proud.'

As Manchester United begin to plot a route to Exeter after surprisingly being held at Old Trafford, Mourinho suggests that such trips should become compulsory. 'When it comes to the cup, the Premiership sides should always play at the stadium of the lower division side if they're drawn against one,' he says. 'If we'd played our game at Scunthorpe, I can imagine we might have lost it. I can understand that maybe it was a great feeling for them to come to Chelsea and play in front of 40,000, especially as their fans made the atmosphere magnificent. I guess it was the same for Exeter when they went to Old Trafford. That would have been a big day out for them. But I think we should all have to play away. It would give the smaller sides a bigger opportunity of winning and give the fans the chance to see Premiership football players which they normally don't.'

Joe Cole, watched by Sven-Goran Eriksson, pleases Mourinho with another fine performance. 'Joe is improving a lot as a tactical player. The talent he has he will always have, but two months ago I told him it was impossible for him to play in my team as a midfield player. Last week he played against Middlesbrough as a midfield player and he was fantastic. Now he can think the game, not as an individual but one of 11 players. He understands the organisation of the game, what the team needs, what he has to do when we do not have the ball. He is improving a lot as a player and is a good boy. He is open and, instead of crying, wants to improve.'

While the FA Cup is a chance for Cole to continue his breakthrough in the side, it provides Kezman with a strike to lift his confidence. Kezman observes, 'There is a feeling we have something really special going on here. Why not win all four competitions! Normally it would be difficult to talk about the Premiership, Champions League, FA Cup and Carling Cup, but the spirit and belief within the club is tremendous. We all want to make history. It is wrong to look too far ahead but we'll just keep going.'

Mourinho admits, 'We needed a lot of luck. Scunthorpe had a great chance to equalise but were unlucky to hit the post. They played not only with commitment but also with a lot of quality and we had to work hard for the win. The atmosphere was fantastic and I hope the experience inspires them to get promoted.'

So concerned was Mourinho that he brought on Robben for the final nine minutes. And it was the Dutchman's turn and shot which Scunthorpe failed to clear that provided the final flourish. Mourinho adds, 'I can see what the FA Cup means now and I think it's fantastic. The good thing was that Scunthorpe came to Chelsea with a dream of winning, not just to look around the stadium and try not to lose too heavily. If we'd had to play at

Scunthorpe, I couldn't have afforded to play the team I did at home. I'd have been pushed to play a better team because I'd be afraid of losing. I have respect for these guys.'

Team

Cudicini, Johnson, Watt, Smertin, Morais, Geremi (Ferreira), Tiago, Cole, Drogba (Jarosik), Gudjohnsen, Kezman (Robben).

Back at Glanford Park, Laws glances through the Mourinho Report: four pages of computer-generated Technicolor triumph, fronted, of course, by a glossy corporate cover. 'The main thing was that he guessed correctly at our formation and how we would play,' Laws says. 'He knew that sooner or later we would give the ball back to them and the dossier is all about our weaknesses. We are at our most vulnerable when we are on the attack. The attention span of players farther down the league is not very long. Instead of concentrating on individuals, Chelsea concentrated on our shape and how we would attack and defend.'

The fourth round draw pairs Chelsea with Birmingham, and the club's owner David Sullivan admits, 'I'm gutted. We couldn't have had a worse draw. Chelsea are the best team in Britain and probably the best team in the world at the moment.'

John Terry helps brother Paul try to spring an FA Cup shock on Charlton. John fixes it for Yeovil to train at the Blues' training ground ahead of the League Two leaders' fourth-round visit to The Valley. Yeovil manager Gary Johnson says, 'It is thanks to our Terry connection. Paul spoke to his brother and I believe John had a word with Jose Mourinho. I am very grateful to PT and JT and of course Chelsea and Mr Mourinho. It will be an ideal place to prepare for our big game.'

Mario Melchiot reached two FA Cup finals in his five years at the Bridge, winning one and losing the other. Melchiot left Chelsea at the end of last season, initially with the intention of playing abroad. He changed his mind after falling for the charms of Brum boss

Steve Bruce! The season has not panned out as expected and Birmingham hover only slightly above the relegation zone. Melchiot says, 'I made my decision before the season finished. I needed something new and fresh. I was at Chelsea for five years. Everyone knew I wanted to go to another country and try there. But I've never played for any coach who wanted me as much as Steve Bruce wanted me. Things are not going like we expected but I have no regrets. I also have no negative thoughts about Chelsea. The club has been waiting for a long time and I want them to win the title. I think Mourinho has got everyone's head straight. He has enough quality to take the team to a different level and I think he's done that already. He is a man who psychologically is strong. He knows what he wants and he knows how to get it and he's going to get all his players to believe in it as well.'

Melchiot vows to give old pal Claude Makelele a good kicking. 'When I saw we were playing Chelsea, I smiled because I thought it was funny,' he says. 'We want to go further and it would be easier to play a team not doing as well as they are. But you can't do a lot about it. This is a nice game and a nice moment to play. When the draw was made my friends started calling me, but this week I've spoken to Claude. He was joking with me. He told me if the chance arose to give me a kick, then he would. I told him, "Don't worry, if I get the chance, I'm going to do the same!"'

Birmingham boss Steve Bruce is the latest to be spellbound by Mourinho. 'He is a breath of fresh air,' says Bruce. 'We've all been watching him. I don't know whether it's his personality or whether he's a maverick but he's very good and his team reflect it. I had a chat with him earlier in the season and he's very interesting. He's only been here six months and we are all intrigued.'

Bruce, in charge of Huddersfield five years ago, reveals he almost lured John Terry to a club that was then going places. Bruce says, 'When I was at Huddersfield I had agreed a fee of £700,000 with Chelsea for him. And I was led to believe he'd join us. I don't know what it was that I saw in him. Potential, I suppose. And who knows what might have happened if I had signed him? I could have made him a star in Huddersfield!' Terry's move to Yorkshire fell through because the Huddersfield board could not raise enough cash.

Now Bruce believes Terry is one of the main reasons for Chelsea's success. 'John and Frank Lampard are the heartbeat of this Chelsea team,' he says. 'He has been a bit unlucky in some respects inasmuch as he has strong competition for a regular England spot. But for my money he's right up there. And he is unbuyable now. You don't come across the likes of him very often. He's brave – as tough as they come – and a leader. Mind you, you can run through this Chelsea side and there aren't too many weaknesses in it anywhere.'

Mourinho approaches the FA Cup with the same attitude he had towards the early rounds of the Carling Cup. 'There, we played every round with a stronger team, and when we reached the semi-final we used our best XI. In the third round of the FA Cup, against Scunthorpe, we rested a few players, now against Birmingham we'll field a stronger side. Fortunately, all our players are up to it, and I don't think three or maybe four changes will make us weaker.'

SUNDAY, 30 JANUARY 2005
CHELSEA 2, BIRMINGHAM CITY 0

John Terry's goal ten minutes from time spares Chelsea a nervous finish with the team effectively down to ten men and only a goal ahead. Mourinho has already put on Lampard, Drogba and Robben as substitutes when Huth, scorer of the opener, is injured. The centre-half eventually goes off straight after Terry's strike. 'In the first half I think we played very, very, very well and we should have been two or three or four goals up,' says Mourinho. 'In the second half we didn't. It was our fault and they improved a bit. The most important thing is to be in the next round.'

In just the sixth minute Terry's cleverly executed block on Taylor gives Huth the space to head home from a corner. Terry heads the second from a Lampard cross ten minutes from time – his seventh of the season. Terry is honest in his assessment of the opener, which he admits was no 'accidental collision'. He says, 'It's not something we work on in training. Robert and I just said one will win it and the other will do the block. I was pleased with my goal. It was good to get on the scoresheet. The lads were a little bit relieved after we went 2–0 up. Birmingham started quite well. Emile Heskey was winning a lot of headers, which was disappointing defensively. But overall I think we deserved the win.'

After Huth's goal Bridge carves out another opening for Duff four minutes before the break, but this time his effort is deflected for a corner. When the ball comes across Huth again finds space but crashes his shot into the ground and against the crossbar.

Chelsea swap one rampaging winger for another during the interval with Mourinho deciding it is Robben's turn to terrorise the City defence instead of Duff.

But it is City who almost got on level terms in the 52nd minute when a cross from Gray falls to Darren Anderton at the far post. The former England midfielder's volley is good enough to bring the best out of Cudicini, who tips the ball over the crossbar.

Terry makes a slip with a back-header that falls short of his keeper, but the chance is wasted, and the Chelsea skipper then strikes to finish off the visibly wilting opposition.

Most of the post-match talk centres not on the game itself but on allegations that Chelsea have made an illegal approach to Ashley Cole. Mourinho makes light of the suggestions. 'I was in Milan with Adriano,' he jokes. 'On Thursday I flew to Milan, so I couldn't be with Ashley Cole.' In case anyone is in any doubt, he quickly makes it clear his words are in jest. 'Steven Gerrard, Adriano, Ashley Cole – and next week it will be another one. I have a perfect and wonderful squad and I don't need any more players this season. Next season I will need one or two. It is names after names with us, because it is Chelsea. Everybody wants to come and everybody wants to connect players with us. But I have no time to meet players. I am concentrating on my job with the club, and that is to get some silverware.'

Team

Cudicini, Johnson, Huth, Terry, Bridge, Cole, Smertin, Jarosik, Duff (Robben), Gudjohnsen (Drogba), Kezman (Lampard).

With all the off-field controversy the FA Cup draw seems to go ahead virtually unnoticed. Chelsea are drawn away to Newcastle, who they beat en route to the Carling Cup final. But Newcastle boss Graeme Souness is confident of stopping Chelsea's charge. 'We were unlucky not to beat them in the League Cup earlier this season and we cannot wait for this one,' he says.

Newcastle's spy in the camp is Celestine Babayaro, who spent eight years at Chelsea and outlasted three managers: Gullit, Vialli and Ranieri. Nothing prepared him for the impact of Abramovich. 'What has happened at Chelsea under Abramovich is like nothing else that has happened before,' says the Nigeria international who, after almost a decade in west London, delivers his words with an accent more King's Road than Kaduna, his family home in Nigeria. 'He came out of nowhere. Nobody expected someone like him to take over Chelsea. The amount of money he has invested is unbelievable. So many players came and went; the dressing room always had different faces in it. Everything changed so quickly.' Babayaro made 197 appearances for Chelsea following a £2.25m move from Anderlecht in 1997. Significantly, though, only five of those were made during this historic campaign.

Having left Nigeria aged just 15, Babayaro was still only 19 when he moved to Chelsea. He grew up at the club and became a familiar face in a river of new arrivals. But, having survived the cull under Ranieri, the first manager given unlimited access to Abramovich's chequebook, he was not so fortunate under Mourinho. 'There was no hesitation when I found out Newcastle were interested in me,' says Babayaro. 'I'd been at Chelsea for eight years, but I had five months left on my contract. I could've stayed, the manager told me that. I'd thought about signing a new contract, but I wasn't playing regularly. I was the longest serving player at the club. I'd seen players and managers come and go. I'd played under four different managers and that is not an easy thing to do.

'Until Roman Abramovich took over Chelsea there was nothing to choose between them and Newcastle. We were at the same standard. Both looked like they might be able to win the title, but never managed it. Then it all changed because of Abramovich. It is not the same Chelsea I joined, but they are doing so well and I'm pleased for them. I'm happy here, though. It was the right decision. Things have not gone as well as we'd like on the pitch, but we can change that.

'Do I think they can do the quadruple? No, because I hope we knock them out of the cup. It would give me a lot of satisfaction. Beating Chelsea is the sort of result which could make a season. Chelsea are nine points clear in the league and still in every cup competition, so you have to say the quadruple is possible. It's our job to knock them out of the cup, though I'd be happy if they win the rest. Chelsea are flying at the moment but no team is unbeatable and anything can happen in football.'

Babayaro won an FA Cup winner's medal and the European Super Cup with Chelsea, and he believes the transformation from also-rans to runaway leaders is largely down to one man. 'Mourinho's great strengths are confidence and organisation. He knows exactly what he is doing. He came into Chelsea and changed everything. Some people say he's arrogant but I just think he has confidence in everything he does. He's instilled that into the boys and they really believe in themselves, which is a big change for Chelsea. Last season we went into games thinking it was going to be hard and we might get a draw, but this year they expect to get three points from every game. No one even thinks about the possibility of losing. Mourinho's approach to the game is so professional – the most thorough manager I've worked with. We used to watch videos before every game, but Mourinho made us watch the same video three times. A couple of days before the game he puts down notes on each player's peg of who you're playing against so that everyone knows their job. There's this incredible feeling of togetherness and belief that they're going to succeed.'

But against Newcastle Mourinho has Robben, Parker and Drogba injured and Terry suspended. Lampard and Bridge have flu, while Cech, Makelele and Duff are rested with the Champions League blockbuster against Barcelona to follow in midweek. Mourinho says, 'We will go to Newcastle to play against a strong team with my second team.' He adds, 'If the match had been on Saturday, as I believe it should have been, I would have played my strongest side. I don't have supermen here, and it would be asking too much of them to play on Sunday, then travel to Barcelona and arrive in the early hours the next morning. Newcastle played on Thursday, and in those circumstances I can understand that they didn't want to play us on the Saturday. I would be the same. But my point is that there are two days allocated for Uefa Cup ties, and Newcastle could have played Heerenveen on Wednesday. If they had played on Wednesday and Saturday instead of Thursday and Sunday, we'd have played our full team in the FA Cup. The FA should have done something. They should defend the interests of all clubs representing England in Europe.

'Nobody can say I don't respect the cups in England, because when others were playing reserve teams in the Carling Cup I was fielding our best team. Ourselves and Manchester United played our strongest sides in the semi-finals, which was the biggest compliment we could pay the tournament. But this time I cannot do it.'

SUNDAY, 20 FEBRUARY 2005
NEWCASTLE UNITED 1, CHELSEA 0

Chelsea's quadruple dream collapses after Mourinho's double gamble backfires spectacularly. Mourinho, who already has Terry suspended, chooses to rest six more key players ahead of the

Champions League trip to Barcelona, a decision he is forced to rethink after seeing Patrick Kluivert head the home side into a fourth-minute lead.

Duff, Gudjohnsen and Lampard all come off the bench at the break, but 'Plan B' is ripped up within two minutes when Bridge is stretchered off with a suspected broken ankle. Chelsea end the game in disarray, with Duff a virtual passenger for a long spell, and even Gallas limping after a collision with his own keeper. With Cudicini sent off in injury-time, Chelsea actually finish with nine men on the field – two of whom are injured. Little wonder Mourinho starts shaking the hands of Souness and his coaching entourage a minute before the end of the five minutes of added time!

It is Chelsea's first defeat in 16 games and only their second in 30. The Magpies' eagerness to clear the snow off the pitch may have much to do with Terry's ban and the absence of Robben and Drogba, although the Chelsea captain is aware a postponement would rule him out of the Carling Cup final.

The Toon Army are in good voice from the off as they sense an opportunity and they are on their feet with just four minutes gone when their side surges into the lead.

Cole is on the attack but falls, and Kieron Dyer and Nicky Butt combine in the middle of the park to find Laurent Robert on the left. He whips in a cross and Kluivert gets in front of marker Gallas to power an unstoppable header past Cudicini and into the top corner.

Kezman is desperately unfortunate to see his lob clear Shay Given but not the crossbar on 24 minutes, and the Newcastle keeper has to make a solid save from Jarosik nine minutes later.

Mourinho's reaction is as decisive as it is swift, replacing Cole, Geremi and Tiago with Gudjohnsen, Duff and Lampard at the break. But he is left to wish he had not been so bold when Alan Shearer tackles Bridge from behind just two minutes after the restart.

The England defender is in agony and, after extensive treatment on the pitch, he is stretchered off with his left ankle in a protective brace, leaving his side down to ten men as he heads for hospital.

Souness makes his own moves as the game enters its final quarter, replacing Shearer and Dyer with Shola Ameobi and James Milner. Kezman and Gudjohnsen both try their luck from distance to keep Given on his toes.

Full-back Stephen Carr has a chance to wrap things up 16 minutes from time after being played in by Milner, but Duff and Cudicini do enough to deny him only for the keeper to injure his own winger. Cudicini, though, has to suffer even more with his dismissal, ending his dream of a Carling Cup final farewell. 'A selfish person would have let Ameobi score a goal,' Mourinho says. 'Instead Carlo thinks of the team and he bets. He bets, he gives away a free-kick and he gets sent off, but Newcastle do not score. I think it showed the professional that he is.

'You can put a big headline: "Mourinho Guilty Of The Defeat",' the Chelsea manager admits. 'Putting three on at half-time is a risk. But I don't regret it. My life is a risk. I have done it before and would do it again. I am the manager and I make decisions. I am responsible for the defeats; my team are responsible for the wins. I thought the subs would be the best thing for my team. We had ten men for most of the second half and we were better than them. Imagine if we had eleven.'

Bridge is now out long term and Duff (hamstring) and Gallas (groin) are doubts for the trip to the Nou Camp. Mourinho refuses to moan about his injury list in the most crucial week of his reign. 'I don't cry about injuries,' he says. 'When we get on the plane I will think about the Barcelona team. It is time for that now. We can do nothing about the injuries. The medical department will do their best. Sometimes you're proud of your team when they win and sometimes you're proud of your team even when they lose, and I was proud of them today.

'I think the mentality was fantastic – the way the team reacted after losing the goal and playing with ten players during the second 45 and then nine and a half men when Duff was injured. Sometimes defeat makes you think your group is a great one and you are not afraid of the future. I know four trophies is possible. I did it in Porto.

But the domestic competitions are more difficult to win here in England. The result is not fair for us. But I have to be fair and say at Stamford Bridge they did better than us in the first half and we won 4–0, so that was not fair. This is football. We played really well for the team I put on the pitch.'

Shearer describes the win as 'huge'. Asked if the home side were under pressure in the second half, he says, 'I don't think so. If you look at the chances we created and the chances they created, I don't think they really troubled Shay. On the Bridge injury, I don't think we touched each other.'

Souness reiterates the importance of grinding out results without the stylish quality football some fans demand. 'The last two games against Chelsea, luck was not with us. This time is was. They controlled possession after our goal. We are not used to holding on to leads and winning 1–0. That is the first time we have done it since I have been here. Football has never been more cat-and-mouse, never been more cagey. We got a 1–0 and we are delighted. We are in the next round of the cup. Chelsea were criticised at the start of the season. But they kept winning, their confidence grew and they started to score goals.'

As Tyneside celebrates a famous win amid the blizzards that blanket the North East, suddenly Mourinho faces his toughest challenge. They must put behind them their third defeat of the campaign, and find the mental and physical resolve to take on Ronaldinho and friends in the Nou Camp and then a fired-up Steven Gerrard and Fernando Morientes in the Carling Cup final, with the first stirrings of doubt and the sense that the good fortune that has been with them all campaign has turned its back on them at the time of greatest need.

Lampard issues a defiant rallying call, insisting greatness is still within their grasp. 'When you've been winning, it really hurts to drop out of one competition, but there's other things for us to concentrate on. We've got a massive week ahead of us with a lot hinging on it and we need to make sure we're on our game. We can still go on to have a great season. We've got great spirit and belief in ourselves here and will always keep fighting to try and win games. There's disappointment at the minute and the defiance will probably come tomorrow. We'll get together and realise that we're on the verge of some great achievements this year. There's a long way to go on a lot of fronts but we have to make sure we carry through the journey and finish it well.'

Mourinho says, 'Today is not a good moment but there is no time for dramas, especially as we're in a fantastic position to win what we really want to win: the Premiership trophy. I have only good words for my players.'

Team

Cudicini, Johnson, Gallas, Ricardo Carvalho, Bridge, Jarosik, Smertin, Tiago (Gudjohnsen), Geremi (Lampard), Kezman, Cole (Duff).

The Carling Cup

'I LIKE JOSE. HE HAS A GREAT SENSE OF HUMOUR AND A DEVILISH WIT ABOUT HIM. HE SEES HIMSELF AS THE YOUNG GUNSLINGER COME INTO TOWN TO CHALLENGE THE SHERIFF WHO'S BEEN AROUND FOR A WHILE. HE WAS FULL OF IT, CALLING ME BOSS AND BIG MAN. IT WOULD HELP IF HIS GREETINGS WERE ACCOMPANIED BY A DECENT GLASS OF WINE. WHAT HE GAVE ME WAS LIKE PAINT-STRIPPER AND I NOTICE THAT HE DIDN'T HAVE ANY ... NOR DID ROMAN ABRAMOVICH.'

Sir Alex Ferguson after the Carling Cup semi-final at Stamford Bridge
against Manchester United, 12 January 2005

The Carling Cup campaign begins when Chelsea are drawn against fellow Londoners West Ham at Stamford Bridge. A trio of former West Ham players – Frank Lampard, Joe Cole and Glen Johnson, all once idolised at Upton Park – are expecting to run a gauntlet of hate. Assistant manager Steve Clarke says the three players are bracing themselves for a rough ride. 'Having spoken to the lads, they are not expecting a very nice reception from the West Ham fans.'

Lampard has played against West Ham since his move in 2001 but it will be the first opportunity for Cole and Johnson to renew old acquaintances. 'They all want to play against their old club – that is normal,' Clarke adds. 'But it won't affect team selection. All three might play, but it could be two or even one.'

Chelsea will field a strong team because Jose Mourinho is aiming to make the League Cup his first piece of silverware in English football. During his final two seasons with Porto, Mourinho won five of the six available trophies and he is intent on ingraining the same winning mentality at his new club. 'The only difference between Porto and Chelsea is that at Porto we won everything but not at Chelsea,' states Mourinho. 'When you win things together, it makes you stronger. We had two and a half years at Porto of winning and winning and winning and winning ...'

Last season Chelsea lost in the quarter-finals of the Carling Cup to Aston Villa and Clarke says Mourinho has already spelled out what he wants this time around. 'He has told the group that he expects us to win this game and then to go all the way in the League Cup. That is a shift from previous managers.'

WEDNESDAY, 27 OCTOBER 2004
CHELSEA 1, WEST HAM UNITED 0

Last week's Champions League match against CSKA Moscow was played out in near silence at times but there's a much more vibrant atmosphere to this cup tie – that is, until a minority in the crowd loses its self-control and the mood sours. Mourinho makes several changes but still fields a competitive side. In come Carlo Cudicini, Celestine Babayaro, Geremi and Tiago, with Scott Parker starting his second successive match.

The game sees Mateja Kezman's first competitive goal for Chelsea, something which has taken an inordinately long time to arrive. Indeed, after appearing to squander a couple of nailed-on chances in the first half, the Serbian has been receiving stick from a section of the Chelsea fans in the 41,774 crowd. In the 56th minute, however, he gets the reward he deserves for sheer perseverance. Joe Cole plays him in and the striker's shot just evades the groping fingertips of goalkeeper Jimmy Walker to shave the inside of the upright and go in. After the game the Serbian's relief is palpable. 'This was an important goal for me,' says Kezman. 'I feel very free now and I am sure I will score more. Although I missed chances I never gave up. I thought from the first moment of this match that I would score and, in fact, I could have scored a hat-trick.'

The game degenerates in the last 15 minutes after Kezman, who has just been awarded a penalty, is struck above the eye by a coin thrown from among the 6,000 West Ham fans massed behind the goal. With blood pouring from a wound in his forehead, the former PSV Eindhoven striker receives treatment for the cut. Former Hammers favourite, Frank Lampard, is then pelted with more coins before missing the spot-kick.

One of Chelsea's substitutes, Eidur Gudjohnsen, deflects a header against the crossbar and West Ham just fail to force a draw in the dying seconds when Anton Ferdinand, sent forward in a last desperate attempt to salvage something, heads against the bar from Rufus Brevett's cross.

In further outbreaks of crowd trouble, at least two plastic water bottles are thrown onto the pitch as West Ham fans target their former hero Joe Cole. During the evening a Stamford Bridge steward is crushed and has to be taken to hospital after riot police clash with fans who have been pelting the pitch with coins and bottles. Violence flares again after the final whistle when West Ham fans in the Matthew Harding Stand's lower tier fight with police, while Chelsea fans in the top tier appear to throw rubbish from above. It takes 15 minutes for order to be restored inside the ground. Rival fans then clash outside Fulham Broadway tube station as the crowd heads home. Police make 11 arrests for public order offences, carrying offensive weapons and possessing drugs.

It's just a pity that the focus of media attention is falling on a second successive night of football violence in London. These unsavoury scenes come only 24 hours after Liverpool fans threw coins and seats at police during their 3–0 win at Millwall.

After the game West Ham manager Alan Pardew says, 'What happened is a shame. There had been some good English banter between the two sides. There is a big rivalry behind these two clubs and both sets of fans were in good voice.' A police spokesman adds, 'The majority of fans behaved well.'

Pardew meanwhile is comparatively happy with his team's

performance. 'It's difficult to get the ball off Chelsea, but when we did our performance level was good.'

'West Ham played well,' admits Steve Clarke, 'but we could have scored more goals and won more convincingly.'

Team

Cudicini, Ferreira, Carvalho, Gallas, Babayaro, Geremi, Parker (Lampard), Tiago, Kezman, Robben (Gudjohnsen), Cole (Duff).

Chelsea's next Carling Cup opponents are Newcastle United. Having spent two seasons as assistant manager with Newcastle, Steve Clarke knows all about the pressures of working in that football-mad city. He says, 'Newcastle have a good squad of players and great support, but they need to win a trophy. They've invested a lot of money in the squad and need something to show for it. They desperately want to be successful and will be smarting from Sunday's defeat by Fulham as they don't like getting beaten on their own ground – 4–1 is a very heavy defeat and they'll come out wanting to make up for it.'

Meanwhile, Mourinho's side have moved to the top of the Premiership for the first time following Saturday's 1–0 win over Everton. Clarke says, 'We've never really thought about being top of the league, second, third or fourth. We just want to win as many games as we can. It's the Carling Cup, so we'll have a totally different psyche. There's pressure every time these boys pull on a Chelsea shirt, because they're expected to perform. I'm sure they can all handle it.

'We'll make one or two changes, but it won't necessarily weaken the team as we've lots of top international players. It's the time of year when we need to rest one or two because we've got a difficult schedule and a lot of games. It doesn't get easier between now and Christmas.'

WEDNESDAY, 10 NOVEMBER 2004
NEWCASTLE UNITED 0, CHELSEA 2 (AET)

Until extra-time Mourinho cuts a frustrated figure in the dug-out. Laurent Robert is the main architect of Newcastle's territorial domination and has three long-range efforts well saved by Carlo Cudicini. Plan A – with Joe Cole up front, Damien Duff down the left and Tiago in midfield – isn't working, so Mourinho switches to Plan B, unleashing Frank Lampard and Arjen Robben on Newcastle with 20 minutes to go. The game is transformed.

Robben immediately looks the greatest threat on the pitch, and so it proves when he jinks down the left wing and dinks a ball to Eidur Gudjohnsen, who has only been on the pitch for three minutes but still manages to power home a drive low past Shay Given in the 100th minute of an absorbing game. It marks the end of the home side's challenge. Twelve minutes later it really is all over after a superb individual effort from wonderboy Robben. He picks up the ball 45 yards out and dribbles at the heart of Newcastle's defence before flashing his shot across goal and into the far corner.

In the post-match press conference, Mourinho admits, 'We were ready for penalties. But I told them Newcastle would be more tired than us in extra-time and we would get the space. The answer was magnificent again. All of my players gave a fantastic performance. Carlo and Glen Johnson gave a fantastic answer. John Terry and William Gallas were great behind this team.'

Newcastle manager Graeme Souness contributes his personal viewpoint. 'It was a very close call. We had better chances than them and this is hard on us. We leave with nothing after lots of hard work. We defended really well and shaded it in normal time. But Chelsea are a really class side. The first goal was important and they got it. Chelsea will be right up there at the end of the season.'

After watching his skipper guide the club into the Carling Cup quarter-finals, Mourinho insists that John Terry is worth every penny of his lucrative new contract. The England international has just signed a new five-year deal, worth £80,000 a week, and Mourinho is convinced it is money well spent. 'He's ready for everything; he's a top player. To be fair, in this country, maybe you have the best central defenders in the world – John Terry, Sol Campbell, Rio Ferdinand, Ledley King and Jonathan Woodgate. But John Terry is the one for me, partly because he's a Chelsea boy – he grew up here, he was born in Chelsea and he feels Chelsea like nobody else – besides he's a big influence in the dressing room and he deserves every coin.'

This is Chelsea's tenth win in 11 games and their seventh victory in a row, a sequence which has seen the Blues concede just four goals in 18 games with only one defeat. The Blues make the short trip to near neighbours Fulham in the next round.

Team

Cudicini, Johnson, Terry, Gallas, Bridge, Ferreira, Tiago, Parker (Gudjohnsen), Duff (Robben), Kezman, Cole (Lampard).

With Fulham next up in the quarter-finals, Chelsea are taking the Carling Cup seriously because they want to lift *all four* trophies this season. Arjen Robben says, 'We are still in four competitions and our aim is to win them all. You can't go into a competition with any other attitude. It will be very hard to win all four but we'll try.'

'We are now in a time of rotation,' Mourinho says as the Fulham game looms into view. Chelsea could showcase the strength in depth that makes them increasingly likely to win the title. Chelsea's second string is truly first-class: Scott Parker (England international), Wayne Bridge (the second best English left-back), Alexei Smertin (captain of Russia), Mateja Kezman (prolific for PSV Eindhoven), Joe Cole (England awaits his imminent development) and Carlo Cudicini (last season's first-choice goalkeeper).

'You can have the top stars; you can have the best stadium; you can have the best facilities and the most beautiful project in terms of marketing, but if you don't win, all the work these people are doing is forgotten. You have to win and especially, as I have, you have to win a trophy for the first time,' Mourinho says.

After scoring four goals in each of their last three away Premiership games, only Arsenal have a better goalscoring record than Chelsea. But Arsenal have not won the League Cup since 1993 and Manchester United's only triumph in the competition came a year earlier. It would underline the opulence of Chelsea's resources if they were to succeed in the Carling Cup while maintaining a push for the Premiership, the Champions League and FA Cup glory.

TUESDAY, 30 NOVEMBER 2004

FULHAM 1, CHELSEA 2

In the first half Fulham's four-player midfield gives them a man over and it is only after a half-time change of formation that Chelsea start to open up their hosts. Chelsea look to be on their way when Damien Duff's 54th-minute shot from the edge of the box takes a horrible deflection off Ian Pearce's outstretched leg and hops past the wrong-footed Edwin van der Sar. This deflection is a cruel blow for a Fulham team bidding to reach the semi-finals for the first time.

Yet Fulham are determined to make a fight of it and gain their reward in the 74th minute when Ghana-born striker Elvis Hammond, who has only been on the pitch a matter of seconds, whips an inviting low cross past John Terry for Brian McBride to force his way beyond Ricardo Carvalho and shoot home.

Unfortunately for manager Chris Coleman, his team do not have the finesse to break down the meanest defence in the business, with front man Andy Cole guilty of failing to hit the target on at least three occasions.

In the end, substitute Frank Lampard strikes the winner with just two minutes to go, after van der Sar fumbles in his 20-yard shot. The marathon man of England's midfield has replaced Duff 12 minutes earlier and simply refuses to let this tie drag on when everyone else is steeling themselves for extra-time.

Lampard nearly didn't play because he is in mourning for his grandfather, Bill Harris, who died the previous weekend. Before the game, Mourinho offers to leave him out. 'I spoke with Frank before the game and asked him how he was feeling. He said he wanted to be here to help his team. He is a great guy and a great professional. His attitude is fantastic. I asked him about this game and next week's tie against Porto because the funeral is next Monday. He will travel separately to us next week. We will go in the morning and he will go later, but he still wants to join us there.'

After the game Lampard comments, 'That goal was for my granddad. Now we want to go on and win this tournament and get a cup in the bag by the end of February.

'We don't consider ourselves to be "The Invincibles". That's the term used for Arsenal last season but we want to get to that level. We're not there yet because we haven't won anything. But all the players want to go on and win the Carling Cup.'

Fulham manager Coleman says he got the reaction he wanted from his team after their weekend disaster against Blackburn. 'We've matched the country's best team and it's a huge disappointment to lose like that.'

Coleman believes Chelsea may not win all the trophies they are after. 'There is certainly enough quality in the squad but I think it will be hard for them to win all four. I think they will win two – the Premiership and possibly the Champions League. They are in the semi-finals of the Carling Cup and they could win this as well. But I think that the games build up towards the end of the season and it is a big ask.'

Team

Cudicini, Johnson, Carvalho, Terry, Bridge, Smertin, Makelele, Parker, Duff (Lampard), Robben (Cole), Drogba (Gudjohnsen).

While the Carling Cup remains at the bottom of Mourinho's list of priorities, he believes that winning his first trophy as Chelsea boss will enable his side to cross the last remaining mental hurdle.

'I have told the players that this is a competition which finishes in February. It doesn't go on until May or June. If we can reach the final, it would be great for all of us, and especially for the club as they haven't been involved in big occasions for a few years. If you can get through to the final, you go. If we can win, we win.'

Following alleged missile-throwing by fans during their Carling Cup tie at Stamford Bridge, Chelsea and West Ham are both charged by the FA. On 15 December, the FA announces on their website, 'Chelsea FC and West Ham United FC have been charged for the behaviour of their supporters during their Carling Cup match at Stamford Bridge. The two clubs have been charged with a breach of FA Rule E22(a) for their alleged failure to ensure that spectators, and/or persons purporting to be its supporters or followers, conducted themselves in an orderly fashion and refrained from threatening and/or violent and/or provocative behaviour.'

The Carling Cup semi-final draw pits Chelsea against Manchester United. Manchester United thus get a chance to spoil Chelsea's perfect season and repair their own at the same time. United have been second best to Chelsea since the very first league game of the season, when Mourinho's fledgling side ground out a 1–0 victory over them at Stamford Bridge. Twenty-one matches later, Chelsea are brimming with confidence, having cast an inconsistent United 11 points adrift in the title race. Not only have they left United third in the table, dropped champions Arsenal to second and qualified for the FA Cup fourth round, but Chelsea have also been resolute in Europe and are the first club into the Champions League knock-out stages after qualifying with two matches to spare and without conceding a goal in the first four games.

Fergie abandons his policy of playing his second string in the Carling Cup and recalls his star names. 'It will be a stronger team at Chelsea, without being my strongest team. I know I said I'd stick with the side that beat Arsenal in the previous round, but injuries and circumstances have changed all that. The team will be a mixture of first-teamers and youngsters. I can't risk all our players because we play Liverpool on Saturday. We've got a fantastic record in semi-finals since I came to this club: I've never lost a domestic semi and, when you get this close to a final, you want to go all the way.'

With Chelsea and United not due to meet again in the league until 16 April, Fergie knows this is one of his last chances to land a psychological blow on the team everyone is chasing. 'Chelsea have had a great season, you can't deny that. They've had great momentum. They are 11 points clear of us and seven clear of Arsenal. That tells you the story. But, historically, what the next few months tell you is that they will have a blip. However, they have a lot of players and a strong squad, so it's going to be interesting.'

WEDNESDAY, 12 JANUARY 2005

CHELSEA 0, MANCHESTER UNITED 0

A goalless draw at the Bridge ensures it will be advantage United when the teams square up again at Old Trafford for the second leg. The way the visiting fans celebrate at the end of the game suggests they think they will make it through.

Fergie has said the Blues cannot win all four competitions – and he may be right. But United are fortunate. Twice they clear off the line in the second half and, after the game, Mourinho is furious at the performance of referee Neale Barry after the break.

Mourinho claims United got all the decisions from then on because Fergie 'got at him'; he cites a shocking high tackle by Quinton Fortune on Drogba just before a mass brawl that went unpunished.

For his part, Fergie reckons United are hard done by in the first half when Barry turns down a tenth-minute penalty appeal. Louis Saha, back in the United team after a 14-game absence because of a knee injury, is sandwiched as Tiago and Paulo Ferreira challenge him in the area. Then, within two minutes, Cristiano Ronaldo goes sprawling as he checks away from a sliding tackle by Terry. Ronaldo's reputation as a diver has gone before him. Lampard flicks a header wide and

Gudjohnsen converts Duff's cross only to be given offside. Wayne Rooney then brings out the best in Carlo Cudicini, who flies to his left to save the young Liverpudlian's firm header.

After the interval Chelsea replace Gudjohnsen with Drogba and Mourinho's side up their game. Joe Cole volleys Tim Howard's poor clearance wide and on 48 minutes Frank Lampard shows great skill to break into the box and beat Howard with a close-range shot but Gabriel Heinze gets back to clear his shot off the line.

Heinze is then booked for a foul on Drogba and from the free-kick Lampard squares to the striker whose deflected shot is saved by Howard. The game may be scoreless but it is far from dull and Lampard goes close as he volleys Drogba's headed flick just past the post from 25 yards. Chelsea deserve better than a draw but you cannot fault the way United get stuck in to keep them at bay.

Sub Jiri Jarosik pops up in the box with a crisp angled far-post snapshot but Phil Neville denies him on the post. Mourinho then finds himself wrestling in the middle of a late melee after Drogba and Ronaldo clash when the ball goes out of play close to the dug-outs. Drogba has Fortune by the throat while Ronaldo is swinging his arms wildly.

Drogba and Ronaldo are booked but that may not be the end of the matter once the FA have studied the video. And they will be wanting a word with Mourinho after he accuses Ferguson of influencing referee Barry at half-time.

In his cool, calculated style Mourinho fumes, 'There was one referee in the first half and a different one after the break and I suggest he didn't walk alone to the dressing room at half-time. He should go to his dressing room with two linesmen and the fourth official but somebody else was with him and, if the FA ask me about that, I'll tell them.

'Maybe one day when I am 60, when I've been in the same league for 20 years and I know everyone and they respect me, I will also have the power to speak and people will tremble a bit. The second half was fault after fault and diving and more diving. There were dozens and dozens of free-kicks; the ball went into the Manchester United end a number of times and he awarded only two minutes of stoppage time. I'm not questioning the integrity of the referee. I'm sure he is a nice man. It was a question of a big personality influencing another person without as much prestige in English football. I told the fourth official what I felt at the end. It was very important for me to understand a few things of what I saw, what I heard and what I felt at half-time.'

Fergie does not deny his chat with Barry but insists, 'Well, I certainly didn't influence him in the first half!' The United boss says his team should have had a penalty when Saha went down. 'I've seen it on TV and it certainly looks a foul. But we were at Chelsea and it was always going to be difficult to get a penalty.'

Mourinho retorts, 'Manchester United should be forbidden from speaking about referees for at least a year after what happened against Tottenham [Pedro Mendes's last-minute, 40-yard shot which crossed the line, a fact never acknowledged by match officials at Old Trafford] last week. That was the most ridiculous thing I've seen for a long time.'

John Terry maintains that Chelsea will still win through. 'I thought it was a good performance from the lads. It was just a shame we didn't manage to break them down and get a one- or two-goal cushion for the second leg. We said before the game that if it didn't work out for us in the first leg, we would go up there and get a result and that's exactly what we have to do now. We're not going to throw it away now. We're treating the Carling Cup seriously because it's the first final of the season and we want to be there.'

> **Team**
> Cudicini, Ferreira, Gallas, Terry, Bridge, Tiago (Kezman), Makelele, Lampard, Cole (Jarosik), Duff, Gudjohnsen (Drogba).

Mourinho initially escapes punishment from the FA for his comments but referees' chief Keith Hackett wants him to apologise.

'What Jose Mourinho has said is rubbish. The truth is that at half-time Alex Ferguson shouted to the referee, "There are two teams out there." Neale is one of our most experienced referees and was not influenced by that. The facts show that in the second half there were 19 free-kicks – ten of them went to Chelsea and nine to United. I'm hoping that Mourinho might reconsider his comments. Managers do not go into the referee's dressing room at half-time and neither did so on Wednesday. Referees are impartial and Neale Barry is one of the best. On this occasion, it is the comments of a manager who didn't get the result he wanted.'

Statistics do, however, show that Barry punishes Chelsea players more often than other clubs. And he is lenient when reffing Manchester United games. Since 1998, he has given Chelsea 17 bookings in seven games. By contrast, he has shown 10 yellow cards to United in 13 matches.

Mourinho renews his war with Ferguson by branding Manchester United 'cheats'. The Chelsea boss is now in deep trouble with the FA after taking his outburst a step too far. Mourinho says, 'Sir Alex was really clever, if you can say that, at half-time by putting some pressure on the ref. In the second half, it was whistle and whistle, fault and fault, and cheat and cheat.'

Mourinho makes his remarks on Chelsea's own TV channel and his use of the word 'cheat' is likely to enrage both Ferguson and the FA. Arséne Wenger was fined £15,000 earlier in the season for branding Van Nistelrooy a 'cheat' and the FA will be under pressure to haul Mourinho to Soho Square.

On the other hand, Ferguson may see Mourinho's rant as a sign that his mind games are beginning to rattle the Portuguese. Having considered Mourinho's comments, Ferguson comes to the conclusion that the main reason behind them is to try and exert influence over Graham Poll who is taking charge of the encounter between Chelsea and Tottenham at White Hart Lane.

The Scot is annoyed enough to recall Porto's diving antics during last season's Champions League clash with United, then to set his sights on John Terry's claim that Barry refused to listen to him during the game. 'I think Mourinho has opened a can of worms for himself. We remember what happened in Porto. Look back a couple of weeks to the penalty decision that went their way against Liverpool and how Rafael Benitez handled that. But I don't think his comments have anything to do with what happened on Wednesday. It was more about trying to influence the referee for tomorrow's game against Tottenham.'

In a fresh charm offensive Mourinho insists he will go mob-handed to Soho Square to fight any disrepute charge and maintains he has no feud with the United boss. Indeed, he reveals he will be taking a bottle of splendid Portuguese wine to share with Ferguson after the return leg at Old Trafford in a fortnight because the United manager complained bitterly about the vintage they had drunk in Mourinho's office after the first leg! Mourinho says, 'I will be happy to go to the FA with the five, six or seven people who were with me in the tunnel. I won't accept any fine; if they fine me, I will have to pay, but I won't accept it because I did nothing wrong. Since the first day I arrived in England, I've done nothing wrong with referees.

'I know I could be punished for pointing out that someone else has done something wrong. So if the FA do it, I think it will be unfair. I don't think they should punish Sir Alex for what he did; I think they should just tell referees not to allow it whether they are the top manager in the country, a guy has who just arrived or a lower-division manager. I always say what I think and feel and I am not worried by the consequences. If Sir Alex can do that in the Stamford Bridge tunnel – and the tunnel at Chelsea is only ten metres long – I can only imagine what he can do in the Old Trafford tunnel, which is 30 metres. If the FA want me to go there and say what happened in those ten metres, I will go.'

Mourinho's 'cheat' comments were not, it seems, directed at referee Barry but at what Mourinho perceived to be the tendency of United's players to fall down at the first touch. He admits that the use of the word 'cheat' may have been wrong in the circumstances, yet he still hints that United's players were diving. 'Maybe the word is not the correct one and it is not in relation to the referee. It was in relation to players trying to get faults after faults. Maybe "cheat" is not the correct word. For me, "cheat" means when a player gets one touch and they dive.'

The last time Mourinho visited Old Trafford he ended up tearing joyfully down the touchline after his Porto side knocked Manchester United out of the Champions League with a late goal. This time he hopes to be celebrating more than just his 42nd birthday, which falls on the day of the game.

Ferguson has not beaten Mourinho in four attempts and Chelsea have lost only three of their 12 visits to Old Trafford in the Premiership. But Chelsea are aiming to win their first cup tie at Old Trafford in seven attempts. Ferguson has never lost a domestic semi-final in his 18 years at the club.

The word from the United camp is that victory is essential to halt Chelsea's title drive; Ferguson is not quite as convinced about the effect defeat would have on Mourinho and his team. 'It would take a lot of damage to allow us to claw back 11 points. That is a big lead at this time of year.'

For an entire week, Sir Alex is full of praise for Mourinho and Chelsea, but the compliments stop when it is put to him that the London club could one day be bigger than Manchester United. 'That's the most stupid question I've heard this year. You should be apologising for even asking it.'

The second leg will be watched by 68,000 compared with the 41,492 who saw the first leg. In two years, Old Trafford's capacity will rise to 75,000. The club museum and the trophy cabinet complete Fergie's argument. Yet overtaking United and Real Madrid as football's greatest income-generators is precisely what Chelsea are aiming for.

WEDNESDAY, 26 JANUARY 2005

MANCHESTER UNITED 1, CHELSEA 2
(CHELSEA WIN 2–1 ON AGGREGATE)

When Mourinho shakes the hands of the Manchester United players in the tunnel before kick-off, they look confused, sheepish and puzzled. Only Ronaldo smiles and grasps his countryman's hand of friendship.

Ferguson's players have set a club record with a sequence of eight consecutive clean sheets but Mourinho has pinpointed a weakness and is as relentless as ever in preying upon it. Didier Drogba persistently pulls out wide, delivering one pass for the opener and providing another from which Arjen Robben should extend the lead.

United find themselves trailing to Frank Lampard's strike just before the half hour. The in-form midfielder gives United an early warning with a typical surge into the box but his effort from Duff's pull-back is scuffed wide. The next chance comes from Lampard again and it gives the visitors the lead. Lampard delivers a straight pass forward from inside his own half to Robben, who in turn feeds Drogba in the United penalty box. He holds the ball up, then picks out Lampard, who bursts past Roy Keane before controlling the ball with his first touch and dispatching the shot with his second past Tim Howard into the far corner.

United enjoy plenty of possession but, with Claude Makelele patrolling the midfield, they cannot break down the Blues back line. They have legitimate claims for a penalty not long before half-time as Bridge sticks out a foot to bring Quinton Fortune down from behind. The left-back has no need to make such a challenge with the ball heading out of the box. Fortunately for Chelsea, referee Rob Styles may be unsighted by Lampard and he waves play on.

Some heroics from Howard save the Red Devils from conceding a killer second not long before Giggs magically brings United back into it. The American keeper may now be a confirmed second choice behind Roy Carroll but his recent form has been excellent, barring his late blunder to allow Duff's free-kick to find the target.

Twice he keeps United in the hunt, scrambling away a goal-bound Lampard effort, before earning top marks for a feet-first stop which denies Robben. Giggs then produces another semi-final beauty to add to his solo effort against Arsenal in the 1999 FA Cup. Gary

Neville clips a curling ball into the box from the right touchline. With Terry back-pedalling and Cech advancing, Giggs slips between them and chips a first-time volley over the goalkeeper and into the unguarded net.

Chelsea respond by rising above the frenzied atmosphere and clinically looking for a second. They get it, although they benefit from Howard's misjudgement as Duff swings a dead-ball in from the right that eludes everyone to find the net.

United rally and it needs a goal-line clearance from Bridge to deny Mikael Silvestre as well as a brilliant Petr Cech save to thwart Ronaldo before Mourinho is able to celebrate yet another famous night at Old Trafford.

Later Giggs points out that Chelsea found themselves on the rack during the game. 'When we upped the tempo of our play in the second half, I didn't think Chelsea could live with us. We all recognise Chelsea are a quality side but I have not seen them rattled like that before. Once we scored it looked like there would only be one winner. We definitely felt we did enough to get something out of the game but I suppose if you make mistakes in a semi-final against a team as good as they are, you will get punished.'

Mourinho says, 'This was perfect. I'll never forget it. We have given everyone a message that we are really strong. The boys were magnificent and we're ready to win the Premiership now. If you can finish your day with such an important victory, it is the perfect day. The plan was just to win the game and be in the final but we knew, with the opponent and the atmosphere, that a semi-final is always difficult and we were ready for anything.'

Ferguson, who has now failed to beat Mourinho in five attempts, is displeased about the defending for Duff's winning goal. He says, 'In 18 years you expect to lose a semi-final some time. But I didn't want it to happen tonight. We're not happy about the free-kick from 50 yards out – you can't expect to win losing goals like that. We played exceptionally well in the second half. It was a great game; you couldn't divide the teams today. They are a threat on the counter-attack but we coped with that well and I thought we had the far bigger momentum in the second half.'

Asked about whether giving Fergie a £240 bottle of Portuguese vintage red was a fair swap for claiming his proud 18-year-old unbeaten semi-final record, Mourinho graciously insists, 'I would love to lose my records at his age, for his records are absolutely magnificent. I would be very pleased if I kept winning and winning and winning and then I lose one semi-final in 20 years.'

Team

Cech, Ferreira, Gallas, Terry, Bridge, Makelele, Lampard, Tiago, Duff (Jarosik), Drogba (Gudjohnsen), Robben (Cole).

A date at Cardiff is the first tangible reward for all the investment and hard work that has been put in at Stamford Bridge. Mourinho says, 'This final is a great gift for Roman Abramovich who has given so much to this club. From the beginning I thought we could achieve good things.'

Mourinho seems genuinely pleased that Liverpool and Rafael Benitez will provide the opposition in Cardiff. 'It's fantastic for Rafa because he had a difficult week and now he's in the final. It's not easy for managers to adapt to a new country. Liverpool is Liverpool, and Liverpool is history, so it's a fantastic final for the clubs, for the pros like we are and for the supporters.'

Attendances at Old Trafford in the last two rounds of the Carling Cup, against Arsenal and then Chelsea, have been the highest, apart from finals, in the competition's 45-year history. This year's final will have a higher profile than last season's, which was between Bolton and Middlesbrough, and will be contested by something close to full-strength sides, allowing for the exertions a few days earlier of Champions League games against Barcelona and Bayer Leverkusen respectively. Chelsea have beaten Liverpool twice already this season – by a single Joe Cole goal each time.

Mourinho believes the opposition will be all the stronger by the end of February when the final is played. 'When we went to Liverpool they had no Morientes, and Baros was injured. In one month's time, maybe they have both and will have a lot of power. And of course there is Steven [note the first-name terms!] and a good defensive organisation.'

Steve Bennett is appointed to referee the Carling Cup final, the first domestic cup final for the 44-year-old from Kent who has been on the FIFA list since 2001.

Mourinho is then charged with improper conduct by the FA for his 'cheat, cheat, cheat' comments after the semi-final first leg with Manchester United. Mourinho denies the FA charge of improper conduct and requests a personal hearing to defend himself.

In a major break with tradition, Mourinho wants to treat the final like any other away match, so there will be no designer suits. Mourinho doesn't want his players distracted; he orders his players and staff to make sure the build-up is low-key. When Chelsea last reached a final, their 2–0 defeat by Arsenal in the FA Cup three years ago, they won style points for their Giorgio Armani blue pinstriped suits. But this time the players will be in the normal Hugo Boss club suits the squad wear to away matches. Mourinho, no doubt, will wear the grey trench coat his wife bought him when the winter weather kicked in, because he believes it brings him luck.

The biggest week in Mourinho's first season begins in the worst possible way, FA Cup defeat at Newcastle, before the team head off to Barcelona for the Champions League with a series of injuries and lose 2–1. Wayne Bridge is left behind with a suspected broken ankle and Carlo Cudicini is ruled out of the final after being sent off against Newcastle.

Chelsea lodge an appeal with the FA on their goalkeeper's behalf. Cudicini has to wait 48 hours to know whether or not he will be cleared to play in the final with Liverpool. The Italian was dismissed after bringing down Ameobi just outside the Chelsea penalty area. Match official Mark Halsey deems Cudicini to have 'denied an obvious goalscoring opportunity', although TV replays indicate

Ameobi was heading away from goal when he was sent clattering to the ground. Mourinho promised Cudicini he would play in the Millennium Stadium showpiece. But Chelsea withdraw their appeal since they stand little chance of overturning the red card without the cooperation of the ref.

Benitez claims Liverpool's 3–1 Champions League victory over Bayer Leverkusen has boosted Anfield. 'The victory gives us confidence for the Carling Cup final. To score three times in a Champions League game is very good and should improve my team's morale. And do not forget that we have Steven Gerrard and Fernando Morientes back.'

Last summer Steven Gerrard's dad Paul, a straight-talking Scouser, warned his son that he was about to become the most hated ex-Liverpool player in the club's history and that his family would become outcasts in their beloved home city if he joined Chelsea. After hearing his words Gerrard stood in the Anfield trophy room and announced he had no intention of joining Chelsea and that his future lay at Liverpool. The club had managed to hold on to its favourite son for one more season at least. Gerrard's decision to stay at Anfield meant he turned down an extra £15m from Chelsea in increased wages.

Liverpool deny it, but Chelsea insiders now insist a deal will eventually be agreed to sign Gerrard. Apparently he made up his mind to join Chelsea while on England duty in Portugal during Euro 2004 and even texted Mourinho and Peter Kenyon to announce his decision. He was 'less than a week' away from completing the move.

Liverpool chief executive Rick Parry is believed to have held at least two private meetings with Paul Gerrard at the exclusive Royal Birkdale Golf Club to convince him that Steven's future lay at Anfield. John Williams, of Leicester University's Football Research Centre, who is also a Liverpool season ticket holder and closely monitors events at Anfield, says, 'The board mobilised his [Gerrard's] family to work on him. It was emphasised that this was more than about football and money; this was about family and loyalty and the fact that Liverpool is where Steven belongs. The family, particularly Gerrard's father, implored him to stay.'

Former Liverpool player Howard Gayle, who is still closely connected to the club and, like Gerrard, was born in the city, adds, 'There was a feeling that, when Gerrard was in Portugal during Euro 2004, his head was turned by some people telling him that he needed to move on. Gerrard's dad soon put him right and had serious words with him. He just told his son, "Look in the mirror, you are a hero around here, can you really turn your back on the club now?"'

This time the mood is different. There is a sense of inevitability about his move and locals are prepared for Gerrard to leave for west London. Gerrard's deal with his father Paul was that he would give the new regime of Benitez one more season and that, if he was still dissatisfied with Liverpool's progress, he could leave. Williams adds, 'Steven is already in the departure lounge and if he was to go this summer it wouldn't be a big surprise to Liverpool fans. Many fans feel he's done his bit and that he should be free to go; it will hurt, but they are ready for it.'

Gerrard leads his side into the final believing that a major upset is on the cards after Chelsea were knocked out of the FA Cup at Newcastle and then stumbled to a disappointing Champions League reverse in Barcelona, with a sending-off in each game. Liverpool hope to make it a treble of misery. Gerrard argues, 'I really think the pressure is on Chelsea now. Everyone is expecting them to go to Cardiff and win the final and that could work against them. We are going there with the intention of upsetting the odds.'

For more years than he cares to remember, Gerrard has dreamt of lifting a trophy as skipper of the club he has supported since he was a boy. 'If anyone wants to know how much lifting a cup for Liverpool as captain means to me, they should just watch my face if I do that on Sunday.'

Benitez's side have been beaten twice by Chelsea but Gerrard is adamant the London side were lucky to come away with two 1–0 victories. Liverpool dominated for long periods in the New Year's Day fixture at Anfield before Cole stole the points with a late winner, just as he had done at Stamford Bridge earlier in the season.

Gerrard says, 'Chelsea are a very good team full of world-class players so it will be a tough game, but we're confident we can win. They were a bit lucky against us at Anfield. It's a big couple of months for Liverpool. We're fighting for fourth place in the league and are still involved in two cup competitions. We are confident we can get to the last eight of the Champions League but our main aim is to upset Chelsea on Sunday. That's our best chance of winning a trophy.'

Mourinho will not receive a win bonus if he leads the club to a first trophy in five years. Although Mourinho's contract includes scope for generous bonus payments on top of his basic £2.25m-a-year salary, they do not cover the Carling Cup, providing a revealing insight into the club's attitude towards the competition. Mourinho will receive huge bonuses if Chelsea win the Premiership, FA Cup or Champions League, but the Carling Cup is not deemed important enough to merit additional remuneration.

But Mourinho is desperate to collect his first trophy in English football and will select a full-strength side.

John Terry is still haunted by the memory of his last visit to the Millennium Stadium when he was ruled out of the 2002 FA Cup final by a mystery ear infection. 'I woke up on the morning of the match and literally fell out of bed. The balance in my eardrum had gone. Apparently it was vertigo. I'd never suffered it before and have never suffered it since. So it wasn't a good day to go down with it! I did come on as a second-half sub but we lost 2–0 and the medal I got that day doesn't mean a lot.

'I got a winners' medal against Aston Villa in 2000 – but I didn't get off the bench at all that day. Now this is a chance for me to go to Cardiff, enjoy the pre-match atmosphere and hopefully pick up a trophy.

'Everyone at the club knows how important it is to get our first cup. Put one in the cabinet and get the confidence to go on. Then, hopefully, we can add a couple more. This is a perfect chance for us to shut up all those people who are saying that this is finally

Chelsea's blip. There is always an element of jealousy in football and people want to knock you down when you're at the top. It's up to us to deal with that criticism. Losing two games is a new experience for us this season but this final is the perfect opportunity to bounce back.'

Terry also has a point to prove to Fernando Morientes after he scored the goals for Monaco that knocked Chelsea out of last season's Champions League semi-final. 'We really thought we were going all the way, so it would be nice to get our revenge.

'Morientes is a tremendous player, good in the air, strong and holds the ball up well for players like Stevie Gerrard to come through from the midfield. We've got to keep those players quiet because we've put a lot of effort into this cup and it will mean nothing if we lose the final.'

Defiant Mourinho, who ordered a media black-out after the Barcelona game, holds a press conference ahead of the final in which he taunts Sir Alex Ferguson and Arsene Wenger, insisting both would want to swap places with him. An indignant Mourinho denies that the Blues are experiencing the blip that Manchester United and Arsenal have been waiting for and insists that, of the three sides, Chelsea are the most likely to go through to the Champions League quarter-finals. 'They can't speak to us about blips because they're not in a better position than us. Do they want to change positions with us? We are top of the league by nine points and in the Carling Cup final; we didn't lose at home in the Champions League to Milan and didn't lose 3–1 in Munich. If you think two defeats makes me doubt our work or what we can do in the future, I tell you: no chance. The only thing they can say they are in a better position than us in is the FA Cup.'

Asked about the importance of his first piece of silverware, he says, 'I'm not the point. I prefer to analyse it as Chelsea's first trophy of a new regime. People speak a lot, and rightly so, about all the money this club has invested in buying players, but the reality is that we are talking about a process – the process of building a team and a football club – and Chelsea are nowhere near a finished product. We are at the beginning of the process. If you can win trophies during our stage in that development, it is fantastic, because normally you have to wait until it is finished. To get a trophy now would be fantastic, and I'm sure Liverpool feel the same. They have not spent the same sort of money, of course, but they have the same ambitions as us. My friend Rafa Benitez hasn't come to England just to visit; he's here to make Liverpool a winning team again. Maybe he has more time to do it, but they also want to win a trophy.

'We're on top at the moment, but not because of the club's financial power. We are in contention for a lot of trophies because of my hard work, coaching sessions and the team ethic I have instilled here. My philosophy is that you don't win a game during 90 minutes. A winning team is made day by day, training session by training session, minute by minute. Winning the Carling Cup will be a testament to that. A team has to play in the image of their coach. They have to be able to do things with their eyes closed. That isn't about money or having people working together for years. It is about me making them work hard and putting on good training sessions. Then the success will come.'

SUNDAY, 27 FEBRUARY 2005
LIVERPOOL 2, CHELSEA 3

Mourinho shows another side of his character before kick-off when Carlo Cudicini leads the team out despite being unable to play. However, first-choice goalkeeper Petr Cech finds himself picking the ball out of the back of his net with just 45 seconds gone as Fernando Morientes arcs over a searching deep cross. John-Arne Riise is unmarked at the far post and produces a thunderous first-time volley to leave Cech rooted to the spot. Steven Gerrard responds by setting a captain's example by winning his first full-blooded, 50-50 tackle with Lampard.

Sami Hyypia comes close to being sent off just after the break.

Already booked for bringing down Joe Cole, referee Steve Bennett looks set to issue another yellow card before realising what this would entail. Hyypia instead escapes and Mourinho starts to lose his temper when he berates both Luis Garcia and Jamie Carragher from the touchline as the match grows in intensity.

The Chelsea boss changes the pattern of the game with his introduction of Eidur Gudjohnsen at half-time, replacing Jiri Jarosik. Gudjohnsen re-energises his team as Chelsea lay siege to the Liverpool goal, even if Jerzy Dudek conjures up a fantastic double save first from Gudjohnsen and then from William Gallas. Benitez brings on Milan Baros and, just moments later, Gerrard comes agonisingly close to putting his side 2–0 up only to divert Antonio Nunez's cross inches wide from close range.

After Didi Hamann brings down Frank Lampard in full flight, the Blues duly equalise from the free-kick. Gerrard jumps highest, challenged only by his own players, to meet Ferreira's mis-flighted delivery but succeeds in diverting the ball past Dudek. At this point Mourinho cannot contain his celebrations and is dismissed from the touchline. Dudek is then injured in a clash with Damien Duff, and, with his side's three substitutes already on, there is a nervous wait for Benitez before he carries on.

Just a minute into the second period of extra-time, Hyypia fails to cut out substitute Glen Johnson's long throw and Drogba bundles the ball over the goal-line from close range. Then Dudek fails to hold Gudjohnsen's fierce cross and Kezman succeeds in prodding the ball just over the line before the keeper can react in time. Liverpool rally immediately, with Nunez just beating Cech to a header as he flicks the ball into the net, but after this there is no more scoring and Chelsea run out 3–2 winners.

Mourinho is guaranteed a hero's reception from the Chelsea fans when he finally reappears after the final whistle. In his first season, Mourinho has just brought the club their first trophy in five years and only the tenth major success in their entire history.

But he has endured a controversial afternoon. He was shocked that it was a policeman who intervened to send him off after he appeared to gesture to Liverpool fans following Chelsea's 79th-minute equaliser. After Gerrard's own-goal, Mourinho turned to the crowd with his finger to his lips and then was ordered from the dug-out by fourth official Phil Crossley, in conjunction with the head of the national group of referees, Jim Ashworth. 'For me it is unusual to be sent off by the police and not by a fourth official. The policeman told the fourth official Mr Mourinho has to go off, so this is a special situation for me. But again if I made a mistake, if I do something I cannot do in English football, I have to adapt.'

A league official confirms Mourinho was asked to leave the technical area to preserve public order.

Earlier Mourinho had been warned for berating Liverpool players, notably when he pointed an accusing finger at Jamie Carragher, and he was then censured seemingly for inciting Reds fans by putting a finger to his lips after Chelsea's late equaliser.

He later tells a news conference the gesture was not to Liverpool fans but to his critics in the media. 'It was a gesture to be cool, to put your pens back in your pockets,' he says.

In the end, it was Didier Drogba who persuaded Mourinho to go back out on to the pitch to celebrate with his players. 'I had to do this for my team-mates,' says Drogba. 'I told him that we win together, we lose together and we celebrate together. It was me who went back for him but it could have been any of us. That is the spirit of this team.'

Drogba 'had to score' as he later explains, 'I knew I had let my team-mates down in Barcelona by being sent off and I had to make up for that. I know I will not be there for the second match but I am confident the team will win through without me. If I had played one or two more matches before Barcelona, then I am sure I would have been quicker and would not have been sent off. This trophy is very important for us though. We have not been down in many matches this season and won. This will give us great confidence now to go on in both the Champions League and the Premiership.'

Mourinho says Chelsea, who dominated possession

throughout, deserved victory. 'We were the best team. They fought a lot. They defended a lot and well and they were very well organised. They did their best. But when we scored with ten minutes to go, at that moment we had a big advantage from the psychological point of view.

'The attitude of my players was magnificent and we deserved to win, no doubt about it.'

Benitez says his side deserved to win after holding on to the lead for 79 minutes. 'If you have clear chances at 1–0, if you get a second goal, you finish the game. We made mistakes and in the end we conceded a goal. I said to the players we must be proud, we have had a good game; they controlled the game but we were organised as a team and had opportunities. It is difficult to play against Chelsea, but we scored two goals and worked hard. I think that after the game we need to analyse things.'

Gerrard's face is a mask of suppressed rage when his name rings around the Chelsea areas of this magnificent stadium: after his own goal, the idea of his defection to the west London club is mingled deliciously with implied gratitude for his contribution to the cause. The clear implication of the chants was that this was his first significant contribution to his 'new club'!

Later Benitez is adamant his captain must not shoulder any blame and praises his side's defiant performance. 'I spoke to Gerrard afterwards, just as I spoke to the rest of the players, and I said that they should be proud. It's a pity for the team and the fans. It's not a problem for any one player. At the end, to score in your own goal is bad luck, that is all.'

Gerrard is distraught at the end of the match and tries to avoid Mourinho, only to be pursued by the Chelsea boss for a handshake. The significance of that is not lost on fans, but Mourinho says, 'I didn't see Gerrard move away from me; he was feeling very down because he had scored the own goal and I was trying to console him. I went to every member of the Liverpool staff and I didn't see that as a negative thing. I didn't single Gerrard out, I just felt for him.'

During the game Roman Abramovich could be seen willing the ball to cross the line, fidgeting and then jumping for joy as the goals went in. This is the beginning: the first trophy for the owner and the new manager, but it won't be the last.

Team

Cech, Carvalho, Gallas (Kezman), Ferreira, Terry, Cole (Johnson), Duff, Jarosik (Gudjohnsen), Lampard, Makelele, Drogba.

In an interview with Portuguese television, Mourinho continues to insist that he was banished to the stands by the police. 'I wasn't sent off by the fourth official but by the authorities. This country is different and has its good and bad stuff. It was all because of a gesture to shut up the British Press. For them this is First World and Portugal is Third World. I won't shut up because Chelsea needed a Third World manager to win a trophy, something that didn't happen in the last five years.'

Captured on Sky TV, Mourinho can be seen telling Jamie Carragher to 'f*** off' *five times*. But another rap for Mourinho looks unlikely as the FA await the formal reports. Sifting through the information has taken longer than expected because of the conflicting stories. South Wales Police say that it had nothing to do with Mourinho's removal after Chelsea's equalising goal, an assertion backed by the Football League. 'The decision to ask Jose Mourinho to leave the technical area came from the match officials and was initiated by the fourth official, Phil Crossley,' a spokesman says. 'The match referee, Steve Bennett, was aware of what was happening on the touchline and was content that it was being dealt with correctly.'

Chelsea's director of communications, Simon Greenberg, says Mourinho has apologised if there was any misunderstanding among Liverpool fans over his gesture. 'The manager apologised, which is something people have not made a lot of. He was measured and said that, if he had made a mistake, he apologised for that. He is a guy who knows his own mind and also a guy who does listen. He knows why he did it and we don't have a view on whether that was wrong or not.'

Abramovich, according to John Terry, was 'over the moon' as he joined the players in the dressing room. 'He was having pictures taken with the lads and the trophy,' Terry says. 'He had a couple of glasses of champagne as well, so it is great.'

Inevitably Abramovich's riches have brought envy and resentment. Terry says, 'We don't get irritated by people having a go at us. It is frustrating at times, because we have done really well this season, but it is up to us to stop people from talking. There is only one way to do that, which is on the pitch. We have shut a few people up. It is a great win for us and hopefully that will stop people talking for a little bit. There is definitely no crisis here. When you are at the top, people want to shoot you down. That is where we are at the minute and we have to deal with that.'

Terry calls it 'a massive cup' and adds, 'This trophy means the world to us. The players, the management, the club, the fans – everybody involved with the club. It is a great achievement and a great starting point for us. We are professionals, we are grown up and we deal with that. We can build from this and, if we keep on showing great fight like that until the end of the season, hopefully it will be a great year for us. This is the start of our trophies.'

What counts above all else is that Chelsea had to recover from their lowest ebb to capture the Carling Cup, as Cech points out. 'Our black week is now over. After our failures in the FA Cup at Newcastle and the Champions League at Barcelona, we were under big pressure but we showed we had the inner strength and will to win. We were in our worst position of the season but we came back and defeated Liverpool. We were like a good working machine.'

As he toasts his first winner's medal, Frank Lampard offers further insight into Mourinho's mentality. 'The manager can handle the pressure. He reacts to it in a positive way. He likes a fight, he likes a battle and he stands up to it. This was our message: we won't give in and we will continue that in the league and against Barcelona because we want to win them all. If we had lost, the pressure would really have been on. It would have been a case of going from the quadruple to almost nothing. But we have thrived upon the fact that there has been so much pressure and criticism from outside.'

Mourinho receives news that he has escaped a fine or touchline ban from the FA after his behaviour in Cardiff but he is reprimanded and asked to behave more responsibly in future. 'Jose Mourinho has been reminded of his responsibility to abide by FA rules governing the conduct of managers,' the governing body says. 'He will not face any formal disciplinary action and the FA now considers the matter closed.'

And finally, Wayne Bridge gets to lift the Carling Cup – from his hospital bed. Led by skipper John Terry, players visit the broken-ankle victim and take the trophy along with them. Bridge, who broke his ankle at St James's Park during the FA Cup defeat, will still receive a winner's medal after playing in four of Chelsea's six ties on the road to Cardiff.

PART TWO:
SUSTAINING SUCCESS

Back-to-Back Champions

CHELSEA 3, MANCHESTER UNITED 0

Mourinho's team save the best until last as Chelsea seize back-to-back championships against the only club to have similarly won successive Premiership titles. After 50 years without winning the League, two titles came along at once, one for each of the two years of Jose Mourinho's reign.

Chelsea start with William Gallas's fifth Premiership goal of the season – a total that means the French defender has equalled the combined output of Eidur Gudjohnsen and Damien Duff. Frank Lampard swings the corner over, John Terry jumps early and Didier Drogba, lurking behind his captain, nods goalwards. Gary Neville, positioned by a post, would probably have stopped it, but is helpless to keep out a more powerful header from the intervening predator Gallas.

Terry, having come off worse in a challenge with Wayne Rooney, overcomes the pain, but is one of two defenders embarrassed by a thrilling surge from the former Everton man which gives United hope. Finding Louis Saha from deep, he sprints and turns the striker's lay-off into a one-two; Terry, diving in, is left on his bottom and Ferreira is nutmegged before Rooney advances on Petr Cech only to pull his shot wide. Later, with a sudden low drive from 20 yards, Rooney brings an outstanding save from the Blues goalkeeper.

Chelsea, though, are in overall control and, when Drogba flicks on a long clearance from Cech, the nimble feet of Joe Cole prove too much for both Rio Ferdinand and Nemanja Vidic, whom he leaves in his wake before shooting past Van der Sar. Rooney is cautioned for a foul on Drogba, before Ricardo Carvalho rounds matters off in style. From his own penalty area, he feeds Lampard and surges forward into attack. He never stops running as the ball moves on to Cole, who spreads it to Carvalho on the left. Carvalho cuts in and sends a smooth right-footer into the far corner.

Even in the 78th minute, with United three down, Rooney remains in brilliant defiant form until he collapses in agony after a tackle from Paulo Ferreira. Rooney's England team-mates – Lampard, Terry and Cole – are visibly anxious when the striker is stretchered off.

Then come the celebrations. Before the 90 minutes are up, Mourinho shakes the hands of all the United staff, including Sir Alex Ferguson, which leaves him free to stride triumphantly on to the turf at the final whistle, a Portugal national team scarf wrapped around his neck. This is more to do with patriotism than a subtle dig at the FA over the Luiz Felipe Scolari debacle.

Mourinho remains as unpredictable as ever. He carries a magnum of Barclay's finest champers with him out on to the pitch, sipping as he walks. Without warning, he goes over to the crowd and throws his personalised club blazer into the chanting crowd, followed by his gold medal and then, when handed a replacement gong, he pitches that in among the fans too. He is showing his appreciation, but in a way that only the idiosyncratic boss of this Chelsea team is capable of.

Indeed, he turns out to be in one of his enigmatic moods. Instead of recognising the great teams he has built, he tells the post-match press conference that his critics can only see 'coins, pound signs, big numbers and transfer fees'. He has, he says, come close to quitting Chelsea twice this season because they are 'the worst club in the world' to be the manager of. 'You can achieve, you can win leagues,' he says, 'but it is never enough.'

His achievements, Mourinho says, have only been recognised by the award of the Manager of the Month trophy, which he has received twice in two years. But there are enemies in Portugal he describes as 'rats', who are out to get him, and every club Chelsea tries to buy a player from, he insists, charges an extortionate price. That elaborate explanation is made with a glass of water as a prop. 'To everybody else this glass is £2m,' Mourinho says, 'for Chelsea £200m.'

Sir Alex Ferguson is magnanimous in defeat. As well as praising Mourinho and his team, he says, 'For the history and for the stats in terms of winning the League, Chelsea have got all the credit. Because it's not easy to win the League and they've deserved to win it because they don't lose goals at home. We had opportunities today and missed them and, if you miss chances against Chelsea, then with the record they've got at home you deserve to be beaten.'

But Chelsea have taken the title in a manner that banishes any doubts as to whether they deserve it or not. Their stirring performance emphasised the margin between the teams. Mourinho reminds anyone listening that he now has four consecutive national championships, the first pair with Porto. 'The result doesn't show how difficult Manchester United made it for us. They were fantastic today.'

Knowing they only needed a draw to win the League, Chelsea set out to attack to ensure there was no chance of a slip-up. Mourinho says, 'It is a fantastic feeling. This is my second title in England and my fourth consecutive one if you include Porto. One day we'll lose, but for now we are the best team in the country and we really deserve this moment.'

In Europe, they might have failed against Barcelona and in their FA

Cup semi-final against Liverpool, but since Mourinho arrived at Stamford Bridge he has been master of the Premiership. Out of 74 matches, they have won 58 and lost only four, out-scoring the opposition by an average of four goals to one and few champions, in any era, have got anywhere near that ratio.

At home, they have dropped a mere two points all season: a record which Mourinho refers to as he explains why he hurled his medal – preceded by his jacket – into the Matthew Harding Stand. 'I think the people behind that goal are the best supporters we have,' he says. 'One of the reasons we are champions is that we have a very good record at home and they are a part of that, so I wanted to share the moment with them. The person who got the medal is a lucky guy. He has a great souvenir – or he can go on eBay and make a fortune!'

Mourinho may be wearing his Portugal scarf as he salutes Stamford Bridge, but he praises the English backbone at the club, players who encapsulate the spirit of his team. 'The next jump for JT is for people to look at him as the big player he really is. And for me he is the best central defender in the world. I could not have inherited a better leader of my side.' But is he a better chief lieutenant than Lampard? 'Frank is a different kind of person,' says Mourinho. 'He is a fantastic JT shadow. Frank is not so emotional, but in the day-by-day squad life he's a fantastic shadow for the captain. I cannot separate them.'

For his part, John Terry says, 'What a season from the lads and to retain it [the title] is absolutely fantastic. We all dug in together, grafted and we came out of it again. That's been the best atmosphere I've ever seen at the Bridge here today – two years unbeaten in the League is fantastic.'

Chelsea's 20-goal, top-scoring midfielder Frank Lampard adds a comment of his own. 'To be champions back to back when we haven't been champions for 50 years before, it's a special day for the fans, for everyone, it's brilliant. This means everything to me.'

Terry hobbles out of Stamford Bridge on crutches, but Mourinho is adamant there is no chance of the defender missing out on the World

Cup in Germany. 'I know he was hurt, but it's not the kind of injury that is a problem for the future. The problem was the pain. Some people have a pain threshold very low and others have it very high. JT played last season in unbelievably bad circumstances. Today he went out and played as a captain on the day to lead us. It is difficult to be a better player. All he can do is keep that standard.'

Chelsea club doctor Bryan English later confirms Terry has come through the title clincher against United carrying two injuries and will have a scan on a sprained ankle to make sure it is not too serious. English says, 'We put two stitches in at half-time, then took them out at the end and replaced them with three. In the second half, he also twisted his ankle a little as well, so he actually had two injuries. He will have a scan tomorrow, but I am not concerned about anything and expect him to be fully fit for England.'

Mourinho joins Liverpool and Manchester United in the exclusive club of back-to-back title winners and remains keen to see his men maintain Stamford Bridge's status as a fortress. They have only dropped two league points at home all season. Mourinho comments, 'The home record is amazing, yes. One of the reasons why we are champions is because we didn't drop points at home. We lost just two points out of 57. For me, it is now four years without a defeat at home. It is unbelievable. Two titles for Chelsea and four consecutive years as champions here and at Porto.'

William Gallas, 28, has a year to run on his contract and Chelsea will have to sell him now or else he can leave on a free transfer. Barcelona and Milan currently head the chase for the defender, who was bought from Marseille five years ago for £4m. The experienced defender says, 'I have not signed anything with Chelsea and don't know if I'll stay because I am a man who wants to win everything. I want to do that in different countries and maybe next season I will be somewhere else. I need to speak with the manager. In my mind I am confused because maybe I want to leave. I've been here five years and maybe that is enough. When I started in football I told myself I wanted to play in every country. In Spain and Italy and England and

France and you are fortunate when you are a footballer that you have the opportunity to play in those places.'

Arjen Robben admits he has not been in top form for Chelsea this season. Robben, 22, says, 'I would have liked to play a more important role for the team. During my first year I could easily make the difference in the game, something that I have not been able to do in the past months. I didn't have a great start to the season. I had trouble with some injuries. I also believe that other players have managed to prepare and defend themselves more against my way of playing.'

Speculation suggests Robben could be among those on their way out. But he denies this to Dutch newspaper *Algemeen Dagblad*. 'I can assure you that that is not true. Right now I'm interested in the fact that we fully deserve this title. It is in the hands of the rightful owners. We built up a large lead early in the season and we managed to keep it up all the way through.'

But this is also an occasion for Mourinho to get all his grievances off his chest at one go. He blames the press for his team's exit from the Champions League and rails against a system that punishes his players, but lets off big names such as Ronaldinho. 'When Barcelona played Benfica, there was a free-kick and Ronaldinho went to measure the 10 yards for the wall,' Mourinho says. 'If another player did that, yellow card, goodbye, disappear. Ronaldinho, a walk, a smile, a laugh and it's done.'

Meanwhile, Roman Abramovich loves nothing better than to mix with the players in the dressing room, enjoying their highs and sharing their lows. Relaxed in jeans and pullover, the club's Russian owner is there as usual, this time to bask in the glory of back-to-back championships.

Chairman Bruce Buck, the American lawyer who has been a member of the Abramovich entourage since long before the Chelsea takeover, observes the club's owner joining in the celebrations after what must be the most satisfying way of landing the second title – beating Manchester United comprehensively at the Bridge. Buck comments, 'I saw Roman in the dressing room and he had the broadest smile on his face. We have accomplished a lot, but there is still a way to go. He agrees with our expectations for the future: to become the biggest, best, most well-known club in the world. We have got to accomplish a lot. We would like to do better on the football front. Many people would say it is hard to believe you can, but we would like to.'

Clearly, Abramovich's ambition is still to land the biggest prize of all, the Champions League. But, in their second year of glory, Chelsea end up with 29 Premiership wins to their name, equalling their own record from last year, with four draws and three defeats. Their points total is 91 and their goal difference an impressive 50. Their early season form was exceptional with 15 wins in the first 16 games and, but for a dip in March, they would have cruised to the Premiership title. As it was, Manchester United hit a hot streak, winning ten matches in a row and cutting down the Blues' lead from 18 to 7 points, before succumbing to the men from the Bridge when the chips were down.

Team
Cech, Gallas, Carvalho, Terry, Ferreira, Makelele, J Cole (Crespo), Essien, Lampard, Robben (Duff), Drogba (Maniche).

Sebastian Kayll, 35, caught the first medal thrown into the crowd by Jose Mourinho. The volatile Chelsea boss then threw a replacement gong to the fans, which was grabbed by delighted Dean Juckes. Recruitment consultant Kayll, 35, of Binfield, Berks, said, 'Not only did we beat United 3–0, we won the Premiership and I got Mourinho's medal. After the match we were celebrating and Jose walked towards our stand. I saw him throwing the medal. There is a barrier next to where I sit, so I used that for extra leverage and caught it. Everyone around me went wild – they all wanted their picture taken with the medal. I am going to frame it and put it in my study.'

Married garage-owner Juckes, 25, of Eastbourne, East Sussex, added, 'A 3–0 win against Man United was fairytale enough. But, when

I caught this medal, it was incredible. I caught it in my left hand and the crowd around me went mental and my picture was up on screen.'

Andrew McAnulty walked off with Jose Mourinho's club blazer stuffed up his jumper after battling several fans for it. His brother Simon helped him keep hold of the jacket in the melee after Mourinho hurled it into the crowd. It has the Chelsea boss's name stitched inside. Dad-of-three McAnulty, 35, of Islington, north London, said, 'There was no way I was letting go.'

2007 Carling Cup Final

CHELSEA 2–1 ARSENAL
DROGBA 20', 84', WALCOTT 11'

Jose Mourinho triumphed again in the Carling Cup thanks to Didier Drogba's two expertly taken goals as substance succeeded over style.

The first 20 minutes were all about Arsenal, whose precision, skill and movement dominated in Cardiff, but Mourinho proved that winning brings its own thrills.

Petr Cech had turned away powerful Fabregas and Baptista shots when, in the 11th minute, he had to pick the ball out of his net. Walcott collected a sloppy clearance 35 yards from goal, fed Diaby at the edge of the area and dashed into the box for the return ball, which Diaby duly delivered. As Cech raced off his line, the 17-year-old kept his composure to slot it past him into the corner.

But then, in the 20th minute, Chelsea suddenly drew level. Drogba peeled away from his markers in the centre and found space on the right – but had seemingly strayed slightly offside when Michael Ballack aimed a dainty chip over the top to him. The flag stayed down, however, and the Ivorian took one touch to tee himself before firing expertly past Manuel Almunia.

Chelsea began to assert themselves.

At the break, Mourinho decided that the best way to keep Arsenal at bay would be to force them on to the back foot, so he threw on Arjen Robben in place of Claude Makelele. The Dutchman's impact was almost immediate, as he slalomed past three defenders in the 48th minute and narrowly failed to find Shevchenko with a clever through-ball.

One of Chelsea's biggest set-backs of the season occurred in the 55th minute, when Terry attempted to head goalwards from a corner but was caught, accidentally, in the face by Diaby's boot. The England captain was knocked out cold and, after several minutes' treatment, was stretchered off and taken to hospital. He regained consciousness before entering the ambulance.

When play resumed, Chelsea lost the forward momentum of Essien, who retreated to defence in place of Terry as John Obi Mikel came on in the middle, but Lampard struck a spectacular shot in the 77th minute, from 25 yards off the crossbar. Seven minutes later, Chelsea took the lead. Essien pounced on a loose ball in the middle and instantly fizzed it wide on the right to Robben, who took one touch, looked up and arrowed a wicked cross towards Drogba in the box. The Ivorian masterfully directed his header into the far corner.

Chelsea almost snatched a third with another simple, devastatingly incisive counter-attack. Drogba flicked on a long Cech kick, Shevchenko controlled it, held off the defender and walloped the ball past Almunia. It cannoned back off the bar.

As the match ticked into the first of 11 minutes of injury time, Mikel tugged Touré's shirt; the Ivorian reacted by pushing the Nigerian in the chest – and then the other 20 players joined the melee. Amid the pandemonium, Wayne Bridge was sent sprawling to the ground, and both managers and several officials had to separate jostling footballers. It took several minutes to restore order. Referee Howard Webb dismissed Mikel, Touré and, after a tip-off from his assistant, Adebayor too.

Chelsea clinched the first trophy of what promised to be a thrilling bid for a historic Quadruple-winning season.

But the after-effects of the blow to Terry's head can be pinpointed as one of the reasons Chelsea surrendered their Premiership crown to Manchester United. Mourinho had run out of centre halves, and Essien's drive in midfield was lost when he played as an emergency centre-back.

Terry couldn't remember anything from the moment he walked out for the second half of the final until he woke up in the ambulance on the way to hospital. Terry swallowed his tongue, stopped breathing and was left concussed; his injury was so serious that players immediately summoned medical assistance from the bench and he was treated for five minutes before being carried off on a stretcher. Yet Terry was fit enough to leave hospital a short time later and join in the celebrations after the game. 'I just said to the lads I didn't remember. I remember walking out for the second half and nothing else until waking up in the ambulance on the way to the hospital. I had the scan and they said it's OK. It was great to be back [with the lads], they were different class. I'm still feeling a bit groggy though. It's thanks to the lads as I didn't have much part to play in the second half. Throughout the competition they've been spot on.'

'Following John Terry's injury in yesterday's League Cup final, the FA can clarify that the rules on head injuries do not set down an automatic rest period for players suffering from concussion, but rather stipulate that each injury must be assessed individually by a doctor,' read an FA statement. 'The FA medical recommendations state that: "since all head injuries are different in terms of the effects on the brain, no fixed time periods are applicable in professional football as to when the player should return to training and playing. The brain's response to the injury determines the time of return and playing and must be clinically assessed by the club medical officer or a specialist neurosurgeon/neurologist. The clinical rule is that no player should return to training or playing until symptom-free and sign-free at rest and on provocation."'

Mourinho urged that there should be no witchhunt after the 18-man brawl that marred the final. 'What happened is not my responsibility or Arsène Wenger's responsibility. If sometimes mature, adult people – managers – lose our emotional control and do things sometimes that we shouldn't do, we cannot kill a player because something happened.'

Mourinho and Wenger had marched on to the pitch in time added on because they feared the fighting would escalate. Mourinho said, 'When I was there I could stop some Chelsea players and when Wenger was there he could help control the emotions of his players. It is what we have to do. We have to try to help.'

Wenger stated that he had 'wanted to make sure nothing major happened'.

Adebayor was also dismissed for his part in the fracas. The Arsenal striker then remonstrated with Webb, and his failure to leave the field and his apparently aggressive gestures were the subject of FA scrutiny. 'I am worried about the FA's response,' admitted Wenger 'With the FA there is always a good chance something will happen, so it is better you worry. I am very disappointed with the brawl because it doesn't reflect the quality of the game. Both teams went for it in a positive way.'

Mourinho added, 'My player with a red card was John Obi Mikel. If he did something wrong, it is not for me to kill him, it is for me to educate him. The last ten minutes was emotional for Arsenal and emotional in the wrong way. I do not think that now is the time to find who is guilty or not guilty. It's time to think about the good things in the game. It had very good things for us, especially the most important thing in finals: that the cup goes home with us.'

Chelsea's own dressing-room inquest into the incident suggested that Adebayor had been wronged and that Eboué had been more at fault. Both managers agreed that the indiscipline favoured Chelsea, who had taken the lead through Drogba's 84th-minute header. 'I felt if we had kept our calm we had enough energy and mental resources to come back,' said Wenger.

Mourinho, who celebrated his fifth trophy of his two-and-a-half-year reign with a five-finger gesture, to the owner, Roman Abramovich, was pleased to have emerged victorious. 'We fought hard,' he said. 'We were losing, they had a much better first half than we had, so to be 1–1 at half-time was good. They were much better than us. The second half was the opposite. We controlled the game and we had two shots hit the post, we scored the winning goal and had control of the game.'

Wenger apologised for his team's part in the fracas. 'I feel we should not have reacted at all. Overall we are sorry for what happened. When you do not behave like you want to, then you have to apologise. We want to focus on playing football well. We want to deal well with the frustrations and want to be exemplary. But we also want to remind people we have been top of the fair play table twice in the last few years. Also this year we are the team who have committed the least fouls in the League and been the most fouled against. What happened was a one-off for us in the last three years and we are sorry for that. It was a good game and that was an incident of one minute. But we do not want to behave like we behaved and that is it.'

Lampard came out in support of Wenger, claiming he was not punched by Adebayor. However, the Arsenal manager had been asked by the FA to clarify his outburst where he claimed that one of the referee's assistants, who was alleged to have reported seeing Adebayor punch Lampard, was lying. Wenger also asked for the Chelsea midfielder to come forward and tell 'the truth' about the clash, which he has now done. 'I've spoken to Frank and he told me that he wasn't punched,' the player's agent, Steve Kutner, said.

The FA found Eboué guilty of violent conduct for his role in the melee, in which he struck Bridge. 'Contrary to Wenger's allegations, the assistant referee's report does not claim that Adebayor punched Frank Lampard,' responded a FA spokesman. 'The report states that Adebayor's attitude was aggressive, that he shoved into Ricardo Carvalho and that he aimed a punch at Lampard. It does not state that Adebayor struck Lampard. Questioning the integrity of a match official and accusing them of lying is a very serious claim to make as it questions the whole integrity of the game. We also reject any accusations of bias or dishonesty within our disciplinary system. We will be asking Arsène Wenger to explain these comments.'

At first it was thought Terry would play immediately but he had to accept it would require a period of recovery. No damage was found during the scan, which Chelsea described as 'routine'. Nevertheless, having accepted that the incident might have been much more serious, he also sought the advice of a specialist neurologist. There was relief that there were no long-term effects but there was also dismay that, since he had suffered a head trauma, he should not have been permitted to discharge himself from hospital after the match. Terry could not remember anything about the incident and it is felt that he should not have been allowed to assess his own situation. He was also allowed to return to the dressing room in the immediate aftermath of the match. However, it is understood he did not drink alcohol and his situation was monitored by Stewart Sullivan, a club masseur. Chelsea sought to play down the significance of the injury. 'We stress that the scan was entirely routine and normal procedure for an injury of this type and raised no cause for concern,' said a statement. 'John's OK. He's still a little shaken but he's improving well,' added the assistant manager, Steve Clarke. 'If you get a kick in the head and it knocks you out, you're going to feel groggy for a couple of days.'

Carling Cup match winner Drogba was named African Player of the Year for 2006, beating Barcelona's Samuel Eto'o by just five votes. The Ivory Coast forward ended the Cameroonian's three-year grip on the title after polling 79 votes from coaches of the member states of the Confederation of African Football. Drogba's Stamford Bridge team-mate and Ghana midfielder Michael Essien was third with 36 votes.

Team

Petr Cech, Wayne Bridge, Ricardo Carvalho, John Terry (John Obi Mikel), Michael Ballack, Lassana Diarra, Michael Essien, Frank Lampard, Claude Makelele (Arjen Robben), Didier Drogba, Andriy Shevchenko (Salomon Kalou)

Jose's Dilemma

With an historic Quadruple challenge still very much on the agenda as season 2006–07 is drawing to a climax, Jose Mourinho wants to focus solely on footballing matters. However, the on-off saga over his future at Chelsea refuses to resolve itself, no matter how hard Mourinho pushes the club's board to clarify his position.

He is clearly agitating for a declaration of support from his board when he says, 'I think, in the same way as I take the pressure off my players by speaking, if the people at the top of me could also speak and leave me free of this pressure in my life, it would be better and easier for me. If I could choose I wouldn't speak. If they speak I wouldn't speak so much. So please speak and give me some free time. Unfortunately, football is like that. Managers and players have an obligation to speak to the public through the media, but the other people, they can make their own choice. From me the supporters know everything. I have said I want to stay. Imagine if at the end of the season I tell them, "Goodbye, I go." What do people think of me then? This guy is a liar? So from me no doubts. I make everything very clear. If at the end of the season I am leaving the club, you then have the right to come to me and say, "Jose, f**k off. You're a liar." I say two hundred times, I want to stay. So every Chelsea supporter believes me.'

The subsequent public declaration of faith from Chelsea chief executive Peter Kenyon is intended to end months of speculation, rumour and counter-rumour. Designed to stabilise the dressing room on the eve of the Champions League semi-final first leg with Liverpool as well as the showdowns with Manchester United for the Premiership and FA Cup; it sadly doesn't achieve the desired effect: the back pages are still awash with intrigue.

Yet, following the statement of intent from Kenyon, Mourinho is at pains to point out that, if it is up to him, then he is certainly going to be around next season. He fervently hopes to see the intense speculation over his future come to an end after Kenyon has moved to draw a line under the long-running saga. But no such luck. Disappointingly, Chelsea draw away at Newcastle. Immediately, one Sunday newspaper suggests it is all a front to settle the camp ahead of a vital period of the season when the chance of so much silverware still lies ahead of them. It is also suggested that Kenyon's words can't be taken at face value because, just weeks ago, he attended a summit in Los Angeles with Jurgen Klinsmann.

Antoine Sibierski, Newcastle's French striker, claims he has spotted signs of tension in the Chelsea camp. Detailed to mark Terry at set-pieces, he does his job so successfully that his opponent repeatedly complains to referee Mark Halsey about his approach. 'They felt the game was going against them because we were playing very well,' Sibierski says. 'We frustrated them. They were very disappointed as they needed three points to have a chance of winning the League. They were worried at the end, and that was a good feeling for us.'

For some time, rumours of profound disagreements with billionaire owner Roman Abramovich have left Mourinho's position shrouded in doubt. However, after seeing his side fail to take advantage of Manchester United's draw with Middlesbrough by beating Newcastle – they draw 0–0 – the Portuguese manager is happy to talk about the resolution of his situation and acknowledge his feelings for the club. 'Of course it is more than a job for me. Maybe the country is special, maybe the country's football is special. Chelsea is my first club in this country and I do not think it would be easy for me to leave Chelsea and go next door [to another club in this country] because we have become part of Chelsea history with the first title for 50 years, the connection with the supporters, the feeling with the supporters, everything together. I like the club; I like the players very, very much; I like the way I work with Peter Kenyon – I think he is top and the way we work together pleases me very, very much.'

Mourinho confirms his commitment to the job, adding, 'I am not saying it was easy, easy, easy, but I am not saying it was difficult, difficult, difficult. I have a job to do and I was always focused on the job. Now you think about the future – that is normal. But it helped me that I opened my mind, I opened my heart and told them I wanted to stay. I was only focused on my job. For the board to say they wanted me to stay and the story was over, that was important.

'It is good, it feels good. Now we can work together for the future. If any story comes again from the media, for me it is not a problem. What mattered for me is they wanted me to stay and my decision was made. I was not thinking much about my future or another club. At that moment I thought nothing because I knew I would be at Chelsea.'

Despite the public utterances from both Mourinho and Kenyon, there is no doubt that Abramovich and Mourinho have brokered a fragile peace as long as Chelsea stay on track for the Quadruple. The timing of Kenyon's backing for the manager, whose future had been the subject of daily doses of media hype, came after news of the Klinsmann meeting leaked. The club then, and only then, issued their first formal declaration about keeping their manager. The announcement, brief as it was, came as a big surprise to many people, even if it did not entirely end the uncertainty. Kenyon said, 'We are not going to sack him [Mourinho]; he has the club's support. That's the situation and we are agreed on it.'

According to the club, the 'we' includes Abramovich himself. However, there remains serious scepticism in some quarters, principally because so much will depend on how the team does at the end of the season in the Premiership, the Champions League and the FA Cup, even allowing for the fact that the Carling Cup was secured back in February.

And yet, after so much controversy, there are still real areas of doubt, irrespective of the supposedly unequivocal statement from Kenyon. The 'deal' is also widely reported to be conditional on the Portuguese coach agreeing to potential new measures implemented by Abramovich. Mourinho himself denies there are any strings attached, but it soon emerges that there could still be problems once the owner and the coach eventually sit down face to face to discuss the new set-up for next season.

The crux of the latest twist in one of football's longest-running soap operas comes when Abramovich realises that Mourinho is such a huge talent that it will be very difficult to replace him. And Jurgen Klinsmann has shown no signs of wanting to leave his stable family existence in LA, not even for the staggering sum of £7m a year.

Equally, it is pretty clear that Abramovich will not tolerate any further public sniping from Mourinho, otherwise the fragile truce will be off and the Cold War back with a vengeance. Besides, Abramovich and his extensive entourage are still considering appointing another senior figure to the club's football staff, with the Israeli coach Avram Grant, who is currently working at Portsmouth under another Russian owner, Sacha Gaydamak, the clear favourite to be chosen.

Mourinho's conciliatory words after the extraordinary Champions League quarter-final second-leg victory over Valencia, stressing how much he wanted to stay at the club, also helped enormously as Abramovich was fed up with his press-conference criticisms. Given that Abramovich missed the game, it is felt by those around the Russian that some kind of compromise needs to be reached in order that the man who has spent over £500m on building the club's success will be present as Chelsea approach a historic end to the season in three competitions. It is felt that every effort should be made to reach a situation where Abramovich will want to attend games.

Kenyon has long been a supporter of Mourinho and it is his decision to go public with the news that the Chelsea manager will be staying next season. 'I would like to be clear on one thing: we support Jose as manager, fully support him, and, given the level of speculation, where we are now is an even bigger achievement,' he says. 'Whatever you have read or heard, no lists of candidates have been drawn up; no one has been offered the job. So let's put that to bed straight away. Jose has a contract to 2010 and he wants to stay. We are not going to sack him – he has the club's support. That's the situation and we are agreed on it. I think we're up to 14 managers we've been linked with, but we haven't got a list. We haven't made any offers and Jose Mourinho is our manager.'

Kenyon's every word is analysed. By saying 'haven't made any offers', was this meant to scotch the rumours that the job was 'offered' to Klinsmann? Is this mere semantics? Maybe the job hadn't actually been offered to the former Spurs star, but will the rumours persist? Yet at least this is the public affirmation of confidence which Mourinho has asked for in recent weeks and the Russian hierarchy are intent on the loquacious coach delivering his side of the bargain by tempering any public comments that can be interpreted as slights against the owner.

As a result, Abramovich attended the game against Newcastle United at St James' Park and, given the latest rapprochement, the atmosphere is clearing to enable him to once again visit the dressing room after games, a tradition he tellingly gave up as hostilities intensified after the home match against Wigan on 13 January.

At this point, Klinsmann, who managed Germany to the World Cup semi-finals last summer, is still being linked in the press with the

Stamford Bridge job, and Franz Beckenbauer, the only man to have won the World Cup both as player and manager, believes the former Tottenham striker will 'fit' at the west London club if he is prepared to give up his California home. 'Jurgen and Chelsea fits, but it won't work if he tries to commute. Nevertheless if the chance arises for Jurgen he should grab it. At 42, he is a young man who can work at a top club. When Jurgen does a job, he is engaging and energetic. He still enjoys great respect in England from his time at Tottenham.'

But now with the Klinsmann option exhausted, Kenyon has staked a great deal of his own credibility on Mourinho staying. If Abramovich later decides that he has had enough, the Chelsea chief executive will be seriously undermined. At the very least, it will become increasingly difficult for him to tell prospective new managers that he is fully aligned with the most powerful forces within the club. Kenyon is reminded that he was similarly supportive of Claudio Ranieri just weeks before he was eventually axed by Abramovich and replaced by Mourinho. There is also a touch of déjà vu, as when Kenyon led a delegation to sound out Mourinho ahead of the Champions League semi-finals – while Ranieri was preparing for his semi-final in Monaco, the search for his successor without doubt seriously undermined Chelsea's quest to reach the Champions League final.

As well as Mourinho's future, Kenyon also moves to play down suggestions that Frank Lampard and John Terry have become unsettled by the delay over new contracts. Terry, who has just confirmed that negotiations over his new deal have broken down, is contracted until November 2009. Lampard is signed up until July 2009, but can buy himself out of his contract this summer under new FIFA rules. This would be at a cost of two years' salary – around £8m – to the purchasing club.

'Every contract is unique; no two contracts are the same,' Kenyon says. 'Michael Essien, Wayne Bridge and Didier Drogba have all signed new deals. That's fantastic news for the future of Chelsea. John Terry and Frank Lampard's are not yet completed. What's important to remember about contract speculation is that there are only two definitive stages: when the discussions start and when they end, either with an agreement or with no agreement.'

Mourinho retains his position as the No.1 media darling, his every word, action and deed filling acres of newspaper space. Snippets surrounding events long since forgotten are dug up and laid out before the public. Two newspapers relate how Mourinho hid in a laundry basket used for transporting the club's kit to get round the UEFA ban imposed two years ago when Mourinho was barred from contact with his players during both legs of a quarter-final Champions League tie against Bayern Munich. He was being punished for indiscretions during the previous round with Barcelona.

On the night of the home leg, observers were convinced that fitness coach Rui Faria was using an earpiece hidden under a woolly hat to communicate with the manager. Mourinho arrived early at the ground and watched the game on a TV in the dressing room where he delivered the pre-match and half-time talks. Ten minutes before the end of the game which Chelsea won 4–2, the manager clambered into one of the laundry baskets. He was then wheeled away to Stamford Bridge leisure club where he spent the rest of the evening. In response to the reports, Chelsea issued a statement saying, 'The situation is very clear. Both matches were controlled by UEFA and they were more than satisfied on both nights that their ruling was intact, hence the statements that were issued by UEFA at the time and subsequently. The only reason to publish this so close to a big match is to serve an agenda that is intended to undermine our team.'

UEFA, it turns out, are unlikely to act on these reports because of the time lapse. And, confronted by journalists at the press conference ahead of the Champions League first-leg tie with Liverpool, Mourinho is about to respond when Chelsea's head of communications, Simon Greenberg, intercedes on his behalf, spelling out yet again the fact that the matter was dealt with by UEFA two years ago. But there has never been any firm denial.

In the build-up to the semi-final, Andriy Shevchenko makes it known that he wants Manchester United to lose the other semi because he prefers the idea of facing his former club AC Milan instead of completing a hat-trick of epic showdowns with United. The Premiership title and the FA Cup already hinge on the outcome of these. If both clubs reach the European showpiece in Athens on 23 May, Chelsea will meet their Premiership title rivals three times in 14 days, following meetings in the League and the FA Cup Final.

It's worth remembering that the Ukrainian striker missed a penalty for Milan during the dramatic shoot-out that saw Liverpool fight back from a three-goal deficit to take the Euro crown two years ago. Liverpool defeated Chelsea in the semi-finals that year with a controversial goal from Luis Garcia – a 'strike' that Mourinho still insists never crossed the line. Shevchenko says, 'This season we are fighting against Manchester United on every front. Besides the domestic League and the Champions League, we will have to play against them in the English Cup, which is also very important. But I have already said it, in Athens I would like to face AC Milan. However, I don't like talking about a game that is not yet even in the programme.'

Shevchenko maintains he wants to shut out all memories of Liverpool's Champions League victory over Milan in the semis. Talking to *Gazzetta dello Sport*, Shevchenko adds, 'There will not be any sporting revenge, why does everyone speak about the past? For me the word is future. I will play against Liverpool without thinking about what happened in that cursed Champions League final. It's going to be difficult. Liverpool are very strong, especially in the Champions League.'

The Ukrainian striker has endured a difficult first season at Stamford Bridge and has been criticised for his poor performances – particularly in the Premiership. He was substituted in the second half of the FA Cup semi-final win over Blackburn after wasting a golden chance to put the Blues 2–0 in front. His miss was embarrassing. The 30-year-old admits having had problems adapting to a new style of football and concedes the criticism has upset him. 'I have had my share of problems but they have all been related to having to adapt to a different reality, a new language, the different style of football, it is not easy. Here you play very competitive football. I am only saddened that so many people have criticised me at the start of the season when things weren't going well. I have also spoken to Michael Ballack about this. I accept any criticism regarding my play, but I cannot accept those personal criticisms. Even Michael has received harsh criticism regarding his performances, without giving him the time to improve.'

Even before Peter Kenyon came out with his statement that Mourinho was staying, it was clear that Chelsea's fans, who constantly sing the name of the manager and the players during games, stand firmly behind the Portuguese coach. Meanwhile, John Terry makes it clear that he hopes the club 'will do the right thing' by the Special One and Shevchenko, too, insists the group remains solid. But, when asked about Mourinho's future, Shevchenko will not be drawn. 'It's not for me to say. I am just a player and I do my job. The rest only serves to create controversy. We are united and we are stronger than everything. He is able to charge up the group in a different way. He has a lot of confidence in himself and his ideas have been very clear to me since the beginning, despite what others say.'

In the week preceding the Kenyon accord, there were numerous hints that Mourinho's days were over. Now the man at the centre of the storm publicly declares that his task is not being made any easier by the number of managers who have been linked with the Stamford Bridge job, the position which carries the biggest pay cheque for any manager in the world. In remarks reported by the Spanish newspaper *Marca*, the Portuguese boss says a number of other managers have been mentioned as possible successors to him at Stamford Bridge – even though he insists he wants to stay at the club at least until the end of his contract in 2010. 'It is harder to work and to achieve results for a team that does not have peace,' he says. 'At Manchester United, there is tranquillity; Arsenal will not win anything this year, but they also live in peace and without any doubts over their future; the same can be said for Liverpool, who have new owners and everyone is talking about their future in positive terms, focusing on the amount of money that Benitez will have to strengthen the team. By contrast, the other day I was calculating the number of coaches who have been named as Chelsea's new manager for next season. We're up to 13. The latest name was Mark Hughes, who appeared last week.'

Mourinho suggests that he will not stay in the Premiership if he is forced to leave Chelsea in the summer, adding fuel to the media's belief that he is definitely on his way out. Mourinho gives an indication of his thinking should he find himself out of work – although he also plays down speculation linking him with a summer move to Real Madrid. 'I don't want my name linked with Madrid or with any other club because I want to stay with Chelsea,' he says. 'I've got a contract until 2010 and I want to carry on.'

But he adds, 'If I have to leave for some reason or because someone wants me to, that's life in soccer. And, if I leave, I want to keep coaching next season at another European club. I like English soccer and I'd like to coach another club in the Premiership, but not now. I don't imagine leaving Chelsea and going straight to another English club. It would be a very strange situation and I don't want it to happen.'

Mourinho is not willing to discuss his relationship with Abramovich, adding, 'My work is with the players – we are the ones that win and lose the games.'

It transpires that Peter Kenyon offered him warm congratulations in the dressing room after Chelsea progressed to the Champions League semi-finals with a momentous victory in Valencia. Kenyon is a huge admirer of Mourinho and it is clear even now that he always wanted him to stay, but that his ultimate loyalty is to Abramovich. 'I have spoken a lot to Peter Kenyon, we meet him a lot,' Mourinho says. 'He is on my side, of course, since the first day, more than ever as always. Fantastic. Peter told me, "Great, I'm very happy with your decision [to stay]." What I've said at least 20 times is that I want to be here, and I can't do more than that. I'm not a liar, I'm honest, so when I say 200 times to my players, my supporters, my board, to you and to everybody in the last two months that I want to stay at Chelsea, that I want to honour my contract, I mean it. I love the club and want to be here. I love English football. I've forbidden my agent from speaking to other clubs. I don't want my name to be linked with other jobs. When I say this 200 times in the last two months I cannot do more than that.'

Mourinho praises Abramovich for providing the best facilities in the country and illustrates his continued personal commitment by saying that he has reserved school places in September for his two children. 'I think leaving Chelsea would hurt me more than leaving other clubs. What I did in Porto was big history, but I wanted to move. I would like very much to honour my contract. I feel everything is great as I am happy in every aspect and families are important. For example, we have made a reservation for next year – we have told the school that we want to keep their place at the school. Everything at Chelsea is the best. If you go downstairs, it's the best health club in the country, amazing facilities. The future of the club is fantastic because the working conditions will be great. What is happening here is the board's job and the boss [Abramovich] is responsible for that.'

The War of Words

Mourinho is always keen to renew his war of words with Rafael Benitez who claims that the Chelsea manager only befriends rivals he can beat, with Mourinho stoking the flames of enmity by taunting the Liverpool manager for being on holiday – a reference to the fact that Liverpool are left with only the Champions League to play for while Chelsea continue their quest for the Quadruple. 'If I was on holidays and only playing Champions League matches, I would answer and would think how to make it nice. But I'm not on holidays. Since January, every game is a final for us, but they have had time to think about this kind of thing because they have only had the Champions League. I have no time and have a big game on Sunday.'

This is the FA Cup semi-final against Blackburn managed by yet another of those 13 names who are supposed to be in line for his job, Mark Hughes. After putting Hughes and Blackburn to the sword in extra-time, Mourinho goes on to suggest Chelsea's quest to win four trophies could play into Liverpool's hands. 'One of my assistants went to watch Liverpool on Saturday and he left after 60 minutes because it was like a testimonial match, and he saw the Champions League game against PSV and it was no different. It is clear they are preparing for the Champions League semi-final. But, at Chelsea, after two hours of playing Blackburn we have a game in two days we have to win and another one at the weekend we also have to win. This is what we fight for though – to be in this position. We can't complain about it.'

Mourinho says Sir Alex Ferguson predicted a possible meeting between his Manchester United team and Chelsea in the Champions League final when they met back in November. 'I met Sir Alex Ferguson at a charity dinner when he invited me. He was telling me he thought it would be an all-English final in the Champions League and I told him I believed him. Now, if we both get there, it will be the cherry on the cake. It would be magnificent.'

Mourinho retains the utmost respect for Ferguson. 'We can't be happy when one succeeds and one fails. Of course we want to win, but we respect each other.'

Rafa Benitez cranks up his rivalry with Mourinho by admitting he won't be having a post-match glass of wine with Chelsea's boss. He gives a clear indication that the Cold War between the pair is unlikely to thaw during their upcoming meetings, but he refuses to be drawn on whether he likes Mourinho as a person. While Premiership title rivals Sir Alex and Mourinho often share a bottle of expensive red wine after games, Benitez has never sat down for a drink with Chelsea's boss. 'I don't know if he goes for a drink after a game with other managers, but I was with Gareth Southgate the other day and David Moyes, so I don't have a problem with other managers,' reveals Benitez. 'After the game, I meet some managers and we talk for five minutes, but you cannot chat for half an hour because usually there is too much to do. I don't expect to go for a glass of wine with him after the match on Wednesday because we have never done. But with Arsène Wenger or Alex Ferguson and other managers we invite them into the boot room for a drink at Anfield.'

It's clear there is still an edge between the pair, which stems back to the debate over Liverpool's alleged 'ghost goal' in their Champions League semi-final, second-leg win at Anfield in April 2005. Benitez subsequently led his stars to an astonishing final win over AC Milan in Istanbul – which wound Mourinho up even more.

The goal still rankles with the Chelsea boss and he brought up the issue again when the teams were drawn against each other. But Benitez believes it's just sour grapes and he is keen to move on. He reckons Mourinho should quit carping that Luis Garcia's 2005 Anfield goal did not cross the line and get over it. 'We don't need to talk about this any more. They can talk about the goal, we can talk about the penalty and the red card! We can talk about it for days – but it's better to think about a new game and a new semi-final. We will see what we can do in these games and that is all that matters to me and my team.'

Asked whether he likes Mourinho as a person, Benitez will only say, 'As a manager, he is a good manager. He is positive for the game because he is a good worker and knows what he is doing. OK, he has a different style and approach to games, but, as a manager, he is good. I have no problem with the other managers – we talk about football and we are focused on our job. Each manager decides how to approach each game or how to do things in his life. I try to be calm. If the other managers talk about football, so will I. I don't like to talk about other teams if possible, but each person decides what to do. It is nothing to do with me being at Madrid and him at Barcelona. He is a good manager for Chelsea and you can see from the records, so I have a lot of respect for him as a manager.'

For a time, the pair refused to shake hands at games and Benitez still won't pretend they are best buddies. 'We shake hands now – so we have finished a debate which made no sense,' he adds. 'It is better to talk about the quality of Steven Gerrard or Frank Lampard or some of the other players than talk personal things together.'

Benitez resists the urge to further ratchet up the tension between the pair when asked if he thinks Mourinho will still be in charge next season. 'I'm not surprised people say he may leave in the summer. I have experience of that in Spain when a manager was eight points clear at the top of the League and he got sacked. But I don't want to start a war with Chelsea. If they are under pressure, I don't know. We have our own pressure, which means we want to win every game and every trophy. I don't get any extra satisfaction for beating him. The joy would be just to be in the Champions League final, not because we have beaten Mourinho and Chelsea – it would be the same with Ferguson or Wenger.'

For his part, Mourinho provocatively predicts Liverpool players will try to provoke Drogba into a booking that will see the striker miss the second leg. Chelsea's manager also accuses Dirk Kuyt of deliberately getting booked earlier in the competition to 'clean' his disciplinary record. Kuyt was cautioned in Liverpool's quarter-final first-leg win against PSV Eindhoven and, according to Mourinho, it was a deliberate tactic to ensure that he did not have any threat of suspension hanging over him. 'They have an easy group in Champions League – they have the chance even to clean cards,' says Mourinho. 'When you see Kuyt getting a card in the last minute against PSV, it's because he does not want to play the second game so he can get clean for the rest of the competition.'

Michael Essien is suspended for the first game against Liverpool, while Joe Cole, Ballack, Diarra, Robben and Drogba are all one booking away from missing a game. Mourinho is most fearful of losing his prize centre-forward. 'It wouldn't surprise me if they chase Drogba for 90 minutes and try to get him suspended for the second game.'

Benitez dismisses the Portuguese's attempts to 'play games'. 'I don't know why he thinks this,' he says. 'Maybe because two years ago he was doing the same with Xabi Alonso, maybe he has these things in his mind. We are thinking about playing football. If it's a message for the referee, the referee has enough experience. If it is a red card or a yellow card, it is the same.'

Mourinho also bemoans Chelsea's recent schedule and a lengthy injury list. Again Benitez is unsympathetic. 'I'm learning a lot of things I didn't know because everyone said we are favourites, they are tired, we have fewer important games than them – I don't know who is interested in telling everybody all these things. I don't want to play games all the time. He [Mourinho] is a great manager, that is clear, but he likes to play these games.'

Mourinho then accuses Benitez of reducing once-great Liverpool to little more than a cup team. 'History speaks for itself and, historically, Liverpool are not even a big club, they are a monster,' says Mourinho. 'But in the last years you can see that they play only one competition and they succeed in knockout competitions. I am not a statistics man, but I think that in the Premiership Chelsea can have 60 points more than Liverpool. I don't know – 50, 55 or 60 – but I would go with 60 points. That's a lot. They are a great team in knockout competitions. We have to admit that and praise them for that: they've won the Champions League, FA Cup, again they're in the Champions League semi-final. But, since January, they have played only one competition: Champions League.'

Liverpool currently trail the Premiership leaders Manchester United by 15 points and have played one game more. According to the Chelsea manager, that luxury of single-mindedness has afforded them freshness he can only envy. 'Liverpool are the favourites because in the year of 2007, three or four months, we have played 27 matches [in fact 24] and Liverpool four,' he says, with a sardonic reference to Liverpool's Champions League exertions. 'Before the game in Barcelona, Liverpool had a week in Portugal preparing for the game. In that week we played three matches. We played the Carling Cup final. We had the FA Cup and two matches against Tottenham; we played 24 hours after a Premiership game. We had Blackburn in the semi-final and extra-time, two games against Valencia. We didn't play PSV. It's a completely different power to fight. But we think we can win.'

Benitez scoffs back that Chelsea's financial resources far outweigh his own, but Mourinho keeps making the same point. 'Liverpool have also played 22 or 21 matches, but they rest players. Do you think Gerrard and Frank Lampard have the same conditions to compete tomorrow? I don't think it will be a fair fight.'

When asked if Benitez would be granted the same patience extended by Liverpool's hierarchy if he was Chelsea's manager, Mourinho expresses his doubts. 'Three years without a Premiership title? You would have to ask Mr Buck,' says Mourinho, looking over to his watching chairman, Bruce Buck. 'But I don't think so.'

Mourinho is also winding up Sir Alex and Manchester United – virtually at the same time as renewing his feud with Liverpool. United director Sir Bobby Charlton brands Mourinho 'silly' and 'senseless' for complaining that there is one rule for Manchester United and another for Chelsea as far as penalties are concerned. Mourinho is incensed that Manchester United have avoided having two spot-kicks awarded against them inside the past week, while his own club had a handball appeal rejected at Newcastle. Both Sheffield United and Middlesbrough had what appeared to be strong claims for penalties waved away on their Premiership trips to Old Trafford, prompting Mourinho to say, 'It looks like there is a rule in football that it is forbidden to give a penalty against Manchester United.'

Sir Alex refuses to be drawn into a war of words with his Chelsea counterpart but Old Trafford legend Charlton tells BBC Radio 4's *Today* programme, 'It's a little bit silly really. Considering he's a very intelligent man, to come out with statements like that is a little bit silly. It's a nonsense really. We've played in so many matches this year when we've not had the decisions and they've been quite obvious really. But you get on with it, you move on. I thought it was a little bit senseless. It makes good copy for the media and he's obviously a marvellous coach. But sometimes, really, I think some of the statements are quite unnecessary.'

At this stage, Chelsea's Quadruple is still possible. 'We just go from one game to another with the desire to win each one,' Petr Cech says. However, the goalless draw in the League at Newcastle, and with it the missed opportunity of closing the gap on Manchester United who had dropped points to Middlesbrough the night before, might prove significant. 'Of course, it would have been better to win, but the race is still on,' Cech adds.

Day of Reckoning

Saturday, 28 April 2007 turns out to be decisive in the chase for the Premiership as second-placed Chelsea take on Bolton at Stamford Bridge and leaders Manchester United travel to Goodison Park. Before the whistle sounds at 12.45 pm for the start of each game, the difference between the two clubs at the top of the table is a mere three points.

For 20 glorious minutes, Chelsea are effectively level on points with Manchester United as they sprint into a 2–0 lead against the Trotters. For the following quarter of an hour, they trail the Reds by only two as Bolton pull back the deficit. But ten minutes later, the gap has grown to five points. The ever-changing scores on the giant electronic scoreboard offer Chelsea a lifeline, but eventually condemn them as Bolton Wanderers draw 2–2 on the same day Manchester United come back from two down at Everton to win 4–2.

Two set-piece Bolton goals lead to Chelsea's first points dropped at home since the turn of the year. Frank Lampard, Joe Cole and Didier Drogba are rested, but all three are called upon before the hour mark. Michael Essien starts in midfield, but within half an hour he is filling in for the injured Carvalho in defence. Meite has already outjumped him to set up Lubomir Michalik's opening goal, and Davies runs off him to head the Bolton equaliser. One of the country's outstanding midfield players is again required to patch up the Chelsea defence at Anfield as the cracks begin to show. 'Of course it's too much, but I always told you that it's very, very difficult to compete in every competition at the same time,' Mourinho says. 'Of course my players are devastated, but Liverpool should also be devastated because they are third, and so many points behind that they lost the title in January. I want my team to remember where we are and what we are doing and what we have to do. They still have a big chance to do something incredible for their careers and for this club.'

Mourinho prowls the touchline clapping and urging every ball on, but his team cannot match the result 200 miles away at Goodison Park on the day the title disappears and Benitez fuels his feud with Mourinho by claiming that tinkering with his team 'cost him the league title'. Benitez must have heard Mourinho's suggestion that the Anfield men had been playing 'testimonials' for weeks because they have only one trophy to play for. The Chelsea manager has also been critical of Benitez's decisions to rest players ahead of Liverpool's Champions League clashes. In response, Benitez claims that, by trying to do the same in the 2–2 draw against Bolton, Mourinho lost Chelsea their Premiership crown.

Two years ago, Chelsea clinched the title with victory at Bolton just three days before losing the second leg of a Champions League semi-final at Anfield. Overcoming Liverpool this time will be harder because Michael Ballack has just undergone ankle surgery and Ricardo Carvalho will also be missing with knee problems. Chelsea's last defeat was at Anfield in January when Peter Crouch and Dirk Kuyt took advantage of a depleted defence and Mourinho quickly points out the fact that Carvalho was missing that day too. Mourinho also notes that both Crouch and Kuyt are missing from the Liverpool shadow team beaten at Portsmouth.

For the first time in his three success-strewn seasons in charge of

Chelsea, the destiny of the Premiership title is beyond Mourinho's control leaving his immediate priority what he calls 'the most important game in the history of this club'. The European return with Liverpool will be a defining moment in Mourinho's Chelsea adventure. 'If we can reach the Champions League final, finish second in the Premiership and reach three finals, that's an unbelievable feeling,' he announces at the end of a turbulent afternoon partnering Bolton on the Premiership-title see-saw.

Benitez takes the opportunity to have a sly dig at Mourinho's 'Special One' tag, saying, 'We have our special ones here, they are our fans, who always play with their hearts.' He adds of Chelsea, 'They know the pressure they have, but everyone has their own problems. We want to win this game, we want to finish third and, as for them, I do not need to put them under more pressure because they know full well what pressure they are under to win things. They try to win everything – that is enough pressure without me saying anything. They know the pressures they are under, you only have to ask Mr Abramovich what he wants: the Champions League or the Premier League. They know. It is clear they will be under pressure because they were talking about trophies, trophies, trophies. Maybe they have one less to win now and that makes the Champions League their priority.'

Mourinho has been critical of Liverpool's fans, but Benitez hits back by saying that, unlike Chelsea, Liverpool do not need to hand out free flags to get their fans in the right mood. He adds, 'At Stamford Bridge, we showed that our supporters won their battle, even though Chelsea had their fans all with flags to wave. But our supporters were there with their hearts. We do not need to give away flags for our fans to wave – our supporters are always there with their hearts and that is all we need. I aim to be concentrating on one competition after the semi-final, and I do not worry whether Chelsea have one or two to think about. They will know that Anfield is a difficult place for them. I know they can say it is not a problem and they have experienced it before, but we know it will be a problem for them. Our supporters, they are the special ones, that is clear. Chelsea know why.'

Two years ago, the Anfield hordes roared their team into the Istanbul final on a memorable night against Chelsea, and Benitez believes they can do it again, though the Merseysiders are 1–0 down from the first leg. He says, 'We can use the memories of two years ago to our advantage because we know what the players and fans can do working together. I remember, before the game in 2005, the Chelsea players spoke a lot about being ready for the Anfield atmosphere, but when the game was played they could not handle it. It's very difficult for any opposing team to prepare to play against 12 men. Our fans cannot give red cards or award penalties, but they can score goals. I like this about our supporters because we know they will show they are the best in the world again tomorrow night.

'The players can also use these positive memories. We will go into the game with a lot of confidence, but we know Chelsea are a very good team and we cannot afford to make mistakes. They are a team which has been built with a lot of money to win major trophies. They spent a lot of money on Andriy Shevchenko and Michael Ballack last year because their priority is the Champions League. Now they have more difficulties in the Premiership, it's clear, if they're going to win a major trophy, this is the one they want to win.'

Benitez reveals he has spent time working on the mistakes which were made in the first leg at Stamford Bridge. 'We are trying to learn from our mistakes in the first leg; Chelsea are very good, but I have confidence because playing with 12 men is a great advantage for us. It is no secret we will try to play with a high tempo from the beginning, something we didn't do in the first leg. If we can keep a high tempo going for 90 minutes, that will be perfect. We did not play to our best level in the first leg, that is the key for me. If we play to our best, we will win.'

Mourinho is still stung by Ronaldo's refusal to admit that penalties are seldom given against United, and he won't give ground in an increasingly toxic war of words. Asked to respond to Sir Alex's accusation that his complaints against referees are calculated, he says, 'It's not even a game between me and him [Ferguson]. It's a game where a kid had some statements not showing maturity and respect. Maybe education, difficult childhood, no education – maybe the consequence of that. That was the reason why I had to give an answer. Sir Alex felt after that he had to protect his boy.'

Mourinho is sure to be further antagonised by the appointment of referee Manuel Mejuto Gonzalez for the game against Liverpool. The Spaniard was in charge during the 2005 Champions League final, when Liverpool beat AC Milan on penalties. It was Mejuto's leniency during that shoot-out that helped Liverpool to success after they had trailed 3–0 at half-time. Mourinho is also concerned that Liverpool will target Drogba, since a yellow card will rule him out of an Athens final. Joe Cole and Diarra are likewise one booking away from missing the final.

Benitez argues that the complexion of the match is already significantly altered by Chelsea's dwindling hopes of retaining the title. 'It's clear they'll be under pressure. If you spend this amount of money, it's to win trophies. That means if they cannot win the League now they will be under real pressure for sure. The League could be difficult for them and maybe also the Champions League. They have spent millions and millions and then they need to win trophies. When you play against a team like Chelsea, who have spent more money than anyone else in the world in the last five years, we must be calm and say, "OK, if we can beat them, perfect." If you analyse the last five years and the value of each player, then we must be the underdogs.'

Portsmouth manager Harry Redknapp expects the luxury of extra rest will be a key factor. 'Chelsea are running on empty at the moment. I don't know how they have kept going. Lampard, Terry and Drogba have played week in and week out and they have all been massive games and they have come back from the World Cup. It's got to take its toll at this stage of the season and that's the big advantage for Liverpool.'

The other factor in Liverpool's favour is, of course, home advantage. 'When they hear our supporters, the players run faster,' says Benitez. 'The fans were a key player for us two years ago – it was the supporters who kept us running and running.'

Boudewijn Zenden adds ominously, 'I know for this one Anfield will be boiling – some Chelsea players will feel the pressure.'

Disaster at Anfield

Liverpool won the 2005 Champions League semi-final on penalties and head triumphantly to Athens by the same route in 2007 – for their seventh final. Pepe Reina saves penalties from Arjen Robben and Geremi and it proves enough. Only four Liverpool spot-kicks are needed, with Dirk Kuyt converting the decisive one. Shoot-out specialists Liverpool take their tally to 11 victories in 12 competitive penalty shoot-outs. 'We have the best goalkeeper in the world,' says Steven Gerrard. 'We saw his penalty saves before he came, so we knew all about him.'

Reina follows his father Miguel in reaching a European final – he kept goal for Atlético Madrid in the 1974 European Cup final. In his last season at Villarreal before joining Liverpool, the Anfield penalty specialist saved seven from nine spot-kicks, going on to make the decisive stop from Anton Ferdinand in the FA Cup Final shoot-out last year.

Chelsea could have settled the Champions League tie in London, but were restricted to a 1–0 win. At Anfield, Liverpool level the tie on aggregate with Daniel Agger's goal in the 22nd minute. Everything happens fast. Joe Cole, a booking short of suspension, is relieved when referee Manuel Mejuto Gonzalez does not raise a yellow card after his foul on Steven Gerrard. In the absence of the injured Carvalho, Chelsea anticipate the routine high ball aimed at Crouch, but a well-worked free-kick catches them out. Gerrard pulls the free-kick back along the deck and the onrushing Agger side-foots a low shot first time into the net at the near post. The centre-half suffered at Stamford Bridge and this is an ideal riposte.

Liverpool are outstanding at the back, but there is a shortfall in creativity from Chelsea. Drogba, inevitably, has the best chance. After 32 minutes, a pass from John Obi Mikel slips the Ivorian striker in behind Agger, but his first touch takes the ball half a yard too far, the angle narrows and he blasts straight at the keeper who is well placed to push out the fierce drive.

For Liverpool, Kuyt hits the bar and has a goal disallowed for a marginal offside. Jermaine Pennant, up against his old friend Ashley Cole, produces a deep cross after 56 minutes and Crouch leaps above Ferreira for a header which is blocked by the legs of Cech. In the 71st minute, Terry misjudges a long ball which skids off his head and Pennant's drive ricochets off the makeshift centre-back Essien for a corner.

Andriy Shevchenko sits watching from the stands, but given his form it is doubtful whether he would have made an impact if he'd been fit. Carragher diverts an Ashley Cole cut-back over his own crossbar after 76 minutes. In extra-time, Mourinho finally makes late changes, first Robben, then Wright-Phillips, for pace down the flanks, and the latter's low cross is almost met by Drogba in a rare opening for Chelsea.

So, as Liverpool reach a seventh European Cup final, Chelsea have yet to qualify for one, and still no London club has won the biggest prize of all.

When the final whistle blows, Terry and Gerrard, England captain and vice-captain, respectively, hug each other, with the Liverpool captain offering words of consolation. Terry sportingly offers his own generous congratulations. Deep down, though, the emotions are more basic.

It's hard to stomach, but Chelsea have fallen to their second Champions League semi-final defeat to Liverpool in three years. 'The first time was special but to do it again from being a goal down against a magnificent squad like Chelsea is fantastic,' says Gerrard. 'The manager's tactics were spot on. We crossed that line and stuck together out there. The players fought for every ball together. If we are through to the final, it has made all of that hard work worthwhile.'

Mourinho had dismissed Liverpool as 'historically a monster', and insisted that their limitations this season make them a little club. After the game, Gerrard admits Jose's words had spurred him on. 'The players read the press,' he says. 'We understand it, but that's Jose Mourinho. He has been a credit to English football. He makes us laugh, but for him to say that we are a little club was a bit disrespectful. Two European Cup finals in three years is not bad for a little club, is it? But credit to Chelsea. Frank Lampard and John Terry were magnificent after the game. They wished us well for the final. I take my hat off to them.'

Mourinho is unapologetic, claiming his team sought to win the tie while a physically fresher Liverpool played for penalties. 'I felt that, even against a team who has only been playing in the Champions League, we were very strong. Physically in the second half and extra-time we were the only team that tried to win in 90 and 120 minutes. But penalties are part of the game. They scored and we didn't score and they are in the final. Chelsea showed more appetite to win the game. We could speak about the first match when we were the best team by far, but history will not remember that we were the best team in that game, the best team tonight, the best team in extra-time.'

With the Premiership slipping from their grasp, Mourinho's players have only an FA Cup Final left to play for, even if the Carling Cup is already sitting snugly in the trophy room. Anywhere else, this would be a fair old return, but for Chelsea it is no longer acceptable. There will be renewed questions about Abramovich's commitment to his manager, especially if they lose to Manchester United at the new Wembley in the FA Cup Final.

Asked what Benitez possesses that he does not, Mourinho is typically blunt. 'What we have they don't have? We have two Premierships in the last three years. They have none.' The inevitable question about his own future is dead-batted. 'The speculation?' he asks. 'Again? More?' Cue for him to depart.

But Mourinho has faith that he will be in charge next season. 'We believe always there is a next chance,' he comments before leaving Anfield. 'Next year is another year. This is heartbreaking because we deserved to be in a final but penalties, penalties... Sometimes football is not fair. It's difficult, but we are strong characters. Next season the group will not be very different to the squad we have now, with maybe one or two changes. Our intention is to keep a big percentage of the players. I've won this competition and I'm very, very sad. I know what the players are going through. The Champions League is important for everybody.'

Former Blues coach Claudio Ranieri fears for Mourinho's future as he tells BBC Radio Five Live. 'Abramovich wants to win the Champions League. He wants Chelsea at the top of the world. Jose Mourinho is working very well, but I don't know what could happen. The Carling Cup wasn't enough for me after four years – is it enough for Mourinho? I don't know. I'm not sure what happened. But he wants it. I think the match was fantastic and the second leg was fantastic. Chelsea lost the match at home at Stamford Bridge when Jose Reina made two great saves.'

Ranieri, who took over at Valencia after leaving Chelsea and is currently with Italian side Parma, also admits he could be tempted by a return to the Premiership. 'England has fantastic atmosphere, great football, great fans. At the moment I am at Parma and in a very good moment.'

Rick Parry, Liverpool's chief executive, takes one final swipe at

Mourinho. 'I don't care what he says, I don't listen. I guess when you've invested £500m it's a fantastic season to win the League Cup. He's welcome to his opinions. We only care about Liverpool.'

Benitez's side trail Manchester United at the top of the Premiership by 18 points, though Parry is confident that Liverpool will challenge for the league title in the years to come. 'For us, the big prize is the Premier League, we've made no secret of that. Every one of us wants to be a Premier League contender. We're not quite there, but we'll do everything in our power to make sure we get there.'

The ramifications for Chelsea and indeed Mourinho are immense. Petr Cech is mortified that he was unable to emulate the penalty shoot-out heroics of his opposite number. 'I am tired and disappointed. A semi-final defeat in such a competition always hurts. It is the biggest disappointment in my career. During the penalty shoot-out, I have always succeeded until now in stopping at least two of the opponents' attempts. This time I had no chance. But life goes on. Time will clearly help.'

Andriy Shevchenko, one of the two superstars bought to deliver the Champions League, sums up the despondency. The build-up was overshadowed by reports that the Ukrainian striker and Mourinho had been involved in a row over a groin injury. Shevchenko says, 'It was a great opportunity. I am really, really sorry and really sad. The team played very well with good heart. But penalties are a lottery.'

The fall-out from this defeat is sure to linger, with renewed speculation about Mourinho's future prospects.

Shevchenko is shocked that no mention is made of his injury in the pre-match press conference at Anfield when his manager bemoans his bad luck, especially the loss of Carvalho, but fails to mention Shevchenko. It is only when the squad come out to train at Anfield, with Shevchenko missing, that the club announces that he has a groin strain. The decision to leave out Shevchenko for such a crucial game and the reluctance to make any mention of his injury does little to convince the striker his future lies at Chelsea after what has been an extremely difficult first season.

But it will be impossible to find a way out if Abramovich does not give a move his blessing.

The question of players continuing to play despite injuries is a major issue with Mourinho, who makes a subtle point in his post-match press conference. Using the unlikely example of Robben, who was making his first appearance since 19 March and has had his run-ins with Mourinho in the past, the Chelsea manager says that the Dutchman had made himself available despite not being completely fit. 'Arjen came here to help the team, he trained for two or three days and he told us, "You have no players, I want to help,"' Mourinho says. Wayne Bridge delayed an ankle operation to continue playing, while Ballack infuriated his manager by making the decision to undergo surgery in Munich on his ankle.

Shevchenko offers his own version of events as to why he did not feature against Liverpool. 'The decision was made on Sunday that I couldn't play when the doctor spoke with the manager and the club. I really wanted to play this game, but the injury didn't allow it. I had a scan this morning and we will see what the verdict is.'

Peter Kenyon, who released the statement that Mourinho's job was safe a fortnight earlier, claims that there is still 'a lot to go for' and that the club has enjoyed a 'great season'. Referring to the title race, Kenyon says, 'I know results did not help but we have a never-say-die attitude and it's not over until it's over. At any stage, Arsenal, Manchester United and Everton are three big games, even more so in the last week of the season. That is an enormous lift for the team. Yes, we wanted all four, but there is a lot to play for.'

Chelsea's dreams of a Quadruple have been shattered by Liverpool's victory and they are falling behind in the battle for a third successive title. If Manchester United defeat rivals City at the weekend and Chelsea lose to Arsenal at the Emirates Stadium, then the Blues really will have just the FA Cup left to play for. But Kenyon declares, 'It was disappointing, but words don't bring home what everybody at the game or who watched the game as a Chelsea fan feels. I know the team was distraught afterwards. A semi-final and we were so close, but I was proud of the team, the effort that went in, and to go to extra-time and penalties in a semi-final, you can't really ask for more than that.

'Once you get to penalties, anything can happen and it went against us. But you have got to look at the season as a whole and, although it will take a good couple of days to get over Tuesday night's disappointments, there is still a lot to go for. Arsenal, Man United and Everton are three big games, even more so in the last week of the season. That is an enormous lift for the team. And then we have got the FA Cup Final against Man United, and the first one back at Wembley, so, as disappointing as losing to Liverpool is, it has been a great season. Yes, we wanted all four but there is still a lot going on. The team is getting better, we've got a fantastic squad, we've lots of things to celebrate and let's put last night behind us and go forward in the League.'

Kenyon also pays tribute to the fans who snapped up FA Cup Final tickets for the new Wembley showdown against Manchester United on 19 May. As Kenyon tells Chelsea TV, 'They have contributed to the success of the team this season. There has got to be a big, big thanks to the fans because they have really contributed to where the team are and I know that it will be a big boost when we go to Arsenal on Sunday and see our away support.'

Black Armbands at the Bridge

Chelsea's players are to sport black armbands against Manchester United at Stamford Bridge next week after the death of the Blues honorary vice-president Phillip Carter. Carter, 44, was killed in a helicopter crash on his way home from the Champions League clash with Liverpool. Carter's son Andrew was also killed in the crash, along with Chelsea fan Jonathan Waller and pilot Stephen Holdich.

A Chelsea spokesperson says, 'Phil will always be remembered as one of our most committed fans and a very popular, larger-than-life character. A lifelong supporter, he was a season-ticket holder in the East Stand for many years, before taking one of the boxes in the West Stand when it was first built. He was then invited to be a vice-president five years ago, an honorary position. He had four seats in the directors' box and was normally accompanied by Andrew, 17, and frequently by his father, Tom. He was present at every home game, travelled to most away games and every European trip. As a mark of respect, the Chelsea team will be wearing black armbands at the next home match against Manchester United.'

Shevchenko needs surgery on his groin at the end of the season. This was the injury that forced him to miss the semi-final defeat at Liverpool. Chelsea are hopeful the Ukraine international will be available for their remaining four matches. Chelsea play Arsenal, Manchester United and Everton in the League, and face another meeting with United in the FA Cup Final at the new Wembley.

Sir Alex Ferguson draws a line under the row with Mourinho and suggests that the Premiership will be a duller place next season if Abramovich dumps him. Ferguson will be happy to share a glass of expensive red wine with him if he is invited into Mourinho's office at the Bridge. 'Recently, I've just responded to the stuff Jose has been coming out with and I have tried to draw a line under it,' says Ferguson. 'But obviously when he made his comments about Ronaldo's background and was bringing class into it, then that necessitated me having to say something because I thought he was out of order. It's finished now and I don't want to talk about it any more because I have important games coming up and there are more interesting things about the football to talk about. I don't think what has happened has damaged our relationship and, if I'm invited into his office for a glass of wine, of course I'll attend – we all have our opinions.'

Ferguson refuses to jump on the anti-Jose bandwagon. 'I don't pay attention to all the talk about Jose's future, I really don't. Just look at the way Abramovich has conducted himself since he came to this country – he never says anything or comments on anything. So how you get information about Jose's future is beyond me and I don't think there is a great deal of substance to these reports that he's going. I think he will probably be there next year and I would like him to be.'

Fergie believes Mourinho's bizarre ramblings offer a colourful touch to managerial life in the Premiership. 'Obviously, there should be a challenge amongst the different groups of players, but sometimes with Jose's continual dialogue as a manager you occasionally quite enjoy having a go back, you know. Maybe it adds a bit more to the game sometimes because you can get too intense and focused about the game itself. Jose maybe brings another agenda and it's one that you can join in if you want to, or just sit back, admire and enjoy what he has to say. But nonetheless I do believe he'll still be at Chelsea next season.'

Despite Chelsea's failure to reach a Champions League final in Mourinho's three years in charge and United's Premiership superiority this season, Ferguson believes the Londoners will continue to be a force – because of their financial muscle. 'But it's been proved time and again that spending big is no guarantee of success. You even go back to the 1950s when Sunderland tried it and got relegated, so there are examples of failing. You see the trouble Leeds United got into with buying players and you see where they are now. But if you are buying the right players with the real quality, which is what Chelsea have done, then of course you expect success.'

Ferguson insists the Premiership race isn't over until it is mathematically impossible for Chelsea to fight back. 'We will just concentrate on our games. I am not counting my chickens because I don't think it is a wise thing to do. I don't know if there are any more twists left – I hope not, in which case we are in a good position.'

Sir Alex joins forces with Mourinho in criticising Liverpool for discounting the Premiership title in favour of Champions League glory. Mourinho has belittled the achievement of Rafa Benitez in reaching the Champions League final by saying Liverpool have only had eyes for one trophy since January. Fergie agrees. 'Rafa's achievement of two European Cup finals in three seasons is fantastic, but sometimes athletes can prepare for one big event. I think he made up his mind in January that he wasn't going to win the League and that Europe would be his target – and he was helped in that when Liverpool got knocked out in the FA Cup third round by Arsenal. His target was simple and his preparation and tactics were very good. There is nothing wrong with that, but it requires patience from your fans and courage to do it.'

Chelsea need to win at Arsenal to keep the season alive, but can only manage a 1–1 draw, with Essien equalising after a Gilberto penalty has put the home side in front. Chelsea go a man down as well as a goal down a couple of minutes before half-time, but storm back with a wonderful Essien goal and a courageous fightback, for the most part outplaying Arsenal despite the numerical disadvantage.

Mourinho labels his players 'heroes' after they reluctantly relinquish their title quest with only ten men at the Emirates. Mourinho strides on to the pitch at the end, walks over to the Chelsea fans and points enthusiastically to his players; the fans cheer the Blues off despite seeing the Premiership title head for Old Trafford. Mourinho paces over to the away end, whips them into a frenzy and ensures his squad will be greeted with an emphatic ovation. Shirts are flung into the stands, hugs and high fives exchanged and congratulations offered all round. Chelsea give up their title for the first time since 2004 with heads held high.

Asked if the best team has won the title, Mourinho says, 'It doesn't matter, what matters is the team with more points is the champion. I have to congratulate the champions, the players, the manager, the fans, the board, all the people that help them be champions. I have to say that maybe I'm prouder today than when I was champion. My players are heroes. All season, against absolutely everything, they did brilliantly. The season was magnificent and I think today is a game to remember. It showed how big Chelsea players are and I couldn't be happier with the way it finished for us.'

Mourinho adds, 'We had a big problem only to play all season only with Carvalho at centre-half, but now is not the moment to talk about that. I'm very proud of my players. Normally when a team has a lot of success and loses a championship, it's lack of motivation, not the same spirit or ambition, but it was exactly the opposite. My team was brilliant.'

Mourinho promises Manchester United a guard of honour at Stamford Bridge next Wednesday, but pledges the new Premiership champions can expect a major battle to retain their crown in 2007–08. Two years ago, Sir Alex Ferguson famously ordered his players to applaud Chelsea on to the Old Trafford pitch following the Blues' first title triumph under Mourinho. And now, after Chelsea's lingering hopes of a championship hat-trick have died, Mourinho confirms the gesture will be reciprocated when Ferguson takes his team to Stamford Bridge. 'They did it for us and we shall do the same for them,' says Mourinho. 'This is not a time for excuses. The title race is over and Manchester United are the new champions. I wish to congratulate everyone, from the manager, to the players, the board – and everyone else who gave them a help to be champions. We still have the FA Cup to play for and I promise we will be ready for next season.'

Mourinho says that he is awaiting with interest the outcome of discussions between United, Everton and the Premier League over the failure of Tim Howard to turn out for the Toffeemen in their home defeat to the Red Devils a week ago; the Premier League said they were satisfied neither club broke any rules.

'I am not the authorities,' observes Mourinho. 'I can't do anything about it. I just have to sit down and wait and see whether I agree with the decision.

Even though he left Drogba, Ashley Cole and Carvalho out of his team against Bolton, Mourinho claims he never abandoned hope of winning a third successive championship until Alan Wiley sounded his whistle for the final time. Certainly, his team have not let him down. Despite playing the entire second half with ten men following the dismissal of Khalid Boulahrouz for the foul on Baptista which earned Arsenal the penalty from which Gilberto put them in front, Chelsea battled until the end. Joe Cole had a goal ruled out for offside. And, with Lehmann denying Kalou with a fingertip save late on, Mourinho feels he had plenty of reasons to be proud. 'I felt the title was still possible,' says Mourinho. 'If we had won today, then beaten Manchester United on Wednesday, the gap would have only been two points going into the final game, when anything could have happened. In the end, it wasn't to be, but I am very proud of my team. I always knew one day I would not be a champion. But when it happened I didn't want to be blaming myself, or the players, or the other people I work with. Sometimes, when you win a lot of trophies, you can reach a point when you do not give everything, the commitment and ambition are not the same or you are not hungry enough. Today has been exactly the opposite and any player who joins us needs to look at the video of this match to see what it takes to succeed.'

Sir Alex admits he was 'in agony' watching the end of Chelsea's draw at Arsenal which confirmed United as Premiership champions for the ninth time on television. With two games remaining, United have a seven-point lead over second-placed Chelsea, gained when they beat Manchester City 1–0 and Mourinho's side could only draw in north London. After the title triumph is confirmed, Ferguson tells MUTV, 'For Cristiano, Wayne and the lads who have not won a championship medal before, it is fantastic for them and, hopefully, it develops and moves them on a bit.'

The Scot hopes to continue at the helm for some time yet, admitting his aborted retirement several years ago was a mistake. 'It's easy to retire. It was a quick decision. I did it years ago and regretted it within days. I feel invigorated by the young players at the club and players like Ryan Giggs, Paul Neville, Paul Scholes turning out every week for me. It gives me the right vibes. I don't know how long I'll last now, but I'm enjoying it.'

Regarding the title race, Ferguson adds, 'It's not easy to keep a lead for six months or something knowing Chelsea are on your coat-tails. The crucial part was the resilience of the players when we started getting all those injuries. Credit to the players who dug in every week for us. It's been a fantastic effort by them.'

Asked how the triumph rated against the previous eight, Ferguson says, 'All of them were good. Maybe the fact that for two years Chelsea dominated the Premier League and we had a big job to do to catch them. The key was a good start to the season and we did that very well. It gave us momentum and from that moment on we did not lose it.'

Shevchenko's miserable season is hit by fresh mystery after he has groin surgery. This means he will miss the FA Cup Final. Initially, it was stated that the Ukrainian would have his operation at the end of the season, but it soon turns out he has played his last game of this campaign. Mourinho had felt Shevchenko exaggerated the effects of the injury, which forced him out of the Champions League semi-final second leg against Liverpool. Chelsea, though, insist the decision to bring forward the operation was made by the club's medical staff, who judged that further games could risk causing more serious damage.

Shevchenko's absence places further strain on Mourinho's squad, who were without Drogba against Arsenal because of an ankle injury. Shevchenko has been dogged by difficulties since his £30.8m move from Milan last summer, scoring only 14 goals all season. His signing is widely believed to have been initiated by Abramovich, and Shevchenko himself is frustrated by his loss of form.

Drogba is the manager's preferred striker and in January it emerged that Abramovich wanted the Portsmouth technical director, Avram Grant, to be brought in to work directly with Shevchenko. That idea was strongly resisted by Mourinho, although Grant is still lined up to arrive at the end of the season in the position of director of football.

'Next year, we have to make sure we're focused on being champions again,' says Frank Lampard. 'If there are kinks, the only way you show the strength of the club is by coming back stronger. That's what United did in the 1990s – they didn't win the League every year, but when that happened they seemed to come back stronger and win it next time round. That's our aim now. It's important for the continuity of the club that the manager stays. What we've done here in the past three years is a huge achievement and you can't hide from that. Chelsea had not won the League for 50 years and we've done it twice on the spin. We've won two cups, gone a long way in others and played great football. We've made the club move on a long way and that's as a result of work done from top to bottom. We've got to make sure it continues in the same way.'

Lampard believes that winning at Wembley will enable the team to put behind them a disappointing season in which their Carling Cup triumph has been overshadowed by the loss of the title and Champions League elimination by Liverpool. 'It's important to bounce back as it's an FA Cup Final. I've never won it and a lot of us have never won it. It's the first one at Wembley, which is a huge thing. For all the disappointment of not winning the League and not getting to the Champions League final, we can still win another trophy. We can't lose our focus in the next few weeks until that comes.'

Chelsea are often depicted as still being the new kids on the block when it comes to tradition. 'Chelsea have got history,' Lampard responds. 'Our short-term history is better than anyone else, and our long-term history is laced with great players, medals, cup competitions and leagues. Arsenal's short-term history isn't very good, so they can shout about it as much as they want.'

Chelsea line up Reading's Steve Sidwell, the former Arsenal midfielder, who is out of contract in June. Sidwell's arrival will raise questions about the futures of Makelele and Ballack, though Mourinho will need central midfield cover in the middle of next season because John Obi Mikel and Michael Essien will be participating in the African Cup of Nations in Ghana.

Though he refuses to mention names, the Chelsea manager clearly believes certain individuals have contributed to the fact that the Premiership title has left Stamford Bridge for the first time since his arrival in the summer of 2004. The unnamed culprits are likely to have been Shevchenko and Ballack, who particularly enraged Mourinho with their reactions to injury problems at a crucial stage of the season.

Arsène Wenger has no complaints about the Premiership trophy heading for Old Trafford. 'The right team won the title,' he says. 'The table doesn't lie. United scored more goals and I can only say they deserved it. They have individuals who can make a difference and they were the most consistent this year, they showed no weaknesses. Chelsea and Manchester United were both strong sides, but there were a few turning points when United didn't show any weakness and they had an offensive ability the others did not have. It is frustrating for us because we only lost one game against the top four all season. But that is also encouraging.'

Rio Ferdinand responds to Mourinho's suggestion that Manchester United only won the Premiership because Chelsea lost key players through injury, and Petr Cech, John Terry and Joe Cole were badly missed by Mourinho. But Rio says, 'There's no bad way to win it. You win the trophy and it's as simple as that. It doesn't matter what anyone else says or reckons what's happened to their team. Everyone's going to have their opinion, but I think we're more than worthy winners.

'We've done it with players all over the park and people have stepped up to the plate when need be. People talk about injuries and go overboard. Every team suffers during the season at some point. We had some horrendous injuries as well. Nemanja Vidic had a broken collarbone and we also lost Gary Neville, the best right-back in the world.'

Ferguson, whose newly crowned champions are about to visit Stamford Bridge for a game which will end goal-less, declares, 'I kept saying to people, "Will somebody please shoot Drogba!" His performances were unbelievable. He carried their team, I thought, and he kept getting these incredible goals. Like the one at Everton with almost the last kick of the ball. He had to play all their games, as they couldn't leave him out.'

Drogba has hit 31 goals this season, including 19 in the title race. Ferguson once thought about buying him. 'I remember us watching Drogba. The price was about £25m, which was a lot at the time. He had had only one season in Marseille. But Chelsea took the risk and paid for him. He is a powerful lad, with a massive physique. He has strength and plays every game. If you look back on the season, you'd say Didier Drogba's excellence really put Chelsea in the race during the first half of the season. But, since January, Cristiano Ronaldo has simply moved into another universe altogether.

'I'm just glad we are going to Stamford Bridge as champions. It would have been some game if we weren't!'

Ferdinand warns Chelsea not to expect to get their hands back on the title the following season. 'We want to win the Premiership again and we want to improve in Europe. We've got the players to be picking up trophies in Europe and we should at least be getting to the final.'

Jose Mourinho issues the strongest indication yet that he will be in charge of Chelsea next season by revealing his plans for the first-team squad. Mourinho will not require a bigger squad for his next campaign despite player fatigue and injuries being widely blamed for Chelsea's failure to win the Champions League or retain the Premiership title. 'It is impossible to have a squad of 35 players,' says Mourinho. 'What we have to do is pray a lot because the situation we have in terms of injuries is not possible to be repeated. We had, I think, seven surgeries and 14 players with traumatic injuries, not muscular or tendon strains – everything we had was a broken bone, a knee ligament, a skull fracture, everything was really bad stuff and we cannot have a bigger squad. Maybe next season I have big, big problems to choose a team because I have 24 players ready to play and everybody is fit. It is something we cannot control and I think the numbers we had this season were correct.'

Chelsea's main problems came over Christmas and New Year when Terry and Cech were out and Mourinho was frustrated in his attempts to bring in defensive cover. He believed that one extra central defender would be sufficient. Mourinho is also aware of the potential impact that the African Cup of Nations might have on his squad in a few months' time with Drogba, Kalou, John Obi Mikel, Essien and Geremi all potentially involved. 'The competition is between January 20 and February 10, so it is around 20 days long,' says Mourinho. 'By the rules the players have to go eight to 10 days before that, so it is around a month. That's one month when there are some Carling Cup and FA Cup games, so I don't think it is a period with seven Premiership matches. I think it will be three, maximum four, league games. We have to look at it like a moment when the players are injured and we cannot use them.'

Mourinho wants to strengthen the quality of young players to complement his senior squad. After a successful loan spell at Plymouth earlier in the season, the 18-year-old forward Scott Sinclair featured in the 1–1 draw against Arsenal. 'What we can have, to give a little protection, is a reserve team with kids with potential and who are ready, like for example Scott Sinclair,' he says. 'It is not an easy game to come on and play for 15 minutes, but I think Scott is improving and we need three or four kids of 18 to 19 who are ready to play for us if we need them.'

And he has finally made peace with Ronaldo. The Portuguese ace says, 'Mourinho has apologised to me and now I have no problem with him. I am pleased that this has happened. As far as I am concerned, the whole thing is now in the past.'

It's a Dog's Life

Perhaps it could only happen to the Odd One. Jose Mourinho's FA Cup Final build-up is interrupted by a shaggy dog story. He admits to being cautioned by police after an incident involving his pet Yorkshire terrier, but pledges to co-operate fully with the authorities. It certainly puts the cat among the pigeons before the final!

As the fur flies, Mourinho is released without charge following a misunderstanding over canine documents. A spokesman for Mourinho says, 'Jose Mourinho can confirm that he was cautioned by police, and released without charge earlier this morning, after an incident involving his pet dog. The incident occurred due to a misunderstanding over documents required for veterinary regulations. Mr Mourinho would like to make it clear that his pet dog was bought in England from a reputable breeder and has had all its necessary inoculations. Full co-operation will be given to the authorities over any animal health issues.'

Officers are concerned the dog has been abroad and has then been brought back into Britain without the required jabs. Reports suggest that Mourinho refused to let police take the dog away and got into an argument with officers. He received a caution for obstructing police. A Scotland Yard spokesman says officers went to an address in central London at 7.45pm on the Tuesday before the Cup Final with an officer from the Animal Health and Welfare Service. He says, 'A 44-year-old man was arrested on suspicion of obstructing police and was taken to a west London police station. He subsequently received a caution for obstructing police.'

Scotland Yard say the dog was to be seized for alleged offences under the Animal Health Act of 1981 and the Rabies Order of 1974. The spokesman says officers discussed the removal of the animal from the address with the owners. Mourinho, 44, was at Chelsea's Player of the Year awards when his wife Tami telephoned to tell him the dog was being taken away.

All in all, it's just another 'ordinary' day in the bizarre world of Jose. But in football terms the Special One is quickly back focusing on a final that is back where it belongs at Wembley. Mourinho is particularly proud to be taking his Chelsea team to his first FA Cup Final on this historic occasion. With the finishing touches still being made to the shiny new headquarters at Chelsea's training ground, Mourinho conducts his press conference inside a much older building a hundred yards away. On the outside of this office block, close to the blue door, there's a sign saying, 'No Dogs'.

Mourinho has made an official complaint about his children being photographed by the press on their way to school. Whether he will end up in the doghouse himself is another issue. There is no sign he will be hounded out of his £5.2m-a-year job. As with all issues regarding his family, he is on the defensive.

Asked whether he is 'hurt' that United are regarded as playing the most attractive football this season, Mourinho says, 'Nothing hurts me and I don't want to speak about it, but, since what happened to my family, nothing hurts me. Especially in football, nothing hurts me because my family compared with football, it is impossible to compare. What hurts me is what happened to my family – not to me, to my family.'

In Manchester, Sir Alex jokes that he has no plans to buy a dog. 'And I certainly won't be taking it to the airport.'

Mourinho discusses the issue of the 'responsibility' both sides have to make sure the FA Cup Final is a fitting occasion. 'The game should be correct – I would be very disappointed if the players were diving and provoking, and trying to get people red cards,' he says. 'I think Mr [Steve] Bennett has enough experience and had a very discreet season. To be low profile is the best quality a referee can have – when you don't remember the referee, it is because the referee was perfect and I think Mr Bennett has been low profile during the season.'

Mourinho must be the first FA Cup Final manager to describe the occasion ahead as 'socially and, as a cultural event, a day to remember'. He pays due deference to tradition, remembering the days he watched the final as a child in Portugal, incredulous that 'the small team could always win it'. Mourinho can remember watching Coventry City in 1987, but not that it was Tottenham they beat 3–2 after extra-time.

'This is something we chased a lot,' Mourinho says. 'It's something that, from the first day, we said we wanted to be there for, to play at Wembley in the first FA Cup Final. Chelsea was in the last final at the old Wembley and we wanted to be at the first of the new one.'

Sir Alex taunts Mourinho by claiming the pressure is all on Chelsea because Manchester United have already won the title. Fergie claims Chelsea will find it hard to raise their game after losing the title – just as United did in 1995 when they lost the title to Blackburn and then the FA Cup to Everton six days later. 'On the one side, you have a wounded animal in Chelsea who have lost the League to us, and on the other hand you have got a team full of confidence. I just have to make sure there is no distinction between the two teams in terms of who has the greater desire. In 1995 we should have won the FA Cup. We should have beaten Everton with the chances we had in the game, but it wasn't to be. There's no doubt coming back from the West Ham trip having lost the title it was hard work. For two or three days everyone was down, but we hoped that by the time we got to Wembley that day we'd be OK. But it wasn't to be.'

Mourinho is determined to end up having the final word on the season. 'From a selfish point of view,' he observes, 'you like to win new things instead of repeating yourself. The point is that it's an FA Cup Final. It's the only title this group didn't win in the years we've worked together. And I can imagine it's a special final because it's the new Wembley. I can imagine that has a lot of meaning for everybody. I'm not English, but for me it means a lot. For me it means remembering my youth. There were a few things I always dreamed of winning and the FA Cup Final was one of those. [This season] I have had to analyse things from the club's perspective and, because of that, I had to say the Champions League was a big target and the Premiership too. But I told you a few months ago that the FA Cup was the one I'd never got before. From a selfish perspective, the FA Cup will have a lot of meaning for me.'

No stranger to controversy, Mourinho is 8–1 in the betting to be sent to the stands on Cup Final day; his great rival Sir Alex is available at 20–1. The fiery pair are 50–1 to both receive their marching orders. But the much more important question is whether Mourinho will receive the Order of the Boot from his club's owner. Despite assurances from Peter Kenyon only a matter of weeks ago – and irrespective of Mourinho finishing the season loudly insisting he will be around for the start of the new one – the rumours inevitably resume, with speculation growing that Mourinho's future at Chelsea will only be decided after the final. So victory over Manchester United takes on even greater significance than simply winning a second trophy in the season.

Roman Abramovich has yet to have a full and frank discussion with Mourinho, who is making it clear that he wants to stay and see out his contract, which expires in 2010. On the plus side for Jose, Abramovich is aware that Mourinho will be difficult to replace and candidates such as Jurgen Klinsmann, Barcelona's Frank Rijkaard and Juventus's Didier Deschamps show little desire to move to Stamford Bridge.

The likelihood is that he will stay, but Mourinho has to accept changes, including the expected arrival of Avram Grant from Portsmouth, plus the fact of having less money to spend on transfers than in previous years. Mourinho acknowledges this when he says there will not be great changes in the squad this summer. 'No big investments, not involved in the big market.'

He acknowledges mistakes have been made during a season in which Chelsea surrendered the Premiership title and again failed to lift the European Cup. 'The thing we can criticise ourselves on is that in the other seasons we had a group of four central defenders,' he says. 'This season, three. The fourth was Robert Huth. Imagine a fit Robert Huth this season, he would have played an incredible role.'

Shevchenko will miss the final following a hernia operation. It hasn't been a great season for the Ukrainian. England's most expensive player scored 14 goals, but only four in the Premiership. Mourinho cuttingly observes, 'Hopefully, he's not happy with the season he has given us. I hope he's not happy with what he gave to this team. If he's not happy, then that's a good start.'

Mourinho is in the market for a new striker, with Benni McCarthy among the possible targets. Mourinho insists he has not run out of patience with Shevchenko though. 'He's a Chelsea player. He has a contract. And if he's not happy and if he wants to try everything for us, it's up to him.'

Drogba fully deserves the Premiership's Golden Boot with 20 league goals. Mourinho says, 'I think it's more than deserved and he's done it with no penalties.'

Mourinho briefly reignites the verbal feud with Ronaldo. When the Chelsea manager is asked whether he has a message for his compatriot, Mourinho says, 'Play good, no injuries, because I don't like injuries in my players or opponents, and, as the big player he is, he wants to be fair with his opponents.'

After Chelsea won the Carling Cup in February, Mourinho made reference to an incident in United's game at Tottenham when Ronaldo won a penalty, intimating that he dived. Later, Mourinho claimed Ronaldo was 'ill educated, disrespectful and immature' after the 22-year-old had said the coach could never admit a mistake. Mourinho later apologised and now calls on all parties to come together to make the return to Wembley memorable. 'I think Saturday, as an event, will be special,' Mourinho says, 'as a sports event and a social event. Now it is up to us, to the managers, players and referee, to make it a sports event to remember.

'The fact that it is Wembley, with 90,000 people there when they could have sold 180,000 [tickets], means that socially and as a cultural event it will be a day to remember, a historical day.'

The Full Monty

The final against United also gives Mourinho the chance to complete the third part of his dream to win four prizes – the Premiership title, the Carling Cup, the Champions League and the FA Cup. Chelsea have missed out on a Quadruple, but Mourinho still wants the full set of trophies. 'If we can win that trophy, we can say we have won every competition in domestic football. As a kid you are more focused on finals, on one-off matches. For me the matches were the Portuguese Cup final, the FA Cup Final – because it was a game everybody was waiting for all year to watch on TV – the European Cup and the World Cup final. If I can realise this dream, then it would be fantastic. But I don't think we can say this game will make us forget what happened in the season.'

Mourinho is still hurt by his failure to complete a hat-trick of Premiership titles, as well as again missing out on the Champions League at the semi-final stage to rivals Liverpool. The FA Cup, he insists, is being taken seriously. 'It's something that, from the first day, we said we wanted to be there, to play at Wembley. All through the competition we always played good teams and good players. I never made rotation. I think we have to enjoy the fact that we are there and we have to play the final with happiness, not with any pressure.'

Mourinho knows his players will be well prepared despite the glut of injuries. 'We have too many injuries, but I believe we're strong enough. Mikel is a big risk. He wants to play and, in a final, where it will be 90 intense minutes and the chance of 30 more, he is a big risk.'

This will be Mourinho's third visit to Wembley, where he has nothing but good memories. 'I was at Wembley only twice. One was to see England versus Scotland in Euro 96, when Gazza scored that goal. The other time was with Barcelona [as assistant manager]. We played Arsenal in the Champions League and won 4–2. Those were the two moments I was there and both of them were absolutely magnificent.'

Apart from one brief week in September, United have led Mourinho's team for the whole of the Premiership campaign. United have also scored 19 goals more than their west London rivals, their stylish play endearing them to those who prefer flair to efficiency. The final is Chelsea's big chance to prove that Manchester United are not the superior side. It will be the Clash of the Titans; not since Liverpool beat Everton 21 years ago have the clubs finishing first and second in the League disputed the Cup Final as well. 'I think it's the right two teams to be playing at the new Wembley,' Ferguson says, emphasising his commitment to producing a showpiece for millions of viewers around the globe. 'We want to see a Cup Final that represents the English game in the right way. We've talked about providing three teams in the last four of the Champions League and it's probably the best league in Europe now. So this is an opportunity for the two teams to give a display that shows that.'

Mourinho has had more than his share of strife since the turn of the year. Little wonder then that £30m misfit Shevchenko is 4–6 not to play another competitive game for the club. But the Stamford Bridge club are 8–13 to pay out more than any other top-flight club for new signings in the close season. Mourinho is determined to be back in the title race.

But for now Sir Alex has the Double firmly in his sights. He tells double Footballer of the Year Cristiano Ronaldo and Wayne Rooney to 'go for it' and ram United's more attack-minded philosophy down Chelsea's throat. Ferguson says, 'I think we've got the future, I really do. Obviously with Chelsea's resources it's possible for them to build another team and, whatever happens, I think they'll be our challengers next year. But, if they play their best team and we play our best team at Wembley, then I'm not worried about what they do. I'm only worried about what we do. We will go there with the confidence of having won the League and we know we've got the players who can win games and I always think you're better having those players than not. We've demonstrated that strongly this season and, if you look at the statistics, they tell you we have more match-winners because 82 league goals is really good going. We've had a great spread of goals from all areas of the team.

'Chelsea have relied heavily on Didier Drogba. They didn't have him on Wednesday against us at Stamford Bridge and that was a big miss for them. The lad has had an incredible season and at times he's kept them going on his own. Winning an FA Cup is a special event. Remember, we lost at Wembley against Everton so we know that the only way you can enjoy Wembley is by winning – and that will be our aim.'

Ferguson, fresh from lifting the title trophy for the first time in four years, adds, 'We are going to go bouncing into Wembley. Winning the title has certainly helped us and now we are looking forward to the FA Cup. It will be great to play in the first final at the new stadium.

'I am looking forward to next season already. I am looking forward to this team developing and maturing and to going on and winning a European trophy along with the Premiership. The rivalry with Chelsea is intense. They spent all that money and won the last two titles at a canter. We had to do something and have done it the right way.'

Surrendering the Premiership title to Manchester United and Champions League elimination by Liverpool are two of the biggest lows of John Terry's career. Five days of hurt have cost Mourinho's side their chance of European and Premiership glory. Terry pinpoints defeat at Anfield as the most heartbreaking moment in Chelsea's troubled campaign. 'Afterwards, for two days, I just didn't want to come out of my house. You experience that and you go through lows in your life where you feel as though you let your family down, your friends, the Chelsea fans and your team-mates. You haven't gone to that next level. We had so many great opportunities to do so – the Monaco game, the two Liverpool games – three great opportunities and we haven't managed to do that. To see Liverpool do it is upsetting, it's very upsetting.'

Having to form a guard of honour for the new champions at Stamford Bridge was pure agony for the England captain. 'I must say I've not been too happy recently. We had to pay United respect – same as they did with us – but what was going through my mind isn't important. Let's just say I certainly didn't like it and I don't think they liked doing it for us last season.'

Failure to complete a treble of successive Premiership triumphs really rankles. 'Overall, that probably hurts the most,' he says. 'I'd love to be lifting that trophy this weekend – it's not going to feel right. There's going to be something missing. It's down to us as a group of players and manager to lift everyone and go again, because that's got to be our base for years to come. The Premiership has to be our base every year, to go on and dominate – [achieve] the dominance to win every game throughout the season.'

Terry knows United will again be formidable rivals next season. 'They won it this time because they were very good all season,' he says. 'And you can pick four or five of their players who've been different class. We can look at games like the one at Newcastle where we missed a chance to put pressure on them, but it was a case of Manchester United being brilliant this season – it's as simple as that. I'm not happy with them winning it and now I want it back. We'll be very determined to do it next year.'

Terry plans to sit down with Mourinho in the summer to give his views on the way forward. 'There will be a bit of an inquest. Certainly, myself and Lamps will have chats with the manager. We've got a lot of time pre-season amongst ourselves, so discussions will be had – little changes and little things to be done to improve ourselves and improve everything around the place. Credit to the manager because he's willing to listen to his players as well.'

Terry insists a victory at Wembley will be reasonable compensation for the Champions League and Premiership disappointments. 'People will say it has been a disappointing season for us, but, if we go and win the FA Cup, then it won't be that disappointing. The FA Cup is a great trophy and for it to be the first one at the new Wembley is another reason to be fired up. This is an opportunity for us to win the FA Cup together. If we can keep building on things like that, then hopefully the Champions League next year will maybe come.'

Terry, whose twins, Georgie and Summer, will be at Wembley a day after their first birthdays, hopes he will be in a fit state to collect the famous trophy this time. While Chelsea were celebrating their Carling Cup triumph over Arsenal on the Millennium Stadium pitch, Terry was in a Cardiff hospital after being knocked out by Gunners midfielder Abou Diaby's boot. 'I can't remember much about the Carling Cup final – apart from getting back to the dressing room and celebrating there with the rest of the lads. So, if we win this one, it would be nice to actually be around and lift the trophy.'

Joe Cole plans to fulfil a boyhood fantasy by lifting the famous trophy. 'For me, the FA Cup Final is as big as the Champions League, if not bigger. After the season I've had with injuries, just getting to the final is incredible – but to win it would be a dream come true. It's been a nightmare time, what with the injury I picked up pre-season in America, but if I went out and had an impact in the FA Cup Final at Wembley and helped Chelsea win another trophy, it would be one of my best seasons.

'I was driving along the Westway the other day and I looked across and could see Wembley with that huge arch, and suddenly I got tingles all through my body. Everyone knows what Wembley means, but to the English lads it's so, so special and I thought to myself, "God, I could be so lucky." I might have the chance to play there a lot over the next five years, the stadium that everybody dreams about, on huge, huge occasions. It will be a privilege to walk out there, to play at a ground that means so much to English football, to fulfil a dream if you like – because my dream has always been to lift the FA Cup. People underestimate the importance of the FA Cup, particularly to us English boys. I remember every single Cup Final, watching them on TV or actually going to the game and, for me, it's as big as the Champions League if not bigger.

'Look at all the great games there have been, you remember every single one of them and my biggest memories are of FA Cups. I've been to all the finals Chelsea have been in since I was born in Paddington. I was at Wembley in 1994 when they got done 4–0 by Manchester United and I was devastated. David Elleray was the ref and he gave them a penalty that was miles outside the box and Gavin Peacock hit the bar before United took the lead. Those sorts of things stay with you all your life.'

Dismissed by Mourinho at Christmas as a long-term injury statistic, Cole has proved his manager wrong. 'I knew people, including Jose, didn't expect me to be fit this season after having surgery. He thought it would be next year when I was back. People ask me if it's been hard to lift myself after missing out in the League. Not really, because I'm in a different boat to the rest of the lads. I'm just happy to be back playing after being out for so long. We have to accept it wasn't our season. Everything that could have gone wrong did go wrong, but we're still in with a chance of winning our second trophy and I think, if we do, then it'll have been a great year for Chelsea. It's the showpiece final, the best two teams in the country, the one everybody wanted. I think it will come down to small details to decide who wins it... a set-piece or the way one side defends, but I'm positive we'll edge it because we're so fired up. For me, just getting there would be incredible, but, if I can help Chelsea lift the FA Cup, imagine how that would feel...'

Michael Essien adds, 'We are going for the win and playing well, but the important thing for the fans is that we go back to Chelsea with the Cup. The week when we lost the Champions League and the League is forgotten. We have to rub it out of our memories and the best way is to win the FA Cup. The final is not about revenge. Whoever we were playing against would not change our aim – to win. I also don't think this final should have a major bearing on whether the manager continues. If the manager has been good in the last two seasons, I don't understand how people can start doubting him now. The players who play will give everything to bring the Cup home and dedicate it to the fans who cried after the Champions League semi-final at Anfield. Then, next season we can only think about winning everything – it is what is expected at Chelsea. The players accept that and it is the challenge for next season, especially in Europe.'

The View from the Other Side

G iggs has won his ninth Premiership title and is out to land an incredible fourth league and Cup double. The Reds veteran says, 'Potentially this team can be the best and I definitely believe that because of the quality and age of the team. There are so many players at the start of their careers or just starting to hit the peak of their form and you can see we genuinely have world-class players in the team. We have the likes of Rio Ferdinand, Cristiano Ronaldo, Wayne Rooney and Nemanja Vidic – that's real quality in the squad and we have quality in depth, too. Beating Chelsea to the title was a fantastic achievement and the players want to make it the Double and go on from there. I'm sure the hunger is there and, although you need things to go right for you injury-wise, potentially this team can be consistently good over the next five or six years. That means winning the Champions League, not just the Premiership, because being the best in Europe is always something you want to achieve. You can't really prioritise, but this season the target was to win the Premiership, then after that the next step is the Champions League.'

Having watched Chelsea and Arsenal dominate the Premiership for the past three years, Giggs might have wondered whether United's glory days were gone for good. 'Over the past three years this team has been developing and it's definitely been good enough. It's just not been as consistent as Chelsea and Arsenal. They deserved to win titles and we didn't, but I think we deserved it this year. We've played great football but also been consistent and had that bit of steel, too.

'You do worry because I'd never gone three years without winning it, but I was optimistic seeing the ability and hunger in the squad and a good mix between experienced players who'd won it and the hunger of players who hadn't. The test now is to go on winning. We've produced great football, but it's no good producing great performances without winning anything. But we have got that taste of success again and I'm sure the players have got the determination to go on and win more. There are certain players who give you a buzz from watching them play, like Cristiano and Wayne. They've given me a fresh lease of life. Especially in the last couple of days I've got a real buzz out of seeing the faces of the lads who've won their first championship. I remember when I won my first championship – it's the best feeling in the world.'

Giggs will set a record if United win at Wembley, surpassing Phil Neal's haul of 16 winner's medals in English football. But, while he's still playing, memories mean little – except, that is, of his FA Cup semi-final goal against Arsenal in 1999. 'Records don't really mean a lot to me while I'm playing. My medals are all in the United museum, which is safe because I wouldn't know what to do with them. I can't really remember watching the finals. I'll probably get the tapes out when I've finished, but not while I'm playing. I've put the Arsenal one on a few times when I'm feeling a bit down or not playing well – I've seen that one a lot of times; that was a great night.'

Giggs accepts United won't stroll to a 4–0 win over Chelsea the way they did in 1994. 'I hope we do, but I can't see it! This is a different Chelsea team. We're a bit more cavalier, whereas they are more patient. They pack midfield and try to get possession of the ball. They have creative players as well, like Lampard, Drogba and

Joe Cole, but they play from a defensive platform. We play with wide men and players who can score from anywhere. That's the way United have always played and it should be a great way to open the new Wembley.'

Referee Steve Bennett wants Manchester United and Chelsea to render him anonymous through the brilliance of their football and their good behaviour. That way he won't be noticed. 'It's a great stage for a fantastic advert the world over and I've got to try to manage the event. Sometimes you are forced to step in and I will do it if I have to. But I simply see it as red versus blue – and it's their game. As long as the players don't take advantage of everybody's understanding of what's at stake, I can take a step back and let them get on with it. Let's hope football is the winner. We all have our jobs to do. For all of us, it's a pressure-cooker situation that will bring emotion because of what's at stake. It's important we all keep calm and don't over-react.

'I try to go into every game with a clean slate. I simply see coloured shirts with great players inside them. Both teams are capable of fantastic football. The only way you notice the personalities is if they become involved in things they don't need to. Then you recognise them for the wrong reasons. Hopefully, it's just a case of managing and cajoling from me. Then I can stay out of the game. I don't want to get caught up in all the rivalry. I have the utmost respect for both managers, who are masters of the game, and for everyone involved. We all want to be successful and someone will be unhappy. Hopefully, there's a bit of respect for us – the officials – at the end of the day.'

Arsène Wenger believes Manchester United take a psychological advantage into the final. The Arsenal manager recalls the mindset of his own players on two occasions to explain the confidence that exists within the United squad as they prepare to face the team they ousted as Premiership champions. 'United are chasing the Double and they will take the attitude of winners and will be on a high. I have twice been in the situation when we could do the Double and in neither game [against Newcastle in 1998 and Chelsea four years later] did I think we played an outstanding game. But the fact is that we were on a winning streak and that pushed us through. We had no doubt that we would win it. Even if our performance on the day was not that good, you win because you are in the winners' position.'

Injured Heroes

Ashley Cole needs an anti-inflammatory injection in his troublesome ankle and will then undergo a small surgical procedure three days after the final that will rule him out of England's games with Brazil and Estonia. Ballack had a similar problem, but elected to have an operation back in Germany. Although this was successful, the stitches have not healed sufficiently to withstand full-on contact and Ballack is ruled out.

Whether Ashley Cole starts remains to be seen, as Wayne Bridge has shone at left-back, but Mourinho is impressed by Cole's determination to make himself available despite the discomfort from the inflammation surrounding the arthritic bone spur outside the ankle joint. Ashley feels as if he has let down Mourinho and his teammates with some of his performances. The England defender has not been at his best since his controversial transfer from Arsenal to Chelsea last summer, with his efforts hindered by an ankle injury that troubled him during much of the campaign.

Mourinho has said as much by describing Cole's season as 'not superb', but the Portuguese maestro praises him as 'one of the heroes who has played injured the whole season'. Ashley comments, 'To be honest, I do feel I've let the team and the manager down a bit because I've not played as well as I know I can and I've had this niggling ankle injury. There have been games where we've maybe been a bit dodgy at the back and conceded silly goals and this season has really taken its toll. But I'm hoping that next season I can stay fit and really prove how good I am.'

Chelsea's unbeaten home league record has been marred by seven draws as opposed to only one last season. Three unexpected 2–2 draws at Stamford Bridge – against Reading, Fulham and Bolton Wanderers – proved crucial, with Cole echoing his manager by blaming injuries for the slip-ups. 'We've had terrible injuries: Petr, Riccy, JT, Joe, Robbie, Carlo – if we hadn't lost all these key players at such vital times I think we'd have been cruising the League, no question. Missing those players when we did more than accounts for the gap in points. No disrespect to Hilario and Carlo, who've both done really well when they've played, but Petr alone wins you a minimum of ten points over a season. If we'd have had our key players fit for pretty much the whole season, I think there'd be a different look to the League. We're only human and there's only so much you can take. It's been exhausting.'

Ashley Cole has sat out the last three matches to rest his ankle, even though he has returned to full training. John Obi Mikel seems to be ruled out, however. Cole is the only member of the squad to have won an FA Cup Final after lifting the trophy three times with Arsenal, but that is discounting the winner's medal John Terry picked up while sitting on the bench as Chelsea beat Aston Villa seven years ago.

Cole is looking forward to his first Wembley final. 'I've played in the FA Cup Final a lot now and it feels great to win it,' he says. 'And, if both us and Manchester United had been in the Champions League final, I think it would have lessened the FA Cup a bit. But now it's absolutely our main priority. For me, it'll just be nice to play at Wembley full stop because I've never played there before. It's always been Cardiff for me. But as much as the new Wembley looks great, when you get there, it's all about the game rather than the stadium.'

Such are Chelsea's injury problems that Mourinho jokes that he'll have to include Hilario, the forgotten reserve keeper, as an emergency striker in his 16-man squad. 'If Ashley is ready, we have 15 players for the final,' Mourinho says. 'I will have to choose between Hilario, because he is not bad playing forward, or one of the kids to make 16.'

Fergie's comments that Manchester United's Premiership title was 'a boost for football' as it was achieved 'with style and great panache' hasn't gone down too well at the Bridge, as Frank Lampard – who has been the subject of much back-page tabloid speculation that he could be playing his last game – makes no apology for Chelsea's plan to continue with their win-at-all-costs philosophy. 'Ferguson's comments are typical banter that comes from most managers, including most of the best ones. It's easy to say those things when you've just won the League. In the last couple of years they weren't saying much about Chelsea because we were the champions. I'll remember it and take it on board for when we're next lifting the trophy.'

Lampard insists Mourinho's men have not got the credit they deserve for winning back-to-back titles. 'We had criticism about the way we played when we were winning 4–0 every week a couple of years ago. How do you win over people when you've spent a lot of money? Everyone wants us to come on and play like the Harlem Globetrotters, but it's not as simple as that. We're here to win games. We want to win well and want to win with great football, but first of all we want to be winners. I respect the sportsmen who are winners, born winners. That's what Jose Mourinho is, that's what Tiger Woods is, that's what these people are.'

Lampard warns that Chelsea's main concern is not to deliver a classic match. 'There's no responsibility to deliver a spectacle. I feel a responsibility to win. Ferguson wants United to win and go out and play the right way, but there's a balance to strike. The stuff that gets talked about, about teams deserving to win the League because they play great football, as if they've brought football back to the planet, is certainly not true. What people respect is a team that plays good football and wins games. That's what Manchester United have done this season.'

Lampard believes adversity has brought the dressing room closer together. 'We want to put the season right. We've got very high standards here. No club can dominate and win league after league after league. It's something we want to come back and win next year, but the FA Cup is the one remaining domestic competition we haven't won under Jose Mourinho. It's a huge competition and no one should underestimate it. The FA Cup's had a bit of a renaissance over the last couple of years with the quality of games, such as the final last year. The FA Cup still means a great deal, even more so being back at Wembley. I grew up with FA Cup days at Wembley, the whole build-up to the game and the game itself. I'm pleased to be there.

'The best two teams in the country will be there, going at each other. What better way to finish the season? We've had some small problems, the period after Christmas was difficult, but we came through strong and weren't that far away from United in the League. It's been our toughest season, a year when you learn more than when you win the League because of the problems you come up against. That's football and that's life. You have to look back on it and take what you can for the future. It's thrown up different aspects than we had in the last couple of seasons when it was plain sailing in the League. It'll make us stronger as an outfit.'

Drogba's aerial power has already brought one piece of silverware to Stamford Bridge, with the stunning header that killed off Arsenal's Carling Cup challenge in Cardiff. Drogba promises at last to find the back of the United net for the first time in his three seasons in English football. Drogba, who has 32 goals in all competitions, says, 'I haven't scored against Manchester United so far. That's because they're a tough team and difficult to play against. There's never as many goals when you play United, apart from the 3–0 last season. It's usually a big battle with one or two goals. But Wembley would be a nice time to change that record. It is what I want to do and I aim to do it.'

Drogba's 20th Premiership goal of the season against Everton secured him the Golden Boot. He has been suffering from a fractured rib since the Champions League semi-final first leg against Liverpool, but still looks fresh and sharp in training. 'This is the only trophy I haven't won in my three years in England and I want to win it. This is what all the team are thinking about. We're excited about the game but a final will only be good if you win. I've won a lot of finals, but I've lost a lot as well and it's always painful to lose. Sometimes you can use the word "revenge" in football. Manchester United beat Roma 7–1 and, if they play again, you can talk about revenge but this is different. There's no talk of revenge for losing the Premiership. It's just a game we have to win. United won the title because they deserved it. It's not only about one game, it's the whole season. We had more injuries than them but they deserved it. Of course it will be good to beat the champions and there will be some strength for us to take from that. We know what we have to do next year. It has been a successful season for me personally, but I will be happy to give back everything I've won individually to win back the League and the Champions League. But we will start with the FA Cup.'

Alan Hansen suggests England now has the best league in the world thanks to Mourinho and Chelsea. The Scottish pundit says, 'The fact that England had three semi-finalists in this year's Champions League is proof that the Premiership is now the best in the world. That is all down to Chelsea. They have raised the bar in this country and forced the other ambitious English clubs to respond. In the 1980s and even in the 1990s, you could win the English League with a better-than-average team. But not any more. To be Premiership champions these days, you have to be top, top class. Chelsea have brought unbelievable quality since Mourinho became their manager and this season United have risen to the challenge and matched them. Liverpool have done the same and that's why they are in their second European cup final in three seasons.'

Hansen's BBC colleague Gary Lineker says, 'If you'd sat down at the start of the season and picked the teams to contest the first FA Cup Final at the new Wembley, you would have gone for United and Chelsea. They are the two best teams in the country, arguably the two best in Europe, and there is absolutely nothing to choose between them. I defy anyone to predict the winner of this game with any degree of confidence at all. A few weeks ago it looked as though this game was going to be the middle of our own little world series – three clashes between bitter rivals to decide everything. Unfortunately, they both got edged out in the Champions League semi-finals and the Premiership was already over when they met at Stamford Bridge last week. But that doesn't detract from this Cup Final and I am sure both teams will give it absolutely everything to prove they are the best.'

When the time comes to pick his team, Mourinho opts not to risk Ashley Cole but to gamble on Mikel. Cole trained but is still left on the bench as he has not been as consistent as Wayne Bridge. Despite starting 26 matches, he was not considered match-fit. A Cup Final place is Bridge's reward for sticking it out. 'I never wanted to leave and always love it here,' comments Bridge. 'Even after Ashley came in I wanted to compete for my place. If I hadn't played as many games, it might be different.'

Gary Neville loses his fight for final fitness. After attempting a return to training, it quickly becomes apparent the ankle injury he suffered against Bolton on 17 March is still too sore to let him play. The Manchester United captain will have exploratory surgery to determine the exact nature of the problem.

Chelsea chairman Bruce Buck speaks in China about the club's new economic plan to which Mourinho must adhere. Much of this has been heard before as Buck talks of Chelsea's intention not to be ripped off in the transfer market and about how 24 players amounts to an adequate squad. But he can foresee next year's African Cup of Nations causing problems. 'We could be pretty stretched in January,' Buck says, before adding of the transfer market, 'We've been going down every year and that's my expectation this year in terms of aggregate spend.'

But 48 hours before the FA Cup Final, the whereabouts of the Mourinhos' pet pooch is making as many headlines as the football. Mourinho discloses the truth behind his arrest and his four hours of detention in a police station. He says, 'I bought the dog in England, the dog was vaccinated in England and he's registered with one of the best dog houses in London. The dog was never in Portugal, contrary to what has been said and what the vet had put into her own head. Therefore, all of this has happened because the vet involved in all the documentation made a statement, when all the relevant documentation was in order.'

Mourinho explains how his children were in tears and how his whole family were petrified when eight policemen turned up on their doorstep. 'Given these policemen don't have the ability to analyse the dog's documents, they were all saying they had to put the dog into quarantine. I suggested I brought them all the relevant documents the following day to show them that they were perfectly legitimate. Instead, they insisted they would have to take the dog away. I answered, "No! You can take me away instead." We didn't come to any agreement, so I said to the police, "Wait a minute." I got inside the house where my children couldn't stop crying.

'I sent the dog to St Tropez! I returned 15 minutes later back to the front door. The reaction of the police was: "Show me where the dog is," and they asked me whether he had gone inside. I said, "Do you mean me? I'm the invisible man."'

After four hours' detention, Mourinho was released at 3am. He says, 'How is it possible there were 20 journalists waiting for me. That's a disgrace that there are such links between some police and some media. That is scandalous. Obviously the police had arrested me for what they said was obstruction and took me to the police station. But I am ready to go to the end of the world for the dog and for this circus that has been created round my family. On the day there was a red alert in London and they catch four suspected terrorists, how can they send eight policemen to my house just for a dog? It's a disgrace. I stressed my total availability to co-operate and provide to the authorities all the documentation that they need. If they want to be honest and see the documentation, all will be well. But I've had a lot of contact from my friends and some have told me they are ashamed to be English. I was all over the front pages of newspapers, but if I was an ordinary person it wouldn't have merited a single line in the paper. OK, let the press follow me, but they must leave my family alone.'

As for preparing for the Cup Final, Mourinho stresses, 'I'll prove I am calm and I have already been calm when I went to the training ground at Cobham. The training was open to the media and everyone could see I was calm. Although privately I still cannot understand why all this happened like it did. I don't believe that it has happened just because we are coming up to a very important match. It happened because I am a public figure. It is clear my children are calm now as well because they know the dog is well, but my children are still suffering because we cannot keep it here close to them. I really abhor having security at my house door, but I have to because I can't leave the place in peace. Is that good?'

According to lawyers acting for the Mourinhos, the family pet now lives in Portugal with the blessing of the British authorities. A statement emerges from Mrs Mourinho's solicitor, Elizabeth Robinson. 'With the full knowledge and assistance of the UK animal health and welfare authorities, the Mourinho family pet, Leya, has returned to Portugal with Mrs Mourinho this afternoon. Once again, the family would ask you to respect their family life, particularly that of Mrs Mourinho and her children. Mr Mourinho asks to be allowed to focus upon his task with Chelsea FC tomorrow, without repeated questions in relation to this matter which has now concluded to the satisfaction of all parties.'

According to others, the matter is far from over. A statement from the Corporation reads, 'Following the issuing of an Article 13 notice by the City of London Corporation, we can confirm that the animal in question left the UK from Heathrow this afternoon in compliance with animal health laws. The City of London's investigations into the incident are continuing.'

Since the story broke, TV news crews, reporters and photographers have been camped out by the Mourinho home – prompting demands for the family to be left in peace. On one occasion, the Chelsea coach claims his children were followed to school by 20 photographers.

Mourinho admits he may be arrested before the FA Cup Final for refusing to reveal the whereabouts of his dog. Animal welfare officers have yet to make checks on the manager's Yorkshire terrier amid concerns about the animal's quarantine status. 'Maybe I'll be arrested before the Cup Final,' he says in an interview for the Portuguese television station TVI. 'The dog is on holiday and will stay on holiday while the people are dishonest and while they won't forget that I am a foreigner, a public person, and while they don't treat me as a normal person, I don't want to co-operate. Basically they want to quarantine the dog and only then investigate. I say the dog won't be quarantined. They should investigate and if it is legal it stays with me. If not they can take it wherever they want.'

Mourinho is willing to provide the authorities with the relevant paperwork, but will not say where the dog is. 'If they want they can see where the dog was bought, the cheque that bought it, all the papers and all the inoculations, and after that they can say, "Mister, you are right." Nobody knows where it is, only me. And I don't want to say where. When a dog with three months of age is the front page of a newspaper in this country you cannot believe the things you read.'

Meanwhile, immediately ahead, is the small matter of an FA Cup Final against Manchester United to be contested.

Route to the Final

Chelsea 6 Macclesfield 1
Frank Lampard completes his first Chelsea hat-trick from the spot, before Shaun Wright-Phillips, John Obi Mikel and Ricardo Carvalho add the gloss.

Manchester United 2 Aston Villa 1
On-loan Henrik Larsson marks his debut with a stunning volley. Milan Baros equalises, before supersub Ole Gunnar Solskjaer hits the stoppage-time winner.

Chelsea 3 Nottingham Forest 0
Another easy win is kick-started by Andriy Shevchenko's deflected volley. Didier Drogba and John Obi Mikel complete the scoring.

Manchester United 2 Portsmouth 1

United are again made to work hard after Nemanja Vidic's headed goal is not given despite crossing the Pompey line. It takes until the 77th minute for Wayne Rooney to tap home the equaliser, before securing victory with an inch-perfect chip.

FIFTH ROUND

Chelsea 4 Norwich 0

Wright-Phillips's 39th-minute opener owes much to luck, taking a deflection on its way in. Drogba, Michael Essien and Shevchenko wrap up the scoring.

Manchester United 1 Reading 1

Replay: Reading 2 Manchester United 3

Both managers field weakened sides. Michael Carrick fires United ahead, before Brynjar Gunnarsson heads a surprise equaliser. Keeper Adam Federici is the star of the first game, so it is ironic that his howler sparks a United siege in the replay, with Gabriel Heinze's second-minute shot squirming under the keeper's body. Louis Saha and Solskjaer add to the tally within four minutes, before Reading stage a desperately unlucky fightback.

QUARTER-FINALS

Chelsea 3 Tottenham 3

Replay: Tottenham 1 Chelsea 2

A thrilling game sees Dimitar Berbatov smash Spurs ahead. Lampard levels, but Essien's own goal and Hossam Ghaly give the visitors a 3–1 advantage. Jose Mourinho goes for broke. Spurs' withdrawal of Berbatov is decisive as Lampard and substitute Salomon Kalou rescue a draw. The replay is surprisingly comfortable for Chelsea, as Shevchenko's sublime angled drive and Wright-Phillips's volley set up victory.

Middlesbrough 2 Manchester United 2
Replay: Manchester United 1 Middlesbrough 0
Controversy reigns at the Riverside as Cristiano Ronaldo's penalty spares United a 2–1 defeat after goal hero George Boateng is adjudged to have deliberately handled Rio Ferdinand's header. An ill-tempered replay is settled by another Ronaldo spot-kick.

SEMI-FINALS

Blackburn 1 Chelsea 2 (aet)
Lampard beats the offside trap to score after just 16 minutes at Old Trafford, but Shevchenko's air shot inspires a fightback, with Jason Roberts deflecting in Morten Gamst Pedersen's free-kick. It takes Michael Ballack to deliver the winner in the 109th minute.

Watford 1 Manchester United 4
An inspired Rooney blasts United in front after six minutes, but Watford hit back via Hameur Bouazza. But it takes just two minutes for Rooney to set up Ronaldo. The England forward strikes again, and Kieran Richardson chips in another for good measure.

Six-Finger Salute

Chelsea claim a 1–0 victory over Manchester United at the new Wembley thanks to Didier Drogba's extra-time goal. Mourinho, who threw his Premier League winner's medal into the crowd last year, promises he will treasure this one. 'This one I don't throw away – it means a lot. We have won every trophy in English football in three years. It is something the players deserve so much because of the difficult season they have had. It is a moment for everybody to enjoy. I think we deserve to go into the holiday period with this cup and a medal. The team played very well, they understood exactly the plan. The players deserved to win this final trophy of the season and the victory is for them and for the supporters.'

Mourinho comes down the 107 steps at Wembley holding up six fingers to underline how many trophies he has won during his time at Stamford Bridge. Referring to the fans who are chanting his name, he says, 'They are in my heart – in the bad moments and the good moments. I love these people.'

Asked if he had felt under tremendous pressure going into the game after missing out on the title and the Champions League final,

Mourinho replies, 'Only the pressure you put on yourself to win... nothing else. We know the game plan and how to beat them and I think the boys deserved this great moment.'

The Portuguese coach adds, 'I am moving to another house in London because after being on TV this week everybody has seen where I live. I am preparing for the new season by moving to a new house so I am not leaving. If people have doubts about my future, what can I do? I have a contract for three years and I want to stay. The club says I am staying. I have had a relationship for three years with Bruce Buck, the chairman, and Peter Kenyon, the chief executive, and if they are saying I will still be the manager then I have no doubts because they are not liars. I am very happy at this club, I love the football in this country and if Chelsea were not happy with me I think I would be the first to know. We start our pre-season with a match in Los Angeles on 9 July and I will be there in charge.'

Mourinho disappears down the tunnel after the final whistle to phone his children who were unable to attend the final. 'I wanted to call my family and my phone was not on the bench, it was in the dressing room. It was a big victory for the team and me and in all the important moments I like to be with my wife and kids and I wanted to speak to them. I made a couple of calls and came back for the celebrations.'

Sir Alex says he feels fatigue played a major part in his side's defeat as Drogba snatched the win four minutes from the end of extra-time, his 33rd goal of the season. 'There was nothing between the two teams – neither deserved to lose or win and it is disappointing we have lost. The pitch was slow and that didn't help, but from our point of view I think we were tired in two or three positions, which didn't help us. What the players have been through in the last few months has been exceptional and credit for that, but we couldn't cross the line today. Maybe the number of games they play eventually gets to them.'

The big moment of controversy came in the first half of extra-time when Giggs slid in to meet Rooney's cross, but failed to get decent contact on the ball, deflecting it into the body of Cech before the winger's momentum took him crashing into the goalkeeper who carried the ball fractionally over the line. Ferguson feels Giggs should have had a penalty for Essien's challenge on the Reds veteran and blames referee Steve Bennett for not spotting it. 'It is a penalty kick. The goalkeeper has spilled it behind the line – it would have been a difficult one for the linesman to call, but the referee should have been in a better position. To lose the game and see a replay of that is harsh to say the least. It is a clear penalty and the referee must be in a better position to see that.'

Mourinho ends the season of turmoil on a winning note and isn't slow to make sure everyone knows. 'I learned that it's very difficult to kill me, very, very difficult,' he says. Victory was imperative given the pressure that he was under and he makes no secret of his tactics; he gathered his players together at the start of the week and presented them with two choices. 'I asked them, "Do you want to enjoy the game or do you want to enjoy after the game? A pretty football match or do you want to win?"'

Mourinho told his players their priority was to frustrate their opponents. 'During the game it was not very enjoyable,' Mourinho acknowledges. 'It was a game where you had to think a lot and control your emotions and control your positions and think about many tactical points to control your opponent. You must have a minimum of six players behind the ball line, so that, if you lose the ball, you have six players behind to stop them. When you can, you double-mark on the wings, with the wingers covering with the full-backs.'

And at least Drogba and Lampard conjured a moment of brilliance with a slick one-two for the winner.

Mourinho predicts that Chelsea will resolve their contractual issues with Terry and Lampard and he will almost certainly have to compromise over personnel on the coaching side too. Avram Grant, the former Israel manager, was watching from Abramovich's private box with his arrival as director of football imminent.

It is another test for Mourinho but, as he notes, he has come through quite a few of those. 'I learned that I am ready for difficult moments, I survive difficult moments and difficult moments do not scare me. A lot of people connected to me told me after the second title that it was the right time to say goodbye. But I told them, "No, I want to carry on. I love the job, so why shouldn't I?"'

John Terry dismisses suggestions that he is about to hand in a transfer request in a bid to force Chelsea's hand over a new long-term contract. Terry's future at the club has come under increasing speculation in the build-up to the big game. Terry is understood to have rejected Chelsea's latest offer and, as I have just reported in the *Express*, he could be on the verge of handing in a transfer request. Terry declares, 'That's ludicrous. I would never do that. Now the season is over for Chelsea, I'd like to think things are going to get sorted out and I'm hopeful we will be in talks. I didn't want to be in talks in the build-up to the FA Cup Final and the build-up to what could have been us possibly retaining the Premiership. I told Chelsea to wait and we would go again in the summer. It was not right to go into important games with things on your mind and being unhappy. Hopefully, it will be resolved as soon as possible really.'

Terry's remarks over talks are echoed by chief executive Peter Kenyon who says the club's message to both Terry and vice-captain Frank Lampard has always been positive. Lampard, also the subject of difficult negotiations over a new long-term deal, insists he wants to remain at the club for life, and his comments have also been noted by Kenyon. He says, 'We are talking about major contracts with many issues surrounding them. Both parties want this to happen and, therefore, you have got to believe this will happen. The key message from Chelsea to Frank has always been: "We want you to stay," and to be fair to Frank his has always been: "I want to stay," so that is a great position to be in. I think it will be settled in the near future. Frank has said he wants it sorting before next season, and we want it sorting before next season. For all parties, it would be the sooner, the better.'

Lampard repeats his statement that he wants to stay at Chelsea despite reports suggesting contract talks have broken down. But the England midfielder makes an emotional pledge of faith. 'These are my people and I want to stay. This is my club and I hope I can sort it out soon because I want to stay forever.'

In the end the country's top two clubs were not able to serve up the thrilling final that had been anticipated and Lampard admits that a long season has taken its toll. 'It [Drogba's winner] took a long time to come because it was such a tight game; we cancelled each other out after a long season. It took a quality finish to do it and we did it in the end. Both teams have been firing on all cylinders, giving it their all. It was a very close game; both of us had fair chances. We got the quality goal that won it and it's massive for us. The lads have put so much effort into it.'

Drogba savours his moment, having scored the first goal at the new stadium to prevent the match going into extra-time, after a neat one-two with Lampard. 'I feel great,' says the Ivorian, who struck in the 116th minute. 'If we don't win this cup, we would be very, very frustrated. I'm just happy to score the first goal in the new stadium.'

Drogba also takes the chance to pay tribute to Mourinho and Abramovich. 'This [another trophy] is what Jose has shown in his three years with us. Special congratulations to him and Roman.'

Terry feels winning the FA Cup helped 'make up' for losing the Premiership title to United. 'This makes up for it. It's not nice losing – but nice coming here [and winning]. It's absolutely unbelievable. It's one of the best feelings I have ever experienced. The way we hung right on to the death. The way Didier took his goal. It was first class. We both started tentative, gave the ball away and made mistakes. But we kept going and going – and it paid off.'

Petr Cech is asked about the incident involving Giggs. 'It [the ball] was behind the line, but it would have been a foul anyway. It was hard for me to know what was happening because the players' legs were in my face.'

Cech feels winning the Cup provides consolation after the

disappointment in Europe and the title race. 'I've heard a lot about the FA Cup and this feeling is amazing. We have been chasing all four trophies. We lost a semi-final [Champions League] on penalties and we lost the Premiership at the last moment, so this cup is a real achievement.'

BBC co-commentator Mark Lawrenson adds, 'The Giggs chance might have been over the line, but forget about the arguments, it was a foul.'

Terry reveals how match-winner Drogba inspired Chelsea with a pre-match speech seconds before kick-off when he called all the players into a huddle in the middle of their own half. Terry declares, 'Didier called everyone together and gave a great speech. He said, "I'm nervous, I know everyone is nervous, but one thing is for sure, I am going to fight, give everything," and he looked every player in the eye. It touched quite a lot of people. I didn't know he was going to do it, he just called everyone together and, when he said he was going to fight no matter what and work so hard for the other players, it was special. He has been unbelievable, not only on the pitch, but off it as well.'

It was out of character for the gently spoken giant from the Ivory Coast, who went on to bag the winner. Normally, it falls to Terry to galvanise the troops, but Drogba refuses to take any credit after his inspirational address. 'We know it's not easy to be a Chelsea player, so we are always together. I had to find the good words to explain. There were so many emotions when I scored. I am just happy. I don't think I will realise what we have achieved for a few days. Maybe over the years... It was a great game in a fantastic stadium. When you win, you have to enjoy it because tomorrow maybe you will lose.'

As for his exit down the tunnel at the final whistle, Drogba says, 'I chased Jose Mourinho down the tunnel because he means a lot to me. The reason I'm here is because of him and Roman Abramovich. They gave me the chance so I have to say thanks to them.'

Terry cannot hide his pride at becoming the first captain to lift the FA Cup at the new Wembley, as well as gaining revenge on United for their title victory. 'I felt really proud walking up the steps, and getting out on the last line of the walkway was really special. To lift the cup was an amazing feeling. I am just so proud and quite emotional. With what has happened this season in the Champions League and the Barclays Premiership as well, winning the cup on the last day of the season means we are going away really happy. I am really pleased with that. I did feel quite tired when we were celebrating on the pitch, but you manage to get your energy from somewhere.

'On an occasion like that, in a stadium like that, it comes from deep inside and that's what we have shown all year, not just me but everyone. Chelsea were the last team to win it at the old Wembley and now we've been the first at the new stadium to win it – that is special in its own right. Maybe a lot of people and the fans wouldn't have accepted us just winning the Carling Cup this season. That's why it was very important to win the trophy. Even though United won the Barclays Premiership three weeks ago, we go away the happiest.'

Chelsea expect to sell three players in the close season, but they will not include Shevchenko or Ballack as Kenyon affirms. 'It's not going to happen [selling Shevchenko and Ballack]. We brought both these players in for three, four years, we didn't bring them in for a season and we knew full well what their capabilities are and their prospects. I'm confident they're going to be here as big players with Chelsea next season. They feel they have a lot more to give. It takes time to settle in. They're two fantastic professionals and I think it's an exciting prospect to see those two guys on top of their game for us next season.'

Kenyon adds that the club want to bring three or four new players into a squad that has struggled to cope with a series of long-term injuries. 'I think we're in the region of moving three out and bringing three or four in. I don't think we'll have big-name signings because I don't think we need it. We're looking for some cover for central defence, midfield and a striker.'

Mourinho has never forgotten the Garcia 'ghost goal' for Liverpool, but now he has had the benefit of the goal-line decision in the final.

Mourinho isn't concerned, either, with 'putting on a show' as he doesn't care how he wins. Bringing off Joe Cole so early surprised many, but it was the right decision because Ronaldo wasn't offering much defensively on that flank and the introduction of the flying Robben suddenly gave Chelsea a threat they had been lacking.

In the press, there is immediate analysis of the season and whether it has been good enough, or not, in the eyes of Abramovich. Shevchenko's contribution is still a matter of great debate. The Ukrainian, who missed the final victory because of a groin injury, insists he should not be branded a flop.

The £30.8m signing from AC Milan argues, 'It wasn't a great season, but it hasn't been the worst. People always expect a lot from me. I wasn't well in the first four months, partly because of fatigue from the World Cup and partly because of the injury I was carrying. But then I had a good stretch in the middle of the season. In the end, despite everything, I ended up with 14 goals and 11 or 12 assists – that's not a bad season. I know people wanted 30 goals but the reality is it can't happen every season. With all the problems I had, I don't think I did that badly.'

Shevchenko believes he failed to deliver in front of goal because Mourinho did not play him as an out-and-out striker. 'I didn't play in my position this year – I wasn't the key of the attack. I was playing further behind, away from goal, which is different from how I played at Milan and maybe that's why Didier Drogba scored so many goals this year. We made a good partnership with me setting him up some of the time. At Milan I played in my natural role. Here I had to adapt to be something else and I did it so I could help the team. The main priority for me is feeling well next season.'

While headlines rage that winning two domestic cups is 'not good enough' for Chelsea, Mourinho has had the final word over United and he doesn't mind rubbing it in. 'We deserved to win totally and it has been a great season for us. We have won two cups, lost on penalties in the Champions League semi-final and have finished second in the Premiership. They have made history, not only by beating Manchester United, but by beating them in the first game at this magnificent stadium.'

Mourinho defends his three-year reign further, saying, 'We have dominated domestically in this country for the last three years and that is why I held up six fingers to show the trophies we have won in my time here. Manchester United have been champions this season, but I can see the same fight between us next time.'

Mourinho thanks his players for rescuing what had threatened to be a disappointing season. 'My first season was very important because we won the title 50 years after we had last won it, and we won it again the second season, but I think this third season was better than the second with the problems we had. I'm not a magician, I cannot predict things, but if we did this with players limping and losing an important player every week, what would the season have been like if Petr Cech and John Terry were not out for four months, if Ricardo Carvalho had not been out? We had Arjen Robben playing with injury, Ashley Cole the same. We deserve this happiness at this historical moment for the country. Chelsea made history by winning the last cup at the old Wembley and special regards to all the boys that won that cup, and a big, big, big hug to every one of my boys because they were brilliant.'

Mourinho's Chelsea become just the third team to win an FA Cup and League Cup Double – following on from Arsenal in 1993 and Liverpool in 2001. If you add the Premiership titles of 2005 and 2006, the inspirational Portuguese manager has now been a winner in all three of English football's domestic competitions in three seasons, but he admits there is something special about lifting the FA Cup. 'It's amazing,' he says. 'I had heard a lot about the FA Cup, about the tradition, about the finals, but this feeling is just amazing. It's such an important victory – it's not just an FA Cup, it's more than that; the first FA Cup at the new Wembley, the FA Cup against Manchester United, and we have now won every competition in English football and six trophies in three years. It's especially amazing after this difficult season when we've been chasing all four trophies. We lost a semi-final [in the Champions League] on penalties, we lost the Premiership at the last moment, so this is a great achievement.'

Asked whether he thought Giggs should have been awarded a goal late in extra-time, he says, 'It was behind the line, but Giggs slid into Cech's face and I think it should have been a free-kick anyway.'

Asked when he will be speaking to Abramovich, he says, 'I will speak with him. There is no problem. He does not need to be at the club day by day because he has people to do that for him. But I mentioned him in the programme and he was in my heart because I knew winning at Wembley was a big target for him.'

CHELSEA/MANCHESTER UNITED FA CUP FINAL STATS

Shots (on Goal):	18 (4)	12 (4)
Fouls:	18	18
Corner Kicks:	1	6
Offsides:	0	5
Time of Possession:	50%	50%
Yellow Cards:	4	3
Red Cards:	0	0
Saves:	3	3
Attendance:	89,826	

Team

Cech, Bridge, Ferreira, Terry, Essien, J Cole (Robben [A Cole]), Makelele, Lampard, Mikel, Wright-Phillips (Kalou), Drogba.

PART THREE:
RETURN OF THE KING

So Special in Italy, Special or Not So Special in Spain?

J ose Mourinho transported his winning mentality to Italy and then on to Spain in the 'gap years' away from the Bridge and continued to collect the usual profusion of trophies, enemies, alongside media-fuelled rows and endless controversial headlines.

He is, to date, the only manager to win the league titles in England, Italy and Spain. He also won in Portugal, claimed the Champions League twice with arguably the weakest teams (Porto in 2004 and Inter Milan in 2010) to lift the trophy in the last 10 years. He has won cups, super cups and holds a remarkable record, which he transports from club to club, of never having submitted to defeat in home fixtures until unexpectedly right at the end of his first season back at the Bridge.

To his detractors, Mourinho is a man prepared to sacrifice style to win, with exuberance, mind games and disrepute charges – a flawed genius. To the players who worship him and talk of incredible relationships, to his proven CV, he is a genuine genius.

Away from the Bridge, he was still never far from the hearts of

Chelsea fans who longed for what seemed an unlikely return, considering the manner of his break-up with Roman Abramovich. But the headlines he created in Italy and Spain reverberated back in England, where the Mourinho brand was sorely missed.

Mourinho took just three months to master Italian but such are his linguistic talents that three weeks after arriving at Inter Milan some were already convinced he was fluent. This is how the story goes, at least, but such is the 'Mourinho Mystique' that it is often hard to distinguish fact from fiction.

With the public utterances of Mourinho as direct and uncompromising as the teams he creates, he is always a headline waiting to happen, whichever the country, or whatever the language.

While some foreign managers come to English football struggling with the language – and often ridiculed as a consequence – Mourinho's use of it is colourful, explicit and cutting. He uses language to his advantage. It is important for him to be word perfect, so, arriving in Italy, it was vitally important he commanded Italian and he worked relentlessly to achieve his goal.

Mourinho gets into the mind of his players, to communicate directly and personally, as well as to manipulate the media in a side-show, to perpetuate the so-called managerial mind games. The players are the 'Important Ones' for Mourinho and his personal style of man management.

The manager says, 'It's important to understand things. Sometimes you have a player and his performance level is going down and you don't understand why. He trains well, he's not injured, everything looks perfect but he's not performing. Why? Why? There must be a reason. But they have to trust you. I'm not a policeman, so I don't chase them outside the club. Even if my clubs are keen to do it, I don't allow them to follow players. It's their lives and their privacy.'

The 'Mourinho Method' is based on being up close and personal with the players, forging relationships, which often linger beyond their time together at a club. A clip of Ronaldo and Mourinho crying on each other's shoulders is typical of the bond he forges with his players, irrespective of the furore he creates and the controversy that often surrounds him.

His former players reveal that constant attention: persistently calling their mobiles, sending texts, wanting to know how they slept, making sure they are 'happy', whether they are eating correctly. Even the girlfriends and wives are under the Mourinho spell as important conduits for his mission to know the ins and outs of his players, so they, too, are made to feel part of his 'team' to ensure his players are happy. Mourinho's mission is to motivate his players to give their all.

When it was announced that Mourinho was returning to the Bridge, Ramires was informed by the new boss that he tried to sign him during his spells as coach at Inter and Real Madrid. This is typical of the 'Mourinho Method', making personal contact with his players even before he meets up with his new squad. Ramires was on a summer break after being omitted from Brazil's Confederations Cup squad by Luiz Felipe. 'I'm hugely excited about getting down to work with Mourinho,' he said. 'He called me a few days ago out of the blue, which was a surprise to me. We talked a lot and he said a lot of nice things to me, including the fact that he tried to sign me from Benfica when he was at both Inter Milan and Real Madrid. Mourinho told me he was very happy to have me at Chelsea. I was very glad to hear that and told him he can count on me. He spoke of his excitement too and knowing how much he wanted to work with me made me even more motivated for next year. I have a feeling that it will be a very good season for us.'

On returning to the Bridge, those rows in Italy and Spain continued to follow Mourinho. On the eve of his new Chelsea playing Galatasaray in Istanbul, accusations flew from one camp to the other. The Turkish team was now managed by Mourinho's predecessor at Inter Milan, Roberto Mancini, once of Manchester City, and the background to Mourinho's appointment at Inter continued to gall Mancini, who was sacked by Inter in 2008, less than a fortnight after winning Serie A for the third time in a row.

Mourinho had taken over the job at Inter Milan and, within two seasons had outshone him by winning the Treble and transforming Inter into European champions for the first time since 1965. Mancini did not agree that this made Mourinho's record superior. 'No,' said Mancini emphatically. 'Mourinho won the Champions League because he took a good team. He took a team that, like Manchester City, I had built. A team that had a strong mentality. When I went to Inter, they played very bad football and we changed this. To win a Champions League you should be lucky. Champions League is a difficult competition but a strange one. Strange because you can win your group in October, November, December and, after maybe February [in the knock-out stages], everything can change.'

Mancini grinned when asked about Mourinho. 'Unfortunately, me and Mourinho cannot play this game,' said the Italian, so at least there's no dispute about who was the better player.

When it comes to who might be the better manager, Mourinho was attempting to reach the semi-finals for the eighth time in 10 years, which he eventually achieved before going out to Atlético Madrid. Mancini made it past the last-16 stage only once and never beyond the quarter-finals, so Mourinho was not happy that Mancini was trying to take credit for Inter's Champions League title in 2010. 'It's funny, it's funny. It's funny because my team in the final had Lucio, Thiago Motta, Diego Milito, Samuel Eto'o, Goran Pandev and Wesley Sneijder. From eleven players, he didn't work with six of them. So he made a five-a-side team because I played with only five players from his team.' Motta was suspended for the final but Mourinho was on a roll making his point.

Mourinho was soon adored by the Italian club. He made history at Inter by winning the league and the Coppa Italia, the Italian Super Cup and the Champions League during his two-year spell at the San Siro after leaving Chelsea in 2007. When Mourinho returned to the Bridge, the Inter president, Massimo Moratti, announced that 'The Favoured One' would return to Inter by 2016. 'I called Mourinho to wish him the best for his return to Chelsea. What did Jose say? He said we'll meet again at Inter in three years.'

Along with Chelsea, the Italian club remains in Mourinho's heart. He still owns the house in Milan where he lived during his spell there, providing Moratti with the hope that he might one day return.

Now at Paris St-Germain, Swedish striker Zlatan Ibrahimovic played under Mourinho at Inter in the 2008–09 season before being sold to Barcelona. In his autobiography *I Am Zlatan Ibrahimovic* he offered a fascinating insight into how Mourinho motivates and into his work ethic. 'He worked us twice as hard as all the rest to get us ready. Lives and breathes football 24/7. I've never met a manager with that kind of knowledge about opposing sides. It was everything, right down to the third-choice goalkeeper's shoe size. He built us up before matches. It was like theatre, a psychological game. He might show videos where we'd played badly and say: "Look at this. So miserable! Hopeless! Those guys can't even be you. They must be your brothers, your inferior selves." And we nodded, we agreed. "I don't want to see you like that today," he would continue. No way, we thought, no chance.'

The vastly experienced Ibrahimovic played for Juventus, AC Milan and Ajax. He described how Mourinho would use props to fire up his team. '"Go out there like hungry lions, like warriors. In the first battle you'll be like this—" – he pounded his fist against his open hand. "And in the second battle—" he gave the flip-chart a kick and sent it flying across the room. The adrenaline pumped inside us and we went out like rabid animals. There were things like that all the time, unexpected things that got us going, and I felt increasingly that this guy gives everything for the team, so I want to give everything for him.'

Mourinho responded, 'It's not obsessive. I think details are important: details make players better; details make the team better; details help to win. Of course, there are a few players in the world who by themselves can make a team look better than it is. But basically, football is about teams and teams are better if you care about the details. So, it's not an obsession, my experience tells me that details can make a difference.'

Mourinho makes the greatest difference in the psychology of his players: telling Ibrahimovic at half-time in an Inter game that he should give his award for best foreign player in Serie A to his mother – 'someone who actually deserves it'. Or his insistence that Sniejder take three days off in the middle of the season to sit on a beach in Ibiza.

Shortly after Mourinho arrived at Chelsea the first time, the gifted striker Adrian Mutu – bought in haste in a whirlwind of Abramovich spending – had a questionable temperament. Mourinho told him he could fight and struggle and achieve something special at Chelsea, or, as he was already rich and revered like a king in Romania, he could be satisfied with that. 'But five years after you leave football, nobody remembers you,' he warned. 'Only if you do big things. This is what makes history.' Not long afterwards, Mutu tested positive for cocaine and was banned from the game for seven months.

One of the highlights of Mourinho's Inter reign was the 'almost perfect' – as he put it – display of winning 1–0 on his return to the Bridge to dispatch Chelsea out of the Champions League, 3–1 on aggregate in season 2009–10.

Mourinho received a warm welcome from the Chelsea supporters prior to kick-off at his first competitive match after returning to the club. Drogba was sent off in the 87th minute for kicking Thiago Motta as Mourinho's side produced a dazzling display, and Chelsea fans were left with the enduring image of Mourinho doing his best to tone down his celebration of Eto'o's second-half goal, which secured Inter's quarter-final place. Mourinho indulged in some fairly low-key fist pumping but the rest of Inter's backroom staff and players celebrated wildly. 'I love Chelsea, I love this stadium, I love these people but I am a professional,' stated Mourinho, who emerged from the tunnel before his players to take his seat in the Stamford Bridge dugout ahead of kick-off. 'I celebrated a lot in the dressing room. I'm happy because I won. I am not happy my ex-players lost, because Roman lost or because the fans go home unhappy. It is a very important victory for me as a coach but it is not the victory of my life.

It was hard to prepare myself to come here as an enemy. I exchanged some text messages with John Terry before the game and I told him someone will go home happy and someone sad. My people will always be my people but I was the enemy – and the enemy won. That's life. Somebody asked if I would still be special if I didn't win. Now I can say I am not so special to the Chelsea supporters, who will probably never forgive me.'

Inter came with a slender 2–1 lead. Mourinho ditched his normally defensive tactics for an attacking formation. 'The team accepted the risks that I took – and you don't always get that as a manager. I don't think it was tactics, it was attitude on the pitch.'

Jose Mourinho left the door open for a possible return to the Premier League. 'Who knows, in the future I may coach another English team and I will come here as an opponent.'

Carlo Ancelotti had no complaints as Chelsea failed to reach the final eight for the first time since 2006, as an early Champions League exit increased expectations for the remainder of the season with the team second behind leaders Manchester United and in the FA Cup semi-finals. A League and Cup double beckoned as Ancelotti commented, 'I'm disappointed because we lost and are out of a very important competition. I want to say best wishes for Inter because I have nothing against Mourinho or against Inter. Now we have two important competitions we want to win.' Ancelotti went on to deliver both those trophies.

Mourinho's affection for Inter, and theirs for him, was cemented when Inter beat Bayern Munich 2–0 to win the Champions League final, ending the club's 45-year wait to regain Europe's top prize. Argentinean striker Diego Milito scored both the goals in a game that was won by brilliant defending and individual magic. Inter became the first Italian club to win the Treble.

Bayern controlled the game from the start and were the better team, keeping possession and testing the Inter defensive line time and again. The Germans, however, failed to take their chances and, in the 34th minute, Milito headed a long clearance by keeper Julio

Cesar to Sneijder, who then passed it back to the Argentine to open the scoring.

Inter sat deep in the second half, defending splendidly and letting Bayern control possession. In the 70th minute an Eto'o pass found Milito, who struck again. Mourinho outfoxed his mentor Louis van Gaal. They had worked together in the 1990s at Barcelona, where Mourinho had started his career as a scout and interpreter. This earned him the nickname of 'The Translator' with which Barcelona fans had taunted him during their Champions League contest.

No one predicted that Inter would become the Champions League holders again after such a long time, let alone beat Premier League champions Chelsea, Spanish La Liga champions Barcelona, and the Bundeslige Champions Bayern Munich, to enable Mourinho to become only the third man ever to have won the Champions League with different clubs.

For Mourinho, though, his management pattern persisted. There followed yet another season of personal vindication, a frosty relationship with the Italian media, and he often admitted to being unhappy in Italy. As usual, the media was awash with speculation that he would move on and his destination was rumoured to be Real Madrid – a rumour that soon became fact.

It was the perfect send-off that his last victory at Inter Milan should come at the Bernabeu, Real's home stadium. The final whistle at the Champions League final saw a warm hug between the protégé and the professor as Mourinho went on to celebrate with his team and lift the trophy, while Louis van Gaal waved impassively at the supporters.

But the switch to Real was not going to be what Mourinho had anticipated. During his three years as Madrid manager, he appeared determined to undermine Barcelona – arguably the finest club side in history – and their coach Pep Guardiola. In 2011 things actually got physical when Mourinho appeared to poke his finger into the eye of Guardiola's successor, Tito Vilanova, during a post-match scuffle. He was filmed walking over to Vilanova during a melee in the closing stages of the Supercopa and attacking him following a bad foul by Marcelo Vieira on Barcelona's Cesc Fabregas. Mourinho referred to Vilanova as 'pito' – Spanish slang for 'penis'.

When Mourinho walked away, Vilanova reacted by pushing his attacker, causing outrage from the Madrid team, which had not seen their manager's actions, and referee David Fernandez Borbalan did not note it in his match report. The shocking incident came at the end of a wonderful game that saw Barca twice take the lead through Iniesta and Messi, with Cristiano Ronaldo and Benzema replying. But, with extra-time looming, Barca won the match when Messi volleyed home Adriano's right-wing cross. Madrid's frustration then spilled over, with Marcelo sent-off for a crude tackle on debutant Cesc Fabregas. It sparked a bust-up, which saw Mourinho and Vilanova clash and red cards for substituted players David Villa and Mesut Ozil. Barca central defender Gerard Pique commented, 'It's a shame, it is not the first time and it's always the same. Someone has to take action on the matter. There is talk about the Catalans, but the problem is with Madrid.'

Mourinho was due to serve a touchline ban in Champions League fixtures after comments he made about Barcelona in the previous season.

The manager was particularly unhappy that the ball-boys seemed to disappear after half-time, with the home side 2–1 up on the night and 4–3 ahead on aggregate. He said, 'Real Madrid gave a spectacular performance from the first to the last minute. We came here to play. What I'm about to say is not a criticism, I'm just stating a fact: there were no ball-boys in the second half, which is something typical of small teams when experiencing difficulties. I'm not going to say we're happy because we didn't win the Spanish Super Cup: that would be hypocritical of me. But we intended to play like men and not fall on the ground at the slightest touch.'

Mourinho was given a two-match ban by the Spanish football federation, and Vilanova a one-match ban. Both men were fined six hundred euros, with the bans only being served in future Supercopa matches, the pre-season competition that pits the reigning Primera Division champions against the Copa del Rey holders. Spanish Federation president Angel Maria Villar lifted the ban on Mourinho as part of a general amnesty so the manager could take his place on the bench for the first leg of the traditional season-opener at Barca's Nou Camp stadium and the return game at Real's Bernabeu arena. Mourinho, some time later, admitted he was wrong to poke Vilanova in the eye: 'I should not have done what I did, obviously not. The person who messed up there was me.'

Vilanova was assistant to Guardiola at the time. Mourinho, whose Real side ended Barcelona's three-year grip on the Spanish title, said his relationship with Vilanova had since been repaired. 'I work a lot with my players precisely on this, control the emotions, only think about playing and work well. The key thing is the negative image. As Tito said a few weeks ago, the footage will be there for ever. There are no problems between him and me. The story is over and what needs to be done now is to make sure nothing similar happens again.'

For Mourinho, the constant discussion of his off-the-field behaviour and his 'dark-arts' tactical mind games is vastly overstated. 'In football, the only game I know is the 90-minutes game. It's not mind games; I don't try to do that. The period before the game can be important to influence opinions, characters, personalities, feelings, and, of course, I use that to touch my players, to touch opponents, to touch supporters. But for me, the only game in football is the 90-minutes game.'

Do the exchanges become personal? 'No, I never have that,' Mourinho insists.

With Guardiola? Wenger? 'I prefer to play against the best players and the best teams and the best coaches. Never personal.'

In his first season with Madrid – after guiding Porto to the 2004 crown and with his success with Inter in the previous season – it was suggested he was grittily determined to hold on to the record of becoming the first manager to lead three different clubs to the

European titles. UEFA charged Mourinho and four players with unsporting conduct after Xabi Alonso and Sergio Ramos appeared to get themselves deliberately sent off in the Champions League, both dismissed after second bookable offences for time-wasting towards the end of Madrid's 4–0 win at Ajax. The result ensured the Spanish giants qualified in first place from Group G and the dismissals meant Alonso and Ramos would miss the final round-robin match against Auxerre, rather than carry the threat of suspensions into the knockout stage. TV cameras caught Jerzy Dudek talking to Mourinho on the sidelines before the substitute keeper went to talk to Iker Casillas, who, in turn, had a word with Ramos. All denied they were transmitting instructions for the players to coax red cards from Scottish referee Craig Thomson. UEFA charged Mourinho, Alonso, Ramos, Casillas and Dudek with unsporting conduct.

After the match, Mourinho insisted, 'I spoke with many players throughout the game, not only with Ramos and Alonso. Stories sell, but the important thing is the 4–0 win and the fantastic game we had. Let's talk about that and not other things.' Ramos, who was dismissed for having taken an age to take a goal kick, maintained, 'We didn't go looking for the cards. Seeing what the score was, the referee could have saved them. But he sent me off and that's that.'

Mourinho had previously clashed with UEFA when he was manager of Chelsea. UEFA banned him from the touchline for two matches in 2005 after he accused Barcelona coach Frank Rijkaard of visiting Swedish referee Anders Frisk at half-time in the first leg of a last-16 clash.

There are a number of previous cases of players deliberately seeking cautions to manipulate the timing of suspensions. Beckham was England captain when he intentionally committed a yellow-card foul against Wales in a World Cup qualifier. He later explained that he'd sustained a rib injury that he knew would sideline him for the next match, so he wanted to serve a one-match ban for his second caution of the qualifying campaign. 'I now know that was wrong and apologise to the Football Association, the England manager, my teammates and all England fans for this,' Beckham said. Australia skipper Lucas Neill admitted to deliberately getting a yellow card against Qatar in a World Cup qualifier, so that he could serve a ban immediately and not risk carrying it into the finals in South Africa. (He told Australian reporters after the match that his yellow card was 'tactical'.) Lyon players Cris and Juninho were both fined by UEFA for deliberately incurring a second Champions League yellow card against Fiorentina in order to miss the meaningless group tie with Bayern and be clear of suspension ahead of the knockout stage. UEFA said in a statement: 'The two Lyon players... have been fined 10,000 and 15,000 euros respectively for deliberately committing fouls in order to get yellow cards.'

Mourinho bemoaned the 'worst season of my career' after seeing his Madrid side slip to a 2–1 extra-time defeat to capital rivals Atlético in the final of the Copa del Rey. Widely tipped to return to Chelsea, he made his feelings clear to the media after seeing his last chance of silverware that season slip away, as Real lost the semi-finals of the Champions League to Borussia Dortmund, and Barcelona clinched the Spanish La Liga title. A season that had started with such promise after beating Barca to win the Spanish Super Cup petered out. 'This is the worst season of my career with a title that is not sufficient to satisfy Real Madrid and therefore it is a bad season. With a final, a semi-final, second place in the league and the Supercup, what for many would be a good season, for me is the worst.'

Pressed on his likely move to Chelsea, Mourinho refused to be drawn. 'I have a contract for three more years [with Real Madrid] and I have still not sat down with the president to talk about my future. I have to be honest. Until the day that the president sits down with me and the club does something official it has to be like this.'

His swansong in the Santiago Bernabeu wasn't the best of nights for Ronaldo either, as he saw red in the dying minutes. Mourinho was ordered by the referee to leave the touchline for protesting a decision late in the second half as Atlético won their first Copa del

Rey in 17 years. Mourinho was teased by the Atléti fans. 'Mourinho, stay!' they implored with heavy sarcasm. The scrappy contest, which featured more than a dozen yellow cards and two reds, was settled by Miranda's header in the eighth minute of extra time on a night when it seemed Atlético, who hadn't beaten their city rivals since 1999, were destined to lift the trophy. After Ronaldo opened the scoring in the 14th minute with a typically impressive header, Diego Costa levelled on a counter-attack in the 35th after superb work by striking partner Radamel Falcao.

Real struck the post three times prior to the game entering extra time and Atlético keeper Thibaut Courtois made two stunning saves to preserve the victory and help end his team's three-match losing streak in Copa finals.

The affair turned ugly, however, in the closing minutes, with Ronaldo given a straight red card for kicking out at Gabi, and players from both benches having to be separated. Courtois fell to the ground when struck by an item thrown from the stands.

Mourinho believed that his team should have lifted the cup and had been plain unlucky. 'The result is 1–1 and it is not normal to hit the post three times. You don't have to be a magician of football to think that the result is not fair, that Atlético are not the deserved winners of the final. The refereeing is forgotten, the shots off the post are forgotten, all that remains is that the winner is Atlético.'

Several of his players cared more about their public appearance than about winning trophies, according to Mourinho, who, after three years in charge at the Santiago Bernabeu, was not impressed by their attitude. 'Lots of times at Real Madrid, the players would be queuing in front of the mirror before the game while the referee waited for them in the tunnel, but that's how society is now. Young people care a lot about this: they are twenty-something and I am fifty-one and if I want to work with kids I have to understand their world. How can I stop my players on the bus doing, er, what do you call?... Twitters and these things? How can I stop them if my daughter and my son do the same? So, I have to adapt to the moment. I'm a manager since 2000 so I'm in my second generation of players. What I feel is that, before, players were trying to make money during their career, be rich at the end of their career. But in this moment, the people who surround them try to make them rich before they start their career. They try to make them rich when they sign their first contract, when they didn't play one single match in the Premier League, when they don't know what it is to play in the Champions League. This puts the clubs in difficult conditions sometimes. You have to find the right boy: the boy who wants to succeed, has pride and passion for the game. His dream is not one more million or one less million, his dream is to play at the highest level, to win titles, because if you do these things you'll be rich the same at the end of your career. So we are working hard to give the best orientation to young players, to follow examples of guys from the past – the Lampards, the Terrys – who were always fanatical for victories.'

For the first time in a decade, since he took the reins at Porto, he endured a term without a trophy (bar the Spanish Super Cup). Mourinho said, 'But I don't know any manager who always has a fantastic season. For others this might be a great season: second in the league, a cup final, a European semi. But for me it is the worst. This season I have failed.'

Newspapers reported an alleged falling-out between Mourinho and two of the 'galácticos': Iker Casillas and Sergio Ramos, globally revered goalkeeper and defender, respectively. After a defeat to Barcelona, stories appeared that Ramos had sniped at Mourinho: 'Because you've never been a player, you don't know that that sometimes happens.' It was suggested that Mourinho and Ronaldo barely spoke to each other at the end of his time in Spain.

Conversely, Ibrahimovic felt his manager made him 'feel like a lion'. Dutch playmaker Sneijder went even further: 'I was prepared to kill and die for him.' When Lampard's mother died in 2008, Mourinho phoned him every day, commiserating and offering advice. Mourinho wasn't even his manager. 'He's the most loyal, the most caring manager I've ever worked with,' Lampard said. 'I might be biased, because I love the man, but he does it instantly. He brings instant success.'

Mourinho says, 'It's impossible to make every player better. With some I don't succeed and with some I cannot improve. But – if I go player by player – my percentage of players who reach the best years and the best moments of their career with me is huge. Of course, there are a few where the connection was not good, because the personalities couldn't find each other, or because I don't enjoy working with them. But that percentage is minimal.'

Mourinho was interviewed for the Barcelona job in 2008 but they opted in the end for Pep Guardiola. Johan Cruyff didn't like the style of football, others find Mourinho arrogant. Manchester United should have pursued Mourinho to replace Sir Alex Ferguson but they went for David Moyes for the long-term, preferring someone far less controversial. Mourinho denies that he cried when he learned he'd been passed over at Old Trafford but he also denies that he was ever approached.

So does Mourinho find the job of being a football manager stressful? 'No. I find life stressful sometimes. Not in London, but in Madrid, in Italy, it was stressful.'

What keeps him awake at night? 'Nothing. Nothing! I sleep seven, eight hours every night. I cannot compare my job with the doctor who is doing heart surgery. The difference is that I have millions of people know the result of my work and the only people who know the result of his work are the family of the person who is on the operating table. But there is much more responsibility for him than for me. That's why I sometimes feel that we earn too much money compared to people who do much more than us to benefit humanity.'

'What is football?' Mourinho continues. 'Football is emotion. No more than that.'

He disagreed with David Luiz's suggestion that it was a failed season without trophies. 'I don't think it's a bad season. I think it's a transitional season and, for a transitional season, to arrive where we did is very good. I would agree I have had four bad seasons since 2010 with Inter.'

Mourinho was sensitive to criticism of his recent record. 'Last year, I won Super Cup against Barcelona. I'm going to tell you something about my career. In 2010, I reached the maximum of my career, I won everything. This is the maximum. In the first season, I won the cup against the best team in the world, I finished second to the best team in the world, and lost the semi-final to best team in the world, then we won the league against the best team in the world, with all the records. We lost in the semi-finals of the Champions League [against Bayern] when two of the best penalty-takers in the world missed penalties. The next season, we beat Barca in all the big matches, and lost the Champions League semi-final by one goal. In my fourth season, I [went to the] Champions League semi-final, I [fought for the] title until [the] last moment, so these are four bad seasons of my career? I [went] wrong by doing year after year like nobody else did. [To] arrive into a level where [you] finish second is not good, semi-final is not good. So if you say it went wrong, it went wrong by going year after year like nobody else did, to be at a level where finishing second and losing the semi-finals is not good. So I'm proud to be guilty of that. This season has been a big step in terms of fighting for the title and for the Champions League. A good step. We are ready for the improvement we need for next season, and we need that. So many teams need years and years to build. We are in a transitional period, but it's not out of context to say this team deserves to start next season with a base to do well.'

Mourinho believes that the basis of the criticism towards him is that he is held accountable by different standards than those of other managers. 'I'm guilty of that [being judged by higher standards], and I'm proud to be guilty of that.'

He added, 'The day I am happy a couple of days after a defeat, it is because there is something wrong with me... and there is nothing wrong with me.'

The Missing Mourinho Years: The First Champions League Triumph

For a while Chelsea had 'Mourinho Lite'. Andre Villas-Boas (AVB) returned to Chelsea after a gap of just under four years after being in the role of scout, responsible for assessing opposition teams throughout Jose Mourinho's time in charge between the summer of 2004 and September 2007.

He was the first at Chelsea to hold the opposition-scout role as a dedicated, full-time position and was innovative in the use of up-to-date computer and video technology to brief the coaching staff and players. It played an important part in bringing back-to-back Premier League titles and FA Cup and Carling Cup victories to Stamford Bridge. AVB remained part of Mourinho's staff at Inter, experiencing more trophy success.

After a year with Portuguese club Academica from the city of Coimbra, AVB moved to Porto and, within his first season, won the Portuguese Super Cup, a domestic league and cup double, plus the Europa League, beating another Portuguese side, Braga, 1–0 in Dublin. He became the youngest manager to win a European trophy, at the age of 33. At home Porto broke their own record, previously set in the Mourinho era, for games unbeaten at the start of the season in all competitions.

AVB was a self-confident young manager at the Bridge, with the brief to perfect a 'project', often referred to as 'transition', which was inevitably going to lead to personality clashes and conflict within a group still dominated by the senior players loyal to Mourinho.

Concern about the AVB reforms manifested itself within the form of Fernando Torres, or rather the lack of it. AVB had been recruited to attempt to maximise one of the most under-performing, expensive stars of all time: a £50m centre forward who had lost his confidence in front of goal, with little sign of improvement.

Abramovich agreed to be patient. He wasn't, however, despite AVB suggesting that his position would not be under threat if he finished the season empty-handed. The owner is not renowned for his patience. Cracks were beginning to show behind the scenes; internal squabbling, which always, inevitably, leaked to the media, eroded that early-season faith in AVB. Worse was the fear of missing out on the Champions League, as Chelsea were destined not to finish in the top four.

The inevitable sacking was the chance for Roberto Di Matteo to take over the reins and lead Chelsea to an improbable Champions League triumph.

Chelsea's decision to axe their eighth manager in eight years came on the brink of elimination from the Champions League – clearly the defining moment in AVB's short reign as manager. It also came immediately after the 1–0 defeat by West Brom, which put their qualification via the league in jeopardy, with a disastrous run of three Premier League wins in 12 games. Abramovich had to act fast to save a rapidly disintegrating season. Di Matteo was put in charge on an interim basis until the end of the season. He had not been AVB's personal choice for assistant manager, originating from the Abramovich camp through the owner's aides and advisers. Di Matteo was in the right place to take temporary control, having had Premier

League managerial experience with West Brom before he was sacked at The Hawthorns.

AVB lasted 257 days: one of Chelsea's biggest-ever managerial flops, certainly in terms of costs, as well as results. He signed a three-year contract after Abramovich sanctioned a £13.3m buy-out payment to Porto in compensation, plus £10m in paying off Carlo Ancelotti and his coaching staff.

AVB was 36 weeks into a three-year deal worth £90,000 a week, pocketing £3.5m for 40 games, plus a further £11m when sacked. Chelsea paid combined transfer fees of around £45m to bring in Oriol Romeu, Romelu Lukaku and Juan Mata. AVB didn't do too badly in his first full month but a four-game winning streak ended with a 3–1 defeat at Manchester United. Between October and November, Chelsea won twice in nine games – a run that included a 5–3 home defeat by Arsenal. Between January and March, Chelsea won one out of seven league games since beating QPR on 28 January. A statement on the club's website read, 'Unfortunately, the results and performances of the team have not been good enough and were showing no signs of improving at a key time in the season. The club is still competing in the latter stages of the UEFA Champions League and the FA Cup, as well as challenging for a top-four spot in the Premier League, and we aim to remain as competitive as possible on all fronts. With that in mind, we felt our only option was to make a change at this time.'

AVB had a difficult working relationship with senior players, several of whom were only slightly younger than him. Anelka, 32, and experienced defender Alex were side-lined and sold off; Lampard was left out of the team. AVB's man-management skills were called into question.

The timing of the sacking was quite remarkable, coming as Chelsea faced two significant and tough games in the FA Cup and Champions League: a visit to Championship side Birmingham for an FA Cup fifth-round replay, then the seemingly impossible mission, to overturn a 3–1 deficit against Italian side Napoli at Stamford Bridge to avoid exiting the Champions League at the last-16 stage. Few people – if anyone – gave them much chance.

Ray Wilkins felt Mourinho was still best equipped to manage the team and should return. 'I would say Mourinho because I think Mourinho will leave Real Madrid. I think he will win La Liga comfortably and he will think his job's done there. He's still in the Champions League, he's got a chance of winning that. He's got a wonderful squad of players there but I think he will leave. He, for me, would be the perfect option.'

The club had taken soundings from a couple of vastly experienced managers but to take the job on a temporary, virtually trial basis until the end of the season didn't fit comfortably with the likes of Rafa Benitez. So Di Matteo – who played for Chelsea from 1996 –2002 and had helped win two FA Cups, scoring inside 42 seconds in the 1997 final against Middlesbrough (the fastest goal in a final at the old Wembley Stadium) – was handed the interim post. He also helped win the League Cup, the UEFA Cup, the UEFA Super Cup and the Charity Shield while at Stamford Bridge.

His managerial career began at Milton Keynes Dons in 2008, guiding them to the League One play-offs in his first season and losing to Scunthorpe on penalties in the semi-finals. Having moved to West Brom, he secured promotion to the Premier League in his first season as the Baggies finished runners-up to Newcastle, but his team were beaten 6–0 in their first match in the top flight – coincidentally at Chelsea – and he was sacked in February 2011. Four months later Di Matteo became AVB's assistant before their partnership was ended, in another ironic twist, following defeat at the Italian's former club.

Former Chelsea star Eddie Newton joined his coaching staff until the end of the season. Roy Hodgson was the last opponent for AVB and the shock victory propelled the WBA boss towards the England job and AVB towards the exit door – such are the ups and downs of management at the highest level.

Ian Wright wondered whether the red-hot favourite Pep Guardiola would welcome such an intricate task as trying to turn around Chelsea. He argued, 'Abramovich is paying more compensation on managers than actual buying of players at the minute. The fact is it's embarrassing. It's embarrassing the way he's sacked managers and what he's done with managers in the past – good managers. Now people are talking about Pep Guardiola, maybe Jose Mourinho going back, but why would Pep Guardiola want to leave Barcelona, whatever money they're going to offer him? He's already said that he wants to have a break if he does leave Barcelona, why would he want the Chelsea job? Why would anyone want the Chelsea job with an owner that does things like that?'

Mourinho was in London buying a house, prompting speculation of a return to the Premier League, but Mourinho was always linked to clubs at that stage of the year. However, there was every chance he would stay in Madrid, although Ian Wright believed there was a chance he could return. 'I'm not sure with Mourinho. People are saying why would he come back, and him and Abramovich don't get on. I think they do get on and I think that that was something that was a massive mistake from Roman in the first place. You just don't know, you just don't know in football. I would never have guessed that they would have got a 33-year-old manager to manage Chelsea in the first place. Abramovich is the owner, he does what he wants and he's done what he wants again.'

Di Matteo, though, pulled off one of the most incredible managerial feats when least expected to do so. Chelsea succeeded for only the fourth time in 45 attempts to overcome a first-leg deficit of two or more goals in the Champions League as the Blues won 4–1 after extra time, winning 5–4 on aggregate on 14 March, 2012. Chelsea joined Manchester United's class of 1957 and Leeds United's 1992 vintage as the only English team to progress in the European Cup after losing the first leg by two or more goals.

Chelsea overcame Benfica to reach the semi-finals against Barca and recalled how unfortunate it was to be knocked out by Guardiola's side in 2009, complaining bitterly about a succession of decisions made by Norwegian referee Tom Ovrebo. The two legs of this semi-final were the ninth and tenth times these two teams had met since that dramatic win in Camp Nou in 2000 – a compelling rivalry riddled with incident and controversy: Frisk forced out of football after receiving death threats following Mourinho's claim that he had seen him speaking with Frank Rijkaard at half-time (a claim that Frisk denied); Mourinho accusing Messi of play-acting to get Asier del Horno sent off ('I don't do theatre,' the then 18-year-old Argentine replied, dismissing the claim) and Chelsea being denied three clear penalties. Di Matteo was a club record signing at £4.9m at that time, and Puyol and Xavi were young players when Barca beat Chelsea that night. The following year Guardiola, then 30, left the club. For all Rijkaard's success, it was not until Guardiola returned that they established themselves not just as the best side in the world but one that has changed the way the game is played.

As Guardiola was letting his contract run down and was constantly linked with a move to Chelsea, Di Matteo was coaching for his future at the club but it was widely known that Abramovich wanted a high-profile, experienced coach. Three years earlier, Chelsea sacked Luiz Felipe Scolari in mid-season and Gus Hiddink came in and lifted the team. They had beaten Juventus and Liverpool to get a shot at Barcelona in the semi-final. Over the two legs, Hiddink's Chelsea subdued Barcelona. They held them to a 0–0 draw at the Camp Nou and, leading 1–0 at Stamford Bridge, lost to a late goal from Andres Ineista. Only an awful refereeing performance prevented Hiddink's Chelsea from winning that night.

Drogba was determined to land the elite prize in Europe, as this was his final season. He answered the critics who said he was over the hill after scoring the winner in the hugely impressive 1–0 win over Barca at the Bridge. The 34-year-old found the net with his team's only shot on target. Few, if any, thought they would survive the barrage of attacks that awaited them in the return leg.

Chelsea were sixth in the Premier League. Their ability to qualify for the Champions League via the league was in such doubt that it increasingly looked like the only salvation to the season would be actually winning the Champions League, despite having to overcome Barcelona, and then take on either Real Madrid or Bayern Munich.

Chelsea produced one of the greatest escapes in the history of European football as they withstood the sending-off of Terry to win a place in the final on a night of drama at the Nou Camp. After surviving a Barca siege from start to finish, which saw Messi miss a penalty, Torres came off the bench to score a stoppage-time breakaway goal as Chelsea avenged their 2009 defeat in the most remarkable manner possible. Terry's indiscretion ruled him out of the final in Munich. Meireles, Ramires and Ivanovic were also suspended after picking up yellow cards. Cech rated the performance as the greatest in his time at the club. 'I don't think you can find in the history of the game a team who were 2–0 down, lost two central defenders and were down to ten men against the best team in the world, yet managed to play that confidently.'

So no magical final showdown with the 'Special One' after all. Mourinho was naturally supporting his 'Chelsea heroes' against Bayern in the final after he was denied a reunion with his former club by a dramatic penalty shoot-out defeat in the second leg of the semi-final. The then Real manager rounded on critics of Chelsea's tactics, telling them: you know nothing.

Ronaldo and Kaká had penalties saved and Ramos blasted his over the bar as Madrid were beaten 3–1 in the shootout after a 3–3 aggregate draw. Mourinho, as usual, defended his players, highlighting the 'brutal' pressure and praising them for having the 'balls' to step up. He continued in a similar vein with an equally spirited defence of his former players from Stamford Bridge over their defensive approach against Barcelona. 'John is missing but Chelsea are there and that is the most important thing. I just hope it is a good final and, of course, I want the Blues to win, even though I have a lot of respect for the reds. I have a blue rib, still. Inter and Chelsea mean a lot to me. I think Chelsea's boys were heroes, absolute heroes. Some people think they are the masters of the game and they will criticise Chelsea in the same way that they criticised Inter two years ago, but they know nothing. Nothing. They know nothing about character and personality. They know nothing about the effort or what it is to resist physically, emotionally and technically, with ten men. They know nothing about organisation. They know nothing. That's why my heroes at Chelsea are in my mind and why Chelsea deserve to be in the final. One of the great things about football is that it is unpredictable. Chelsea have fantastic fans and so do Bayern Munich so I hope they enjoy the final. And I hope Chelsea win.'

The Bayern coach, Jupp Heynckes, was surprised Chelsea had reached the final but praised them for a 'tactical masterpiece' against Barca. He insisted the four suspensions picked up by Chelsea did not constitute an advantage, noting that Bayern were also without key players: Alaba, Badstuber and Gustavo. 'It is a pity that the best players cannot play in the final,' Heynckes said, 'both for Chelsea and for Bayern Munich. We have to rethink the rules. We have lost three players who have played stupendously in this year's competition. I do not think it is an advantage. It was a surprise Chelsea were in the final but in the last few weeks Chelsea have made a very good impression. They are a team of wonderful professionals and if they reached the final it is because they deserved to. I thought Barcelona suffered from immense fatigue; they were exhausted. Chelsea did it that way because they knew that they could not play offensively against Barcelona and we have to congratulate them. It was a tactical masterpiece.'

Mourinho announced that he intended to stay at the Bernabéu, ending speculation about a return to the Premier League. He was handed greater authority than any coach in Madrid's history but he also made it clear that he demand further changes. Asked if defeat made him determined to stay at Madrid and attempt to win the competition again next year, Mourinho replied, 'Absolutely.' He added: 'If I have anything in my mind, it is to try to win with these [players]. Winning the cup last year was important and if we win the league this year that will be important too. Two [Champions League] semi-finals is also not bad, but we want more. My feeling is that we still have the ability to grow as a team and the club can grow too. Clubs have to adapt to the evolution of time and to changing mentalities. A fantastic car in the 1980s is not fantastic in the 1990s or the 2000s. If the club thinks that I can still give something – and I know that they do – and if the players think so as well – and I think they do; I feel like the empathy is increasing – I will continue.'

Chelsea were hopeful of persuading Guardiola to postpone his break from football after announcing his decision to quit Barca. Abramovich had desired for some time to replicate Barcelona's playing style and youth development. He had meetings with Txiki Begiristain, Barcelona's former director of football, about taking up a similar role at Stamford Bridge, only to see his offer rejected. Guardiola denied ever having had similar meetings with Abramovich. The manager, who won 13 of the 16 trophies he contested since taking charge at the Nou Camp in 2008, would be replaced by his assistant, Tito Vilanova. Guardiola's decision came following their midweek Champions League exit to Chelsea and their defeat to Real Madrid. Although he announced that he planned to take a sabbatical, speculation was rife that Abramovich would try to make him an offer he could not refuse.

Michael Ballack believed that Bayern had an 'emotional advantage' over Chelsea as the showpiece final was played at the German side's home ground, the Allianz Arena, and Ballack, who left Bayern to join Chelsea in the summer of 2006, recognised that was a difficult obstacle to surmount for the Londoners. 'I think Barcelona would have been the only team capable of contesting a final abroad and winning it. It is a huge advantage when you are at home in a final, where a lot of emotions play a role. This is an emotional advantage that Chelsea cannot compensate for,' Ballack insisted, though showing that he was entirely neutral, added, 'I have my fingers crossed for both sides.'

Drogba became the first man to score in four FA Cup finals as

Chelsea overcame Liverpool. Terry became the first captain in the modern era to lift the trophy on four occasions. Cole collected an incredible seventh winners' medal. Despite victory over relegated Blackburn in their final league game, Chelsea ended the season a shocking sixth, so they would only qualify for the Champions League by beating Bayern. Equally, Bayern were under pressure to deliver the club's fifth European Cup, having been eclipsed domestically by Borussia Dortmund, losing the German Cup final 5–2 to the league champions.

Bayern, beaten in the final by Mourinho's Inter in Madrid two years earlier, were the first side to play in a Champions League final in their own stadium and it was Bayern's last chance to win silverware that season. Lahm believed that the club had progressed since Louis van Gaal's side lost to Mourinho's Inter and that home territory could be the key. 'We believe we can win the title more this time around. We're more experienced now than we were two years ago, and what Jupp Heynckes has done with us is get a much better grip between the mix between offensive and defensive style. All that will make a big difference but so would the thought of a team coming here, to our house, and winning it at our expense. Naturally, that would be awful for us.'

Arjen Robben enjoyed three years at the Bridge under Mourinho, being involved in the winning of successive Premier League titles, two League Cups and enjoying an FA Cup success. His dazzling wing play in combination with Damien Duff and Joe Cole produced Mourinho's most exciting counter-attacking side. His last Chelsea appearance, as a substitute who had to be replaced, was in the 2007 FA Cup final.

He reflected on that spell and eventual £24m move to the Bernabéu in the summer of 2007: 'Overall, I had a great time, especially in the first season when I was part of the team who won the league for the first time in fifty years. It was great to be there, and I played my part in the time I was fit, and showed what I could do on the pitch. Of course I wanted to show them more, but because of the injuries I couldn't always do that. They've changed the way they play in the time since. But when I was there we were nice to watch, with two wingers and attacking football. Maybe, tactically, they're a bit more defensive these days. They can still play football, but it's not always the most technical football like you see at Arsenal or Manchester United. For a lot of their players, this will be their last chance to win the Champions League. People say their team has not evolved, and that may be a failure, but it could also be a strength. A lot of their players have been at the club for a long time, which can make them strong. They have experience and a lot of leaders in their team, even if the biggest leader [John Terry] will be missing in the final. We know the threat they pose. They've come close in this competition before, and it's still a big target for Mr Abramovich. They were in the final four years ago against Manchester United and, when I was there, we played two semi-finals against Liverpool. But, in the end, it's about winning the trophy. If you want to enter the history books you have to win it. We're in our second final in three years and, for us, it's our time to win it.'

As Di Matteo led his players up the seemingly never-ending flights of stairs to reach the presentation podium high in the stands, he embraced the man he called 'The Boss'. 'I won it,' Di Matteo could be heard telling his boss. For the tenth time, an Italian manager won the European Cup; the first Italian to achieve the feat with a foreign club. For Chelsea, it was the first time they had won the European Cup – the first London club to win it and the second side to win the FA Cup and the European Cup in the same season, along with Manchester United in their 1998–99 treble-winning season.

Chelsea lost on penalties when Terry slipped and struck the outside of the post four years earlier and who knows what would have happened to the then manager, Avram Grant, who was clearly out of the door when Manchester United took the domestic crown. It looked as though Chelsea were going to lose the shoot-out again when they started two goals down. Mata missed the first penalty. The German side went 2–0 up in a penalty shoot-out. Surely game over? But Luiz,

Lampard and Cole were all successful. Lahm, Gomez and goalkeeper Manuel Neuer were all on target. After Robben's saved penalty in normal time, he was unable to take part in the penalty shoot-out, leaving it to his keeper, who scuffed the shot slightly but still found the corner. Cech was guessing each penalty correctly; it was only a matter of time before he saved one. The momentum shifted decisively when Cech denied Olic, and Schweinsteiger hit the post to present Drogba with his moment of destiny.

Drogba composed himself, then took three strides to strike the perfect penalty just inside the post. Signal wild scenes of elation among Chelsea's players, staff and supporters. Drogba ran the length of the pitch, swirling his shirt above his head before finally slamming it onto the pitch. Nine cup finals, scoring in every one.

Back in the dressing room, Drogba spoke to the trophy. With the flag of the Ivory Coast draped across his shoulders, Drogba leaped on to a table in the centre of the dressing room and said, 'Why have you avoided us for such a long time? Flirting with us, eluding us.' He spoke of 'Barcelona in 2009', of 'Moscow' the year before, eventually focusing on the dramatic events of that evening and how they had unfolded. Rarely the other players interrupted but, when they did, it was a clear message to Abramovich that they wanted Didier to stay; they chanted to Drogba, to Abramovich, to the members of the Chelsea board.

'It was like he was praying to The Cup,' said chairman Bruce Buck, 'It was almost a religious experience. He talked about Barcelona – not this year's Barcelona, but the previous time – and about Moscow. It really was a lot of fun.'

Abramovich gave a speech, using director Eugene Tenenbaum to translate. 'Roman gave a little thank-you speech in the dressing room,' said Buck. 'The message was it was all down to the boys. They did it. We've had a tough season, a bunch of highs and lows, but they grasped it and deserved all the credit. And they do. It was very difficult when Andre left because Andre's a really good guy. I guess we just felt it was something that had to be done and, obviously, it's turned out correctly for us. The spirit in the dressing room after the match was unbelievable. The camaraderie; they were sitting and talking for the longest time. They didn't get back to the hotel until almost three o'clock in the morning.'

When Abramovich addressed his European Champions, he made it clear that 'this is just the beginning' for Chelsea.

Drogba informed his team-mates of his decision during the club's open-top-bus parade. He struggled to get the words out and burst into tears. After eight years, 157 goals in 341 appearances, 10 titles, including the Champions League late equaliser in normal time and the winning kick, his time at the club was over.

Mourinho had signed him for £24m in July 2004 from Marseille. Drogba said, 'Me, Frank, John Terry – we were part of a new era and created an identity. Now, wherever you go in the world, everyone is wearing Chelsea shirts. It's been a pleasure and an honour to wear the blue shirt and to achieve everything we did here with all these trophies. The best for me was to finish on a high with the Champions League final. As we say in French, it was the crème de la crème.'

Drogba's relationship with Mourinho lasted beyond his time at the club and continues. 'Everyone knows he is the man who gave me the strength and the man I learned a lot from. As a human being and a manager I learned a lot from him. He gave me this winning attitude and this desire to make history. He created this, it's in our DNA now. It would've been nice to win it for him, but we tried so many times. As I said after the game, the Champions League is for all the managers who have been chasing the trophy.'

Ron 'Chopper' Harris, told me, 'Having been at Chelsea most of my life, more than twenty years as a professional and on the first European trophy by beating the greatest ever club side of that generation, Real Madrid, I have to say that winning the Champions League is the ultimate prize – and, therefore, I would have to say that was the club's greatest ever achievement in their history. You have got to put it all into perspective and, no matter how much we love to look back and say this team or that team was the greatest team, when I was at Chelsea we won the League Cup, the FA Cup and the icing on the cake was the Cup Winners Cup beating Real Madrid in a replay in a major European competition. Real Madrid were the number-one kings back then, so it was some achievement to beat them in the final. But the first time winning the European Cup: that is the ultimate. Nothing compares with the European Cup; it is the club's great achievement.

'I know a lot of people will say that Chelsea rode their luck and, of course, they did, not just in the final but in a few years' time when we all look back on Munich, it will say "Bayern Munich 1, Chelsea 1, Chelsea won on penalties". No one will dwell too much on how lucky or unlucky they were. The body language of the players told you that they were not happy under the previous manager. A blind man could tell that the players didn't seem happy. Certain things were going on but there was a lot being said at the time about what was going wrong. I work at the Bridge in the hospitality lounges and you hear quite a bit – keep it all to yourself, of course – but there were plenty of rumours, plenty of stories, but you knew that too many important players were not happy. Roberto Di Matteo changed all that. Once he took over, certain players found themselves again; they performed under him whereas they were not performing before, so that cannot be a coincidence. You see this in a dressing room, you have to have harmony, you need everyone pulling together.

'Di Matteo got everyone pulling together and you could see that from the first game in the Champions League once he took over against Napoli and it was there from there onward, the players were playing for him. When a car breaks down, it is easier if all eleven are pushing it; if only half a dozen are behind the car pushing, it's a different story. Let's be honest, Di Matteo transformed what had become a very, very ordinary side. They finished some twenty points behind the Premier League winners, which tells you how bad it was for a team that had always been challenging for the title but, worse still, were in danger of finishing outside of the top four and ended up so low that they would not have qualified for the Champions League unless they had won it. That was unheard of since Roman Abramovich took over from Ken Bates and took the club to another level of success, challenging for titles and determined to win the biggest prize of them all, the Champions League.

'When Chelsea made it to the Champions League Final, the chairman Bruce Buck spoke to me and then I received a phone call from the chief executive, Ron Gourlay, inviting me to lead the team up to collect either the losers' or the winners' medals and, if they won, the trophy itself. Peter Kenyon did it in Moscow but they clearly wanted a football persona and they came to me, having been so long at the club. I couldn't do it because each year I attend a dinner in Ireland and, when I make a commitment, I don't let people down, no matter how much I wanted do it, so I had to turn down the invitation to be flow over to Munich and to lead the players to collect their medals. What an honour that would have been. After they won the trophy, I left a message for Ron Gourlay asking him if they will have me next year to lead the team up to collect the trophy and the medals!'

For Abramovich, the Champions League was the Holy Grail: one billion pounds, eight managers in eight years, a penalty-shoot-out defeat in Moscow against United – finally, after all the frustrations, Abramovich got his hands on the trophy he craved; *the* trophy that had always eluded him; the one piece of silverware all the gold of the Russian oligarch's £16-billion wealth could not buy, no matter how much he threw at buying players – even the £50m lavished on Torres.

As Drogba was finally handed the trophy at the presentation ceremony, after all the players had frantically got their own hands on the precious silverware, he handed it straight to the guy at the end wearing a cardigan and looking as though he had gate-crashed the party: Franco Zola.

Drogba runs Franco Zola close as the all-time most popular player in west London. Zola charmed off the field and dazzled on it but the powerful goal-scoring brute of a centre-forward was sometimes unplayable in his prime. In his twilight years, recovering from the long-suffering, lingering effects of malaria to regain his form and fitness, he summoned up all of his old force to take the Champions League Final by storm. At 11.29pm local time in Munich, Drogba delivered the trophy with the coolest-looking final penalty, which turned out to be his last-ever kick for Chelsea. Drogba had the bleakest moment of his career as he was sent off in extra time and United won the Champions League in a penalty shoot-out. He should have been taking the penalty that fell, instead, to Terry, who slipped on the sodden surface, sending the ball sliding against the outside of the post.

But Drogba will always be affectionately remembered at the Bridge for the night when an English team beat a German team on penalties.

The Happy One

Jose Mourinho described his return as a 'great moment' for him almost a decade since he was first unveiled at the club. Mourinho first joined Chelsea in 2004 and the impact of 'The Special One' was instantaneous: back-to-back Premier League titles in 2005 and 2006.

He was conscious of the possibility that his return might not spark the same level of success and that it might ruin the memory of his original achievements. 'When I decide to come back, there is some risk of things going wrong, but I'm not afraid. I trust myself, I think I can do it again. I'm not afraid to lose my job and when you're not afraid, you don't feel any pressures. You are not too worried, you can express yourself in a different way. It makes you better, I think.'

He embarked on the season giving the impression he had changed; that he had returned older and wiser, and that it would be less 'sexy football', but the motivation was there – the thirst for more success. At 41, he first turned up in west London suave and tanned without a trace of grey. His media debut provoked a quote that will forever live with him: 'I'm not one who comes straight out of a bottle – I'm a special one.'

Manchester City fans spread a rumour when he first arrived that his distinctive slate-grey overcoat was from Matalan. It was Armani. His first Chelsea experience was all silverware, even if he failed to deliver the real pot of gold – the Champions League: the trophy that eluded Roman Abramovich and was, ironically, delivered in Mourinho's absence.

Now he was back, in his fifties, his hair grey. More than half the managers in the Premier League were younger than him. Mourinho was no longer the fashion icon. 'I wear clothes to feel good, not to look good. Sometimes I can wear a tracksuit, other times I need a tie and a jacket, it depends on the circumstances, but I'm never worried about being fashionable or looking good or something like that. Feeling good.'

The self-styled 'Special One' remained stylish and a trend-setter, however. His flat was in the highly fashionable Eaton Square. He likes cars, and owns a few, and he has lent his name to a new Mourinho supercar, which comes in an edition of 11.

The media were eagerly looking for a new tag on the manager's comeback, and the man who inspires a million headlines didn't disappoint, branding himself 'The Happy One'.

But that was received with a huge dose of scepticism; contentment in the Mourinho mind is never far away from outbursts of ego, anger, moodiness and controversy. The tranquillity he sought back in west London after the turbulence of life in Madrid didn't last too long.

However, comparatively speaking, life was far easier. Mourinho was back among the Chelsea faithful that adored him and, once he had knocked his side into shape, despite its shortcomings in attack, the old Mourinho song was soon ringing out at home and away. He was back where he is loved and appreciated by the fans.

The fans, too, recognised that Mourinho had inherited a Chelsea far from the one that satisfied him and, as the season unfolded, the lack of a genuine out-and-out goalscorer within his squad was the team's ultimate downfall, as they lost the Champions League semi-final and the chance of the title in the space of five days. Apart from the Spanish Super Cup at the start of the previous season, it was back-to-back seasons without a major trophy; something that forced Mourinho into a passionate defence of his entire career record. Having branded Arsène Wenger a manager who specialises in failure, it was not the right time to fail but, given the shortcomings of his squad, it was not exactly unexpected.

Mourinho parted company with Real Madrid after three years in which he won La Liga and the Copa Del Rey and, while it seemed he might be heading to Old Trafford, he wasn't their kind of guy, with Sir Alex recommending David Moyes instead. Despite the Scot's uncanny warm relationship with the Portuguese and their endless banter about the quality of red wine afforded him in previous Bridge visits when Mourinho was their coach, the Old Trafford board would have been reluctant to risk their reputation on such a controversial manager. They played safe with their chosen one. But Moyes' six-year contract was brutally cut short when it was clear he was never going to turn around the team's fortunes. United have now turned to Louis van Gaal, every bit as controversial as Mourinho.

Before Madrid, Mourinho took Inter Milan to Champions League glory and two Serie A titles between 2008 and 2010. He disclosed that he been offered the chance to manage Real Madrid after he won the FA Cup in 2007, his last trophy during his first spell at Chelsea. He stayed, however, and was sacked in September.

A fondness for Inter remains but not so for Real, where antagonism and confrontation reached an unprecedented peak. Yet Mourinho badly wanted Real on his already impressive CV and left Inter for the opportunity. Unfortunately, though, the love affair ended in an ugly divorce. The Real hierarchy were glad to get shot of a coach who had become far too high profile for all the wrong reasons. Mourinho split opinion about his merits as coach at Madrid – not necessarily about his ability to lead a team but because of the headlines that appeared at times. His time in Spain was punctuated by a series of rows with the press and issues with key players.

Mourinho's return was remarkable given the nature of the fall-out that saw him leave in the first place.

Nevertheless, he signed a four-year contract, replacing the hugely unpopular Benitez, who had guided Chelsea to third place and won the Europa League after taking over the helm on an interim basis in November from the hugely popular Roberto di Matteo.

Mourinho explained on his return how he had repaired his fractured relationship with the Russian oligarch. 'I'm very happy. I had to prepare myself [to] not to be too emotional at my arrival at the club but obviously I'm very happy. It was an easy decision. I met the owner and I think in five minutes after a couple of very short but pragmatic questions we decided, I think, straight away. I asked the boss, "Do you want me back?" and the boss asked me, "Do you want to come back?" and I think in a couple of minutes, decision made.'

Having won the 'grand slam' of titles in Portugal, England, Italy and Spain, he felt it was the right time to return. He added, 'I love it here and I have big connections with the club. I think we are ready to marry again and to be happy and successful again.'

Of his split from Chelsea, he explained, 'I think my departure was not easy for the club but, if you analyse it in a cool way and leave emotions a bit apart, I think it was fantastic because in my career after that I had what I was aiming for in that period of my career. By the other way, Chelsea football club got important trophies after that, had important moments in the history of the club and now we are back together in a great moment for both. In my career I had two great passions, Inter and Chelsea, and Chelsea is more important for me. It was very, very hard to play against Chelsea. Now I promise exactly the same thing I promised in 2004, with the difference that I'm one of you.'

Clearly Madrid had left its mark in a negative way. However much Real were delighted to push Mourinho to the exit door, it was a relief for him to be away from the constant turmoil that dogged his life there.

Mourinho sought stability back in west London. His insistence that he 'will stay for the long-term' was interesting considering that the longest he has managed at any club is the three years and two months he spent at Chelsea between 2004 and 2007. 'Every day you have to think about yourself and about evolution. I have the same nature but I'm much more mature with a different approach to things, I'm more ready to be in a club and stay for a long time.'

After seven permanent managers and two temporary appointments during Abramovich's 10-year ownership, the club could now do with stability as they set off at the outset of the second Mourinho management era but it seemed a contradiction in terms that they could possibly find it with the nomadic Mourinho.

The manager led Chelsea to a Premier League points-tally record of 95 in the 2004–2005 season; a feat that remains unsurpassed. His departure was mourned and his return eagerly anticipated.

Despite being the most successful manager in the club's history, in terms of domestic trophies, he would not rely on his popularity with the fan base to see him through. 'I'm not coming here to sleep on what I did in the past and be comfortable just because we [Mourinho and the supporters] have a great relation, and probably the first day I put my foot in Stamford Bridge again they will sing my name. I'm not that kind of person and professional. I'm very demanding of myself. I need, of course, their support, but I want to start from ground zero. I need to work hard again and build a different team from the team I built in the past.'

Mourinho tried to sign Frank Lampard when he was at Inter but now he was glad it never happened, explaining, 'He is Chelsea. This is where he belongs. It was close, very, very close. When he eventually turned me down I told him he had made the right decision.' Mourinho spoke of his high regard for Chelsea's old guard: John Terry, Ashley Cole and Lampard – players he once called 'untouchables'. 'They have made my life easier. Some managers bring in four or five guys they know well when they first arrive at a club. I didn't need to. They were already here.'

They helped him to get his ideas across to the team because they had the benefit of playing under him several years ago. 'It was a help for me, the way they communicated with other people, the way they know me and the way they helped others understand my ideas. They are good guys, they are professional and the relationship they have with me is perfect for the time of their career because they trust me.'

Mourinho inherited an evolving Chelsea, with a number of missing links and some problem areas. He had some familiar old friends in Terry and Lampard but his rock of a captain and leader, Terry, was no longer in favour. That would change, however, with his old manager back. How to integrate Oscar, Juan Mata, Willian and Eden Hazard was a conundrum. Mourinho was saying all the right things: 'I like the profile, I like the fact we have five players from the beginning of the winning Chelsea, and I think they have to be always a part of the Chelsea soul, so I'm pleased we kept some of these boys. The profile of the younger players with long-term space for improvement, I like. I've come with a four-year contract so with the immediate age of Hazard, Oscar, Luiz, it will be good for me to work with them and good for them to work with me. Together we can improve.'

From his own staff Mourinho brought coach Rui Faria and goalkeeping coach Silvinho Louro, who worked with him in his first spell at the club, and scout Jose Morais, keeping Christopher Lollichon, Steve Holland and Chris Jones from the existing staff. In the build-up to his official unveiling he remarked, 'I'm not happy, I am very happy. I was preparing myself in the last couple of days to control emotions, to come here in a cool way but I'm really emotional. I feel the people love me and in life you have to look for that. Life is beautiful and short and you must look for what you think is best for you.'

Before Mourinho starts a new job, he sends an open letter to the players. The first time he did it was at FC Porto in January 2002. Back then it was written on old-fashioned paper but times move on. 'In this moment, we have an application [on] our telephones and [on] our iPads,' he explains. 'So not anymore a paper letter.'

The basic instructions have not significantly altered in more than a decade of management. An outline of his belief that football is a collective; that all the individual's personal ambitions are put aside for the team mission to flourish. He promises to be fair but reminds the players that every decision he takes will be in the best interest of the club and the team. If they fully commit to his way of working, he'll devote himself totally to improving them and he prides himself on leaving a club with the players much improved from when he joined them. 'There is no more, "I respect you because you are the manager,"' he explains. 'I respect you because you are good. I respect you because you are honest with me. I respect you because you are making me better and I feel that. But no more, "I respect you because you are the manager".'

Mourinho noted how three of his protégés were now rivals, including Brendan Rodgers, no doubt, but no one could have imagined how much of a rivalry it would turn out to be. So every dossier containing his tactics and methods would be freely available. But he then made a point of tapping his head and stressing that they could not put a USB stick 'in my brain'. Much of his genius is spontaneous and, as the season progressed, he became 'The Silent One'. Although he still managed to rack up three FA charges for savaging match officials, one being an attack that was pure sarcasm.

Mourinho was fined £10,000 for sarcastic appraisal of officials. The manager's comments did not question the officials' integrity but amounted to disrepute and improper conduct. An FA statement read, 'Following an independent regulatory commission hearing, Jose Mourinho has been fined 10,000 pounds in relation to comments he made after Chelsea's game against Sunderland on April 19, 2014. While the commission did not find that Mourinho's post-match comments called into question the integrity of the referee appointed to the above fixture and/or the integrity of Mike Riley, general manager of the Professional Game Match Officials Limited, they did find that the comments brought the game into disrepute and the charge for improper conduct was found proven.'

At the same time, Mourinho also failed in an appeal against an £8,000 fine for his conduct towards referee Chris Foy at the end of a defeat at Villa. The FA statement went on, 'Meanwhile, Mourinho has lost his appeal against an independent regulatory commission's decision to fine him 8,000 pounds in relation to Chelsea's game against Aston Villa on March 15, 2014. Mourinho denied a breach of FA Rule E3 in that his behaviour in re-entering the field of play and approaching the Match Referee in an attempt to speak to him, in or around the 90th minute of the game, amounted to improper conduct. The charge was found proven by an independent regulatory commission and that decision was upheld by an appeal panel.'

'The Silent One' also, on one occasion, refused to give a half-time talk to his team because his players had been so bad in the first half of the match!

Chelsea's chief executive Ron Gourlay greeted Mourinho's return as you would expect, with typical boardroom speak, but he did make this valid point: 'His continued success, drive and ambition made him the outstanding candidate. He was and remains a hugely popular figure at the club and everyone here looks forward to working with him again.'

Reacting to the news of Mourinho's return, former Chelsea assistant manager Ray Wilkins said, 'Having lost from our game Sir Alex Ferguson, who has been absolutely unbelievably good, it is nice we have got another fantastic personality coming back. It is not only good for Chelsea, it is good for the Premier League as well.' Former Chelsea captain Ron Harris added, 'I think ninety-five per cent of the Chelsea supporters are pleased Jose is back. I feel that the supporters will be more than happy and I think it is a pat on the back for Roman Abramovich in bringing Jose Mourinho back to the club.'

One fan tweeted, 'I started supporting Chelsea because of the team Mourinho created and to see him return is so exciting. This is going to be big!'

The fans had wanted him back and now they had him back, turning out in their 'Special 1' T-shirts for his return game at home to Hull City. His 'signing' was more anticipated than that of any multi-million-pound player, inspiring confidence that another trophy haul was about to start.

Mourinho was greeted at the match with a sign that read 'Jose

Mourinho Simply the Best'. In the match-day programme he wrote, 'The boss [Roman Abramovich] celebrates ten years of amazing work. I celebrate my return, but this match is not a testimonial! It is great to write again to my Blues brothers.'

He told Sky Sports before kick-off, 'I feel good. I want to play. I try not to feel [emotional]. But I think when I go and sit [in the dugout], there will be thirty seconds of emotion, for sure. After that I have to focus on the game.'

Pitch announcer Neil Barnett was 'looking forward to introducing this manager more than I did the last one'. That was tough on Benitez, who had delivered a trophy and qualification for the Champions League.

Mourinho tried hard to keep things low-key when he finally emerged from the tunnel to take his seat. No chance. Nearly 40,000 people sang his name, some wearing Mourinho masks. He stood up and sat down three times, eventually blowing kisses to the supporters and then, as the game started, he began writing his customary notes on a pad. His unbeaten home record in the league was never going to be challenged that day.

Mourinho's first line-up:

Cech, Ivanovic, Cahill, Terry, Cole; Ramires, Lampard, Oscar, Hazard, De Bruyne, Torres.

Up in his executive box, Abramovich gave a shy wave to the supporters when his face was beamed up on the screen. Earlier he had imparted a rare message to the fans on the cover of the programme: 29 words in all, thanking them for supporting the club over his 10 years in charge.

Mourinho said that the billionaire had been in the dressing room before the game to speak to the players – the first time that he had done so during Mourinho's time in charge on the first day of a season.

De Bruyne was selected as the number 10, between Hazard and Oscar. The 22-year-old, who was making his competitive debut for

Chelsea, was impressive. He passed to Oscar on six minutes, after Hazard had carried the ball from the left wing, and the Brazilian scored beautifully.

Mata's absence could be noted: it was clear there would be a tough period of transition, with Schürrle coming on after 69 minutes.

It was obvious from the start that Mata would need to convince Mourinho that he could conform to the team ethic despite his billing as the team's best player for two years. Equally apparent was the lack of a genuine goal-scoring threat, alongside Mourinho's persistent courting of Wayne Rooney. Mourinho talked around the subject of the United forward after the game because the penny had dropped that he would not be sold to Chelsea, so there was no point in aggravating the situation any further.

Romelu Lukaku was a late replacement for Torres but Mourinho was again less than convinced and the young Belgium was destined for another loan spell, this time with Everton. Without Mata and David Luiz, it was an impressive start. But as goals became hard to come by, there was a great deal of head-scratching as to why Lukaku was farmed out to Goodison, as he hit a rich vein of goal-scoring form while his strikers were misfiring.

Lukuku had put in a request for a move after his decisive penalty-shootout miss in the Super Cup defeat by Bayern. With eight goals in nine league games for the Toffees, he told BBC's *Football Focus* that he would be interested in staying for another season. Mourinho responded by suggesting that it was Lukaku's choice to go on loan. 'Maybe there is a new rule in football where when the season finishes every player is able to decide their own future. Romelu likes to speak. He's a young boy who likes to speak. But the only thing he didn't say is why he went to Everton on loan. That's the only thing he never says. And my last contact with him was to tell him exactly that. Why do you never say why you are not here? So it's something he should [talk about] because he likes to speak. It's something he should say, the reason why he's not with Chelsea and is in Everton.'

Mata was surprised when Mourinho sold him for £37.1m to United. 'To be honest it is a bit surprising, but I have to say I'm really grateful to Chelsea, to the owner, everyone who works at the club and the fans – they voted me the best player in the last two seasons and I will always be grateful. They have been amazing with me. The last six months were difficult as I didn't play as much as I wanted to. I understand it's a team sport so I respected that situation. But the chance to come to Manchester United was a great moment for me to carry on with my career and join another massive club. I think I can play in the three positions behind the striker. I played on the left when I arrived at Chelsea, this season I have played on the right and last season, which was probably the best season of my career, I played behind the striker. But it doesn't matter as long as I play.'

Mourinho was convinced Chelsea were doing the right thing and that he would also have sanctioned the sale to title rivals Arsenal and Manchester City. Launching a detailed explanation of the reasons behind the transfer, he said, 'sooner rather than later' and criticised Wenger for suggesting it was a way of undermining fellow challengers for the title. Asked if he would have sold to Arsenal or City, the teams directly above Chelsea in the table, Mourinho said, 'Yes, honestly. A team can only play with eleven players, not twelve. City, Arsenal and United are full of top players, so if Juan plays for them it means somebody else is not playing. So why not? It's the same in other countries [that players move among top clubs], so why not here? We had clubs that contacted Chelsea, but with a real offer adapted to the potential of the player, and to what the player means to Chelsea, only United offered that.'

To Wenger's complaint that Chelsea benefited from Mata facing Arsenal and City in a United shirt in the second half of the season, Mourinho said, 'Wenger complaining is normal because he always does. This is the market. We don't do the market, we don't do the rules... he should be very happy that Chelsea sold a player like Juan Mata. But I think it [complaining] is also a bit of his nature.'

Pellegrini did not agree with the principle of Mata joining United in mid-season. 'I think if a player plays for a club for more than half of the season, a club with money can take the best players from the other teams. But the rules allow it, so [there is] nothing to say.' He clarified that his complaint was not because United were still to play City at Old Trafford, while they have taken on Chelsea twice already. 'I think in this transfer window, players that play more than five or six games for the same club should not change to another.'

The inevitable abrasive managerial confrontations began to dominate the agenda for the season.

Sam Allardyce defused this row by suggesting that the new incarnation of Mourinho was far more sociable, as the Hammers boss brushed off Mourinho's criticism of West Ham's style. Mourinho savaged the Hammers' willingness to get men behind the ball after the 0–0 draw at Stamford Bridge seemed, at the time, to put Chelsea's title chances backwards with a big step. Mourinho said Allardyce had his side playing 'nineteenth-century football'. Big Sam was understandably a trifle peeved. Surprisingly, though, he heaped some praise on his adversary by suggesting that he had mellowed. 'His comments apart, Jose was OK after the match. He seems less tense this time than during his first spell in England; perhaps more sociable. He says he is the "Happy One" now and perhaps he is. He has achieved so much in his life, he should be happy. He knows how to change his teams and when to change them. You survive in this management game only if your man-management skills are good and you are tactically aware. Jose has both those qualities. What he said about us I take as a great compliment. Jose invented parking the bus, don't forget. I've played against his Chelsea side at Stamford Bridge when they've gone 1–0 up and he has put on two defensive midfielders. It's perhaps a bit sad when he says things about teams who have played well against Chelsea but that is just his character.'

For the next game – one of the most significant of the season – Mourinho deployed two defensive midfielders with devastating attacking effect. He was also reminded about Inter's performance in their semi-final Champions League second leg in Barcelona in 2010, as he joked, 'In the second game, when you start 3–1 up and play with ten men, you put the airplane in front of the goal!'

First Mourinho engaged in typical mind games, dismissing Tim Sherwood's assertion that City are the best team in the world after tearing Spurs apart and continuing with their mountain of goals. Mourinho took a swipe at City, suggesting a true measure of their worth would out in the Champions League. 'Maybe, for the Tottenham manager, the planet is England,' said Mourinho. 'You will see [how good City are] in the Champions League. You will see in a couple of months.'

Mourinho continued on the attack. 'They are lucky. The reality is they have many crucial decisions in their favour. Against Liverpool, the Sterling "goal". The penalty on Suárez. Against Newcastle, the goal that is a clear goal. Against Tottenham, Dawson's goal, the penalty, the [Danny Rose] red card. They are having everything. I repeat, because I don't want to be misinterpreted, [it is] just pure coincidence. The referees, they try to do their best and sometimes they make mistakes and normally during the season the mistakes are split between teams. In their [City's] case, they have everything in their favour.'

Mourinho insisted his side were not yet ready to win the title. 'Next pre-season, day one, I will say we are candidates to win the Premier League. This season, the speech is we are candidates to win the next match. It doesn't matter where, it doesn't matter the opponent. We're just trying to win. I tell you now, before Man City... I will tell you before the Newcastle game next week, and then West Brom. I will repeat this.'

City were escaping the public criticism his Chelsea had to face 10 years ago, according to Mourinho. 'I don't know why they are so popular when we weren't. I don't know why. In my time we were accused of buying the title, no? Because our owner was Mr Abramovich; just arrived in the country. Maybe now people see City in a different way. I'm not sure if it's because it's taken them six years to get to this stage while we won straight away. And I don't care. I don't envy the fact that they have this kind of protection, of whichever word. It's the way it is. Teams with success, people tend not to like them, no? If they want to make it impossible for us to compete with them in the market, yes, it's impossible. Financially, no, we can't compete. Back then it was a free world. There was no Financial Fair Play. If your club was a rich one, your owner a rich one, there were no rules. It was an open situation. But times change. Many things people considered wrong fifty years ago are something very normal now. Maybe ten years ago a huge investment in the club was something people hated, but in this moment it's something people accept in a different way.'

Mourinho claimed that not all clubs were showing the same commitment to UEFA's Financial Fair Play regulations as others. On the day £11m-signing Mohamed Salah trained for the first time and 19-year-old Kurt Zouma completed his £12.5m move, loaned straight back, Mourinho hinted that some clubs were finding ways to mask their spending. Of course, Abramovich personally funded the recruitment when Mourinho guided the team to back-to-back titles in 2005 and 2006; City are funded by their billionaire owners from Abu Dhabi.

City recorded a loss of nearly £51m for the financial year ending 2013. Losses for the last two years were £150m, millions written off against the FFP rules because they invested in facilities and youth development. The annual wage bill at City is £233m but they used a loophole to avoid taking wages into account on contracts signed before 2010.

Chelsea declared a loss of £49.4m but recorded a small profit in the previous year. They, too, wrote off part of this and were able to satisfy the FFP rules. 'Some clubs are feeling FFP as a fair FFP, and some others are feeling FFP as a dodgy FFP,' said Mourinho. 'We don't want emergency plans, it's not our profile now. The players we're signing now are the right ones for our future: Matic, Salah, Zouma, a young kid for the future.'

When Abramovich first arrived, they would not have sold Mata mid-season and would have fought with City for Porto centre-half Eliaquim Mangala, rather than conceding defeat to sign teenager Kurt Zouma. Chelsea now find it 'impossible' to compete financially with City. 'We are working, thinking and believing that FFP is going to be in practice,' he added. 'So there are things that are impossible for us. We can't sign Mangala. We signed Zouma, who is even younger and has comparable figures. We have the central defender of the Brazil national team, the centre-half of the English national team and the best central defender in the Premier League 2013–14. So we're fine.'

He added, 'We don't sign a striker now as an emergency plan to score half-a-dozen goals to give us half-a-dozen extra points, whatever they mean for us. We're waiting for the summer to do the right thing in that area. We know basically what we want, and we know what we want is impossible to get in this transfer window. Many people don't understand why we did other things and not a striker, but in the summer you will understand why.'

Mourinho was astutely removing the pressure from his players ahead of the Etihad clash with typical divisive tactics. Asked if he might have to accept second to City, Mourinho replied, 'Yes. But if we finish second it's fantastic. If we finished second doing the formation work, it's an acceleration of our process. It's good.' He suggested City had a 'complete' team in comparison to his own, which requires 'a bit more time, a little bit more players. Just a little bit. Our objective is to finish in a Champions League spot. That's the competitive objective, because the greater objective is the improvement of the team and preparing the team for the future. Next pre-season, day one, I will say Chelsea are a candidate. This season I won't say that. It's not what we feel or what we are working for. If we win or if we lose at City, I don't think we're candidates. If we win, obviously, we're [on] the same points as City. If we lose, the distance is six. It doesn't matter. It is not what concerns me. What concerns me is my team playing well and trying to get the best possible results, feel the improvements. And next pre-season, you will hear me say something completely different. I don't give up. I'll try to win the next match, against whoever. We will try to win.'

Mourinho agreed City's midfield power axis of Yaya Touré and Fernandinho provided the platform for their goal-scoring feats. Touré, Dzeko, Negredo and hamstring-victim absentee Aguero all notched double figures already in goals scored, while only Hazard scored more than 10 for Chelsea. City have not dropped a point at home this season, winning 11 matches and scoring 42 goals but Chelsea were not planning all-out defence. He added, 'I don't know if other teams have been scared of City; whether it's not so much that they don't attack them and more that they can't. Maybe they can't. I want to attack them. I can tell you that. But after ten minutes, people might say I'm not attacking. If I don't, it's because I can't.'

Almost seven years before, when Stuart Pearce was City's manager, Chelsea were the side splashing millions on the world's best players, winning trophies and challenging for European glory. Pearce fielded a team made up of academy players and bargain buys as visitors Chelsea ran out 1–0 winners, courtesy of Frank Lampard's first-half penalty. Pearce's side cost just £13.5m, compared to £160m for a team then seeking to leapfrog Arsenal and regain top spot in the Premier League. Although Chelsea now remained one of the elite, City were now on a level playing field after a huge investment from billionaire owner Sheik Mansour. City finished 14th in 2007, 41 points behind Chelsea, who ended the season second behind Manchester United. Brazilian midfielder Elano was the club's top scorer with just eight goals all season; Aguero, who joined City from Atlético Madrid for £38m in 2011, had already found the net 15 times in the league, 26 in all competitions.

Pellegrini's high-scoring side had attack as their best means of defence. City had found the net 115 times already this season but were without main striker Aguero.

Despite beating City at Stamford Bridge, Mourinho had long since hailed Pellegrini's team favourites for the title. 'They're complete. The players are amazing, the squad is fantastic but you also need the manager to do a good job and I think he is [doing that]. The players are experienced. They were champions two years ago and a big nucleus is the same. They have everything and we need a bit more time, a few more players. Just a little bit.'

City were still smarting from a 2–1 defeat at Stamford Bridge in October after a 90th-minute winning goal from Torres. Pellegrini's side had been practically unstoppable since then, particularly at home, and Fernandinho knew that victory would represent a massive step towards clinching the title. 'It's not about revenge,' he insisted. 'The result down there was a very bad one but now things are completely different. The whole team is better. If we beat them, we'll be six points ahead.'

Mourinho masterminded a defining 'double' over City by delegating the pre-match team talk to team masseur Billy McCulloch as a first-half Ivanovic strike gave them an outstanding victory. McCulloch, who has also been involved in the England and Scotland set-ups in the past, is a popular figure within the Chelsea dressing room, with a reputation as a funny-man for his pranks at Stamford Bridge. Mourinho attributed the credit to McCulloch for inspiring the players. 'I didn't speak. It was Billy the masseur that spoke to the team. He was screaming so much in Scottish I didn't understand him. I am serious. But the players were clapping. It was Billy's team talk. The last time I spoke to the players was midday.'

At midday Mourinho walked into a team meeting and told his players what he was planning: Oscar and John Obi Mikel left out from the 0–0 draw with West Ham, Matic and Luiz as the holding midfield pair. The players practised something completely different before travelling to Manchester the day before, believing Willian was the odd man out in a system designed to stop City getting a grip in midfield. Mourinho was making sure there would be no leaks of his surprising team plans. No one in the Chelsea squad believed that Oscar, with nine goals this season, could not start a game of this magnitude.

As the teams were announced, many believed Mourinho had set

his team out to 'park the bus' but his team had the better of the chances, hitting the post three times. Mourinho said, 'I think they did amazing. When the team lost the ball, they all sacrificed for the team. Our record was not good against City in the last few years. This season we managed to win these two matches, especially this one. Today we won because we were the best team – I am not saying we are better, I am just saying we were today.'

Victory at the Etihad was the first time in 61 home league games that City had failed to score, dating back to a 0–0 draw against Birmingham City in November 2010, as City suffered their first home defeat in the league that season after 11 straight wins – the first team to do the double over City since Everton in 2010–11. It put Chelsea level on points with their rivals behind leaders Arsenal.

Still Mourinho played down his team's chances of winning the league. 'There are two big horses and a little horse. A horse that next season can race. We can win it if they lose it. Arsenal [have been] working for many, many years for the evolution of their team. What we are doing this season is what Arsenal have been building [up] to for years. We are there, but are not favourites. We are preparing the team to be one of the favourites next season and this is a very important step. We lost points at home against West Brom, against West Ham, we lost at Stoke, we lost at Newcastle. We are a team in evolution but this is the kind of performance that helps the team to grow up a lot, tactically, mentally, I think it was fantastic. It's not our objective to win the league. Our objective is to build the team and complete the puzzle and formation of the players. Some managers, because of their nature and DNA, say they need two or three years.'

Mourinho's master class of tactics was universally applauded. Sky Sports expert Gary Neville praised the way Mourinho set up his team to nullify the threat of the title favourites and said that even his demeanour on the touchline had an impact on the result. 'He doesn't mind us praising him, does Jose Mourinho. He loves the attention of big matches. You saw him tonight and he was like the conductor of the orchestra. He walks out at the start of the match and sits on the bench before his team have even come out. He comes alive on big-match days and that's what the best managers do. He is the best in the world at the moment at affecting big matches, absolutely brilliant. He thinks about every small detail, things that I don't think many would think of because he's been around the block. He's shrewd, he's smart and he calls it on. He's good and he knows he's good.'

Mourinho chose to sell Mata to United and many were surprised by his treatment of the man who'd won Chelsea's Player of the Season award for the last two years, but Neville spotted how the manager was putting his stamp on the team, and an important aspect of his success this season has been using wide players who are willing to work hard; something he feels is increasingly common at Europe's top clubs. 'You can see the way in which Jose Mourinho is taking this team. You can see it in this last month or so: Willian and Hazard have energy, desire, power and strength. We are seeing it with our eyes. Tonight he left Oscar out because he's got players in the team like Ramires, who was big tonight. When you put a world-class centre-forward in that team, which I'm sure Chelsea will do in the summer, you have got a real top-class team on your hands. Jose Mourinho has said they are not quite there yet and thinks Manchester City are still ahead of them. I can't disagree with him but they're not far behind. They are coming on the right lines – for what he wants anyway. Would he tolerate a David Silva? I don't think he would. You see Willian and Hazard and the way in which they work and the work of Ramires tonight. I think Chelsea were brilliant all night. Full-backs have got to be wingers and wingers have got to be full-backs. There's no excuse any more. There is too much evidence in the way the game is going to say "we will have a luxury player on the left or right". Unfortunately not – not at the top level. There's a lot of evidence in the last twelve months, watching Dortmund and watching Munich and tonight with Chelsea; that's the way the game is going.'

Mourinho claimed his side were 'not ready to win the title this season' but should be considered as favourites next year. Neville agreed that Chelsea could suffer for the lack of a top-class striker, with Eto'o, Torres and Ba scoring 11 Premier League goals between them so far, but he said, 'I have a tendency not to believe a word Jose Mourinho says, but I actually believe him. I think the odds reflect where it probably still is at. In his mind there's that niggling doubt that he's just that little bit short. He was criticised earlier in the season for parking the bus in big matches, but his team are now starting to play very well in big matches and his journey is on an upward curve. His team are getting better, you are starting to see Mourinho-like performances but is he going to fall that little bit short? The bookies suggest he is and I think he possibly might because of that lack of a devastating centre-forward.'

Stung by Mourinho's typical jibes that City had been 'lucky' with refereeing decisions, Pellegrini accused him of trying to brainwash the public. Asked if he thought it was a fair assessment, Pellegrini said, 'No, it isn't. It is very easy to say every week what is best for your team, but there is a very famous sentence: "Lie, lie and something will remain [in people's minds]." In fact, the only time there has been an apology from a referee for an important mistake was when Mike Riley said sorry for the ninety-third-minute penalty that saved a point for Chelsea against West Brom after Ramires dived.'

Pellegrini ridiculed Mourinho's assertion that Chelsea were a 'little horse' compared to City and Arsenal. 'Maybe it is a small horse if the manager thinks like that but it is also a very rich one. This is the team that spends the most money in the last ten years, it is the team that spends the most money this year and the team that spends the most money in the transfer window, so a little bit rich. He shows in the last two games he has a strong team with some great players, but he thinks it is better not to talk about it. Why? Because if he wins [the title], he has all the merit, while if he loses, he does not have the responsibility. It is the way he acts. It will be very close with Chelsea and Arsenal. Arsenal is the favourite because they have a two-point lead in the table, an important advantage.'

Mourinho accused Negredo of trying to get Matic sent off. Matic already on a yellow card, Negredo held his face after an aerial challenge. 'That simulation has to be punished the same way aggression is punished. I had an exchange of words with one of the City players. I was not happy because he was trying to get Matic sent off. He knew he had a yellow card. Matic jumped in front of me in a very clean way and the other guy immediately [holds his face]. He knew Matic had a yellow card. Mike Dean, the fourth official and the linesman were all there and they decided between them no yellow card. But if it's no yellow card for Matic, then for me it's a yellow card for the other guy. He deserves the punishment if he's trying to get the guy sent off. You have to attack the guys who try to get people sent off.'

Hazard was delighted when Mourinho called him the best young player in the world but believed his best form was yet to come. 'I'm very happy because it's very pleasing when a coach gives praise but I'm still aware of what I need to do to make the next step up. It's a nice compliment but I'm not going to rest on my laurels. I know I have to keep working hard every day. It was a great atmosphere in the dressing room [after the match] but we weren't getting carried away because we know that there are plenty of big games ahead. We beat possibly the best team in the league but we know that, if we then go on to lose against Newcastle, then it's no use whatsoever. It's up to us to pick up the maximum points from the games that are coming up.'

Hazard made the switch from Lille in the summer of 2012 and was humbled by talk that he could be the best young player in the world, but predictably looked to Cristiano Ronaldo and Lionel Messi as the benchmark.

Hazard enjoyed working under Mourinho, 'He's made me focus on my work ethic even more. He aspires for one thing – that I become like them one day. It's time for me to work hard together with the coach and the club to achieve that objective. Results have been going well so he is happy and perhaps a little more relaxed. I think as long as we're all working hard, he's happy. And the most important thing is to make him feel happy.'

After an emphatic home win against Newcastle, Jose was full of his impish smiles and title-avoidance despite City drawing at Norwich, now back-to-back games goalless, while earlier in the day Arsenal were toppled from the top with a crushing 5–1 humiliation at Anfield. Chelsea were top, installed as title favourites for the first time, with Hazard looking every bit the best young player in the world with a hat-trick in a 3–0 win.

Mourinho wanted to kill all talk of a horse race, as he switched metaphors to cars, likening City to a 'Jaguar' wearing 'L-plates'. Interpreted as a swipe at Pellegrini, Mourinho said, 'A Jaguar: you wouldn't put an L on it.' He went on, 'It's time to kill [talk of] the horse. We are playing well. Players individually are in a good moment, we are getting results and we are top of the league. That is something that we can't hide.'

Of match-winner Hazard, Mourinho said, 'His performance was no different [to how he has been playing]. The only difference was he scored a hat-trick for the first time. He's had a big evolution, he's got consistency, he's got ambition – it's fantastic.'

Jose criticised the panel that chooses the Player of the Month, pointing out that it was improbable for the best young player in the world never to win that award this season. 'He's the best young player in the world, I don't want to compare him with the "monsters", because they have ten years of career, winning trophies, scoring goals, and it's not fair on them or the kid to make that comparison. But I don't see a better young player.'

Pre-season brought demands for industry and greater professionalism, the message clear that even the team's most mercurial talents must accept more mundane duties, tracking back, marking, committed attitude to training. Mata was sold. Hazard, a prankster with a carefree approach, was reformed. A late return to training after an invite to attend his former club Lille's Ligue 1 game against Monaco in November (Hazard said he had mislaid his passport) was make or break

– 'an isolated episode' according to Mourinho – but the manager left him out for the next game against Schalke. 'He accepted that immediately and understood he was wrong, but was wrong in a naïve way. He hadn't thought about the possibility of being late and missing a training session. I remember perfectly in that [Schalke] game he was in the dressing room, he was behind the dugout, even if he was not selected. The reality is that, since pre-season, he has understood the levels of professionalism I demand from my players. The kid is a good kid. He's a married man, he has sons, he's a family boy, he's a guy with a fantastic life. Not many players his age have the kind of family life he has. Many of the young talented boys, they are still a bit... you know. The kid is a nice guy.' The manager now demanded more ruthlessness in front of goal, yet 14 goals – 12 in the league – was already more than Hazard had managed the previous season.

Pardew believed that this current Chelsea vintage was the best he has ever faced under Mourinho, having taken on his friend as boss of West Ham, Charlton Athletic and now Newcastle. Pardew said, 'This is as good as he's had. They've got a real chance [of winning the league].'

Mourinho continued to talk down chances of silverware in his first campaign back in charge but Hazard said, 'We're at Chelsea, in a club where you're obliged to try and win something every season. We will be involved in the title race right to the wire.'

Chelsea have secured 11 major trophies since Abramovich bought the club in 2003 and Hazard claimed his first winners' medal in the Europa League last term. Cech played a part in all those triumphs, including three league championships. Like Mourinho, he still felt it was City's title to lose. 'At the moment we are playing well and picking up plenty of points. We are first in the table now and we hope we can stay there until the end of the season. I think we are less well-armed than City even though when we played there we won. Arsenal lost heavily at Liverpool but they are a great side too, so we will see. There isn't a lot of difference between the teams so it will be in the details. The best will come out on top.'

Pellegrini's view that Chelsea were a 'rich little horse' in response to Mourinho saying his team were a 'little horse', promoted a stampede of cross-fire from both camps. Mourinho questioned his adversary's maths. 'Mata was sold for £37m and De Bruyne for £18m – that's £55m,' said Mourinho. 'Matic bought for £21m and Salah £11m. In this window, we are plus £23m.'

Mourinho added, 'We are building a team for the next decade and City have a team to win now. They have experience, potential, power and no worries about [UEFA cost-control protocol] Financial Fair Play, because in summer they just spent. We don't need a calculator for this.'

Former Malaga boss Pellegrini, who faced the Portuguese when Mourinho was coach of Madrid, questioned Mourinho's view and drew reference to Chelsea's spending since Abramovich bought the club. Chelsea's net spend during the previous two summer and winter transfer windows was £49m. City did not change their squad during the winter window but had a net spend of £80m last summer. Mourinho was interested in signing Falcao and Cavani in the summer but did not go through with the deals, to keep the Blues in line with the new Financial Fair Play rules. Chelsea did sign Schürrle, van Ginkel and Willian. When asked if Financial Fair Play was the reason moves for Cavani and Falcao never got off the ground, Mourinho replied, 'Correct. Because of transfer fees and salaries. Players are not just about transfer fees but big wages. Of course there's a certain profile of player we don't go near.' Mourinho relishes the challenge of the financial restraints and added, 'It's even better and even more enjoyable work, I think.'

Mourinho said of Pellegrini, 'He has been speaking about winning four competitions, so there's no reason to change the speech. But the only thing that is funny [is] that he keeps saying he never responds to Mourinho; he never comments about Mourinho. He said that in Spain too. So he's changed.'

Yaya Touré kicked out at Norwich striker Ricky van Wolfswinkel at Carrow Road, with the incident missed by referee Jon Moss. It was therefore referred to the FA's new video panel. Speaking just before the verdict, Mourinho warned Touré that escaping a ban would be taken as a message that players could get away with anything on the pitch if it was not seen by officials. Asked how he would feel if Touré escaped, Mourinho said, 'I don't understand why you say "if". If he's not suspended, the message is clear: the players can do what they want if the referee doesn't see. The message is normally that, if the FA defends football, he'd have to be suspended. Of course, I would be disappointed if he is not punished. If he is not, it has to be the same for everyone: if the referee doesn't see, a player can do whatever he wants. It doesn't matter about cameras or others seeing, I can do whatever I want. If they make the rule that action can be taken if a referee has missed something, they have to apply that rule.'

Touré escaped after all and was free to face Chelsea in the FA Cup fifth round. Mourinho's mood was not improved by the panel agreeing to charge Cardiff forward Craig Bellamy retrospectively after he struck Swansea's Jonathan de Guzman.

Pellegrini refused to react. 'I answered just once to Mourinho because, if you remain in silence always, [people] may agree with those things. He started talking about referees and Financial Fair Play. I don't think it is the way [to do things]. I don't talk about other teams, whether the FA should suspend players from other teams or whether the referee has given bad decisions for the other teams. I think the best way is to work with your team and leave the referees and the FA to do their work. The fair way to do it is for everyone to work with their own club.'

Mourinho often draws rival managers into a tit-for-tat but Pellegrini said that differed widely from his own approach. 'It is not my way to act, so I will not do it. I don't think everyone should act the same way. I answered once what Mourinho says because he was talking about the referees but I won't be answering every week because we would just continue to give an answer and get one from the other side.'

Of Mourinho's statement that Touré should have been banned,

Pellegrini added, 'I repeat, I don't respond to things Mourinho says every week because he will continue every week to try talking about things that are not from football. I suppose the FA acts the way they think is better for all the teams. I trust in the FA and I trust in referees.'

Mourinho lamented the lack of a 'killer instinct' as Victor Anichebe's late goal saw two points slip through Chelsea's hands when West Brom's striker cancelled out Ivanovic's opener with three minutes left. Ivanovic and Cech were also involved in an on-field spat. Having seen his side give Arsenal and City the chance to overhaul them, Mourinho said, 'We were comfortable in the game, maybe too comfortable. We didn't kill the game when we had the chance. For sixty minutes the game was completely in our hands, West Brom didn't put one foot in our box. In the first half we had complete control without creating many chances, but complete control. Petr [Cech] not one save, their strikers not one shot, everything in control, waiting for spaces. It opened in the second half, but we were not strong enough to kill the game. A ready team, a complete team, kills this game. 2–0, goodbye. We didn't. They had a reaction and we couldn't cope with the reaction. In the last twenty minutes they put us under pressure and they scored a goal as a consequence. Maybe they deserved that point. A point is a point and at the end of the season we will see.' He brushed aside the row between his two players. 'I don't know what happened but I like it. I like the players to have emotion and, if someone has made a mistake, I like [that] they speak between them.'

Mourinho insisted one point was still better than none on a ground where Liverpool and Arsenal drew. 'In this moment we have one more point than before. If Arsenal and City win tomorrow, they go above us but that is their job. Every game is difficult.'

Responding to Wenger's claim that other bosses are playing down their title chances because they 'fear to fail', Mourinho delivered an acidic riposte. 'If he is right and I am afraid of failure, it is because I didn't fail many times. Eight years without silverware, that's failure.'

Arsenal had not won a trophy since the 2005 FA Cup. 'He's a specialist in failure,' continued Mourinho. 'If I do that in Chelsea, eight years, I leave and don't come back.'

Lineker felt Mourinho had gone 'over the top'. 'Mourinho is out of order and wrong with Wenger comments,' Lineker wrote on Twitter. 'He's won trophies galore all over the world, playing delightful football. Yes, Wenger hasn't won anything for a number of years, but he hasn't, until very recently, had the budget of others. Club is in great shape.' Gary Neville waded in. 'Getting to the business end!' he wrote on Twitter. 'Jose lobbing grenades out! Anyone going to take him on?'

Of the nine matches where Pellegrini and Mourinho faced off, Pellegrini won just one. In their first two encounters in La Liga in 2011, with Mourinho at Madrid and Pellegrini at Málaga, the aggregate scoreline was 11–0. 'Look at the average of all those games and history tells you that Real always beat Málaga,' Pellegrini pointed out, recalling the subsequent 3–2 victory at La Rosaleda that restored faint pride. But City's two defeats to Chelsea so far this season turned the screw on rampant City.

He shot down arguments that Mourinho had exploited the absence of Fernandinho in the match 12 days earlier, or that Willian and Matic had been expertly deployed to negate Touré. 'Look at the options that Chelsea had in the second half of that game,' Pellegrini explained. 'There was a shot by Matic from twenty-five metres and a corner from Gary Cahill that hit the outside of the post. They didn't have any more chances. In the first half they had one, where we missed a pass on the counter-attack and they scored. It was not because Fernandinho was not there but because we made a mistake. I don't have any concerns.' Pellegrini rejected that tactical defeat. 'We made sure we moved Martin Demichelis up into midfield,' he said. 'We had enough holding midfielders. We had sixty-four per cent possession.'

With more than a hint of a dig at Mourinho, he added, 'For me, it's more important to score goals. If we had scored one against Chelsea, we would have won; one against Norwich, we would have drawn. I continue thinking in exactly the same way.'

Pellegrini was careful to avoid any more personal distraction. When Mourinho was appointed at Real after Pellegrini's solitary season at the Bernabéu – in which the club finished runners-up behind Barcelona despite amassing 96 points – Mourinho said with a sneer: 'Second place is just the first loser.' In almost the same breath, he added, 'If Madrid were to fire me, I wouldn't go to Málaga.'

The 'Special One' revels in his superiority over the 'Silent One'. Asked whether he could inflict further psychological damage on his main title rivals by knocking them out of the FA Cup, he said, 'If Chelsea win, they [City] can't win four trophies, which their manager said was their target for the season. Just that. But if you can't win four but win three, that's a lot. I don't think it will affect their confidence. Big teams know they can lose against big teams.'

As for his dominance over his Chilean rival, he said, 'I don't like this history of records between managers. It's between teams, not managers. I don't like it. If I have a record in favour or against, I don't like it either way. I don't look at it in any aspect.'

Pellegrini refused to take any more questions about Mourinho. Did that suggest he was running scared? Mourinho couldn't resist. 'If he doesn't like to speak about me, perfect. I hope he does what he says and doesn't speak. I also don't like a lot to speak about other managers. I think he's right. So if he doesn't want to speak about me, that's perfect.'

So, Jose doesn't like all this chit-chat before games? Pull the other one!

He did not think the Cup tie would follow the same tactical pattern as the league game. Asked if, whoever played, he would once again be instructing his players to negate City's attacks by man-marking Touré, he insisted that stopping Pellegrini's team was not as simple as that. 'They are good all over. You close the right side and Kolarov makes fantastic crosses the other side. They are good at everything – in set pieces and every aspect of the game.'

There came a final barb. Recalling his recommendation that the FA suspend Touré, he commented, 'Is Yaya Touré important? Yes. He's so important that the FA decided he has to play this game.'

An attempt on the Friday by a reporter to elicit Pellagrini's opinion on whether Mourinho should be reined in by the FA for his comments was stonewalled. 'I will not answer questions on Mourinho or the way he acts because I don't want to continue with this controversy. The important thing is that every institution, the FA or whoever, do their duty. To say whether to suspend [someone] or not, I don't think it's right.'

Chelsea at home to Arsenal in a month was likely to have a significant bearing on the title fight. Wenger insisted the title was 'Chelsea's to lose' but said that Arsenal would 'give everything' to win it.

Mourinho highlighted the 'many, many years' Wenger has had to turn his squad into champions. Wenger admitted after the goalless draw with United that his team were 'nervous' but Mourinho believed that they should now be mature and ready to deliver. 'Arsenal have spent many, many years working together. Many, many years making these players grow up and achieve this maturity level. These guys, Jack Wilshere and Alex Oxlade-Chamberlain, Theo Walcott and Kieran Gibbs, they are not kids any more. They were kids but in this moment they are mature players. The manager with this group of players, four, five or six years working with these players and then adding fantastic players like Mezut Özil, Santi Cazorla or Per Mertesacker to the team, these last pieces of experience.'

When asked why he thought Wenger was obsessed with Chelsea, he replied, 'Ask him.' When asked why Arsenal had not won anything in eight years, Mourinho said, 'Ask him. Not me.'

Mourinho would not hang around at a club if he was not accumulating silverware. 'If I don't win a trophy in four years, I don't want a new contract. It's as simple as that. I don't think a manager should be embarrassed when he gives everything, tries everything, dedicates himself to the club, the project and the collective dream. If you don't get results, that's football. But for my mentality, there is a limit. And you have to be strong enough and proud enough to admit when it's enough.'

The pair have history, Mourinho having described the Frenchman as a 'voyeur' in 2005 after his rival questioned Chelsea's transfer policy. 'He likes to watch other people,' Mourinho said in October 2005. 'There are some guys who, when they are at home, have a big telescope to see what happens in other families. He speaks, speaks, speaks about Chelsea.' At the time Wenger retorted, 'He's out of order, disconnected with reality and disrespectful. When you give success to stupid people, it makes them more stupid sometimes.'

Wenger had his moments hitting out at Mourinho, and vice versa. Wenger quoted in August 2005 on Chelsea's tactics: 'I know we live in a world where we have only winners and losers, but once a sport encourages teams who refuse to take the initiative, the sport is in danger.' Mourinho quoted in November 2007 on Wenger's foreign policy: 'Unlike Arsenal, we sought success and tried to build it through a concept of the game using English players.'

Brendan Rodgers, manager of fourth-placed Liverpool, continued the horse-racing analogy by saying his side 'may be the Chihuahuas that run in between the legs of the horses' as they looked to make a late challenge. Mourinho then compared Liverpool to a 'privileged Chihuahua', with Rodgers' side moving within four points of Chelsea.

Mourinho believed Liverpool had a 'big advantage' because they were free from the constraints of European competition. 'I am sure it is a four-horse race now. They have a big advantage because they don't play in the Champions League. If Brendan has a Chihuahua, it is one that trains a lot and rests a lot. The other dogs, they don't train a lot because they play a lot and they don't rest because they play every three days and, when the Barclays Premier League goes to the crucial point, we all will have to play Champions League at the same time. To play, for example, like we are going to do in Istanbul against Galatasaray on the Wednesday, Fulham on the Saturday. Brendan's Chihuahua doesn't do that. During the week it sleeps, eats and trains a little bit. So I have to say his Chihuahua is a privileged one. Next season he will see what it is like to play in two, three, four competitions. This season he has this privilege, which gives him a big advantage.'

Rodgers once described working under Mourinho for three years at Chelsea as 'like being at Harvard University'.

Mourinho's genius was finding a solution to the lack of a top-class centre-forward, with Torres, Ba and Eto'o contributing just 11 league goals between them. 'If you are talking about the team that looks really solid, the team that defends well but at the same time creates a lot – that is my team. But when I say we're not the top candidate everyone thinks, "Here he is again", with what you like to call the mind games. But it's just my feeling. The matches I have lost were matches we should have won. They were the easy ones to win. The match against Everton was so easy to win but we couldn't score a goal out of I don't know how many chances. But we conceded and we lost. We went to Newcastle; it was so easy to win. In the first thirty minutes we hit the post, we had chances but we lost the game. We went to Stoke; it was so easy to win. Against West Ham we had twenty-five shots on goal. We are a team that, if we had that last "click", that click is to put the ball in the net, then I would say to you that we are favourites. Our team is going in a very good direction but at this moment I would not say we are favourites, but we are candidates.'

Chelsea crashed out of the FA Cup with a 2–0 defeat at Etihad Stadium but, although he had a day earlier, branded Wenger a failure, Mourinho insisted that his team hadn't failed him. 'I don't say my team failed. I would say that City played much better than us and deserved much more to win. The game was simple to analyse – they were the best team and they won.'

Mourinho felt City's second goal was offside but conceded that it made little difference, as his side only managed three efforts at goal, with none on target. 'They were the best team and when the best team wins I think football is at peace. Two weeks ago, the best team won and this time the best team won. What happened in this tie gives more credit to my players because it proves it is difficult to win twice against City in a season, and to win here. Was the referee's team poor in the second half? Yes. But even with [a] perfect refereeing team, would Chelsea have won the game? No. Their second goal was an offside but they would win 1–0 anyway because we were never close enough to score or to be dominant or to scare City in the game.'

As for his jibe at Wenger, Mourinho said, 'I don't accept that one is always "Monsieur Polite" and the other one is always the bad guy. I don't accept, I'm sorry. The only thing I feel was that I was very quiet in my place and somebody spoke not in a nice way about us.'

Pellegrini felt his side were refreshed because they rested instead of playing in midweek, as their home league game with Sunderland was victim to high winds. 'We were not fresh after eighteen games in two months. But in training on Thursday and Friday we were fresh again. I knew then we would have a good day against Chelsea.' Mourinho agreed that extra time off was a factor. 'It was clear that there was a difference in freshness between the teams. One team played two days ago and another team played last week and had one week without competitive football.'

Pellegrini faced a lot of questions when City had lost to Chelsea but insisted, 'I also don't think we had any tactical problems against Chelsea before, it was just that they scored before us and then made it a difficult game. We did not have any tactical problems against them and this was not a master tactical victory for me, because I don't believe in those things.'

The Gunners beat Liverpool to reach the quarter-finals and, just before the tie, former player and coach Bob Wilson savaged Mourinho for his views on the Arsenal boss. 'I think at its best it's disrespectful, at its worst despicable. I find him boring in the extreme. I think it's personal. He is a hugely talented, amazing manager but a self-publicist and it's mainly inaccurate. To say West Ham play nineteenth-century football, to give Manuel Pellegrini the abuse he has: this is a weekend when we honour a gent – Tom Finney – I don't like bullies.' Wilson, an ever present feature of Arsenal's double-winning side of 1970–71, says Wenger has 'opened eyes and ears' during 17-and-a-half years in England and is frustrated by Mourinho's 'dismissive' comments. 'He's out of order, disconnected with reality and disrespectful... It's not the first time he has singled Arsène out. A few years ago he called him a voyeur, which is a disgusting claim – albeit thankfully with a belated apology. I like people who have within them some humility as well. Bill Shankly was in his day, like Jose Mourinho. He took every opportunity to psyche you out. He would get at you, but in a lovely, sort of competitive way.'

Lord Coe defended Mourinho. 'All he's doing is answering the questions that he gets asked,' said Coe, a Chelsea supporter. 'I'm not sure these are mind games, I know they're not mind games. He's answering the questions he's being asked and he's actually doing it with honesty.'

Wenger escalated the feud, although he stressed that he did not specifically mention Mourinho when he claimed that a 'fear to fail' was why so many managers were saying they were not contenders to win the league title. 'I do not want to go into those silly, disrespectful remarks. I never spoke about him in my press conference and I will not start now. The only thing I know is it is more embarrassing for Chelsea than for me. I am embarrassed for him. Honestly. I am more disappointed for Chelsea than for me. I am not interested in the subject at all. If you are interested, and you have nothing better to do in your life, you are free to do it. I love football. What is interesting for me is what happens on the pitch.'

Asked for his final word on Mourinho's comments, Wenger said, 'There is no final word on that, unfortunately.'

Cesc Fabregas told Mourinho to 'mind his own business' after he criticised Barcelona as being the worst they had been for 'many,

many years'. The former Arsenal star added, 'If we have to get motivated by Mourinho's comments, we shouldn't play football. We are top of the table, in the Cup Final, in a good moment in the Champions League. Some people want us to fail all the time, some people have been talking a bit too much, for a few days they will have to shut up.'

Ahead of the next game, it was a very contrite Jose refusing to answer questions beyond his own team so, after weeks of taunting his title rivals, he suddenly clammed up.

The questions Mourinho was reluctant to answer (as reported by the *Daily Telegraph* on 21 February):

What did you make of the Champions League problems for Arsenal and Manchester City?

'My Champions League starts Wednesday.'

Will the Champions League affect the Premier League title race?

'I play Wednesday and I concentrate on that.'

Arsène Wenger said your comments were embarrassing. Do you have anything to say on that?

'No.'

Manchester United have agreed a new contract with Wayne Rooney. Are you disappointed?

'I don't react. We did show an interest in the past. It doesn't bother me at all.'

What do you make of the job Roberto Martinez is doing at Everton?

'I don't comment.'

How do you think Romelu Lukaku has done on loan at Everton?

'I don't speak about Romelu Lukaku until the end of the season. Until then he is an Everton player. He is our player but I prefer to see him as an Everton player for now.'

Wayne Rooney will earn £300,000 a week at Manchester United. Is he worth that?

'Not my problem.'

What do you think of the red card decisions in the Champions League this week?

'It's for the coaches that go to the UEFA meetings to speak on that. I accept the way it is.'

What does this week's Champions League games say about the quality of the Premier League?

'I don't comment. The Champions League for me starts on Wednesday.'

What about the competitiveness of the Premier League?

'I don't want to comment.'

How do you think Roberto Martinez has managed Lukaku?

'I don't comment. I prefer to understand that Roberto is in charge of Lukaku. He speaks, comments, play him, not play him.'

You seem unhappy. What's up?

'I'm fine.'

Have you taken a vow of silence?

'No.'

Are you unhappy about criticism you have received?

'No.'

Do you have a reaction to the criticism you have received?

'I have no reaction.'

Is there anything you would like to talk about?

'No. If I've finished, I go.'

Can Chelsea benefit from other English clubs being knocked out of the Champions League?

'I don't speak about other teams.'

Did you watch the Champions League games?

'Yes. I watched all four. Nothing stood out.'

How difficult is it for a manager like Roberto Martinez to go into a club and change the playing style?

'Ask him.'

Do you see your relationship with Pellegrini ever improving?

'I'm not in the mood.'

Is your determination not to say anything today a sign that you accept Arsène Wenger had a point?

'No comment.'

In the final 10 minutes of Chelsea's 1–0 win over Everton, with the Blues still locked at 0–0, Mourinho got so carried away with giving instructions that he walked on to the pitch, very close to where the ball was, nearly impeding winger Aiden McGeady as the Scot ran up the wing! Mourinho insisted that his team deserved the late lucky break, which saw his side consolidate their position at the top. Two points would have been dropped until Jagielka fouled Ramires. Lampard's in-swinging free-kick just cleared Ivanovic's leap. Terry, returning from a three-game absence due to a gluteal muscle problem, slid in as the ball squirmed past Howard, then Terry ran off, claiming it for himself. But whoever scored (it ended up as Lampard's goal, direct from the free kick), Mourinho didn't care. He was just delighted that his team had finally notched a goal. 'When you score [in] minute ninety – [it's] something you can speak about being lucky,' he said. 'The reality is that the boys chased that. We were the team that was really trying to win, which is our responsibility. We deserved it. I never thought we would score so late. I had hoped that we could score a goal before that. Destiny wanted last minute.'

Martinez was frustrated with referee Lee Probert's decision to award Ramires the free-kick, suggesting Chelsea are cute in winning set-pieces around the area. 'It's an incredible know-how, using every single trick in the book to get dangerous positions. We had to defend dead-ball situations well, but unfortunately in the ninety-third minute they got a goal that I don't think reflects the performance. We defended really, really well. In that one, John Terry throws himself, brave, and he gets the luck of the bounce and they score.'

Mourinho had sympathy for Everton as it appeared Chelsea's win-less run would be extended to three games. Instead, Chelsea stayed top entering the Champions League last-16 clash at Galatasaray. 'I feel sorry for them [Everton] because maybe a point for them is fair after their good performance. If today we had only one point, if the teams that are behind us win, we lose that position. Every victory keeps us there, every defeat or draw we lose a position. We just want to try to keep the position, not to give [it away] for free to the opponent. We have to fight, we have to play and it's a good feeling to win in the end. The team wanted to win. You score, it's fantastic. Even if you don't score, my feeling would be a positive feeling with them. They tried everything.'

Mourinho praised Azpilicueta's all-action performance as 'representative of the desire the team put into the game' and bemoaned an injury to Oscar, which brought the Brazil playmaker's afternoon to a premature end.

Terry's return was an obvious boost and Mourinho added, 'Again one great defensive performance by the whole team. It was not [just] John. The defensive organisation is good and strong, but when you captain, your voice, the stability, the complete understanding of him with [Gary] Cahill. I think it's good. He didn't play three matches and we clearly missed him.'

He praised Lampard after the midfielder went second on the all-time list of appearance-makers in the Premier League, equalling David James's 572 games in England's top division. 'He's fantastic. To be one of the top scorers in the Premier League with all the players who have been in its history is fantastic. The others are strikers and he is a midfielder and for him to be amongst them is amazing. He is now level with a goalkeeper and that means a lot because they play more games and years.'

Chelsea conceded twice in Terry's last nine appearances and three times in his three-game absence. Terry believed Mourinho's methods were bearing fruit. 'Maybe the year before we were a little bit open and everyone was gung-ho. We were left three or four at the back at times and overloaded. The manager's come in and reshaped us, reformed us, added a different dimension to the wide boys. Look at Eden [Hazard]. Even though it looks good on the back four, it's a collective unit.'

Chelsea were still unbeaten at home in the league, extending Mourinho's overall record to 74 games. Mourinho, whose first objective is Champions League qualification, said it is essential for Chelsea's challenge at the top of the table. 'Any objective you have, to have a good home record is important,' he told Chelsea TV. 'We've lost four points at home – [drawing with] West Brom and West Ham – and if you can arrive at the end of the season without dropping many points at home, you have a better chance.'

Terry was a key figure for Mourinho during his previous spell at the Bridge, lifting five major trophies, including two Premier League titles, but Benitez dropped him down the pecking order. On returning to the club, Mourinho needed to be convinced that Terry was still the talismanic figure he had placed so much trust in before. He has been left in no doubt that that is still the case, with the 33-year-old becoming a key performer once more. Mourinho said, 'I didn't know [what to expect]. And I told him that. I told him I wanted to understand what had happened. Some players lose form, lose their performance level and lose condition. I wanted to feel if that was the case. I wanted to see if it [him not playing] was down to other managers' options. That is something you always have to respect. So I didn't know. I started pre-season with him, analysing the situation. With me he has always played well, except when he had back surgery and lost an important part of the season. But in my first two seasons here he had a fantastic level. Now? This season he is doing very well.'

After waiting until 93 minutes for a goal, it was time to joke about the Galatasaray tie and his reunion with Drogba. 'Ideally, I would prefer to go there and win 10–0!' Very droll, as Chelsea found goals hard to come by. 'Obviously we have some limitations,' Mourinho accepted. Drogba was approaching 36, not quite as prolific, although still capable of leading the line. 'He's still good, still a threat,' Mourinho said. 'It will be a strange feeling playing against him because we know him so well but as a manager I have come up against him before. We played Chelsea when I was at Internazionale and he was at Galatasaray when Real Madrid played them last season. We [Madrid] lost in Istanbul. They had us in trouble but Galatasaray is always a difficult place to go to; the crowd is difficult too. Before the game and after the game it will be big respect for

Didier. We will always be big friends because he is a real legend of the Chelsea club. But during the game we will not be friends and we know as well that Galatasaray have a very experienced team with many more big players.'

Yet, another extraordinary row erupted over a series of unguarded but highly disparaging remarks by Mourinho about the club's strikers, recorded by the French television company Canal Plus in what he thought was a private conversation with the owner of the Swiss watch manufacturer Hublot. 'I have a team but no striker,' said Mourinho. 'The problem at Chelsea is that we are lacking a goalscorer. I have one but he is thirty-two, possibly thirty-five, who knows?' The remark about Eto'o was controversial for the supposed doubt about the true age of some African players. Chelsea 'briefed' that the remarks were light-hearted and not meant for broadcast or publication, with Mourinho unaware that Canal Plus, there to conduct an interview, were filming the exchange. The conversation was then posted online, with Mourinho's comments soon being translated from French and then published around the world. The footage was subsequently removed from the Canal Plus website. Mourinho was furious that what he thought was a private conversation had reached the public domain. With Rooney having signed a new contract at United, Chelsea were pursuing other options and, in the same 'private' conversation, Mourinho said of Falcao, 'He doesn't have a team. Who wants to play in front of three thousand supporters? If I was one day to go to Monaco it would be the end, perhaps to prepare for retirement.' Mourinho admitted that it would be impossible to prise Cavani or Ibrahimovich from Paris St-Germain but was adamant that any bid for Eden Hazard would fail. 'Eden is our boy,' Mourinho said. 'We want him to stay for ten years. We want to build the team around him. He's a player with the style of football that we want to have in our team. Zlatan to Chelsea? It's impossible. He's happy at Paris. I know because he is my friend and we are in touch. PSG, with all its wealth, would never open the door. That's mission impossible.'

Mourinho admitted that he had once met the owners of PSG but that there had been no direct offer and that he saw his long-term future with Chelsea. 'I am very, very, very happy, I am at a club that represents for me more than a club. It is a project that I love. I could work in France in the future, why not? I did not say no, or yes [to PSG], there was not a true, direct offer. We met, I had the honour of visiting the Emir at his house in Qatar three or four years ago, before he bought the club. We have a respectful relationship but, after Real Madrid, I said to everyone what I wanted to do, which was to return to England. I want to stay; I have four years on my contract.'

Eto'o was naturally said to be 'very annoyed' following Mourinho's jibe about his age, according to former Cameroon coach Claude Le Roy. Eto'o was the last to arrive at Chelsea's team meeting in Istanbul, arriving 15 minutes late. Speaking to the Canal Plus show *Talents d'Afrique*, Le Roy said, 'I had [Eto'o] on the phone just before I came on screen and he's very annoyed.' Le Roy, 66, coached Cameroon twice. 'Actually, Mourinho went to see him before he saw the pictures and told him to not believe everything that was going to be said. And that he had said nothing about him. But I can tell you that Samuel didn't like it.'

Eto'o's former partner, Anna Barranca, claimed that the striker was actually 39: 'I think Samuel is not thirty-five. He is more thirty-nine. Samuel was born in 1974 and so that makes him thirty-nine now. It was evident Samuel was older than the age he said he was when he first came to Europe.'

Mourinho said at his press conference in Istanbul that the media should be 'embarrassed' by Canal Plus airing an off-the-record conversation. 'It was a funny conversation between me and somebody who doesn't belong to the football world and we were laughing. It's a disgrace that someone is taping and recording a private conversation when, obviously, we don't know. From my perspective, the comment is obviously not a good one and obviously not something I would do in a serious way; an official way in an interview. I don't make fun. I am one of the managers who really defends their players and Samuel Eto'o is a four-times Champions League winner. It was with him I had the best-ever season of my career. He is one of the few players who is working with me at a second different club and a manager doesn't do that if he doesn't like the player or the person. He has no reason to be upset. Also, a few years ago, he said Mourinho was the only manager in the world he would never play for and after a year he was playing with me at Inter and now here.'

The French TV station argued that Mourinho was fully aware the comments were being filmed. 'These are not stolen images,' Herve Mathoux, the presenter and chief editor of the show that broadcast the Mourinho interview told *footballmercato.web*. 'The camera wasn't ten metres away, it's not on zoom. You could see the red light and he was clearly aware he was being filmed, especially as he's someone who comes across cameras so often and who is used to the media. Mourinho perhaps did not want to fully assume what he had said. He could have come and seen the journalist and asked us not to use the images. He did not make any special request.'

Torres revealed how his manager has never explained his selection decisions to his players since his return but said he has grown used to Mourinho's way of working. 'You just get used to it and try to respect his decisions,' Torres told Marca. 'Mourinho has shown that everybody will get a chance and we've all been through the same thing. He likes to rotate the squad and shake up the team depending on the opposition. There are two months left in the season and we have to stay focused.' Torres has a very good relationship with Eto'o, despite competing for a place. 'It's great, he's a genius, he's doing what he's always done, scoring goals. Under Mourinho you don't know if you're going to play or not, so you have to be fully fit and ready.'

Sneijder, Drogba and Hamit Altintop all played under Mourinho during the course of their careers. 'Mourinho knows us well and that is an advantage but the same applies for us,' Sneijder argued. 'We know Mourinho very well, perhaps better than the Chelsea players know us. Chelsea is a great side, everybody has to accept that, but if we show the same spirit we did against Juventus, we could achieve another big result.' Mancini confessed, 'We don't have a lot of chance even at home because Chelsea are better, one of the best teams in Europe. But for Galatasaray to just play Chelsea is an important moment and we need to do a good job. Didier was an important man for Chelsea. Wesley won the Champions League under Mourinho and they have a good relationship but for ninety minutes they will be enemies. After that, they can go for dinner together. Didier and Wesley will be very important for us.' Mancini had no doubts who would win the league. 'It will be a fight with Chelsea because now Chelsea has improved a lot but City will win.'

Drogba and Sneijder, like Eto'o, have strong emotional connections to Mourinho. 'It's a strange feeling,' said Mourinho. 'When players belong to my career, they belong to my life and the feeling is not the same when you come up against them. I played against Chelsea once and the feeling was not the same, but during the game you have to do the best you can. They want to win, we want to win. That's the basic principle of football: you do your job and try to forget.'

Asked about Mourinho, Sneijder shrugged and replied, 'What can I say about him? We won this cup together.'

As for the game, Mourinho commented, 'When it comes to the knockout, you add the pressure of the detail: the goal, the post, the offside, the mistake. The stadium is difficult, the crowd is difficult, even at Stamford Bridge they will bring lots of fans and put pressure on the opponents and on referees. Drogba and Sneijder are two of the best in the world, two Champions League winners. If the pitch was not in the best condition, I think it favours them because they are a very competitive side, very physical, very aggressive. They will prefer a fighting, aggressive match. They play with their strength and their experience, with their know-how. For my people, like Oscar and Hazard, it is an experience to catch with both hands and learn.'

Chelsea young and inexperienced? What did Mancini make of it? 'Chelsea are on top of the Premier League because they are a good team. They have fantastic players used to games like this. They are eighty per cent to go through.'

Chelsea became the first English team to score in the last-16 Champions League round of games, and a draw was a reasonable result. 'Some other teams have three chances and score three goals. We have five and score one,' said Mourinho. 'That's not a critique of the strikers but it's the profile of the team we have. We create but, when we arrive in the final third of the pitch, the correct pass and right movement is something we don't have. We are paying for that. In the Premier League we are losing points and in the Champions League we could have had a different result.'

But Mourinho, whose team drew against West Brom and West Ham in their past five league matches, said that the draw in Turkey was 'acceptable'.

On their return, Chelsea won 3–1 at Fulham. Arsenal, second at the start of the day, lost 1–0 at Stoke as Mourinho's team moved four points clear of Arsenal and Liverpool, who won at Southampton, and six ahead of Manchester City, who were preparing for the league cup final. Mourinho said, 'The gap to Man City is a fake advantage. If they win their games in hand, they're top.' City's goal difference was 12 better than Chelsea's. 'I prefer to have the destiny in my hands, and only City have destiny in their hands. If I win every game until the end of the season, all ten – which we won't – maybe we are not champions. If they [City] win all twelve games they have, they are champions. They have their destiny in their hands.'

After a very poor first half Schürrle netted a second-half hat-trick, Mourinho made one of the most bizarre half-time team talks ever – he didn't talk! He explained later: 'At half-time, I told them nothing – nothing – not a word. I walked in, then I walked out. I don't know if anyone else gave a team talk. I was not inside the dressing room. The second half was a great reaction to the worst performance of the season. The players knew the first half was really poor. I haven't had many first halves like this one – it was very bad. The second half was one of the best performances of the season. We moved the ball around well. If I could've made eleven changes, I might have done, but I could only make three – so I did nothing. Schürrle is still in a learning process about the Premier League. You play aggressive teams and players – but he is cold blood in front of goal. He always shoots in the corner.'

Mourinho later elaborated on becoming the 'Silent One'. 'Normally I give the players two or three minutes to arrive, to change boots or shirts and after that they know that I start talking, and they were there, ready for me. But I was not ready for them. I decided not to speak – because if I start speaking about the first half, I would need more than ten minutes. I think they showed they are very intelligent – without words, you understand what is in the mind of a person, especially if you know the person. I think they understood the first half was really poor and they transformed it into a fantastic second half.'

Schürrle estimated that Mourinho spent about 10 seconds with his players. It was suggested he had said, 'It's your shit – sort it out.'

Mourinho is unpredictable: one game he will rant like Sir Alex, or he will be surprisingly calm. Against Manchester United in January, his team talk lasted less than 10 seconds.

He put it this way: 'Big games are for big players. If you are a good player, go out there and win.'

They did just that: 3–1.

'Simple. Nothing more to say.'

The response was a brilliant second half, especially from Hazard and Schürrle. Mourinho was delighted at how his best player took responsibility. 'I think he felt in the second half that the team needs someone to create. I think he had that responsibility. If the team is not producing for you, you either wait and the production never starts or you decide "I have to try by myself". He dropped back and he started getting the ball in deep areas, started beating people and we started having more spaces to play. He made the "click" and after that the team followed him.'

The 'click' was evident in Schürrle in his first Premier League start since New Year's Day. Mourinho stressed how he must develop physically to realise his potential. 'We talked a lot,' said Schürrle. 'He told me I needed to change; to change my game and my body. That's what I've done over the last two months. I did a lot in the gym. I've really worked very hard to be aggressive. Now I'm ready to play more often.'

Eto'o, despite having scored the most league goals of any of Chelsea's three senior strikers, did not make the bench. Explaining why he opted for Torres, Mourinho said, 'There's nothing wrong with Samuel. I just felt in this kind of match – away from home, against normally defensive teams, aggressive defenders – I thought to go with Fernando and, if I need to risk in the last part of the game, I'd use Demba. You see, Eto'o scores goals but at home. He scores in the league, in the Champions League but all of them at home. Playing away is more difficult for him. I think he is our best striker to play at home because of his technique, his movement and his understanding with Eden and Oscar. For me, he is best to play at home. Away he is showing some difficulties.'

After being named in the PFA Team of the Year last season, Hazard was enjoying a coming-of-age season: 12 goals and nine assists in 28 league games. Asked by Belgian reporters about his relationship with Mourinho, he said, 'He might be called the "Special One" but to me he is the "Normal One". I prefer it if people say things to my face. I find we have a normal relationship. If there are things to be said, he says them. If you are playing well, he says so. But if you are not, you also get to hear about it.'

Belgium faced Ivory Cost in a friendly and Mourinho was hoping that Hazard would not play as, 'he needs a rest'. Hazard always wants to play. 'I don't need rest. As I've said before, I'm at my best if I can play a lot of matches. But I must be aware that I don't let myself burn out. I'm in a good rhythm, I'm getting a lot of game time. I did feel a little down in the first half against Fulham but it went much better in the second half.' Belgium manager Marc Wilmots ended any speculation, as Hazard was not going to start. 'Whether Mourinho had asked or not, I wasn't planning to play Hazard for ninety minutes.

I was already planning to rest Hazard for a longer time. He has played so many games that he can use some rest. It is possible that he will play for twenty minutes.'

The rehabilitation of Terry and Lampard was significant. André Villa-Boas and then Benítez dismantled reliance on the old guard. Mourinho explained, 'Terry and Lampard are very, very important. It was very important for me to recover them.'

Mourinho went to Paris to repair a fractured elbow, having aggravated an old childhood injury, but returned in time for training. Just before he flew to France he had also picked up an award at the Football Writers' Association dinner at the Savoy Hotel, where he told his audience: 'Without love and happiness, I could not do my job. The best thing football gave me was to make a decision about my future. Some managers go where they have to go, where the club comes, and sometimes it is not the best move, not what they want to do, but they go.

'I sat down with my wife and family, and said, "Where is the best place for us? Where can we be happier as a family? To be happy as a manager and enjoy more the family and life socially?"

'We decided England, after that, for the situation to be perfect it would be Chelsea and I was lucky because the door was open for me. The principles you have in relation to football and life are absolutely amazing. I love this Chelsea football club, which has been the only club to have ever sacked me. We as a family belong to you [in] England. I belong to Chelsea, Chelsea belongs to me, and hopefully we will stay for many, many years.' He added, jokingly, 'It is not a threat, but if you sack me, I will stay in England and go to another club, a possible rival.'

Chelsea went seven points clear after giving Spurs the elbow all right, with a whacking 4–0 win at home: goals from Eto'o and Hazard, and two from sub, Ba. Eto'o scored first and poked fun at Mourinho's latest leaked comments about his age with a celebration mimicking an older man. Eto'o's goal marked his 300th career-club goal – an incredible record. After the match, Ba posted a photo of himself, Eto'o and Hazard in the dressing room. The veteran striker mimicked a backache and slow walk as he bent double by the corner flag, though Mourinho enjoyed the humour, which he felt defused the situation, as he commented, 'Eto'o's celebration was fantastic. We knew he was preparing something. It's amazing how well he's coped with the situation in the last couple of weeks. I told him today he was certain to score.' Ironically, Eto'o wasn't in the starting line-up and only played when Torres hobbled off with a groin injury in the warm-up.

Mourinho was still reluctant to admit his team were title favourites, despite going seven points clear at the top. He argued, 'I think the top four is in our hands. Now the objective is the top three. If Man City win their three games in hand, we are second, not first.' He was aware that City would go top on goal difference if they won all three of those games and believed that until they had played those three matches, City were actually top of the league. 'I would like to be in that position because, if they win those matches, they are top of the league. If we win the next nine matches, we maybe are not champions. If Man City win the twelve matches they have, they are champions. They have their destiny in their hands and we don't have ours. I just know that I would prefer to have my destiny in my hands. If you tell me you win the next nine matches and you are champions, I say "OK, great" – it depends on us. But it doesn't depend on us. It depends on them.'

Mourinho was sent to the stands in stoppage time following the dismissals of midfielders Willian and Ramires, as the title challenge lost its momentum with a 1–0 defeat at Villa, with City winning 2–0 at Hull earlier in the day. City moved six points behind the league leaders with three games in hand.

Mourinho vented his fury at Chris Foy, as his team finished with nine men and also had their manager dismissed. 'We must be very, very unlucky to have another refereeing performance like this one. This is not about one mistake from a referee. This is about a performance from minute one to minute ninety-four.'

Villa became only the third team, after Newcastle and

Middlesbrough, to beat Mourinho's Chelsea more than once in the Premier League. All three teams have two Premier League wins against the Portuguese manager. Foy had now sent off six Chelsea players in the Premier League – only Mike Dean (seven) had shown more Premier League red cards to Chelsea players. The game's biggest flash-point occurred in the closing stages as Ramires was shown a straight red card for a two-footed tackle on El Ahmadi. Mourinho was dismissed in the fracas that followed, insisting as he rushed onto the pitch that he was trying to alert Foy to a push by Villa striker Agbonlahor on Ramires. Agbonlahor had already been substituted but rose from the bench to confront Ramires following his challenge. Mourinho said, 'It is a big occasion for me to know about the character of Mr Foy because I want to know what he is going to write about my sending-off. If it was because I was on the pitch, it was two or three metres inside the pitch, then there should be ten people sent off. I don't know why I was sent off. I asked but the referee refused to speak to me. Gabriel Agbonlahor was on the bench, he jumped onto the pitch, he was aggressive towards Ramires. Then everyone jumps onto the pitch: me, Paul Lambert and my assistants, lots of people there. There are no statues in a football match, so if I was sent off, everyone should have been sent off.'

Reminded about the convention that managers should not approach referees for 30 minutes, Mourinho said, 'This is not about conventions, it's about common sense. If you see someone out of control, OK: convention. But if you see someone is calm, is not screaming, it's not the convention. Simple people from football don't need conventions.'

Mourinho denied reports that he and Terry had tried to force their way into Foy's dressing room. He did admit to attempting to speak to Foy again after the match. 'In the dressing rooms I tried to ask politely, can you give me five seconds? And he refused.'

Mourinho questioned whether Foy should ever officiate a Chelsea match again, suggesting there were 'problems' when Foy previously took charge of matches involving the club and that his players had been discussing the appointment in the build-up to the game at Villa Park. Foy had issued six red cards to Chelsea players in his last eight matches involving the club. Mourinho compared it to the controversial defeat by the same score to Queens Park Rangers in October 2011, when Jose Bosingwa and Didier Drogba were dismissed by Foy. It was pointed out that Foy officiated that match too. 'I didn't know,' Mourinho said with a smile. 'It's a coincidence.'

Ramires was homing in on goal when he was brought down by Joe Bennett and should have been dismissed. Willian committed a minor foul and a free-kick was the most that should have been awarded, not a second yellow. Ramires was correctly shown the straight red card for his shocking challenge on El Ahmadi.

Mourinho commented, 'The players were speaking about it during the week. My philosophy is that I never care who the ref is, I don't want to know. If for some reason I know the referee is Mr Anthony or Mr Jon, I always think that the referee is a good referee, I look always positive. But during the week the players were speaking about the situation and I think from now on, the next time we have Mr Foy, I have to work my people in a different way because I don't want this. But do they have a reason? Maybe it is helpful that the committee doesn't send him to our matches. I don't have the right to request. It's just I think they have to analyse the situation and see if, every time he has Chelsea – or not every time – but many times he has Chelsea and problems are there, I think maybe it would be a good decision.' He added, 'I went to the pitch, as everybody went, with one single objective, me and Paul [Lambert] and my assistants and Paul's assistants – that was to calm one situation in the last minute of the game. I was angry but calm. Completely in control of my emotions. That's why I can control myself and say I will refuse to comment. I'm completely aware that if I comment, I will be accused of bringing the game into disrepute. Donations I prefer to do anonymously and to people who really need the money. I don't think it would be a problem to make a donation to help young referees to have better conditions to improve – a referees' academy.'

Lambert laughed off Mourinho's comments about Foy. 'I know what Jose's doing – he's been around the block. If you go on about decisions, it deflects from the performance. Of course Jose thinks we didn't deserve to win. His team is trying to win the league and that's his problem. How can this team, a Villa team of young kids, beat a team that's vying for everything going?'

Mourinho let rip again when asked in the media conference ahead of the Champions League tie whether he had spoken to Ramires about his two-footed challenge on El Ahmadi. 'Don't you have other things to ask about that game more important than Ramires' tackle in minute ninety-two? You think that in that game the most important thing was Ramires' tackle in minute ninety-two? I don't want to answer because I feel what happened in minute ninety-two was a consequence of the other ninety-two minutes we played before that. I'm sorry if I'm wrong or if you don't agree but I think, if you want to ask, you should ask about what made that tackle happen. But that's just my opinion.'

Asked specifically what he was referring to, Mourinho added, 'Everything that happened.'

Earlier, Mourinho was asked if he expected a reaction from his players. He answered a different question. 'We can't have a reaction to Villa Park because, if we have a reaction, we bring the game into disrepute,' said the Blues boss. 'We just close our mouth and we keep going.'

With Chelsea due to play Galatasaray in a Champions League game at the Bridge, Mancini jokingly offered to pay for a meal should the Turkish side come away victorious, but Mourinho didn't see the funny side of the proposal. Asked if he would join Mancini for a bite to eat, he bit back, saying, 'No. Why? Because I have no interest. After the match I don't do things because I win or lose. After matches what I have in my mind to do, I do. It doesn't matter if I win or if I lose. I won't have a meal with somebody who has the same job as I do and the only thing we have in common is the fact we're both football managers.'

Drogba prepared for his first appearance at Stamford Bridge since his 2012 departure. Mourinho anticipated the next comeback to be of a more permanent nature. 'He is a Galatasaray player. We know he is a free agent and we know he finishes his contract at the end of the season but we think it is not the right moment to speak about him. I think it has to happen one day. When, I don't know – as a player, as a coach, as an ambassador – next year, in four or five years, in ten years – I don't know. But when a person represents so much to a club and when a club represents so much to a person – and that's the case – I think he has to be back one day.'

Drogba's last kick in a Chelsea shirt won the club their first Champions League title, with the 36-year-old netting the winning penalty against Bayern Munich at the Allianz Arena. 'Undoubtedly he is one of the most important players in the history of this club – that is not a doubt. I think all Chelsea supporters, we agree with that,' Mourinho commented. 'We don't say the most important one because that is not fair for other people that were in the same level and in the same generation, but for sure we all agree one of the most important players in the history of our club. Is he the same player at thirty-six that he was at twenty-six? I think nobody is, but he is one of the best strikers in the world, that's for sure.'

Mourinho declared that Chelsea were back among Europe's elite after they cruised into the Champions League quarter-finals with first-half goals from Eto'o and Cahill, securing a 3–1 aggregate win over Galatasaray. Chelsea succeeded where Manchester City and Arsenal had failed the previous week to reach the last-eight draw. Chelsea were knocked out in the group stage in the previous season before going on to win the Europa League under Benitez.

Mourinho said, 'It's different from last season because last season was the Europa League: a different level. To come from the Europa League to the quarter-finals of the Champions League is important for the club. We are a Champions League club and now we are among the best eight – the best clubs in the world – and the players deserve to be there. We wait for the draw. It doesn't matter who. All the big candidates to win the competition. Welcome to any one of them.'

Drogba was presented with a silver boot ahead of kick-off, Mourinho presented with a kiss on the cheek from the Chelsea legend, but that was as good as it got for the Galatasaray striker, as the best he managed was a shot so far over the bar that it struck an image of himself high in the stands. Mourinho said, 'The most difficult thing was the way his team played. If your team doesn't produce attacking football, you feel like a lonely man. So I think he couldn't do much.'

Mancini admitted his side had been well beaten but fired a parting shot, tipping former club City to beat them to the title. 'I was confident we'd do a good game, have chances to score. Instead, we did nothing on the pitch. Who will win the Premier League? I think City are the best team.'

Should United fail to overcome a 2–0 deficit in their second-leg meeting with Olympiakos, Chelsea would be the last English team standing in Europe's elite competition.

Mourinho was willing them to make it. 'I hope it's not true. I hope United do it tomorrow.'

And United finally had something to cheer about in their season of gloom but their success over Olympiakos was short-lived with a draw against Bayern Munich and van Persie's twisted knee to keep him out again for a long spell.

Mourinho claimed he was singled out for harsher treatment than other managers after being charged with improper conduct. 'Look, you see the charges from the last match, and you see that I'm different than anyone else. In the eyes of people, I am different. That, I think, is obvious. It's obvious there's a measure for some, there is a measure for me. There is a way where I can feel the differences, all the time.' He contested the charge, which could see him hit with a £10,000 fine. 'It can be £1. It's the principle.'

The old feud with Wenger rumbled on ahead of the Arsenal manager's landmark 1,000th game in charge of the Gunners, in what amounted to a play-off for the title. Mourinho had never lost against Wenger in 10 meetings. The Arsenal manager said, 'You cannot be friends. It is impossible. If I start any game, I have to win. That is our job. The real sport on that front is rugby. They do not kiss each other before the game when they walk in the tunnel. They go out and are ready for war. We are not friends. I don't know if you can be friends with somebody you see three times in a year and when you see them it is for five minutes.'

Mourinho struggled to compliment Wenger and could not resist a swipe at Arsenal's nine years without a trophy. 'I admire him and I admire Arsenal. It's not possible to have a thousand matches unless the club is a fantastic club and supports the manager, especially in the bad moments and especially when the bad moments are quite a lot. There are many ways of paying tribute. For me, to pay tribute is to say he's in a position where many people would like to be. I love my career and the experiences I've had in my career, but he's in a position where everybody would love to be.' In response, Wenger teased Mourinho's reputation for unattractive football. 'The ambition of a great club must be to win with style.'

Arsenal were FA Cup favourites after reaching the semi-finals and Mourinho believed Wenger's men were performing well this term. 'This season they are better than last season. Last season, in this moment, they were struggling to finish top four. This season they are safe in a top-four position and in condition to fight for the title.'

Mourinho again played down title chances, despite the 6–0 thrashing of Arsenal, wrecking Wenger's thousandth game and setting all sorts of new records. 'Jose Mourinho', the fans chanted as Mourinho enjoyed his best win with the club, Chelsea's best-ever win over their London rivals and Arsenal's heaviest defeat in line with their 8–2 defeat by United. The victory kept Chelsea clear at the top. 'City have everything in their hands,' Mourinho said, referring to the idea that Pellegrini's team could overtake Chelsea if they were to win all their games in hand. Mourinho's team rattled in three goals between the fifth and 17th minutes, described as 'ten amazing minutes' by Mourinho. 'As we used to say in football, we came to kill. In ten minutes we destroy... after that, easy.'

'We pressed very, very high,' said Mourinho. 'We know they want the ball, they want to build from the back and they want to be comfortable with the ball. We pressed them very high immediately, recovered the ball and we were attacking the space very, very fast. We got the result with some numbers which are special for our fans, which makes it even more beautiful. Last Saturday [in the defeat at Aston Villa] the momentum was broken, and now we are trying to build more momentum.'

Mourinho pointed out that, of the four teams vying for the title, only Chelsea remained in the Champions League quarter-finals, adding to the strain on his players. Asked whether he thought he had any chance of winning his third Premier League crown, he finally conceded, 'Just a little.' Classy goals from Eto'o and Schürrle put them 2–0 up before Hazard added a penalty. Oscar added two more either side of half-time before Egyptian substitute Salah ran clean through before sliding the ball under Szczesny for his first Chelsea goal. To compound Arsenal's misery, Gibbs was wrongly sent off after 15 minutes when referee Andre Marriner punished him for saving the ball on the line when it was actually Oxlade-Chamberlain who committed the offence.

Mourinho chose to disappear down the tunnel just before the final whistle, explaining that he needed to phone his wife with the score, as he regularly does, but consequently avoiding shaking hands with Wenger.

Asked whether Chelsea could still win the league for the first time since 2009–10, after the shock 1–0 defeat with a Terry-headed own-goal at Selhurst Park, Mourinho said, 'Now it's impossible to win the title. We depend too much on other results. When you depend a little it's possible, when you depend a lot I don't think it is possible. Mathematically it is still possible but one thing is mathematics and another is reality.'

Palace won their first in six games, as Mourinho admitted his side deserved nothing against a Palace team who were still five points clear of the relegation zone despite a hugely impressive win. He praised defenders Ivanovic, Azpilicueta, Terry and Cahill but said the others players lacked the correct 'mentality and a little bit of quality'. He explained, 'Mentality because the opponent beat us clearly on that. Crystal Palace had a strong mentality, were aggressive and committed with every one of them playing to the top of their potential. Ivanovic, Azpilicueta, Cahill, Terry – they perform in the sun, on small pitches, on big pitches, against aggressive teams, not aggressive teams, possession teams and not possession teams. They perform every game from day one to [the] last day. But you have other players who are fantastic in some games and they disappear in others. It is clear to everybody that Chelsea next year want to bring a striker. What's the future for the others? The ones who are staying are competing with the striker we are bringing in. It is normal at the end of the season if players who are not playing a lot or players who are not happy and prefer a change will go. That is also part of the market. We want to improve the team and the players and make some surgical movements in the transfer window. It is also clear we want to improve our players. I can't and I don't need to improve Ivanovic, Cahill or Terry, but there are others I need to improve. We are doing that step by step. But that's not enough to be champions.'

Mourinho marched on to the pitch, hauled up Cahill and told him to leave with his head held high. 'I told him he was one of the guys who should not be on the floor. I told him he was one of the guys who should walk to the dressing room with pride, that he had another performance where he gave absolutely everything. I don't think it's down to courage. It's down to the qualities that make personality profiles. You have some players for everything and other players who are in their habitat in some circumstances. So Stamford Bridge is better than away. Playing away against Arsenal, City, United or Liverpool is one thing and another thing is to play at Crystal Palace, West Bromwich or Stoke City. Clearly, we have players who are up and down in relation to the profile of the match.'

Mourinho explained why he ran to a ball-boy in injury time after the youngster failed to release the ball to Azpilicueta promptly. 'It is not right to educate kids to do that. I went to stop [Azpilicueta]. I was afraid he would lose control of his emotions and push the kid or do something like Eden did last year at Swansea. I told the boy to not do that. I told him if he does this, "one day somebody will punch you".'

Hazard was red-carded in a league cup game at Swansea the previous season when he tried to kick a ball away from underneath a ball-boy who had fallen on top of it. Rather than telling the assembled media at the Selhurst Park press conference, Mourinho preferred instead to scribble his message down on one journalist's notepad. It read – 'Balls!' The one-word answer was later revealed on Twitter by the chosen scribe, Paul Lagan.

In the evening kick-off, City dropped two points at Arsenal, who remained in fourth, five points adrift of Mourinho's side. 'Of course Arsenal are in the race. They are behind the leaders, but not by much. Four teams still have a chance to win the title,' said Pellegrini. 'All four of them will drop points before the end of the season. It is always difficult when you play against the top sides, or ones fighting to stay in the division.'

Second-placed Liverpool were a point ahead of City, taking over from Chelsea at the top of the table, comfortably beating Tottenham at Anfield the next day, but City had two games in hand on the rest of the top four. City were two points adrift of Chelsea and would have gone top had they won at Emirates Stadium.

Mourinho responded to speculation in France that PSG wanted Hazard and Oscar by claiming that Chelsea could sell – for £300m. Former Newcastle midfielder Yohan Cabaye hoped to be reunited with his former Lille team-mate Hazard, while Lucas Moura thought PSG should move for his Brazil team-mate Oscar. Mourinho believes the astronomical spending of Manchester City, PSG and Monaco should be scrutinised by the footballing authorities. However, if FFP is not applied to PSG, the pair could be sold – at a price. Mourinho said, 'No. It's not irritating. No problem. If there is Financial Fair Play, they don't have money to buy them. If there is no Financial Fair Play and they threw something crazy – £300m for both – I think Chelsea has to think about it.'

Mourinho was determined to be upbeat coming out of defeat at Palace, surrendering the lead to Liverpool. 'It would make no difference if his team win in France against Paris Saint-Germain in the first leg of the Champions League quarter-final on Wednesday. Paris is the kind of match they feel comfortable to play. It is a big match in a great stadium against opponents of top quality and a referee who stops the game and doesn't let aggression into the game. I prefer the English ones but normally this is the profile of referees in UEFA competitions. I do not need to do a lot. They will be fine. They will be in their natural habitat in that match. They can do a good match there.'

As for the final six games, 'The easiest thing to do is to perform when you are not playing for something big. If, in the last part of the season, we have an unbelievable performance and some player is going to perform in a beautiful way, that's easy. The difficult thing is to perform when you feel the heat. Because of that, some are big and some are not so big.'

Tight at the top, unlike the last two seasons, when Chelsea trailed 14 points behind the champions United in the previous season and 25 points behind in 2012. Mourinho said, 'To be where we are is an important step and, when you are there, you have in the back of your mind the little feeling that you can still do it, but the reality is different.'

Mourinho criticised his team's sloppy defending and lack of a cutting edge after they went down 3–1 in Paris. Having recovered from the loss of an early Lavezzi goal to equalise courtesy of a Hazard penalty just before the half-hour mark, the Belgian then struck the post before half-time. PSG seized the initiative again in the second period and a Luiz own-goal put them back in front before Pastore's stoppage-time effort handed the Ligue 1 leaders a potentially decisive two-goal advantage.

'I think by the strategical point of view, the team had great discipline and the most difficult things to do in the game they did very well,' said Mourinho. 'They stopped Ibrahimovich. Cavani was under control. The positional play from Motta and Verratti in the centre of the pitch was completely under control. But we couldn't transform the half-chances that we created into goals and on top of that we made defensive mistakes; individual defensive mistakes. So we paid the price.'

PSG's opening goal came from a poor defensive header by Terry. Luiz gave away the free-kick which led to his own goal and Cech was beaten at his near post for Pastore's third. 'In the first goal the ball goes to Lavezzi – control, half-volley, boom. It's like this at this level – one chance, one goal,' admitted Mourinho. 'The game was under control and we had the chance to go 2–1 up at the end of the first half. But we didn't score and then after that we scored in our own goal and after that the third goal, it was a joke. It was not a goal, it was a joke.'

His decision to select Schürrle in attack rather than Torres in the absence of the injured Eto'o reflected a lack of confidence in his misfiring strikers. 'I'm not happy with my strikers' performances, so I have to try things, and with André at least we know we have one more player to associate with the other players. But football is not just about that. It's about scoring goals and getting in behind. And that is for strikers; real strikers.' Mourinho insisted that his team had 'nothing to lose now'.

When asked whether Stoke would be a difficult side to face because they had nothing to lose, he said, 'Of course. We lost there. Obviously we lost because we made a couple of mistakes; one of the not many matches where we've made defensive mistakes. But we played them in the cup at Stamford Bridge and won 1–0. It was not an easy match; it was open until the end. So I can imagine that tomorrow is going to be difficult. They are fresh, they play one match a week, they have no pressure. They will fight for a result to finish the season in a more beautiful position. So I think it will be difficult.'

Mourinho continued to play down his side's title chances after they returned to their winning ways, going top with a 3–0 win over Stoke with goals from Salah, Lampard and Willian. 'I think we played well. Normally after defeat you start slowly and that was probably our problem. In the first half we should have been 2–0 or 3–0 up because we played well. After the second goal, the game was over. Our position is not correct because Manchester City have two games in hand and we are not in control of our destiny. We also still have three points to discuss with Liverpool. It is going to be difficult.'

Thirty-five-year-old Lampard returned to the line-up and the scoresheet – although his goal came from a rebound after Begovic saved his penalty.

Mourinho first burst into prominence in this country with a touchline dash 10 years ago, a brazen fist-pumping jig of 2004 at Old Trafford. He repeated the 'Jose Dash' after Ba scored Chelsea's second. Was he celebrating or passing on tactical instructions, as he claimed? When asked what he was doing after the goal, he said, 'No, it was not to celebrate. It was to tell the players how we had to play the last ten minutes. I knew at that moment they wanted to celebrate, to think the game is over. They forget that they had three plus three or four other [injury-time] minutes to play, and the way we were playing we couldn't carry on winning 2–0. I had to go there because it would be the only chance I'd have to tell Demba, Fernando and Schürrle what to do in the last seven minutes. But you could see I can still run!'

Ba was brought on after 66 minutes, scoring 21 minutes later to turn the tie. Ba, restricted to only four starts since he joined, putting up with Mourinho's claims that Chelsea do not have strikers, turned match-winner in the most crucial of ties. Mourinho said, 'I'm happy for him. A good guy, a good professional, a good group man. I'm very happy, very happy for him. The fact I played him before Nando made him feel that he doesn't have the number-three striker on his back. His enthusiasm was fantastic and he started giving Paris problems that, normally, they don't have in their league where it's a completely different style. I'm so happy he scored the goal because it means a lot for him and a lot for us.'

Just like Ba coming off the bench to score, so did Schürrle. He came on after only 18 minutes for star man Hazard, scoring Chelsea's first. Hazard was carrying an injury from the warm-up. A third substitute, Torres, also contributed as Mourinho again proved the master of the art of substitutions.

By the end of the match, Mourinho had all three maligned strikers on the pitch and all were working hard for him. Whether it is to prove the boss is wrong or prove themselves right, Mourinho has the knack of cajoling performances from players who know they are not his first choice.

Ba, who grew up in Paris, said, 'I'm not out for revenge. Maybe he [Mourinho] doesn't have strikers to his liking but I know that we have three great strikers and I think that a lot of clubs would like to have them. I'm happy to have liberated us. I haven't been given my chance much this season and I've taken it. It's the first time I've wished PSG to lose, and it's me who scores the goal, luckily for Chelsea. I'm happy for Chelsea but it's hard to see them lose.'

Hazard is a long-term PSG transfer target and a move was touted to the French capital, and he was pictured in a PSG shirt after the 3–1 defeat. He complained of a thigh injury to the bench and hobbled off after 18 minutes, leaving the field to applause from the home faithful – and Laurent Blanc was the first to greet him after he left the field, shaking his hand.

'Patience' was Mourinho's buzzword in the build-up and they played with it despite being 3–1 down after the first leg. Being without Matic, Ramires and Salah was a blow Mourinho overcame. The direct ball into PSG's area also had a clear effect. Mourinho said, 'The players followed our plan, our ambition. All we win, all we lose, but without any energy to go home. We have to be, at the end of the game, either so happy with the result or so happy with ourselves. And we were lucky because we have the result we fought for. But, if for some reason we hadn't scored the second, or if they had scored from the last corner in the last moment to send us out, everybody in this club would still have been proud of the boys.'

Mourinho labelled Luiz a 'monster' after doing a job in front of the back four, alongside Lampard. He commented, 'They worked like animals, my midfield. David Luiz is a monster.'

Gary Lineker was less than impressed, tweeting, 'Does David Luiz realise the game has kicked off?' midway through the first half. That didn't look the wisest remark.

Mourinho hurled a barb about Laurent Blanc's approach. 'I think we did enough in the beginning of the second half to score before but we couldn't and after that there were a bit of contradiction to what they were saying on Monday. They played pure counter-attack, no ball possession.'

With one of Mourinho's finest accomplishments since his return to Chelsea, he became the first manager to reach eight Champions League semi-finals.

Drawn against the Primera Division leaders, who knocked out Barcelona in the quarter-finals, Chelsea had a chance of reaching the final. Real faced Bayern Munich. The draw set up an intriguing situation with goalkeeper Thibaut Courtois, on loan to Atlético. Real's pairing against Bayern brought together two clubs who have won the competition 14 times between them. Five-times winners Bayern, quarter-final conquerors of Manchester United, were the defending champions, beating fellow German side Borussia Dortmund at Wembley.

Real, who booked their place in the last four with a win over Dortmund, had won European club football's top prize nine times – but not since 2002. UEFA told Chelsea they could not stop their own goalkeeper Thibaut Courtois playing against them in the semi-finals. The 21-year-old Belgian, in the third season of a loan to Atlético, found himself in the middle of a huge contract row after the two clubs were pitted against each other in the draw. Atlético said there was a clause in his loan agreement stipulating they would have to pay a total of £5m to field him in both legs. But a strongly worded UEFA statement insisted that the clause contravened their regulations and so could not be applied. Courtois was always eligible to face them;

whether or not they would look to invoke the clause privately remained unclear. Atlético wanted to secure another season-long loan deal for the Belgium international, while Chelsea wanted to sign Diego Costa from the Vicente Calderon Stadium and were watching midfielder Arda Turan.

Chelsea's Premier League game against Sunderland was moved forward by one day to help Mourinho's quest for Champions League glory. The first leg was scheduled for Tuesday, 22 April in the Spanish capital, 48 hours after the home game with Sunderland. It was brought forward to the Saturday at 5.30pm, live on Sky Sports, affording Chelsea an extra day to prepare for their trip to Spain. The return leg was three days after Chelsea's away fixture at Liverpool.

Mourinho ordered his players to end their three-match losing streak on the road by demonstrating more of the togetherness that saw them to a famous win over PSG as the Blues travelled to Swansea on the back of defeats to Aston Villa, Crystal Palace and PSG in successive games on their travels. Looking ahead to the Liberty Stadium, Mourinho said, 'They are a good team, they play good football. Especially at Swansea it is never easy and Chelsea knows that better than other teams. They still need the three points, they are not in big danger like other teams but they still need a couple of points to stay in the Premier League and, of course, they will try to get points out of this game.' Ba could be given a first Premier League start since October at Norwich after his midweek heroics against PSG. 'People are working well and hard,' Mourinho added. 'The ones that are not playing so regular, all of them are being good professionals to try to be ready. You could see Demba, as an example, as a player who doesn't play a lot and was ready to try to respond. All of them, they were ready. They are a good group, they are good friends; they have a good relationship. I think, when one of them goes onto the pitch, he goes to help the other players.'

Chelsea played after the crunch game at Anfield, although Mourinho did not plan to watch Liverpool versus Manchester City. 'Maybe it is a historical day for football and they both win!' he said.

Salah made his second start in the 1–0 win at Swansea, following Chico Flores's 17th-minute sending-off. Chelsea were two points behind leaders Liverpool with four games left following Ba's winner with the title decider increasingly looking like it would be at Anfield, although City had two games in hand despite their 3–2 defeat at Liverpool.

Mourinho told assistant Steve Holland to attend the post-match press conference, and admitted that Chelsea had to win their remaining four matches, that it had been a good day for Liverpool, and that it was an exciting climax to the season. A week's break from the stress of the Champions League was a boost to Chelsea's chances.

The media's only access to Mourinho was via the club's official magazine, where he wrote, 'I think he [Mohamed Salah, on an £11 million signing from Basle] has the potential to be a very exciting player. He has come from a different situation to most of the squad, because he was playing in Switzerland before he came here, and in Egypt before that, so he has to adapt to his surroundings here. He has incredible pace and he is comfortable receiving the ball in space, like a traditional winger, so he offers us another way to beat the defence.' Mourinho insisted Salah was not bought to occupy Mata's place on the bench. 'Every player has to work for the team, both with and without the ball. All of our players contribute defensively and for the attacking midfielders there is a big responsibility to press the opposition when they have possession in their own half. It is extremely important to try to win the ball as high up the pitch as possible because, when you do this, your opponent is usually less prepared for the counter-attack. Usually, when you win the ball back close to their goal, the opposition defenders are not positioned to deal with a quick attack, so you have a good chance to find space, to exploit it and, hopefully, to score.'

The fallout from remonstrating on the pitch with Chris Foy over the dismissal of Ramires during the defeat at Villa lingered as Mourinho refused to show up for the pre-match press conference, having cancelled an obligatory media briefing in the previous week. But Ramires was caught up in another major incident as Chelsea surrendered their realistic chance of the title, their 77-match unbeaten home league record under Mourinho, with an incredible self-destructive defeat to the bottom club, Sunderland, in astonishing circumstances.

The ugliest incident erupted in the last few moments, after referee Mike Dean awarded a hotly disputed match-winning penalty converted by Fabio Borini, a Liverpool player on loan to Sunderland. Rui Faria, assistant coach, repeatedly tried to attack the referee, as Mourinho clutched first his arm then his hair to restrain his fellow Portuguese. Three Chelsea assistants, as well as Mourinho, hauled back the furious Faria.

Mourinho produced one of his most bizarre TV interviews, the content of which he repeated in the main press conference, declining questions, opting for heavy sarcasm. He insisted that he would make four points and take no questions. Each point was preceded with 'congratulations'.

He congratulated Dean: 'I think his performance was unbelievable and I think, when referees have unbelievable performances, I think it's fair that as managers we give them praise. He came here with one objective, to make a fantastic performance. And he did that.'

Having congratulated both his side and opponents, Mourinho turned his attention to Dean and Mike Riley, head of refereeing body Professional Game Match Officials Limited, which represents officials. 'Congratulations to Mike Riley because he's the referees' boss and what they are doing during the whole season is fantastic, especially in the last couple of months, especially in matches involving the teams that were in the title race – it's absolutely fantastic.'

Mourinho had twice been sent to the stands this season, for his protestations over Ramires' red card in March and for persistently questioning Anthony Taylor's decisions in October in the win over Cardiff. Earlier this season, he also referred to the Premier League's 'kings of the penalties', a veiled reference to Liverpool, who had won 12 spot-kicks that season: five more than any other side in the top flight.

Mourinho has never been a good loser. The idea that he had become more mature and more relaxed went out of the window along with his amazing home record.

Ramires faced an FA charge after an off-the-ball punch to the face of Seb Larsson, missed by the ref, although it occurred right in front of him.

In Madrid, ahead of their seventh last-four appearance in 11 years, Mourinho's mood had darkened. He started the season as 'The Happy One' but he was back to his siege mentality, the world against him. So what had changed? 'Just the weather,' he snapped.

Back in the city where he won La Liga with Real Madrid and took Los Blancos to three successive Champions League semi-finals, he was a less-than-happy return traveller.

In the auditorium at the Vicente Calderon, his assistant Rui Faria in a corner, he was less than effusive. 'My reaction is simple,' Mourinho began. 'Today, tomorrow and Wednesday are Champions League days. It is difficult to speak about the Premier League. You have nineteen other teams to do that but today and tomorrow is the Champions League. We are only available to speak about the Champions League.' He was asked politely by a local reporter to respond to her question in Spanish – he answered in English.

Two weeks earlier, when Chelsea were in with a chance of winning the title and on the verge of a Champions League semi-final, you couldn't stop him talking. Suddenly, there was the possibility that Mourinho would finish a second season in a row without a trophy.

'I'm not here to talk about Atlético Madrid's qualities,' he added. 'No one arrives in a Champions League semi-final without being a good team and they are no exception. They are a team we respect, and analyse, but I'm not ready to speak about my vision and my feelings about Atlético.'

The question of Chelsea's on-loan goalkeeper also irritated him. 'I don't speak about players from other teams. I think that, with UEFA decisions, it's better not to comment. You just accept or, if you don't accept, you don't make any comment. UEFA decided, so managers don't comment.'

'We all know Mourinho and we all know that, if it is necessary to crank up the pressure before a game in order to win it, then he will do that,' said Tiago. 'Jose just wants to win. He knows that Courtois is very important for us and he protects his own interests, as any coach would. He wants to weaken us, as any opposing manager would.'

Mourinho brought up Chelsea's 2005 semi-final defeat to Liverpool as an example of how his side have been unlucky in the competition under his stewardship. In reference to Luis Garcia's controversial winner in the second leg, before Liverpool went on to win the competition, Mourinho said, 'There's no unfinished business. I did my best, always did my best. In my other semi-finals with Chelsea one was lost on penalties [in 2007] and that was because Liverpool scored one more than us. In the other semi-final we lost with a goal that was not a goal but that's part of football.'

Mourinho stressed that Torres would be highly motivated against his former club. 'Those picked to start will be full of motivation for sure. I'm not saying Fernando will start. I'm saying that he never hides and he is a real Atlético supporter. Every day we speak about Spanish football. But he is a professional. I have no doubts that the minutes he is on the pitch tomorrow he will try to do everything for Chelsea as the fantastic professional that he is.' Eto'o picked up a knee injury in training so Torres played.

Simeone found it impossible to agree with Mourinho's claims that Chelsea suffered without a top-class striker. 'With respect to the coach, Chelsea have very important strikers in Samuel Eto'o and Fernando Torres,' he said. 'They are great champions and have shown that hundreds of times with the trophies they have won, like the Champions League and the World Cup. They have great talent.'

For Torres, it would be an emotional homecoming to a club where he started his career and the stadium where he stood and cheered his beloved Atlético to the La Liga and Copa del Rey double in 1996, with a certain Diego Simeone in midfield. 'He is a lad who will belong to Atlético no matter where he is playing,' said the Atlético boss. 'He has great memories and loves this club, and the people of this club. Before kick-off and after the game he will have the ovation he deserves, because this is his home and he is one of us.'

The £50m striker might return to Madrid if Chelsea complete their swoop for Costa. Mourinho covets the Brazilian-born Spain international, who has a buy-out clause of £31m. 'It would not surprise me if a team with financial power and every chance to have a great player like Diego Costa think of him,' said Simeone. First, though, he had faith in Costa to lead Atlético to their first European Cup final for 40 years.

As for Swedish referee Jonas Eriksson, the man pilloried by Manchester City manager Manuel Pellegrini earlier in the season, Mourinho remarked, 'I don't speak about referees before the game. I hope he has a good game. I hope he is happy.'

Mourinho was given a torrid time by the fans on his return to Madrid but it was a tactical master class again in the Champions League, with a goalless draw. Mourinho parked the bus. David Sullivan's young son took the piss on Twitter, asking him about nineteenth-century football. Mourinho blanked media questions on that one, as you'd expect. His Champions League semi-final record with Chelsea shows that stalemating an opponent is his forte: 0–0, 0–1, 1–0, 0–1, 0–0, one goal in 480 minutes including extra-time. 'We don't start the game thinking of a 0–0, but the game goes in a certain direction where you feel that you have to be safe, don't concede and try to score in one of the few chances you create. We had three or four corners; we had two free-kicks in dangerous situations. If we score one goal in one of those situations, the result would be very good. We didn't but we go with a result that decides everything at Stamford Bridge.'

The desired result, albeit without a preferred counter-attacking away goal, came with a price of bad injuries to Cech, who dislocated his shoulder in the opening minutes and that was it for the season, and Terry, who twisted an ankle and might only return for the final, if they made it there.

It left Mourinho threatening to rest virtually his entire team and potentially hand Liverpool the title after consultation with Abramovich to pick a deliberately weakened side in protest at being made to play on Sunday, with serious ramifications for Manchester City, relying on Chelsea to beat Liverpool and throw the title race back open. Mourinho was furious that the game was not switched to Friday or Saturday when Chelsea had the second leg against Atlético at Stamford Bridge the following Wednesday. He was willing to risk sacrificing their slim chance of the title unless Abramovich objected. 'I can't decide by myself,' Mourinho replied when asked how the injuries would influence his team selection at Anfield. 'I have to listen to the club. I'm just the manager and I have to listen to the club. The fact that the match is on Sunday, I think that puts the problem not in my hands but in the hands of those who decide the game should be Sunday, not Saturday or Friday. We represent English football and are the only [English] team in [the] European competition. Spain have four and give them all the conditions to try to have success. So I know what I would do. I would play the players who are not going to play on Wednesday. My priority is the Champions League. But I'm not the club. I have to speak to them.'

Chelsea were five points behind Liverpool with three games to play. City, in third spot, were another point behind Chelsea but had a game in hand and could potentially win the league on goal difference if Liverpool lost to Chelsea and City won all their fixtures. Mourinho should have the final. 'I'm not the most important person in the club,' he said. 'Roman and the board... everybody is above me. I work for them and have to follow what my club decides. I'm just a piece. I'm the manager, no more than that.'

Lampard and Mikel John Obi were booked and now suspended for the second leg. 'We had problems before the game and during the game,' Mourinho continued. 'We lost four players – two with injuries and two with yellow cards – but we will fight. If we have to play the kids, we play the kids. But Branislav Ivanovic is back. Mark Schwarzer showed we can trust him. People such as Ashley Cole, with an amazing performance, giving an example. Before the game we were speaking about the game of their lives for Atlético Madrid. Now the game of their lives is at Stamford Bridge.'

Mourinho became the first manager to be charged for sarcasm. He was furious with the FA decision to hit him with his third misconduct case. Faria was charged with using abusive/insulting words, Ramires charged with violent conduct. According to *The Independent* of 29 April: 'Mourinho challenged a charge related to his dismissal at Aston Villa last month as a point of principle and is considering his options after being hit with an £8,000 penalty, his second of the season after his sending-off against Cardiff.

'The Portuguese was tight-lipped on Friday following the charge.

'"Every time I speak there is a consequence," Mourinho said. "Even if I say that a referee was amazing that was a reason to be with a charge. I can't say the truth. I don't feel free at all. If you want a better press conference, speak with the FA."

'Asked about the British sense of humour and sarcasm, Mourinho said: "So Mr Bean is in jail... I told the referee he was amazing, and I repeat: the referee was amazing. I was not surprised (by the disciplinary action). In football I'm never surprised.

'He is again unhappy he could be forced to pay a fine. "When I have to give money, I prefer to do it privately," he said. "My wife says that charity is anonymous. I prefer to do that than give money because people decide to take money out of my pocket."

'Midfielder Ramires received a retrospective four-match ban, ending his domestic season, for striking Sebastian Larsson during the loss.

'Mourinho was sarcastic in commenting on Ramires' ban. 'He's a lucky guy. We accept the charge because we are happy with it,' [he] said.'

Rodgers prepared to lock horns with the man who advised him to join Liverpool. They had remained close friends since Rodgers' time as a Chelsea youth coach but that was not going to be a distraction as he focused on Liverpool's biggest domestic fixture in 25 years.

Rodgers was also wanted by Tottenham but, after an exchange of texts, Mourinho steered his protégé in the direction of Anfield. 'Jose told me to take the job, and what a great club Liverpool was,' Rodgers revealed. 'He encouraged me about the sheer scale of the club. We have kept in contact. He has been supportive of me wherever I have been, even in my time here. We might be considered a rival but I know that if they didn't win the league, he would want us to.'

Tension stems from Mourinho's first spell in England, when the clubs played each other 15 times in three years. 'I understand the history because I was on the opposite side,' said Rodgers. 'In that period maybe it was made to be the managers [Mourinho and Rafa Benitez] and that was the rivalry, but I am a different person and man. I am sure it will be a brilliant atmosphere because of the past, but, more important, how we are doing now. But for me there is no drama, no issue with him. The advantage I have is I know Jose behind the manager, a man who is humble, respectful, has real good values and ethics, but he is a winner and he wants to win.'

Mourinho almost took the Liverpool job, according to Rodgers. 'There is no doubt that there was a period back in the early 2000s, that this club was a possibility for him. Maybe resources were different and he had a better opportunity to go elsewhere but, make no mistake, he knows the size and prestige of Liverpool. There has been a history there, what with the rivalry, and it was a great rivalry between the clubs but, beneath it all, he knows the power of Liverpool for sure.' Mourinho was in pole position to replace Gerard Houllier in 2004 and made it known he would love the chance to manage a club he has always regarded as one of the biggest in the world.

Mourinho insisted that Chelsea were the most important English club in Europe and fans believed their team deserved more respect for their continental exploits. 'Chelsea fans would like Chelsea to be respected and get the respect they think they deserve for what they have done for English football in the last ten years,' said Mourinho. 'Chelsea has been the most important club in Europe in terms of being the last to be European champions, the record presence in semi-final, last club to win the Europa League, they think Chelsea deserves more respect than they are getting. They want us to go to Liverpool giving the maximum. Which players? That's our decision.' Arsenal and City crashed out at the last-16 stage, while United succumbed to Bayern in the quarter-finals. Chelsea were the only English side to win a clean sweep of European trophies.

Mourinho added, 'You are right to point out that every club takes the money from television. Every club does. And every club will do, until maybe one day, when for seven, eight, nine, ten years you don't have a European champion or a team in the semi-finals, and then the people who pay the big sums say, "The big teams, the most important teams in Europe, aren't here." I love English football. I love it. But you know what is English football? It's the fans. The stadiums. The yellow ball in the winter. The white ball in the summer. The FA Cup final with Hull City. The FA Cup semi-finals with Sheffield United and Wigan. All of this is English football. I love English football, but the most important thing for me is my club, and the supporters of my club. I have to defend my club, and I have to defend Chelsea supporters, and, if we are not helped to try to follow our dreams and our objectives? One more reason for us to close ranks. To try and think about us and only about us. The priority is the Champions League because, if we win two matches, we win the Champions League. For Wednesday I have lost the goalkeeper, maybe John Terry, Eden Hazard and Samuel Eto'o. And I've lost John Obi Mikel and Frank Lampard. You think if I lose one more player I have any chance to try to play the final? I don't think we have a chance. I can't lose more players, especially in the defence.'

That could see 38-year-old keeper Hilario, whose last appearance was in August 2011, and one-start teenager Nathan Ake in the team at Anfield, but Mourinho vowed, 'Chelsea is Chelsea. We have to work in the maximum of our possibilities, to give everything to our club, to make our families proud of us as good, professional honest people, and we have to sleep well at night. That is all. But we care about English football, and I'm telling you something now: if, next season, Chelsea plays against an English team that is playing the Champions League semi-final two days or three days later, we will play the game one or two days before to give the best chance to the English team. At that time, we would be protecting English football without creating any problem for Chelsea.'

Mourinho was worried about playing Schwarzer. Asked whether, with Cech facing the prospect of shoulder surgery, he could risk Schwarzer, he said, 'It's a big dilemma. Yes. With players that are always looking for penalties and they go for contact with the goalkeeper, it is even more dangerous. When the goalkeeper comes [out] and this kind of striker [tries] to hit the goalkeeper and dive for a penalty, it is even more dangerous.'

Mourinho accused Suárez of 'doing an acrobatic swimming-pool jump' to try to earn a penalty during Chelsea's 2–1 win against Liverpool in late December – the last time Rodgers' side, who led the table by five points, were defeated in the league.

Liverpool disputed Chelsea's claim that they refused to move Sunday's fixture forward by 24 hours to help the Londoners prepare for Atlético. Rodgers said, 'I think the Premier League should have helped them this weekend. It's not Liverpool's fault, it's the Premier League's. They should have had the game on the Saturday. That is nobody's fault bar the Premier League. That is what happens and you have to deal with it.'

After finishing his last season at Real trophy-less, another barren season was a possibility. Would Mourinho also regard that as a failure?

'No.'

Why?

'It's different in every sense.'

Rui Faria and Silvino Louro, two of his coaches and closest allies, were in the back of the auditorium. 'You can't have a squad of forty players because we are afraid that fifteen of them are going to be injured,' he said. 'You cannot avoid it. It's circumstances. We have injuries, we have two players who are not eligible to play in the Champions League – the two players we bought in January as an option because, for us, the future is more important than the present. We decided to buy the players we want to buy even if they cannot play in the Champions League. Because of the nature of our matches, we have a certain accumulation of yellow cards that is leaving us now without two more players. Those circumstances you cannot control.'

It was pointed out that Liverpool scored 24 goals in the opening 20 minutes of games. 'If the kick-off is our ball, we have to go forwards,' he said, before bursting into laughter.

It was a classic Mourinho performance on and off the pitch, his side at their imperious best to claim an unlikely 2–0 victory, while he insisted that the title was still beyond Chelsea. 'We are not in it,' said Mourinho, whose side had two games remaining. 'The champions will be Liverpool or City. We have nothing to celebrate. Today was an important three points and we need one more to finish third.' Third place would ensure they wouldn't have to play any qualifying matches in Europe's elite club competition next season.

Defeat would have ended Chelsea's hopes of winning the title they last claimed in 2010 but late goals in each half ensured they were still contenders, despite Mourinho's reluctance to admit so. 'Now we can say we have won both matches against the champions,' added the manager, whose side had beaten Liverpool and Manchester City twice in the season. 'The team that deserved it more won. Obviously many people would be expecting us to come here and lose three-, four- or five-nil, like others. Many people thought it was impossible to get this result.'

Mourinho gave 20-year-old Czech Tomas Kalas a debut in central defence and praised 'a giant' performance from goalscorer Ba, who took advantage of a Gerrard slip as Chelsea claimed 16 points from 18 against the top four sides.

Rodgers attributed his team's defeat to 'time-wasting' and 'parking two buses'. He, who had worked for three years under Mourinho at Stamford Bridge, would never embrace the style that proved so effective for his old boss, suggesting it was 'not difficult to coach to play defensive'.

Mourinho dismissed suggestions that there was anything negative about his tactics. 'When a team defends well, you call it a defensive display. When they defend [badly] and concede two or three goals, you don't consider it a defensive display and sometimes they are. My team played brilliantly, every player was magnificent.'

Rodgers' friendship with Mourinho would survive the rivalry but there was little respect with a post-match handshake notable by its absence. 'They virtually played from the off with a back six with the wingers coming back,' Rodgers said. 'It was ten players behind from the first minute and we found it difficult to break down. You don't just see it against Atlético Madrid, it's against most. It's the style of football, it's defensive, and the polar opposite of the way we work. It gets results. Jose has got his today and he will be happy with that. It's the opposite [of] how we work and, hopefully over time and with preparation, it will get us long-term results. It's not difficult to coach to just get ten players right on your eighteen-yard box and it is difficult to break through, but they defended well. I think they got booked for time-wasting in the ninety-second minute but you could see from the first whistle that the plan was to frustrate, but teams work in a different way. We are a team that tries to win in a sporting manner, try to work and initiate the game with the ball. I understand if it's late in the game and players are taking their time. It can be frustrating from the first whistle but that is how teams will set up and the nature of some coaches and managers, you have to deal with it. Jose is happy to work that way and play that way and he will probably show his CV and say it works, but it's not my way of working. I like to take the initiative in games and let players express themselves. They have some fantastic players. They defended well. We tried everything we could but our game is based on being offensively creative as opposed to stopping. This game will prepare us for Crystal Palace.'

Mourinho revelled in the siege mentality, targeting TV pundit Jamie Redknapp, a former Liverpool midfielder, for particular criticism.

Chelsea's players were subject to a series of crank calls at the base in nearby Formby Hall on the eve of the game, while fireworks were also set off in the early hours. Mourinho was riled by a guest appearance before kick-off of Luis Garcia, to whip the Kop into a frenzy with the reminder of the 'ghost goal' of 2005. It motivated his side.

'They brought Luis Garcia for us to remember the ghost goal. But Chelsea was the big team in this country in Europe and we will try once more to go to the final,' Mourinho said. 'The best team won and deserved to win. That's it. When you say it was "defensively strong", I'm a bit confused about what the media thinks a defensive display is... Every player was magnificent with no mistakes and the zonal play, covering spaces, was a fantastic performance by my players. A beautiful victory. Now we can say we won both matches against the champions. If the champion is Liverpool, we won both matches; if the champion is Man City, we won both. We are back in nothing. We are almost third. Now with these three points we need one to finish third. It was a good season for us and the boys, an evolution in many aspects. We were waiting for this to be the title match but for some reason this match did not become the title match. It is three important points.'

Mourinho argued previously that TV coverage is against his club and he continued his assault. 'Speak with Jamie Redknapp – he tells you everything about it. You have your pundits where Jamie Redknapp is a brilliant football brain, they can explain everything. Now we have to think about Wednesday and only Wednesday – to play [the] Champions League semi-final at Stamford Bridge is something big. The result is 0–0, not a very good result. This club is doing [magnificently] over the last ten years.'

Rodgers sent Mourinho a message to clarify his post-match

comments. 'Of course I know his words after the match, but I also know his words today. And today he told me congratulations for a great victory and a great performance. So, especially because I consider him a friend and someone I like, I prefer to forget the words after the match and I keep today's word. He's an intelligent guy. He watched the match for sure on video and, now, I think he understood what happened. Brendan is somebody I consider my friend. I met him a long time ago when he was coaching kids.'

Rodgers reflected, 'I was a bit frustrated but I don't regret what I said. I am big enough to respect the man Jose is and the manager he is. He is a great man, I know that. It was never personal; it was a professional look at the game. I am never one to say that my way is always the best way. I have a huge appreciation for the way he works and his team. But I still think what I said was right. I knew exactly what I was saying.'

Mourinho was frustrated with criticism of his team's defensive tactics. 'Football is full of philosophers – people who understand much more than me. It's amazing. But the reality is always the reality. I remember to say in my first period here, if you have a goalkeeper like Petr Cech who puts the ball in the opponents' box, and a striker like Didier Drogba who wins everything in the air, why play short? Because you are stupid? If your opponents are very fast on the counter and want space behind your defensive line, if you give them that space you are stupid. In this moment, depending on the coach and the club obviously, the critics they speak. But, no problem. When Atlético has the ball, we have to defend. When we have the ball, we have to attack. This is football, the football that I know. You have the ball, you have to try and play according to the qualities of your players and the qualities of your opponents.'

Mourinho was ready to commit to Chelsea 'forever'. He commented, 'My future is Chelsea and if Chelsea decides it's time to stop our relationship, it's Chelsea that decides, not me. I want to stay forever. When Chelsea decide it's time to stop, it's time for me to think about my future.'

Mourinho felt the game hinged on a whirlwind passage of play when Courtois made a fine save to deny Terry's powerful header and, in the next attack, Eto'o fouled Costa to concede a penalty, which the striker converted. 'The difference was one minute in the second half, where Atlético's goalkeeper makes an impossible save and, instead of 2–1 to Chelsea, a few seconds later a penalty, which I'm happy people tell me was a penalty. And they scored to go 2–1 up. In one minute, two actions decided the game. After that, there was only one team on the pitch. My team played with pride, honour and professionalism, but after that moment the game was controlled by Atlético. Complete control.'

Likely to finish without a trophy, Mourinho defended the campaign. 'We need one point to be third. You know, we know we are realistic. But at the same time we are optimistic. At the same time, when things go in a certain direction, there is a moment where you can dream and you think that things are possible, even if things are not so. Because we did well in the Champions League and in the Premier League, there was a moment where we felt we could do it. In the Premier League it was the match against Aston Villa that made me believe that we had no chance to be champions. After that we built the momentum again and we were waiting for the Liverpool match to be the title match, but we had another surprise against Sunderland. But I think the boys did a very good Premier League. In the Champions League, it's the same. We knew that there were teams with more potential than us and more ready than us to win the competition, but because you go step by step and beating PSG you build your dream. We had our chance. Until minute sixty-one we were completely in the game. From that moment, the game was over.'

Mourinho pointed a finger at Hazard over their Champions League exit, as he prepared for the Norwich game, making light of Hazard's post-match comment that Chelsea were 'not set up to play football', insisting it had been taken out of context. 'As far as I am concerned, he was reported as being critical, but there was nothing critical in what he said. It's the same type of words he said in relation to the Belgium side a few weeks ago. There is nothing there. But normally you get this kind of comment from players like him: from players who can't resolve a problem like we had with the first goal. Against Atlético in Madrid, Willian played on the left side and Ashley Cole was protected [throughout the] game. Against Liverpool, Schürrle played on the left and a dangerous player like Glen Johnson was completely under control. Eden is the kind of player who is not so mentally ready to look back at his left-back and lay down his life for him. If you see Atlético's first goal, you understand where the mistake was and why we conceded that goal. That doesn't mean I want him to change. I just say the perfect team at the top level cannot make this kind of mistake. Normally, in this game, if you go to half-time winning 1–0, the game is another game. Atlético have to chase the game and we, with stability, have conditions for more. When the comments come from a player like Eden, it's normal. He's not the kind of player who is ready to sacrifice himself a hundred per cent for the team and his mates. But at the same time, the comments were not critical. I'm not happy when a player doesn't sacrifice himself and I've spoken all season and I've tried to improve him.'

Mourinho didn't accept that the title was possible; maximum points in their last two games with Norwich and Cardiff plus Liverpool and City slipping up. 'The only thing we can do is win both matches. Imagine if we are not champions because we don't win these two matches. That wouldn't be a good feeling for the players. So we have to win both matches. On Sunday, Norwich are playing for their lives, to decide if next season it's Arsenal, Chelsea and United or midweek games in the Championship. They are playing the game of their lives.'

Mourinho was playing to 'finish the season with the feeling of victory'. He went on, 'We need to win both matches for the fans, whose support deserves that we finish with two wins.'

Mourinho set out to play more expansive football but, when results were lacking in December, he had to change. 'I made the decision to stop that evolution in the style and philosophy of play,' Mourinho explained, 'and went in the direction where I felt it was the only way that we could get results. I felt we had no conditions to arrive in the Champions League if we did not have a transformation in our style of play. So the team became more strategical and less intuitive because we went for results.'

Mourinho knew they did not have the efficiency up front required to play in that style. 'To play in an attractive way is when you create seven chances and you score five goals, and you can concede two or three and still win. If you create twelve chances and score one, if your opponent scores before, you are in trouble. We had lots of matches where we created lots. At Everton we should have been 5–0 up, but we were 1–0 down. Things are not sometimes like people like to say.'

Mourinho pursued a 'critical signing'. He explained, 'That's what I'm going to do after the season: work, think, think about next season.'

The manager was confused by relegation-threatened Norwich's defensive tactics as his side's fading title hopes ended with a tame goal-less draw with the Canaries at Stamford Bridge.

Neil Adams' side sat three points off safety before kick-off, knowing that seventeenth-placed Sunderland would have a game in hand, even after Sunday's match, but Mourinho felt they did not play like that was the case. 'We had one team that needed three points to survive and they didn't play to win. We tried everything but at the end of the day we knew we had no chance of being champions. We knew we needed a point to finish in the group stages of the Champions League [by securing third place]. That is no trophy for us, but it was important to finish third.'

Mourinho stormed down the tunnel at half-time to blast a number of players, including Matic and Salah, for their performances, accusing his team of being 'lazy'. Mourinho told Matic he was having serious reservations about the decision to bring him back in the January transfer window. Salah was replaced at half-time and told to make sure he returned for pre-season 'ready to be a footballer'. Mourinho stormed out of the dressing room and appeared in the dugout a few minutes before the start of the second half, sitting alone until his players came out.

Despite the disappointment of dropping two points, the squad completed a lap of the field. Cole was in tears and had to be consoled by Terry. Cole, Terry and Lampard could leave as all three had contracts that expired with 1,609 Blues appearances between them. Mourinho believed they would stay. 'Will they play at Stamford Bridge again? I think so, but the summer is a long summer for us. For the players at the World Cup, it's a different story. But for us, as a club, it's a long time to be calm, to sit and discuss and analyse the market and possibilities. A long time.'

Mourinho admitted the season could have been better, 'We lost games where we had them under control but didn't kill them and we were killed. But from day one, never in danger, never outside the top four or outside the title race.'

Chelsea finished the season third with a win at Cardiff, as both Liverpool and newly crowned champions City won their final games. Chelsea finished without a trophy for the first time in three years; their 82-point total the worst under Mourinho.

Mourinho will label Chelsea title challengers if they 'work in a successful way' in this close-season transfer market. He denied being hurt by missing out on the title in his first campaign back in England, saying City were worthy champions. Evolution and transition were buzzwords, so third-placed finish 'is not a drama'.

He said, 'Next season, if we do our work in a successful way in the summer market, which I know the club is trying to do everything to make that a successful period for us, then if we do that I want to start day one saying we are going to fight for the title. We don't need a new spine, a new structure. It is there. The fundamental for us now is a couple of players of a certain level to help the team immediately go to a different level. After that the additional is if someone has to leave then someone has to come. Our work in the summer is not a big amount of work; it is just the right choice.'

He also needed to forge the mentality required to win matches like those against Villa and Sunderland, to which he referred six times in his press conference. 'Manchester City are champions and they deserve it,' he said. 'They have four more points than us and two more than Liverpool. They are not guilty of defeats like ours to Aston Villa and Sunderland. It has nothing to do with them. Am I hurt? No, because it is part of the process. One thing is to play clearly to win the title. Another is to be in a transition phase. It was an easier job for me to get a team ready to win [not Chelsea] and I promise you I had chances to do that, not just in this country but others. My decision was this and I am happy with that. It is part of a process in a dangerous league where you can finish fifth and be out of the Champions League. Third is not a drama, it is a position you have to accept in this transitional period. We are not asking for eight, nine, ten years to achieve success but you can't just click your fingers and success arrives. This season it almost happened.'

The manager penned a heartfelt message to his son Jose Junior in the match programme. He would normally have used his column to discuss the defeat to Atlético but, instead, he wrote, 'I know this space is to communicate with you fans, but one of you is my son. I want to tell him thanks for being with me every second of every match, a few metres behind me, jumping for every goal; hurt by every difficult moment. Thank you, kid, for being my kid. Every time I look at you, I see you, but I also see your sister and your mum, both at home but also playing with us, both waiting for us to go home and to be what we are – an amazing family... like the blue family, supporting each other.'

Jose Mario, a goalkeeper, decided not to follow his father to Chelsea and signed for Fulham under-14s in September.

Mourinho indicated his desire to land a prolific goalscorer. 'Against the teams that are more defensive, more aggressive, more worried about trying to keep a clean sheet than really to play, we keep saying the same. We have good players, but we don't have the kind of striker able to, in a short space, to make an action, to score a goal, to open the gate. In these [kinds] of matches you just need to open the gate. When you open the gate, the gate is open and you win much more. We weren't able to do that. We have to try to win as a team, to improve as a team, but also add the attacking player with that killer instinct and the number of goals that push teams to different levels. It's something our club is going to try, respecting obviously that we have good strikers.'

Chelsea beat City twice, Liverpool twice, took four points from matches with Arsenal, Everton, Tottenham and United but defeats to Villa, Palace, Sunderland and the draw with Norwich proved costly. 'It's much more difficult to get results against the big teams. Mentally you have to be stronger, by the strategic point of view you have to be stronger too. When we have that amazing record against the top teams, I think it's a fantastic achievement and a good base to start next season.'

The loss to Sunderland saw Mourinho relinquish his 77-match unbeaten league record at home. 'If you forget the Sunderland festival, because for me it was not a football game, it was a festival, the record was good. We lost six points at home, with three draws, which is still a good record. The matches with the top teams, the record is really amazing, difficult to repeat next season even if, like we expect, we are stronger.'

Prospective new United manager van Gaal revealed how Mourinho first came to his attention at Barca. At a meeting attended by Mourinho and Bobby Robson, it was announced that van Gaal would be taking charge at the Nou Camp. Van Gaal revealed, 'Mourinho thought he'd been promised the youth academy job and even that he might be the next manager and hadn't been told. He was so angry and shouted so much about not being consulted that I was impressed. On that day he was a "Special One" and because of that I hired him. I learned that day he was special. He told me who he was and we worked together for three years. After one year he could have left but he stayed. He was an excellent co-trainer, a substitute coach. He carried out all the analysis for Barcelona and studied all the opponents. Also, and I don't do it very often, I let him coach matches, because I was convinced he had specific qualities. We have been observing each other ever since and been sending text messages. Little did I know he would be such a great coach. He was an excellent coach then but now he is one of the best in the world. And I don't think many coaches can make that declaration.'

Mourinho stated that he plans to leave the game at 65, normal retirement age, after a dozen years turning 'my Chelsea' into the dominant outfit in global football and then two years taking a national team to the World Cup. He views international management as a symptom of growing old. 'It's not a job I like. You have to wait two years to have a competition! You have easier matches, many friendlies, qualification matches! Training two days a month! I don't need an escape from football. I just need a couple of weeks in the summer to be somewhere, a beach. That's fine for me.'

He is very much a family man, and you can see him taking the Portuguese national job to spend more time with them. His 17-year-old daughter Matilde has a budding interest in photography. During a magazine interview, Mourinho spent the accompanying photo shoot quizzing the photographer on how much such work pays and what editing programs Matilde might need. 'In our house, it's two and two. Mum and daughter isolated of football. They like me to win and they care about my happiness, but they don't live for football. And obviously the boy [Jose Jr] is a boy, and at this age – 13, 14, 15 – he gets involved in the game, too. So, it's two for football and two who are more intelligent than the men of the house.'

The Premier League is a duller place without Mourinho's old foe and friend Sir Alex Ferguson. 'I miss him,' he says. The odd couple had mutual respect and friendship, swapping bottles of expensive red wine after each encounter.

'Sir Alex is seventy-something, no? He just finishes his career and in the first year he retires, he's in football every weekend. Hahahaha! I thought he'd go to enjoy other things, but he's in football every weekend!'